ROAD TRIP
USA
NEW ENGLAND

FIRST EDITION

JAMIE JENSEN

Contributors:

Paul Blair

Andy Coe

Larry Cultrera

Peggy Engel

Elizabeth Meister

Doug Pappas

Jeff Perk

ROAD TRIP USA: NEW ENGLAND
FIRST EDITION

Jamie Jensen

Published by
Avalon Travel Publishing, Inc.
5855 Beaudry Street
Emeryville, CA 94608, USA

Text and photographs © copyright 2001 by
Jamie Jensen. All rights reserved.

Cover and maps © copyright 2001 by
Avalon Travel Publishing, Inc.
All rights reserved.

Some photos and illustrations are used by
permission and are the property of the original copyright owners.
A list of photo and illustration credits appears on page 335.

Lyrics from the song "Roadrunner" are reprinted on page 88 courtesy of Jonathan
Richman and Rounder Records.

ISBN: 1-56691-282-2
ISSN: 1532-3927

Contributors

Paul Blair	Elizabeth Meister
Andy Coe	Doug Pappas
Larry Cultrera	Jeff Perk
Peggy Engel	

Editors: Ellen Cavalli, Grace Fujimoto
Graphics Coordinator: Erika Howsare
Production & Design: David Hurst, Kelly Pendragon, Marcie McKinley
Map Editors: Naomi Dancis
Cartography: Katherine Kalamaris, Mike Morgenfeld

Front cover photo: © Diane Cook and Len Jenshel

Distributed in the United States and Canada by Publishers Group West

Printed in China through Colorcraft Ltd., Hong Kong

Please send all comments,
corrections, additions,
amendments, and critiques to:

**ROAD TRIP USA:
NEW ENGLAND**
AVALON TRAVEL PUBLISHING
5855 BEAUDRY STREET
EMERYVILLE, CA 94608, USA
e-mail: info@travelmatters.com
www.travelmatters.com

Printing History
1st edition—May 2001
5 4 3 2 1

When you come to a fork in the road, take it.

—Yogi Berra

CONTENTS

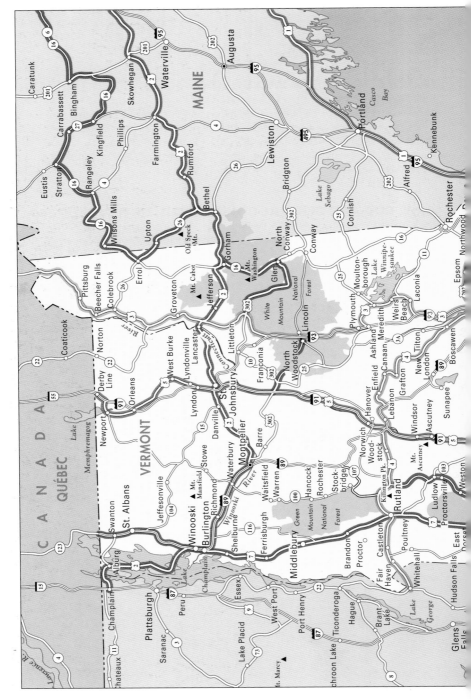

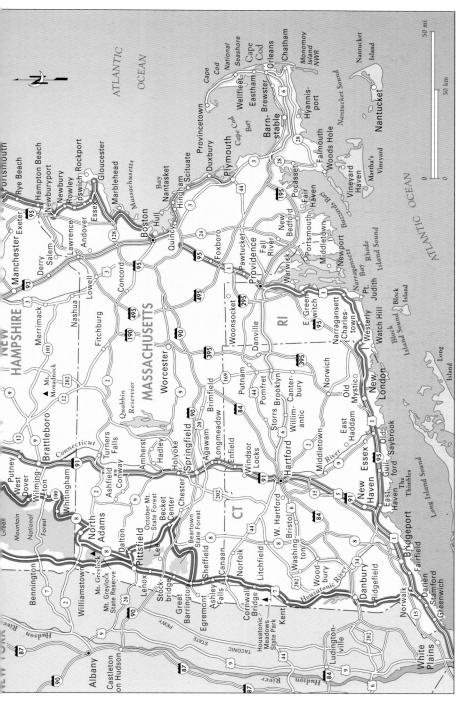

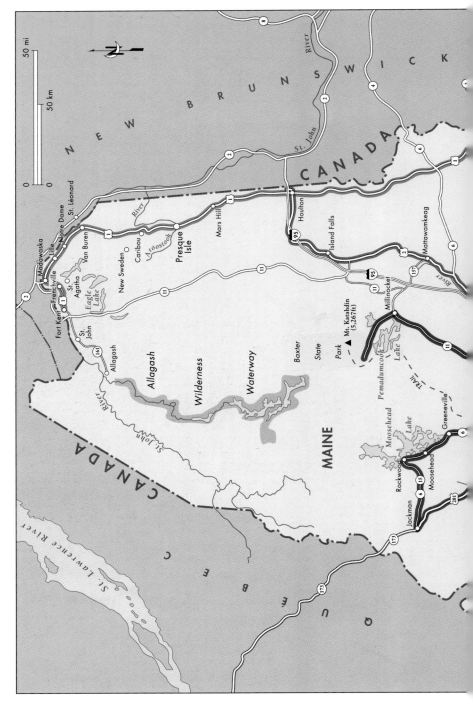

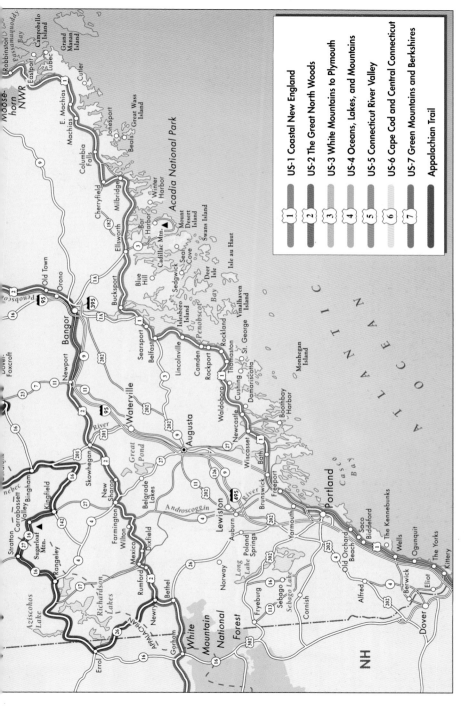

US-1 Coastal New England
US-2 The Great North Woods
US-3 White Mountains to Plymouth
US-4 Oceans, Lakes, and Mountains
US-5 Connecticut River Valley
US-6 Cape Cod and Central Connecticut
US-7 Green Mountains and Berkshires

Appalachian Trail

UNDERSTANDING NEW ENGLAND

N ew England means different things to different people. History buffs know it as the birthplace of the United States and as a living museum of vanishing Americana, including country towns, village greens, and covered bridges. Skiers dream of its snow-covered slopes. Arts and crafts collectors think of the region's Shaker furniture, Norman Rockwell prints, and innumerable roadside flea markets. Foodies ache for fresh blueberry pies or maple syrup–slathered pancakes. Others flock to its mountain forests to celebrate the fall color or head to the many miles of sandy beaches to romp in the surf. The locals, of course, quietly call New England home, and few seem to have much of an urge to leave.

All of this makes for an intriguingly diverse scene in a remarkably compact area. No matter where you are or what you expect to see, or whether you're a resident or visitor, you'll be awestruck by the juxtapositions of nature and industry, wealth and poverty, history and the modern age. There's always something totally new and different right around the next bend. Placid Shaker villages sit alongside stock-car racetracks. Stately summer mansions of Boston and Manhattan financiers alternate with tumbledown rural trailer homes, while Ivy League colleges rub shoulders with roadside diners, minor league ballparks, and nearly abandoned mill towns. Even the forests hold surprises: walking in the dense woods you're bound to come across centuries-old stone walls and mills, or the remains of a 100-year-old logging railroad that's been converted to a hiking and cycling trail.

It is estimated that somewhere between 15,000 and 30,000 people lived in New England when Europeans first arrived, but there is little left of these diverse Algonquin-speaking Native American cultures. Only some very small reservations survive in Maine and on Cape Cod; the most prominent signs of Indian presence are the garish Indian casinos of Connecticut, especially Foxwoods, which is among the largest and most profitable in the world.

For all its popularity, New England has few, if any, singular sightseeing attractions—no Disneylands or Grand Canyons you can cross off a list once you've been there, done that. In fact, the pleasures here are quite the opposite. It takes time to appreciate New England's towns and other highlights, and if anything, the enjoyment of them increases over time. This may be why in New England, more than anywhere else in the United States, people return to familiar haunts over and over again, year after year, visiting the same places generation after generation. This social stability gives even the most touristed resort a homey, settled ambience, in stark contrast to the manufactured personalities of most modern hotels and vacation destinations. All over New England there are lots of these beloved spots, which, despite the famously taciturn character of New Englanders, give the region an unusually welcoming and civilized feel. It also means that, during the main tourism seasons at least, the comforts of home are never far away. You'll never have to search very hard for a great restaurant, a trendy boutique, or a good bookstore.

Even if the natural landscape is not generally as dramatic as in the wild West, there are still some sublime scenes in New England. Apart from tiny Rhode Island (whose highest point is the Connecticut border), each state has its own mountain range—the Whites in New Hampshire, the Greens in Vermont, the Berkshires in Massachusetts, the Litchfield Hills in Connecticut. They are all part of the great Appalachian chain, which ends in central Maine with the mile-high peak of Mount Katahdin. In the White Mountains, the deep canyons of Franconia Notch and the other wild areas were carved into some of the oldest and most rugged rocks anywhere, and hulking mountaintops rise up into the clouds. Along the coast of Maine, tall cliffs and walls of solid granite stand guard against the raging Atlantic Ocean, protecting tiny coves where lobstermen trap their catch. Meanwhile, further south, expansive estuaries and marshlands protected by broad sandy beaches provide rich habitat for seabirds, seals, and other wildlife. Not even the briefest description of natural New England could finish without a mention of its most identifiable denizens, moose, but the region is also home to a wide range of animals, from bears and coyotes to humpback whales.

New England, especially in rural areas and most especially in the northern tier, is demographically the most homogenous region in the United States. The populations of Vermont, New Hampshire, and Maine are all more than 98 percent white.

In addition to the natural scene, testaments to American history are an essential part of the new New England landscape. Massachusetts, where Plymouth Rock is just down the road from the Old North Bridge at Concord, is jam-packed with monuments and edifices that bring to mind historic events. However, often the most moving historical monuments and memorials are the ones you've never heard about: the countless Civil War memorials in Maine, which provided more soldiers per capita to the war than did any other Northern state; the monuments to lost sailors in fishing ports such as Gloucester; the preserved homes of Revolutionary figures and regular folks throughout the area that show us how people once lived; or the many cemeteries all over the Vermont and New Hampshire countryside that remind us that a hundred or more years ago, waning rural hamlets had more inhabitants than they do today.

Honoring and preserving history is part of the New England fabric and way of life, and dates back to well before Revolutionary times. Thus, at times it can be hard to tell the truly old and significant sites from their restored and reconstructed cousins, but at the end of the day, what difference does it make? Though die-hards may mourn the few changes that have taken place, most things in New England are still done the tried and tested ways. This veneration of tradition, whether in making maple syrup, handcrafting furniture, or keeping the countryside free from the Wal-Marts and megamalls of the modern world, animates almost everything. It's the sort of place where, by and large, you still get a strong sense of how people lived generations ago. Sure, Boston has all of the computer companies and high-tech industries you could ever want, but most of New England is decidedly old-fashioned.

However much New England as a whole is seen as some symbol of Yankee Americana, what's also striking is how different the various states are from one another. Yes, they are more like each other than any of them is like Nebraska, but seen up close, or side by side, the differences are revealing and frequently worth savoring. Residents and frequent visitors pride themselves on being able to tell a

Maine accent from a Vermonter's, and after spending even a short while here, new-comers will start to notice the little differences. Perhaps most telling of the con-trasting characters of the states are the sentiments expressed on the various license plates and "Welcome to" signs. Maine is Vacationland, or The Way Life Should Be. Vermont is the Green Mountain State; Rhode Island, the Ocean State; Massachu-setts, the Bay State; and Connecticut, the Constitution State. And then there's New Hampshire, whose state motto gives you two clear choices: Live Free or Die. Sub-tler are the ideological differences, such as Vermont's antiestablishment attitudes contrasted with Connecticut's more commerce-driven lifestyle. Much is in the landscapes themselves: the soft lapping of waves against the piers in some historic Rhode Island harbor, compared to the massive seas of Down East Maine. The crazy traffic of busy Boston, or the rustic idyll of Vermont's Lake Champlain Valley. The gentle rolling hills of rural Connecticut against the sublime drama of New Hampshire's White Mountains.

In 1614 New England was so named by Captain John Smith, who explored and mapped the coastline in the employ of the Plymouth Company.

This endless variety means no book could ever hope to paint a complete picture of New England. Besides, summing up the parts wouldn't come anywhere close to describing the whole gamut of things that make up each passing scene. Instead, I'll try to encourage you to see things not as you expect them to be but as they are. To explore less-publicized attractions, along with those the tourism bureaus recommend. To take time to smell the proverbial roses, whether they be actual roses or maple syrup or pungent cheddar cheeses. When you see one of the covered bridges, stop and get out of the car, walk across it, and listen to the river flow beneath. And most of all, when you have a choice between a pair of routes, do as New England's poet laureate Robert Frost suggests and take the road less trav-eled. It will make all the difference.

Maine

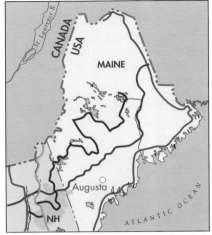

Covering more than 33,000 square miles, the state of Maine is as big as all the other New England states combined, yet its total population is barely a million people, about the same as metropolitan Hartford, Connecticut. Most of Maine's population is concentrated along the southern coast, leaving the vast forested interior to be shared among hikers, hunters, paper companies—and maybe a few thousand moose.

Best known for its natural landscape of lakes and mountains, Maine also has what's probably the liveliest and most enjoyable city north of Boston—**Portland.** A historic port with one of the most vibrant waterfront areas in the country, Portland has excellent museums, great restaurants, and all sorts of cultural life, and it serves as the hub of the state's most developed and most visited corner. South of Portland are a wide range of beach resorts: high-style **Ogunquit,** patrician **Kennebunkport,** and wild and crazy **Old Orchard Beach.** To the north and east spread the many slender peninsulas that hold some of the state's most picturesque sights, from historic towns like **Wiscasset** and **Waldoboro,** to the stunning land- and seascapes of **Pemaquid Point** and **Monhegan Island.**

The other half of Maine's 2,500-mile-long coastline, forever known as Down East Maine, revolves around **Acadia National Park** and its striking combinations of granite cliffs, crashing seas, and sedate glacial ponds. Once the summer domain of the nation's wealthiest people, the Acadia area still draws its share of well-heeled visitors, especially around **Bar Harbor,** which serves as an effective bookend to the park for most tourists. However, the edge of Maine continues for another hundred miles through a series of smaller, lower-key, but more authentic-feeling waterfront communities before bending up for another 200 miles through the diverse, frequently French-speaking potato-farming and logging communities that line the Canadian border.

Getting away from the coast doesn't mean leaving the water behind, since inland Maine boasts more rivers and lakes than you could explore in a lifetime. Some of these you can appreciate from the road, but to get the most out of them you have to take a hike, or better yet, hop in a boat, a kayak, or a canoe, all of which are readily available for rent. At the heart of Maine, **Moosehead Lake,** the largest in the state at more than

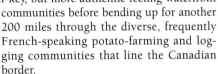

BEST OF MAINE

40 miles long, is one of the most popular; further west, **Rangeley Lake** spreads at the heart of another very picturesque region, surrounded by dense forests and rugged mountains. To the east, protected at the heart of the state's largest park, **Mount Katahdin** rises majestically over the rolling forests, offering an enticing start or finish to hike along the backpacker's legendary Appalachian Trail.

Maine is the only state that borders just a single other U.S. state.

MAINE TIMELINE

1544: Sebastian Cabot publishes a map of New England and Nova Scotia showing the discoveries he and his father, John Cabot, had made.

1647: Kittery, the first town in Maine, is established.

1739: Although Maine is still legally part of Massachusetts, the border between New Hampshire and Maine is fixed along the current line. Estimated population of Maine: 12,000.

1820: As part of the Missouri Compromise, Maine separates from Massachusetts and becomes the 23rd U.S. state. Estimated population: 300,000.

Sebastian Cabot

1912: L. L. Bean opens a shop in Freeport, selling his innovative rubber-soled hunting boots.

1947: The first Maine Lobster Festival is held in Rockland, celebrating the famous crustacean that now serves as the state's tastiest and most lucrative export. Some 30 million lobsters are harvested annually.

1968: Rumford native Democrat Senator Edmund Muskie runs for vice president alongside presidential candidate Hubert Humphrey.

1970s: Alan Alda stars as Captain Benjamin Franklin "Hawkeye" Pierce, fictional native of fictional Crabapple Cove, Maine, in TV's long-running Korean War comedy show, *M.A.S.H.*

1984–93: Vice President and later President George H. W. Bush spends frequent vacations at his family estate in Maine, putting Kennebunkport on the national map.

George H. W. Bush

New Hampshire

From its short, sandy seacoast to the region's highest mountains, New Hampshire has a little of everything people look for in New England. One day you can enjoy the hormone-fueled parade of youthful energy strutting along the summer sands of Hampton Beach; the next you can ride a historic steam train to the summit of Mount Washington and play in the freshly fallen snow. One of the most idyllic college towns imaginable, **Hanover** is a slow-paced, erudite support system for the Ivy League halls of Dartmouth College. In contrast, bustling **Portsmouth** has become a minimecca of lively restaurants lining up along the docks and winding streets of one of the country's most historic places. In and among this are historic mill towns, hundreds of country

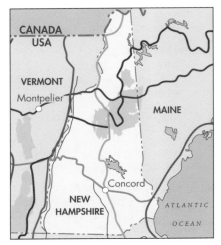

hamlets, and miles and miles of winding country roads, offering greater variety than you'd expect from such a compact place—under 100 miles wide and 200 miles north to south.

The high point of New Hampshire, literally and figuratively, **Mount Washington** stands a mile or more above the picturesque valleys and "notches" below, and the surrounding White Mountains offer a wonderful combination of wilderness and civilization. Everything from stately grand hotels to rustic mountain huts stands ready to welcome you home after a hard day's hiking, so you can spend the day breathing in pine-scented air then while away the evening unwinding by a raging fire. The White Mountains are rich in wacky roadside amusement—kids will like the living fairy tales on show at **Story Land,** and who could resist the chance to "See Live Bears" at **Clark's Trading Post**? Even more fun can be had nearby, on and around the various lakes that fill the heart of the state, from massive (and massively popular) **Lake Winnepesaukee** to quieter **Squam Lake** and **Newfound Lake.**

NEW HAMPSHIRE TIMELINE

1623: English colonists establish settlements along the Piscataqua River, near present-day Portsmouth and Dover.

1679: Breaking off from Massachusetts, New Hampshire becomes a separate royal colony.

1774–76: New Hampshirites claim various firsts in the moves toward American independence, including the first capture of British armaments, from Portsmouth's Fort William and Mary (December 14, 1774), and the first declaration of independence (January 5, 1776).

1880s: Railroads are built to haul logs from the White Mountains, and tourists to the resort hotels that are built in their wake.

1916: New Hampshire holds the first presidential primary election and for the rest of the 20th century continues to play a vital role in shaping the national campaigns.

White Mountains, N.H. *Frankenstein Trestle*

1956: Author Grace Metalious publishes the steamy novel *Peyton Place,* inspired by her life in the small town of Gilmanton. Millions of copies are sold and the book is made into a movie and a TV show.

1963: New Hampshire establishes the first state-run lottery in the United States.

1986: Concord schoolteacher Christa McAuliffe, chosen to be the first civilian in outer space, is killed when the space shuttle *Challenger* explodes seconds after liftoff.

If Ben & Jerry's trademark black-and-white–splotched ice cream packaging gets you interested in the different bovine breeds, here's a short primer to help you tell them apart: Black-and-white splotches: Herefords; Brown-and-white splotches: Guernseys; Brown all over: Jerseys

Vermont

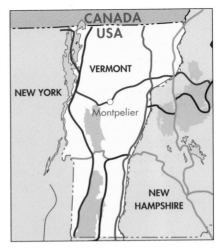

When many people think of Vermont, three names come to mind: Norman, Ben, and Jerry. Illustrator Norman Rockwell lived and worked in the Green Mountain State for much of his life, and his depictions of Vermont life embodied all that was great about America. Sentimental as they may be, Rockwell's images are still played out all over the state, in small towns and rural scenes, where men are men, women are women, and kids can be kids. Today, a generation or two later, Rockwell and his images have been superceded by gourmet ice-cream makers **Ben & Jerry,** whose quirky flavors and antiestablishment ethos have made them an unusual success story. Ben & Jerry's is Vermont's biggest company and the state's most popular tourist attraction, which says more about the state's lack of amusement parks and similar tourist traps than it does about our national love for ice cream. Nevertheless, Ben & Jerry's packaging image of happy cows feeding on lush pastures has promoted another fairly accurate image of Vermont, one of a truly "green," environmentally friendly, life-sustaining place. (However, due to ongoing doldrums in the dairy industry, Vermont no longer has as many cows as people, but it still has the highest cow-to-human ratio of any state.)

The scale of things in Vermont is small enough that you'll rarely feel overwhelmed; if you're looking for bright lights and nightlife, don't go to Vermont. The state's largest city, **Burlington,** has fewer than 40,000 inhabitants, and most of the Vermont's 590,000 residents are spread out over the state's 9,250 square miles, making it officially the most rural state in the nation. Traveling around Vermont, don't expect many strip malls and late-night fast-food joints. Instead, you'll come across picturesque red barns and covered bridges, white church spires and picket-fenced commons, rolling fields hemmed in by rocky hills and mountains. A small town store, an early-opening diner, a few people. Cows, cornfields, and more cows.

Vermont's country charms are genuine for the most part, but thanks to an ongoing invasion of well-heeled urbanites looking to escape the stresses of modern life, there are also many parts of Vermont that seem to have more to do with Gianni Versace than with John Deere. Most of this rural gentrification is concentrated around the state's many top-notch ski areas that dot the Green Mountains along Route 100 in the southern half of the state and around Stowe in the north. The rest of Vermont is (so far) blissfully free from the sprawling suburbia that has covered so much of North America, which may be why more than a few fans of the state propose preserving the whole thing as a living museum of how life used to be.

VERMONT TIMELINE

1609: Following the explorations of Samuel de Champlain, the first European to visit what is now Vermont, France lays claim to the region. The name, which literally translated means "worm mountain," is taken from the French *vert mont,* or "green mountain."

1763: France cedes Vermont to Britain, and both New York and New Hampshire begin granting tracts of land to settlers.

1791: After contentious land claims are settled in favor of New Hampshire (due primarily to the bullying tactics of Ethan Allen and the Green Mountain Boys), Vermont joins the United States as the first new state after the original 13. Estimated population: 85,000.

Samuel de Champlain

1864: Confederate soldiers attacking from Canada raid the town of St. Albans.

1978: Friends since the 7th grade, Ben Cohen and Jerry Greenfield open Ben & Jerry's, an ice cream stand, in an old gas station in downtown Burlington. Five years later, they help build the world's largest ice-cream sundae in St. Albans; it weighs more than 13 tons.

1993: Worried by the increase in ski-resort and other large-scale development in Vermont, the National Trust for Historic Preservation adds the entire state to its list of Most Endangered Places.

2000: Vermont becomes the only state in the nation to pass a civil union law, which legally entitles same-sex couples to the same benefits, privileges, and responsibilities granted to married couples. Ben & Jerry's Ice Cream is bought by Anglo-Dutch conglomerate Unilever for $326 million.

Massachusetts

Located at the center of New England, Massachusetts has a little of everything—industry and farmland, small towns and big cities, golden sand beaches and dense mountain forests. At under 8,000 square miles, the Bay State is smaller than both neighboring Vermont or New Hampshire; however, with more than 6 million in population, it has almost as many residents as the rest of New England combined.

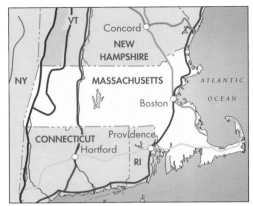

If you remember your high-school history classes, you know that Massachusetts stakes a preeminent claim to historical and cultural importance in the region. **Boston,** its capital and biggest city, has long held itself in the highest regard, viewing itself as the birthplace of American independence, and through its many colleges as keeper of the flame of creativity and social concern. In a day's drive around Boston ("the Hub"), you could have a look at **Plymouth Rock;** spend the afternoon exploring **Salem,** site of the notorious witch trials; then follow in the hoof steps of Paul Revere's horse to **Concord** and historic North Bridge; or watch the sunset over Henry David Thoreau's beloved **Walden Pond.**

There are those who'd say you could learn all you need to know about Massachusetts and America without ever braving the big world beyond Boston's I-495 ring road, but for my time and money, many of the most lasting travel revelations come from the state's less celebrated sights. One example is **New Bedford,** the fishing port where Melville's hero Ishmael started his great adventures in *Moby-Dick.* Another is the brawny old mill town of **Lowell,** preserved as a National Historic Park and shrine to early American industrialism (and favorite son, beat writer Jack Kerouac), and home to some great old diners and a wonderful baseball stadium to boot.

And then there are the college towns of **Amherst** and **Northampton,** or the many artsy communities of the upscale **Berkshires.** Or heading east, the earthly paradise of **Cape Cod,** where Atlantic breakers massage thin barriers of golden sand, overlooked by picturesque lighthouses and historic villages. Massachusetts has a seemingly endless supply of such places, all just a quick drive away from the Hub.

MASSACHUSETTS TIMELINE

1620: Puritan colonists sail from England, arriving at Plymouth after a short stay on Cape Cod.

1770: British soldiers shoot at an angry mob and kill five colonists in what becomes known as the Boston Massacre. Three years later, another step toward American independence is taken at the Boston Tea Party.

1810: Sister Tabitha Babbit, of the Shaker community at Harvard, invents the circular saw.

1820: Women's rights activist Susan B. Anthony is born in Adams, Massachusetts.

Susan B. Anthony

1891: Springfield physical education teacher James Naismith invents the game of basketball.

1928: Playing to common perceptions of thriftiness and reliability associated with puritanical New England, Chrysler names its new line of low-priced cars Plymouth.

1961: Massachusetts Senator John F. Kennedy, of Brookline and Cape Cod, becomes president of the United States.

1982: Set in a basement bar off of Boston Common, the TV show *Cheers* debuts.

John F. Kennedy

2001: Attempting to ease car traffic through the heart of historic Boston, the ongoing Big Dig is the biggest construction project in the United States. One highly visible success so far: a stunning new bridge carrying I-93 over the Charles River.

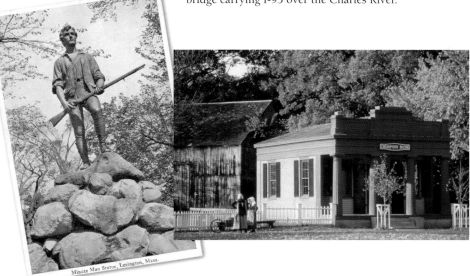

Minute Man Statue, Lexington, Mass.

Rhode Island

Rhode Island is something of a surprise. With about one million residents, it has nearly twice the population of Vermont, at one-tenth its size. With more than 400 miles of waterfront, the Ocean State has more coastline per square mile than any other U.S. state apart from Hawaii, and in summer the sheer numbers of boats and jet skis being towed along its roads can make you think you're in Florida not New England.

Its state capital and biggest city, **Providence,** was recently named the "Best Place to Live" in the United States by *Money* magazine, which cited good jobs, inexpensive real estate, and excellent restaurants and cultural amenities in awarding this honor to the city. Most famous for the massive vacation homes of its main resort city, **Newport,** Rhode Island also has perhaps the richest industrial heritage in America, with more historically significant old mills per square mile than any other state. All of this variety is found in the smallest of all 50 states—barely 20 miles wide.

RHODE ISLAND TIMELINE

1636: Roger Williams, banished from Puritan-led Massachusetts, establishes a colony at Providence.

1790: A year before the Bill of Rights guarantees freedom of religion to U.S. citizens, President George Washington upholds this right in a letter to the congregation of Newport's Touro Synagogue.

1890s: The Gilded Age elite builds massive mansions at Newport, inspiring the expression "conspicuous consumption."

1930: First America's Cup yacht races are held off the shores of Newport.

1952: The country's favorite spud, Mr. Potato Head, is born in Pawtucket, headquarters of toy company Hasbro.

1980: The streamline-style Modern Diner in Pawtucket becomes the first diner to be listed on the National Register of Historic Places.

BEST OF RHODE ISLAND	
Block Island	99
Newport	96
Pawtucket	93
Providence	94
Watch Hill	98

Connecticut

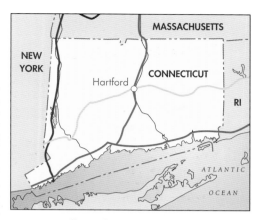

Officially known as the Constitution State, unofficially as the Nutmeg State, and often derided as one huge suburb stretching between Boston and New York City, Connecticut is the hardest of all the New England states to characterize. Statistically speaking, Connecticut is the wealthiest state in the United States, home to more CEOs and highly paid people than anywhere else. (And with more carefully propped picket fences, stone walls, and colonial-style homes than anywhere else!) However, by New England standards especially, it's also an industrial, urban powerhouse. (Toolmaker Stanley is based here, for instance.)

This residential versus industrial dichotomy makes for some fascinating contrasts. The suburban areas within commuting distance of New York City hold some fabulously fancy homes, but this is also where you'll find **Bridgeport,** a heavily industrial center and the state's largest city. (Bridgeport is worth a look for the eccentric P. T. Barnum Museum, which commemorates the circus magnate and former Bridgeport mayor.) Just up the coast is another big city, **New Haven,** a historic port that's home to the excellent museums and libraries of Yale University and also has **Louis' Lunch,** which claims to have invented the hamburger.

Away from the more densely developed coastline and the ever-busy I-95 freeway corridor, Connecticut can seem like another country, where rolling hills and quaint towns define the scene. For any number of reasons, Connecticut can make for some great road-tripping adventures.

CONNECTICUT TIMELINE

1630–39: British settlements at Windsor, Wethersfield, and Hartford unite to form the Connecticut Colony.

1764: The oldest continuously published American newspaper, the *Hartford Courant,* debuts.

1806: Hartford's Noah Webster publishes the first significant dictionary of American English.

1954: The USS *Nautilus,* the world's first nuclear-powered submarine, is launched at Groton.

1998: Adjacent to their massively popular and immensely profitable Foxwoods Casino, the Mashantucket Pequot Indian tribe opens the nation's largest museum dedicated to Native American culture and history.

BEST OF CONNECTICUT

EXPLORING
NEW ENGLAND

N o matter how or why you find yourself in New
England, there's a lot to be said for traveling
with an open mind. It's the sort of place where
the best things are usually just off the beaten track,
where finding adventure is not so much a question of
traveling far and wide but in recognizing the potential
for fun when it's right in front of you or just around a
corner. Whether you're in Boston with a company
rental car and an extra few days after some tedious
convention, touring around and checking out college
towns for yourself or your grandchildren, on your way to a family reunion—or
none of the above—this book is packed with road-tested tips and advice to help
you make the most of your time.

Traveling around New England you'll encounter many of the same things as
elsewhere in America, but you'll experience them to a more extreme degree. From
the utter peace of the pastoral countryside, to the crowded bustle of Boston and the
coastal resorts on the 4th of July, almost everything here—the wealth of history, the
changing weather, the jam-packed crowds, even the quiet—feels somehow more
extreme, and the contrasts are much sharper, than in any other U.S. region. Everything is older, the landscapes are more picturesque; the popular places feel more
popular, and the solitude feels more existential. Compared to most of the country,
places of interest here are much closer together, often side by side, or on top of one
another. Virtual wilderness often backs onto densely pop-
ulated towns or is dotted with tacky tourist attractions,
and the quaintest-looking country hamlets sometimes
have the rusting remains of a burly factory town for
neighbors. Such contrasts typify New England, in the
countryside and along the coastline, and in some ways
can be a little disturbing. At the same time, this intermin-
gling is a big part of New England's charm. After all,
where else can you wake up in a colonial-era B&B, hike
all morning through seemingly pristine forests, drive
down a country road to have lunch at a classic streamlined diner, then spend the evening watching a minor
league baseball game or listening to a world-class string
quartet playing Bach at a music festival?

All of these opportunities can make for great fun and
endless interest, but it can also be a challenge to your pa-
tience and pocketbook. Generally speaking, your travels

around New England will be much more enjoyable if you come prepared for a variety of situations. While advance planning is a very good idea if you have your heart set on certain experiences, things will work out best if you are flexible. Whenever you come and wherever you go, your visit will be more positive if you can go with the flow. If you get to a town and find it's packed because of some big event, go somewhere else for a while and come back again two days later. A big event at Tanglewood in the Berkshires, a lobster festival in Maine, or car race at the New Hampshire International Speedway outside Concord can fill every room for miles, but come the following Monday and these places will have reverted to their comparatively somnolent selves. If it's cold and raining, wait a day or two until the sun is shining to go whale-watching, for example, and spend inclement days inside a museum or savoring an extended brunch. On the other hand, if you see a newspaper or a sign advertising a barbecue cook-off, a parade celebrating a local centenary, a county fair, or what-have-you, take the time to stop and check it out—these sorts of serendipitous, spontaneous experiences often end up being the highlights of a trip.

This is certainly one of the driving forces behind this book. As Yogi Berra said of baseball, 90 percent of the game is half mental. On the road, once you get your mind out of the fast lane, the fun is just around the corner. Get out of the 70 mph mainstream and start exploring the slower roads, and you're bound to find all sorts of fascinating things to enjoy, in addition to those sights you came to see. So stop being merely destination oriented, and start enjoying the ride. For you locals, I hope the following pages point you toward some surprising new treats in your own backyards. For the rest of you, take advantage of how jam-packed the possibilities are in New England, and take the time to see them as they are. You'll find yourself wanting to come back again and again, until you too feel like you belong here.

Happy Trails!

FESTIVALS AND ANNUAL EVENTS

February ..... World Championship Dog-Sled Races; Laconia, New Hampshire
Can-Am Crown International Sled Dog Races; Fort Kent, Maine

March .... St. Patrick's Day Parade; South Boston

April .... Patriot's Day (April 19) in Massachusetts: Boston Marathon, reenactment of Paul Revere's ride, plus staged battles at Lexington and Concord

May .... Lime Rock Grand Prix; Lakeville, Connecticut
MooseMainea; Greenville, Maine

June . . . . Soap Box Derby (Saturday before Father's Day); Camden, Maine

Harvard-Yale Regatta; Thames River between Groton and New London, Connecticut

Loudon Classic motorcycle races; New Hampshire International Speedway, outside Concord

Acadian Day (June 28); festivities all over northern Maine, especially in Madawaska

July . . . . 4th of July: Independence Day celebrations all over New England, ranging from small-town parades (including the nation's oldest, in Bristol, Rhode Island) to big-city celebration like the Boston Pops concert along the banks of the Charles River

Lowell Folk Festival; Lowell, Massachusetts

August . . . . League of New Hampshire Craftsmen Fair; Mount Sunapee State Park, New Hampshire

Wild Blueberry Festival; Machias, Maine

JVC Jazz Festival; Newport, Rhode Island

Brooklyn Fair; held annually since 1852 in Brooklyn, Connecticut

September . . . Fryeburg Fair; Fryeburg, Maine

Highland Games; Loon Mountain in Lincoln, New Hampshire

Fall foliage festivals aplenty

October . . . . Head of the Charles Regatta; Cambridge, Massachusetts

Topsfield Fair; Topsfield, Massachusetts

November . . . . Thanksgiving Day celebrations; Plimoth Plantation and Old Sturbridge Village, Massachusetts

December . . . . Christmas at Hancock Shaker Village, Pittsfield, Massachusetts

Christmas by the Sea; Camden, Maine

WHEN TO GO

New England, stable and old-fashioned as it may often seem, is also a surprisingly dynamic place, especially when it comes to the weather. The weather here seems to change more suddenly than it does in most of the country, going from sunny and warm to cold and wet and back again (if you're lucky) in a matter of minutes. The climate varies tremendously from place to place as well, and a half-day's drive can take you from muggy heat at the coast to bracing fresh air in the mountains.

Be aware that while temperatures and relative humidities can hover in the mid-90s (or higher), very few lodgings in New England have air-conditioning.

That said, there's no bad time of year to travel around New England, but there's really no "best" time, either. The region is comparatively compact, but since the climate varies from place to place so much—even when it's hot and sunny on Cape Cod, it can snow that night in the White Mountains—so no matter when you visit, you can probably find the weather you want if you go to the right places. On the other hand, this extreme regional variation also means that if you're planning to see a lot of different places, you should also be prepared for a lot of different weather—basically all four seasons, at any time of year.

For visitors and residents alike, the fact that seasons are shorter and sharper in New England has an upside and a downside. Peak times can be impossibly crowded, especially in the most popular areas like Cape Cod or the Berkshires. However, this serves to make the off-season feel even more quiet and relaxing. Some places, on the coast in particular, have a very short season and seem to make their full year's earnings in July and August. (In the mountains, the same seems true for those few weeks in early fall, when the leaves on the trees are at their most brilliant.) A homey motel on the coast of Maine that may charge $40 a night in early June can get $140 for that same room a month later. On the other hand, in many of the accommodations around the ski resorts of the Green Mountains, the opposite is true: rooms that are inexpensive and easy to come by in August can be impossible to find once the snow starts to fall.

At any time of year, travel conditions are subject to change on almost a daily basis. Roads that are nearly empty on a Thursday can be clogged to a standstill the next afternoon, when city dwellers escape for the weekend. The rates and availability at hotels and motels vary swiftly with this changing demand; it's not usual for rates to double (or halve!) from day to day.

In most of New England, the most popular time to visit is summer, when schools are out and all of America seems to hit the highways. But summer is by no means ideal: the weather is too hot or ruined by frequent afternoon thunderstorms; the beaches are swarming with visitors; campgrounds and restaurants are full; and all but the most distant back roads are clogged with fellow travelers. That said, even in the middle of August you can still find a place of your own—you may just have to hike a bit farther to get there.

From mid-March through the end of April, maple trees get tapped and their sap turned to syrup. You can witness the proceedings and taste the results at roadside sugar houses all over New England.

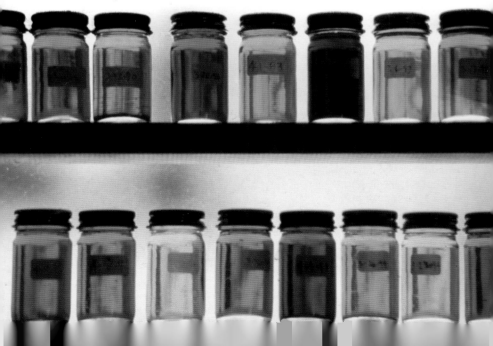

Fall, especially the two weeks on either side of October 1, is another peak time, and for good reason. Apart from the occasional hordes of other travelers, this is as close as it gets to an ideal time to be on the road. In the mountains, the aspens turn gold against the evergreen forest backdrop, and an occasional light snow dusts the peaks. On the coast, "Indian summer" means warm days and clear nights, with no sign of the summer crowds.

Winter, naturally, is the prime time for the region's many ski resorts. There is great skiing all over New England—at mammoth Killington or old-school Mad River Glen in Vermont, Sunday River and Sugarloaf in Maine, and at smaller resorts in Massachusetts and New Hampshire. A full list of New England ski resorts appears in the Index, under "ski areas." Even if you have no intention of skiing, wintertime in New England can be particularly charming if you go for sleigh rides around village squares or cozy up to a raging fireplace at some country B&B.

Spring, commonly referred to as "mud season" in New England, is not generally a prime season for traveling. Unless you're keen to experience the conversion of maple sap into maple syrup, stay put during the spring. The days are too short, the hillsides are bare, the trails muddy, and many attractions are closed, often until May.

GETTING THERE

No matter where in the world you're coming from, getting to New England will be a lot easier than it was for the hapless Pilgrims, who took three months to reach Plymouth Rock. These days, even without the Concorde, it's a quick five hours flight across the Atlantic, so when you factor in the time zones, it takes basically no time at all.

If you don't want to fly and you don't want to drive and you don't already live in New England, your choices come down to riding the rails with **Amtrak** (800/872-7245; www.amtrak.com) or zooming along the Interstates with **Greyhound** (800/231-2222; www.greyhound.com).

Boston's Logan Airport is the main hub for flights coming into New England, receiving more than a dozen daily nonstops from Europe and dozens more from other U.S. cities. But like most of Boston, Logan is generally a frustratingly chaotic place to pass through, so you may want to look into flying into one of the other main airports in New England, like Hartford, Connecticut's Bradley International or the ever-expanding T. F. Green State Airport outside Providence, Rhode Island. Budget carrier Southwest is one of the main companies using Providence, and its bare-bones, ultra-low-fare structures have really shaken up what was long a very expensive corner of the country to reach.

Travelers from the western United States or overseas might also want to think about starting their New England north of the border in the beautiful city of Montreal, which makes a good starting point for a fly–drive tour of New England, especially if the exchange rates continue to keep car rental and accommodation prices lower north of the border. Montreal is a mere hour from northern Vermont,

AIRLINE RESOURCES

Air Canada: 800/776-3000
American Airlines: 800/433-7300, www.aa.com
Continental: 800/525-0280, www.continental.com
Delta: 800/221-1212, www.delta.com
Southwest: 800/435-9792, www.southwest.com
TWA: 800/221-2000, www.twa.com
United: 800/241-6522, www.united.com
US Airways: 800/428-4322, www.usair.com

and Dorval airport gets flights from all over the North America and Europe.

Finally, although distances in New England are nothing near as long as they can be in the western United States, you may prefer to fly directly to one of many regional airports, such as Burlington, Vermont, or Bangor, Maine. This way, you can start or finish your trip in relative calm, rather than dealing with the confusing urban hassle of Boston. You may have to change planes in New York or Chicago, but it brings you that much closer to the New England countryside.

To keep your rental car costs low, insist on unlimited free miles, rent and return your car at the same location, and rent in weekly increments. And always ask for the best deals and resist pressure to upgrade to a bigger (more expensive) car.

Some of the best maps of New England are published by Yarmouth, Maine–based **DeLorme** (207/846-7000 or 800/452-5931). Its double-sided *Highway Map New England* ($4.95) shows the main roads and most topographic features in all six states, but for the best detail pick up copies of its state-by-state atlases ($16.95). These are drawn at a scale of about an inch to the mile, which means that if you cut out all 80 pages and stuck them together, the map of New Hampshire would be about six feet wide and 10 feet tall.

GETTING AROUND

Having a car is definitely a key to happy traveling in New England—and as you probably guessed from the title of this book, driving is by far the best way to get a feel for the region. By all means ride a bike, paddle your kayak, and get out and hike, but since in some places public transit is nonexistent and even tiny towns can be a hundred miles or more apart, you definitely need a car to get around.

Up until the 1960s, when the Interstate freeways were constructed, the roads we highlight in this book (US-1, US-2, US-3, and so on) were the main roads in New England, linking the big cities with the hinterlands. Although they have been largely bypassed by the modern world, they still offer a viable network, and traveling along them can quickly return us to a time when driving was a pleasure and travelers were encouraged to stop and stretch their legs (and maybe buy a postcard or a cup of coffee) along the way. These old roads follow the lay of the land, passing through the center of towns rather than their outskirts, and crossing rivers on covered bridges rather than on high-level viaducts. At the very least, these old roads offer relief from the efficient but bland Interstate system, which, to paraphrase the late Charles Kuralt, has made it possible to drive anywhere without seeing anything. In New England, some of the Interstates—especially I-91 along the Connecticut River or I-93 through the White Mountains—are fine drives by any standard. And in many ways the Interstates are a blessing, especially at night if you're doing a marathon drive to get somewhere by dawn.

The best thing about traveling by car is the flexibility it offers. Everything in New England is within a day's drive of anywhere else, so in some ways you can be more relaxed about planning. If you find out about something going on the next day, you can get there, or if the fall color is peaking in Maine and you're in Connecticut, you can get there that afternoon and still have time to enjoy the drive and the destination. (If you live in Boston or New York City, the smallness of New England makes playing hooky all the more attractive: you can call in sick on Friday morning and have your lunch at a country cafe in greenest Vermont rather than endure the same old same old....)

Bicycle touring companies: Bike Vermont: 800/257-2226, www.bikevermont.com Backroads: 800/462-2848, www.backroads.com

The railroads, which built many of the grand hotels in the White Mountains, were in many ways the creators of the tourism industry in New England, but rail travel these days is not a very practical option. Amtrak offers a handy service between the big cities—the corridor between Boston and New York City has 150 mph, state-of-the-art trains—and

CAR RENTAL AGENCIES

Alamo Rent-A-Car: 800/462-5266, www.alamo.com
Avis Rent A Car: 800/331-1212, www.avis.com
Budget Rent a Car: 800/527-0700, www.budget.com
Dollar Rent A Car: 800/800-4000, www.dollar.com
Enterprise Rent-A-Car: 800/325-8007,
    www.enterprise.com
Hertz: 800/654-3131, www.hertz.com
National: 800/227-7368, www.nationalcar.com
Payless Car Rental: 800/729-5377,
    www.800-payless.com
RentAWreck: 800/421-7253, www.rentawreck.com
Thrifty Car Rental: 800/367-2277, www.thrifty.com

there is also service via the Connecticut River valley between New Haven and Burlington, and across Massachusetts roughly parallel to I-90. Rail travel doesn't work all that well on its own, but in conjunction with a rental car or two it can be great fun: fly to Boston and get a car for a few days to tour around there, then hop on the overnight train to Burlington to rent another car for your tour of the Green Mountain State. There are also a few historic railroads—like the Green Mountain Flyer in Bellows Falls, Vermont—which make a nice change of pace from being behind the wheel. These all travel through glorious scenery, but they all bring you back to where you began.

The best way to get up close and personal with the outside world in New England is to get around under your own steam. Riding a bike along a country lane or paddling across a placid mountain lake does wonders for the soul. If you don't have your own gear, rentals and guides are usually available, and if you want someone else to plan the perfect trip, look into joining a guided tour. Offered by companies like Backroads or Bike Vermont, these tours usually feature the comparative luxury of staying at B&Bs, and follow routes chosen from years of experience (usually along the sorts of roads we recommend for drivers). Best of all, you can choose your desired level of exertion, and cycle as much or as little as you want, availing yourself of a ride in the van if you get tired or sore. Vermont in particular has some heavenly cycling tours, and many New England ski areas are open to mountain bikers in the summer months.

WHERE TO EAT

Apart from the superior driving pleasure, the real advantage of avoiding the freeways and following the roads described herein is clear: the food. From taco stands to four-star restaurants, the best food is almost always well away from the freeways, and usually along some scenic back road like the ones in this book. Besides highlighting the most interesting roads, I've also tried to point out the best places to stop and eat along the way, with a definite focus on characteristic regional specialties. The range of restaurants in particular is as diverse as the varying land-scapes, so I've tried to include everything from fried-clam stands in Massachusetts and diners serving stacks of fluffy pan-cakes laden with maple syrup, to more high-end places serving the finest and freshest meals. I've listed the best of the bunch, but one of the greatest plea-sures of traveling is discovering some great place all by yourself, so be ad-venturous—this is a land of good food, and you're unlikely to go wrong.

Eating options vary tremendously depending upon where you travel—in the wealthy, densely populated parts of coastal New England, all kinds of good food can be found around every turn, but in the middle of the rural Maine nowhere, your choices are not so plentiful. Almost everywhere, though, great

---

SOME NEW ENGLAND FOOD SPECIALTIES

p

Lobster Rolls—Shredded lobster tail meat, served up in a toasted bun. Om-nipresent in Maine, where even McDonald's sells them.

Blueberry Pie—In Maine especially, this finishes off most meals. Blueberries, har-vested fresh toward the end of summer, are also available in pancakes, muffins, and milk shakes, and at "U-Pick-Em" fields in the more northerly climes.

Maple Syrup—Made in Maine, New Hampshire, and Vermont, this laboriously concentrated nectar comes in grades varying from light to dark (in color and taste), and is the only thing you should pour on your pancakes or over your Ben & Jerry's vanilla ice cream.

Fried Dough—Deep-fried pizza dough coated in sugar and cinnamon and sold at beachfront stands, amusement parks, and county fairs all summer long.

Frappe—Always pronounced monosyllabically ("FRAP"), this is basically an extra-thick milk shake.

Whoopie Pie—Like a giant Oreo, with creamy white frosting slathered between a pair of cakelike chocolate cookies. This burger-sized concoction is sold at bak-ery counters and diners all over northern New England.

meals can be found, thanks to the presence all over New England of the hungry travelers' best friend: the diner. "Diner" can stand for all sorts of places, from nondescript roadside shacks to classic stainless-steel–encased streamliners. Design students study them, and great books have been written about all of the many different styles and makes (like Sterling, Worcester, Fodero, Silk City—please see page 236 for a more detailed introduction to this incredible edible world). But the one thing all true diners have in common is that they serve hearty, few frills meals and offer a genuinely warm welcome, whether you eat there once and move on or come back every day for most of your life.

While diners are an essential component of the New England food scene, there are others to delve into as well. Along the coast, especially in Maine, you'll come across homespun lobster pounds—wooden shacks sitting along the docks, serving up freshly caught, boiled-to-order lobsters, usually accompanied by potatoes, corn-on-the-cob, and blueberry pie. (The whole combo is sometimes called a "Shore Dinner.") Inland, especially in the more remote rural areas, more unlikely places to eat are the many general stores that stand at the crossroads or in the center of country villages. These have everything you could need (some have ancient-looking signs saying, "If we don't have it, you don't need it!"). In addition to groceries, maps, newspapers, and hardware, general stores usually have full delis, sandwiches, and shelves full of picnic-perfect local treats, including apple ciders, blueberry muffins, local beers (see page 201 for more on New England's many excellent beers), cheddar cheeses, wonderful fresh jams and jellies, maple candies, and more.

Hotel Wentworth, New Castle, N. H.

WHERE TO STAY

Throughout this book, I've tried to recommend a range of quality accommodations in all price ranges, but when it comes down to it, I find there are basically two types of places to stay. The most common is the sort where you simply want a clean bed in a quiet room, so you can sleep soundly and get back on your way the next morning. This type of accommodation—copiously offered by that all-American roadside icon, the motel—is available throughout New England, and unless there's some major event going on, it's very rare that every room in a given town will be taken. Rates in New England are quite high by U.S. standards, and during the peak summer months two people sharing a room should count on spending around $80 a night including the usual array of taxes for a standard

For help finding that perfect B&B, check out the ***Innkeepers' Register*** (800/344-5244), a guidebook listing more than 400 distinguished inns around North America, including more than 85 independently owned historic inns around New England.

motel—much less in some out-of-the-way places, considerably more in bigger cities. I've listed a few favorite motels throughout this book (usually ones with a particularly fine neon sign in addition to the requisite clean bed!). But the best guarantee of finding something to your liking is to stop driving when the sun goes down and find a place to sleep then and there. The later you put it off, the less choice you will have.

The second type of place to stay I've tended to include are special ones, places worth planning your trip around—a historic lodge in the North Woods, a romantic Victorian-era B&B in some idyllic Vermont setting, that sort of thing. I recommend mixing in at least a few of these into your travel plans and staying put for two or more days straight, so you don't have to pack up and hit the road so quickly. Although many of these are often booked solid for months in advance, it never hurts to ask if they happen to have a vacancy; in the best case scenario, at short notice innkeepers may even offer you a discount, rather than take the risk of having the room go unoccupied.

Another thing to keep in mind as you travel is that you can often save significant cash by staying in less "desirable" towns near the prime destinations. In the Berkshires, consider places like North Adams, next door to Williamstown, Massachusetts; in Vermont, look into White River Junction, in between upscale environs of Hanover and Woodstock. Rates are generally much lower and availability much higher, making them well worth the short drive. Also, many of the most popular sorts of places may generally be available only by the full week. A large percentage of New England's accommodations look and feel more like an old-fashioned sum-

---

LODGINGS

Appalachian Mountain Club: 603/466-2727

Best Western: 800/528-1234, www.bestwestern.com

Budgetel Inns: 800/428-3438, www.budgetel.com

Comfort Inns: 800/228-5150, www.comfortinn.com

Courtyard by Marriott: 800/321-2211, www.marriott.com

Days Inn: 800/325-2525, www.daysinn.com

Distinguished Inns of North America: 800/344-5244

Econo Lodge: 800/553-2666, www.econolodge.com

Friendship Inns: 800/453-4511

Hilton Hotels: 800/445-8667, www.hilton.com

Howard Johnson Lodges: 800/654-2000, www.hojo.com

Hostelling International—American Youth Hostels (HI-AYH): 202/783-6161, www.hiayh.org

Hyatt Hotels: 800/233-1234, www.hyatt.com

Marriott Hotels & Resorts: 800/228-9290, www.marriott.com

Motel 6: 800/466-8356, www.motel6.com

Quality Inns: 800/228-5151, www.qualityinn.com

Ramada Inns: 800/228-2828, www.ramada.com

Red Lion Inns: 800/547-8010, www.redlion.com

Rodeway Inns International: 800/228-2000, www.rodeway.com

Sheraton Hotels: 800/325-3535, www.sheraton.com

Super 8 Motels: 800/800-8000, www.super8.com

TraveLodge Hotels: 800/578-7878, www.travelodge.com

mer camp than a full-fledged resort—these are the sorts of places where families return year after year, planning their visits every January and staying for a week or more each summer. If you're lucky, though, a cabin or room may open up when you're in the area, and it never hurts to ask.

Alternately, I've also included hostels, which offer cheap but spartan accommodations often in beautiful locales. Not only can staying in hostels save you money, it's also a great way to meet fellow travelers. Camping is the best way to experience the wide open spaces. Even if you don't intend to backpack, you may want to wake up at one of the many huts operated by the Appalachian Mountain Club; some of these are full service, with meals and hot showers, while others are rustic lean-tos deep in the wilds. At all of them, the wonders of Mother Nature are right on your doorstep, and most are within a hour's walk of the road.

SAMPLE ITINERARIES
American History Tour
Day One: Start at the beginning, Plymouth Rock, which marks the site where the Pilgrims settled in New England. For a living picture of what life might have been like, tour the nearby Plimouth Plantation, which re-creates the original Puritan colony on the eve of the first Thanksgiving.

Day Two: Head to the Hub, Boston, where every street holds significant historic sites. Board the Tea Party Ship, visit Paul Revere's house, pay respects to heroes of the American Revolution at Bunker Hill Monument, then follow in the footsteps of the Redcoats on their ill-fated way to Concord.

Day Three: Go west to the immaculately preserved colonial-era frontier settlement of Deerfield, and then follow the scenic Mohawk Trail west to the history-rich resort towns of the Berkshires.

Day Four: Cruise scenic Route 100 into the Green Mountains of Vermont to visit Plymouth, the wonderfully evocative home of former President Calvin Coolidge, whose 90-plus-year-old son John still minds the family business—making cheddar cheese the old-fashioned way. Continue on to picturesque Woodstock, where the Marsh-Billings National Historic Site commemorates the birth of the ecological conservation movement.

Day Five: Drop down into the idyllic Lake Champlain Valley, touring historic towns and setting aside most of the day to explore the incredible array of vernacular Americana on display at the magical Shelburne Museum. In summer, enjoy a Vermont Expos game at historic Centennial Field, one of the oldest ballparks in the nation.

Day Six: Head east into New Hampshire to enjoy the incredible scenery and historic resorts of the White Mountains, riding an ancient cog railway to the top of New England's highest peak, perhaps staying at the landmark Mount Washington Hotel.

Canterbury Shaker Village

Day Seven: Head south to the perfectly preserved Canterbury Shaker Village, one of the last of these 19th-century religious communities. Continue on to the Atlantic coast, where the remnants of colonial settlements and the nation's oldest shipyards survive in the lively city of Portsmouth. After dark, commune with the supernatural in bewitching Salem.

Summer Fun

Day One: Enjoy everything from an antique hand-carved merry-go-round to modern roller coasters at the region's largest amusement park, Six Flags New England, outside Springfield. If you don't get your fill of thrill rides, stop by historic Canobie Lake Park, which has a clickety-clacking wooden roller coaster and its own beachfront water park.

Day Two: Head north to New England's summer vacation central, Weirs Beach on magnificent Lake Winnipesaukee. Soak up the sun, take a boat tour, play air hockey and arcade games, and when the sun goes down, watch a movie at a thriving drive-in theater.

Day Three: Cruise north from the lakes to the White Mountains. Hike up the Flume, look at the Old Man of the Mountain, ride a slide down a ski run, and watch the dancing bears at Clark's Trading Post.

Day Four: Head down to the coast. Take a scenic cruise of the Casco Bay Islands, watch a Portland Sea Dogs baseball game, surf the waves at the sandy beaches of Cape Elizabeth, or ride the roller coasters at Old Orchard Beach (fireworks every Thursday!).

Day Five: Cruise south along the ocean, bowl on the beach at York Beach, join the adolescent strut at Hampton Beach, watch the whales off historic Gloucester, or enjoy a baseball game at Boston's historic Fenway Park.

Day Six: If you can time your trip to avoid spending the day in traffic, Cape Cod has to be the ultimate summertime destination in New England. Hang out on the endless sands, ride a bike along country lanes, watch the sun set from the tip of Provincetown, then join the nightly pageant at the bars and cafes.

Day Seven: If you happen to be in Rhode Island on the 4th of July, enjoy the country's oldest and largest Independence Day parade at Bristol. In August, take in the great music at Newport's JVC Jazz Festival. At other times, eat at the area's many great old diners, catch a Pawtucket Red Sox Triple A baseball game, or hang out on the beach at Watch Hill, home of the country's oldest carousel.

HOW TO USE THIS BOOK

*R*oad Trip USA: New England is a concise and complete guide to this most historic and fascinating corner of the country. Covering broad swathes stretching across all six states and organized along the major travel routes, this book gives full background as well as descriptive and practical information for anyone touring around New England. Out of the many thousands of miles of highway crisscrossing the region, I've selected these roads because they offer consistent peaks of driving pleasure. Although the chapters are organized along established, mostly two-lane highways, in all of them I frequently suggest many scenic or interesting alternatives or detours to visit significant sites. For instance, I repeatedly recommend veering off old US-1 along the coast of Maine to explore the dozens of stunning peninsulas and less-traveled spots that make this state such an addicting place to travel.

Road Trip USA: New England has been designed to work both as an entertaining armchair read and as a helpful mile-by-mile guide when you're out on the road. The **chapters** are organized in geographical order, so that the words track the changing scene. Each route is subdivided into small enough stretches that, with a little practice, are easy to use even if you're traveling in the opposite direction to the flow of the text. **Interstate highways** and places where two routes intersect are clearly cross-referenced throughout the book, so you can organize an itinerary to suit yourself, no matter where you're starting from or where you want to go. Seven of the eight chapters are broadly organized along a single non-Interstate route—starting with US-1, then US-2, US-3, and so on through US-7. All of these routes track the original 1920s federal highways, whose sequential numbers reflect the preeminence New England has always seemed to have (politically speaking, at least) when it comes to national status. A final chapter suggests a driving equivalent to the hikers' beloved Appalachian Trail, following a series of country roads from near Mount Katahdin deep in the Maine woods to south across the White Mountains and on into the Berkshires—with guaranteed fall color excellence if you're looking for autumn leaves.

All of the background and practical information on each place is woven together in each segment of text, so there's no need to flip through the pages to find a key piece of information. Throughout each chapter we've included a series of detailed **maps,** so you can keep on track whether you're searching for moose in northern New Hampshire or looking for colonial history in the heart of Connecticut. Odds and ends of trivia and local history are given in the **margins** of the text; this is also where we've listed selected radio stations, short-but-scenic detours, and other details of passing interest. Longer **sidebars** or special topic essays are sprinkled throughout the main text, covering in greater detail some of the many fascinating aspects of each place, giving a taste of Shaker style, an introduction to diners, or tracing the Midnight Ride of Paul Revere.

To guide you along the roads less traveled, one of the most important ways in which this book differs from traditional travel guides is that (so we could have space to write about the really fascinating stuff) we have limited coverage of major metropolitan areas to short **Survival Guides.** These two- or three-page miniguides are intended to give essential tips on what to see and where to eat and sleep in the handful of relatively big cities—Boston, Hartford, Providence, and the like—so that you can make the most of a passing visit. Similar Survival Guides are also used to key you into the many Interstate freeways that crisscross New England, so you can get here quickly then leave the big roads behind.

Finally, at the very end of the book, there is a collection of **Road Trip Resources,** which includes tips on recommended reading, details on some helpful organizations like the Appalachian Mountain Club, as well as contact information for the various state tourism departments and road conditions hotlines. An extensive **index** follows, so you can quickly find your way to a specific place. Interspersed throughout the index are thematic boxes, which highlight such special subjects as minor-league baseball teams and covered bridges—and tell you where to find them in the book.

INTERSTATE HIGHWAYS

While this book concentrates on covering scenic drives, it's hard to ignore the Interstate highways, which run across New England along long-established routes. I-95, for example, runs alongside historic US-1 for almost its entire route; we cover I-95 in three main chunks, across Maine (on page 65), across New Hampshire and Massachusetts (page 79), and across the route blazed by US-3, while I-91 (see page 198) follows the path of US-5.

At points in the text where two routes intersect, a bold banner gives the cross-referenced pages for the other route, so you can easily switch from route to another.

To make it easy to find where you are, throughout *Road Trip USA: New England* the prose is broken up into blocks of text, describing a certain town, state park, section of highway or detour. Each of these segments tells you all you need to know: some history, something of the layout of the town, the main attractions, and necessary practicalities of where to eat, sleep, and find further information.

Short tidbits of text in the margins point out odd facts and interesting pieces of information about the area the route is passing through. Marginal comments throughout the book may recommend a local radio station, a nearby restaurant, or a scenic detour, or offer a piece of roadside trivia.

US-1 becomes a freeway around Revere, about five miles north of downtown Boston. If you want to stay down on ground level, follow Route 60 and Route 1A (signs will say Logan or Airport) and detour east through Revere Beach, a historic resort area that's now home to petrochemical refineries and the Suffolk Downs horse racing track. If you want some up-close views of jets taking off from Logan, wind out to Winthrop, which sticks out into the bay right beneath the flight path.

If you take US-1/I-93, you'll cross the Charles River into downtown Boston on a nifty new cable-stayed bridge, designed by Swiss engineer Christian Menn; if you follow Route 1A, you come in via the Sumner Tunnel, entering downtown more or less underneath the Paul Revere House in the historic North End. The ongoing Big Dig construction, which is eventually going to replace the downtown I-93 expressway with a new tunnel, may send you along any number of detours, compounding Boston's traditional impossibilities for drivers. If you really want to see the city, park wherever you can and take public transportation.

To the south, US-1 starts off as Huntington Avenue past the Museum of Fine Arts and some nice parks, then hops on the VFW Parkway to the I-95/Route 128 beltway, and then runs parallel to the freeway for the rest of the way to Rhode Island.

Boston marks the junction of US-1 with our road-trip route along US-3, which runs north into New Hampshire and south along the coast through Plymouth towards Cape Cod. For more on this historic route, see pages 138–167.

BROOKLINE

Brookline (pop. 54,700) is very much a part of Boston but legally and in many ways socially separate from the Hub. Located off US-1 and well off the main tourist trail, the town has some little-known and truly fascinating historic sites and museums. Car-culture fans will want to visit America's oldest and most stylish collection in the **Museum of Transportation,** 15 Newton Street (Tues.–Sun. 10 AM–5 PM; $5; 617/522-6547), where some of the finest examples of early touring motor cars are housed on a sprawling 65-acre estate. Brookline is also the place where President John F. Kennedy was born in 1917; his family home at 83 Beals Street has been restored as the **JFK Birthplace National Historic Site** (Wed.–Sun. 11 AM–4 PM; $2; 617/566-7937).

On the south side of Boston, US-1 runs through the town of Dedham, where the notorious trial of **Sacco and Vanzetti** was held in 1921. Accused of murder during a robbery of a payroll truck, the two "anarchist bastards" (as the presiding judge described them) were executed after a trial most historians agree was a total miscarriage of justice.

The final pilgrimage place in Brookline's pantheon of history is in many ways the most significant: the home of landscape architect Frederick Law Olmsted, who did more than anyone else to shape the look of the American landscape. The idyllic suburban home where the designer of New York's Central Park lived and worked for the last 15 years of his life has been preserved as the **Frederick Law Olmsted National Historic Site,** at 99 Warren Street (Fri.–Sun. 10 AM–4:30 PM; donations; 617/566-1689).

COASTAL NEW ENGLAND: US-1 93

PAWTUCKET

US-1 eases across the Rhode Island north and east of Providence at the blue-collar city of Pawtucket (pop. 72,644), which has played a vital role in American industrial history. Located in a waterfront park at the center of town and tiny by 19th-century factory standards, **Slater's Mill** (Tues.–Sat. 10 AM–5 PM, Sunday 1–5 PM in summer, weekends only March–May; $4; 401/725-8638) helped launch America's Industrial Revolution. Following the Revolutionary War, England banned exportation of goods to America. However, when English-born Samuel Slater, who apprenticed at Richard Arkwright's cotton mills in Derbyshire, moved to the United States, he brought with him the knowledge of the latest mechanized cotton-spinning technology. Slater also brought with him significant management skills, and in partnership with others, he transformed American manufacturing from handicrafts to mass production.

Numerous exhibits trace the historical context of Slater's efforts, but the real reason to visit is to watch and listen as the eight-ton water wheel creaks and groans around and around, powering the many belts and pulleys that still turn the machines as they did in Slater's day.

Pawtucket's other significant historic site is also well worth a visit, though it can be more difficult to find: the **Modern Diner,** 364 East Avenue (401/726-8390), just east of I-95. A classic streamlined Sterling diner, the Modern was the first diner to be registered as an official historic landmark. It's open every day from 7 AM–3 PM (from 8 AM on Sunday) for breakfast and lunch, with dinners available Tuesday–Friday until 8 PM. Check it out—the cranberry pancakes are great.

Boston has the Museum of Fine Arts; downtown Dedham has the **Museum of Bad Art** (Mon.–Fri. 6:30–10:30 PM, Sat. and Sun. 1:30–10:30 PM; free; 617/325-8224), a changing display of truly terrible paintings housed in the basement of the Dedham Community Theater, 580 High Street.

For every 50 to 150 miles of highway, we have included a detailed map. On these maps, which appear every few pages throughout the book, we have highlighted the route as well as major highways and landmarks to help you get around. All the towns and points of interest described in the text are printed on the maps in blue.

COASTAL NEW ENGLAND: US-1

THE SOMEDAY MAYBE

COASTAL NEW ENGLAND: US-1

More than any other highway in New England, US-1 offers a grand overview of this diverse and often beautiful region. Running along the Eastern Seaboard all the way from Canada to Key West, Florida, US-1 was once the main—and most important—road along the New England coast. Linking the colonial-era capitals of Boston and New York, the route is still often called the Post Road in reference to its historic use as a mail route long before the automobile was invented. Now that 99 percent of the traffic takes the parallel I-95 freeway, by following US-1 all the way or in short stretches, you can still get a feel for what life was like in New England before there was a fast lane to escape from.

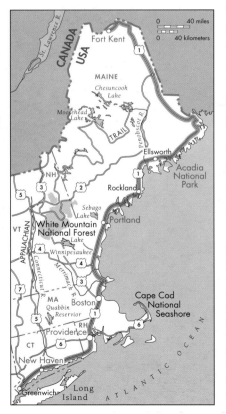

Maine accounts for fully half the length of US-1 across New England, and the route there is fairly equally distributed between the hardworking countryside of the northern interior and the generally awesome southern coastline. From its start at Fort Kent in the northernmost reaches of the contiguous United States, US-1 winds south along the lush valley of the St. John River. It's a pretty, relaxed drive, but once US-1 hits the Atlantic Ocean on the Sunrise Coast (so called because it's the first part of the country to see the sun rise), things only get better. The crashing waves and rugged coastal cliffs and coves reach a peak at Acadia National Park, but the whole shoreline here is wild and wonderful—and a lot less touristed than is much of New England, thanks to its comparatively remote location. US-1 is a beautiful drive, and gives access to a series of even more stunning smaller roads that loop off closer to the ocean.

By New England standards, Maine is huge; it's at least as big as all the other five states put together. If you followed every nook and cranny of Maine's amazing coastline, you'd cover up to 5,000 miles. Even if you cut across the more remote peninsulas, US-1 still takes more than 230 miles to get across, or around, coastal Maine, compared to a mere 50 miles more across New Hampshire and Massachusetts to reach Boston.

Acadia National Park is one of coastal New England's true "must-see" places. It also serves as a handy dividing line between the less-hyped northern half of Maine and sometimes frustratingly popular southern half of Maine, where picture-perfect town after picture-perfect town seems to line up along the rugged shoreline. There are no freeways in these parts, so US-1 is the main road, which means that it can get quite busy during peak season. This central section of the Maine coast is where you'll find scenic towns such as Camden and Wiscasset, as well as brawnier cities such as Bath and Rockland. Ultra-quaint little hamlets, often consisting of little more than a bed-and-breakfast or a crossroads cafe, dot the many peninsulas south of US-1, along with the inevitable port full of bobbing lobster boats. At Portland, the coast's one really big city, US-1 meets I-95 and the coastal character changes again, geographically and demographically. The rugged granite shoreline gives way to a glaciated landscape of broader, sandier beaches, while the influence of summer tourism is felt in such diverse destinations as elite Kennebunkport (summer home of former President George H. W. Bush) and Old Orchard Beach, New England's brashest beach resort.

For the 20-odd miles it takes to get across New Hampshire, US-1 is neither the fastest nor the most enjoyable road. Therefore, you'll probably find yourself using either I-95 (a $1 toll road that races uneventfully across the state) or the prettier and more interesting Route 1A, the coastal route on which you can take your time and follow the water from Portsmouth all the way to Massachusetts.

The same is true of US-1's journey across Massachusetts, which includes some of the most gloriously tacky roadside chaos (especially just north of Boston) along with miles of surprisingly rural countryside. For scenery, the longer and more winding Route 1A is superior in every way, and for speed, you can always hop onto I-95. However you get around, the coast north of Boston contains dozens of significant places (from bewitching Salem to *The Perfect Storm* fishing port of Gloucester), as well as some great beaches.

South of Boston, however, US-1 doesn't have a lot to offer, and there isn't much worth stopping for until you cross the border into Rhode Island. There the wealth of offerings in Pawtucket and Providence belies the state's tiny stature. The Rhode Island coastline is also superb, as are the stately homes of historic Newport, so this is another place where you'll want to steer well clear of I-95.

By contrast, driving US-1 across Connecticut can feel tortuously slow, although the upside is the nearly continuous sense that there is much more to the place than meets the eye. Best known for its isolated temples to tourism, including Foxwoods Casino and the historic ships at Mystic Seaport, the Connecticut coast also has dozens of truly historic towns and more than a few fine beaches.

> At Fort Kent, the St. John River marks the border between Maine and New Brunswick, Canada. The international border also marks the dividing line between the Eastern and Atlantic time zones.

> In the middle of Fort Kent, near the bridge to Canada, is a sign reading: This Site Marks the Historic Terminus of US-1 Originating in Key West Florida.

FORT KENT

Far-north Maine, especially the international St. John River Valley, is Acadian country. Acadians were French Catholics who moved here after the British kicked them out of Nova Scotia in 1755, and even today, French is the native tongue for anywhere from half to nearly all of the inhabitants in many communities. Fort Kent (pop. 4,300) is the largest of numerous small frontier towns in the region, and the population more than doubles during its most popular event: the annual **Can-Am Crown International Sled Dog Races** at the end of February. Braving the freezing weather, dogsled racers compete in a 60-mile, one-day event, in addition to a tortuous, multiday 250-miler, both of which start and end right downtown.

> A quicker and perhaps more scenic alternative to the long loop US-1 makes down the St. John River is to follow Route 11 south from Fort Kent along the Fish River to lovely Eagle Lake. It takes you through open, rolling countryside, and remains pretty all the way to Portage, where you can head east along Route 227 into Presque Isle to rejoin US-1.

The one real sight to see in Fort Kent is the historic **Blockhouse,** built along the riverfront in 1839 during a border war and now preserved as a small museum, with an adjacent picnic area leading down to the riverside. For more on the region's lively history, the small **University of Maine Fort Kent campus,** on Route 11 just off US-1, has a good collection of Acadian and other historical materials.

Food and accommodation options line up along US-1 downtown, where you can tuck in to burgers and french fries at **Sirois Restaurant,** 84 W. Main Street (207/834-6548). If you're brave, try a heartwarming (and artery-clogging!) plate of *poutine,* a traditional Acadian treat that consists of french fries topped with cheese and soaked in gravy. The "nice" place to stay in town is **Daigle's B&B,** on US-1 at 96 E. Main Street ($50–75; 207/834-5803). In summer, rooms are available at the **University of Maine Fort Kent campus,** 25 Pleasant Street ($15–30; 207/834-7513).

MADAWASKA AND THE ST. JOHN RIVER

From its terminus at Fort Kent, US-1 winds north and east then south along the St. John River through a series of small crossroads communities, whose names (like Frenchville and Notre Dame) testify to the predominance of French heritage in the region. The largest town hereabouts is Madawaska (pop. 4,800) which hosts the annual **Acadian Festival.** The event, usually held on June 28 (recognized throughout Maine as Acadian Day), draws francophones and Acadians from all over Maine and Quebec. During the rest of the year, life in Madawaska revolves around the massive **Fraser Paper Company mill,** which offers free tours (Mon.–Fri. 9 AM–4 PM). Larger mills sit across the river in the Canadian town of Edmunston.

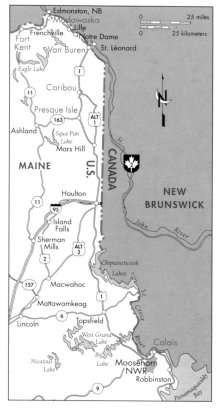

US-1 south of Madawaska is rural and open, until you suddenly come upon a miragelike sight: cathedral-sized St. Luke church, standing somewhat forlornly along US-1 near Lille. Further along, five miles north of Van Buren

In Madawaska, a sign outside a hardware store has the enigmatic slogan, "Oldest trustworthy store in Nation."

in tiny Keegan, is the 2.5-acre **Acadian Village** (daily 9 AM–5 PM, in summer only; $3), a reconstructed town, complete with schoolhouse, barber shop, chapel, and blacksmith's forge.

CARIBOU AND PRESQUE ISLE

Separated by a dozen or so miles off US-1, the rival towns of Caribou (pop. 9,415) and Presque Isle (pop. 10,500) form two points of what is locally known as the Potato Triangle for its impressive production of spuds—some 2 billion pounds annually. Both towns sport a full range of services (gas, food, and lodging) and main attractions. The more northerly of the two, Caribou, has the eccentric **Nylander Museum**, 393 Main Street (Wed.–Sun. 1–5 PM, in summer only; free; 207/493-4209), a museum with several thousand fossils, shells, and taxidermied creatures collected from all over the world. Presque Isle boasts **Double Eagle Park**, located four miles south of town and two miles west of US-1 on Spragueville Road. Here a 10-foot-high replica of a hot air balloon commemorates the first successful trans-Atlantic balloon flight, which started here in 1978 when the *Double Eagle* launched from the park and landed in France a week later. Not to be outdone, Caribou has erected a monument to Joe Kittinger, who in 1984 broke the hot-air balloon distance record previously held by the *Double Eagle*. The monument is two miles south of town along US-1.

Aroostook County, which covers all of northernmost Maine, produces more tons of potatoes annually than anywhere outside the Pacific Northwest. Aroostook County is also among the biggest broccoli producers on the East Coast.

Back down to earth: along with the usual franchised fast-food candidates, you can choose from a good variety of eating places in these dueling towns. In Caribou, consider stopping at **Mainer's Omelette Trap,** 7 Prospect Street (207/496-8727), open all year for lunch on weekdays, and breakfast and lunch on weekends. In Presque Isle, **Winnie's Dairy Bar** is open all day at 79 Parsons Street (207/769-4971), along Route 227 on the west side of town. In winter you can witness the unusual sight of snowmobilers cruising up for Winnie's beloved burgers and lobster stew. Less casual but highly recommended is the **Governor's Restaurant,** on US-1 at 350 Main Street (207/769-2274). The eatery is famous for its strawberry pies—even stodgy AAA calls the desserts "wonderful."

If you're near Caribou on a Saturday night in summer, you might want to check out the action at the **Spud Speedway,** outside town. Here you can watch drivers take 25 laps around a dirt track at speeds above 75 mph—and at a constant noise level of 120 decibels—for only $5.

Presque Isle has the upper hand on the motel scene. Check out the hilltop **Keddy's Motor Inn** (207/764-3321 or 800/561-7666), right on US-1 a mile south of town, has an indoor pool, a restaurant and bar, and doubles for under $60.

If you have time and want a more scenic trip than US-1 offers, try Route 164, which bends west from Caribou then follows the Aroostook River into Presque Isle. It'll add a half-hour to your trip, more if you stop at the fascinating little history museums in tiny Washburne.

The intriguing border city of Houlton is the start of our jaunt west along US-2, and is covered on page 112.

CALAIS

After a long and uneventful journey south from Houlton, US-1 reaches the waterfront at Calais. Named for the French port but pronounced "Callous," Calais (pop. 4,100) is an industrial town with a history going way back to 1604, when French colonist Samuel de Champlain launched an ill-fated settlement on nearby St. Croix Island where 35 people died during the first winter. The following spring, the survivors fled to Nova Scotia. Calais didn't really get going until more than two centuries later, when it began to evolve into a busy shipping center. Nowadays, the community's fortunes are tied up with the giant Georgia-Pacific paper mill, though remnants of its Victorian-era self survive in the Main Street Historic District, downtown.

Southwest of Calais (though technically heading north because of the curving topography), about three miles from downtown, US-1 runs along the boundaries of the 17,250-acre **Moosehorn National Wildlife Refuge.** Along with many mammals and hundreds of species of birds, bald eagles are the big draw here, especially in summer when you're likely to spy newly hatched or fledgling birds. There's an observation area right on US-1, and platforms have been built nearby to aid the great birds in their nesting and reproduction. For further information or for maps of the many hiking and cross-country ski trails in the refuge, contact the ranger station (207/454-7161).

One of the more interesting places to stay in the area is the **Redclyffe Inn** ($70–80; 207/454-3270), on US-1 a dozen miles south of downtown Calais. Perched on a bluff overlooking the river and Passamaquoddy Bay, this inn has a little bit of everything to do with roadside architecture—a Gothic-style Victorian main building, some 1930s cabins, and a more modern motel. There's an on-site restaurant, too.

DETOUR: EASTPORT

One of the few industrial-strength ports in northern Maine, Eastport is a welcome change of pace from the upscale ambiance of so much of the coast. If you prefer tugboats to yachts, you'll like it here at the southern end of Passamaquoddy Bay. Huge tankers and container ships often moor right along the 100-year-old downtown waterfront, making photogenic contrasts with the historic architecture of Water Street, where the **S. L. Wadsworth & Son** store at 42 Water Street is Maine's oldest business and the oldest ships' chandlery in the United States. Eastport (the onetime "sardine capital of the world") used to be a big deal in these parts, but the canneries closed 25 years ago and the downtown area is now more than a little depressed, with lots of vacant storefronts. One upside of so much open space is that there's room to display one of the town's treasures, the scale model of a massive but ill-fated tidal power plant that was slated for construction in the mid-1930s. Today you can study it at the small **Quoddy Maritime Museum** (hours vary; free; 207/853-4297) next to Quoddy Crafts on Water Street. The New Deal project was on a par with the Grand Coulee Dam and other reclamation projects out west, and

About midway between Presque Isle and Houlton, at the junction of US-1 and Route 1A, is the flyspeck crossroads town of **Mars Hill.** Here you'll find a trio of gas stations and an abandoned Newberry's Five & Dime, all lit up by the flashing neon sign fronting Al's Diner.

Along US-1 on the north edge of Houlton, keep an eye out for the chrome-and-steel sculpture garden also known as **Hubcap Heaven.** Nearby, you can stretch your legs at a vintage Roller-Rama.

In Weston, along US-1 about 30 miles south of Houlton, a summer-only restaurant known as the **Million Dollar View** serves up burgers, seafood, and a grand panorama over the Chiputneticook Lakes.

Running between Calais and Bangor, Route 9 is known as the "Airline." It's a busy artery but there are few services and even fewer sights.

Between Calais and Robbinston, US-1 is marked every mile by a red granite milestone, installed by a horse trainer more than 100 years ago to mark the distance. Near Perry, another five miles south, a roadside marker along US-1 points out another distinction: it's on the 45th Parallel, the exact midway point between the North Pole and the Equator.

Whitlock Mill Lighthouse, built in 1892 and visible from a rest area along US-1 four miles southeast of Calais, is the northernmost lighthouse on the Atlantic coast of Maine.

The powerful, 30-foot tides of coastal Maine have inspired efforts to harness them to generate electricity but with little success. The remnants of a New Deal–era power project can be seen on the way to Eastport from Route 190, which runs in part over a series of hydroelectric dams. For a better sense of the scale of this ambitious tidal power venture, see the scale model in the Quoddy Maritime Museum in Eastport.

If you're in the market for a cool wood scooter to rival the trendy metal Razor models, check out the inventory at **Wood, Wheels and Wings**, 108 Water Street (207/853-4831), down by the fishing pier in Eastport. This wood shop has everything you can imagine, from long-board skate decks (for downhill cruising) to authentic pine coffins (for use as tongue-in-cheek guest bedroom furniture, apparently). Great stuff.

Eastport played a role in the War of 1812, when it was seized by the British and held as part of New Brunswick. In 1818, Eastport was the last piece of land returned to U.S. possession, and in 1820 it became part of the new state of Maine.

would have turned the entire coastline of Cobscook Bay, and eventually everything from here across to Canada's Bay of Fundy, into one huge electrical generator.

Outside along the water, you can still grab a coffee at the crusty old dockside **Wa-Co Diner** and go wandering around the creaking quays. "The Easternmost Mexican Restaurant in the USA," according to a sticker above the doors, **La Sardina Loca** at 28 Water Street (207/853-2739) is a real treat, serving up very good food in a room that suits a restaurant named after a crazy sardine. Here you'll find plastic Christmas trees as well as pipes decorated like palm trees—climbing up them are stuffed teddy bears reaching for fake coconuts. Crazy, indeed.

For a place to stay, try the unambiguously named **Motel East**, 23 Water Street ($70–90; 207/853-4747), or the older **Seaview**, 16 Norwood Road ($40–60; 207/853-4471), which has bay-view kitchenette cabins and a relaxed, family-friendly feel.

THE SUNRISE COAST: CAMPOBELLO

Between Calais and Machias, US-1 runs along Passamaquoddy Bay then veers inland, for the most part missing out on one of Maine's most interesting and least visited quarters, the Sunrise Coast at the easternmost edge of the United States. Numerous state and local parks make this an excellent, albeit unheralded, place to get a feel for what makes Maine so special. Many of the places here haven't yet been tidied up for tourists, which means you may have to search through some rust and grime. However, the highlights, in particular the rugged but easily accessible coastline, are on a par with anywhere in the state.

Reached from US-1 by way of Route 189 from Whiting, the biggest community in the area is Lubec (pop. 1,853), a fishing port with a long history of smuggling goods from over the Canadian border. Sardines were another mainstay of the economy, but as elsewhere most of the packing plants and canneries have closed, leaving empty wharves and wooden warehouses along the bay, and a line of semi-abandoned storefronts along Water Street. On the upside, there's a new marina, and best of all is the photogenic lighthouse that stands on an island offshore.

The real reason to visit is linked to Lubec by the FDR Bridge: Campobello Island, which is technically in Canada but for the past 35 years protected as the **Roosevelt Campobello International Park,** in memory of Franklin Delano Roosevelt, who spent summers here as a boy. The massive Roosevelt family home is furnished with mementos of FDR's times here, and miles of scenic drives and hiking trails wind through the island's still unspoiled (but often foggy) 2,800 acres. There's also a small **visitors center** (9 AM–5 PM; free; 506/752-2922), which tells the story of Roosevelt's life, focusing on his battles with polio, which he contracted here in 1921 at the age of 39. Though paralyzed, he went on to be elected governor of New York (1929–33) and president of the United States (1933–45), returning to Campobello rarely and only briefly.

Back on the mainland, the official easternmost point of land in the United States is a 480-acre park with an unusual name: **Quoddy Head State Park** (9 AM–sunset; $1; 207/733-0911), six miles south of Lubec. The park features the photogenic, candy-striped **Quoddy Head Lighthouse,** superb coastal scenery, and many hiking paths and nature areas. The headlands around Quoddy Head are a prime place for enjoying the lush fields of purple lupines growing wild and hitting peak color in July and August.

For more information about visiting Lubec and the Sunrise Coast, contact the Washington County Promotions Board (800/377-9748).

Along with its early dawns, the Sunrise Coast also gets some of the largest tidal ranges of anywhere in the United States, with high and low tides differing by as much as 30 feet. Obviously, you should check tide tables and take extra care when exploring the shore, but when there are no storms, the surf is fairly mild.

ROUTE 191: CUTLER

One example of Maine's many beautiful coastal drives follows Route 191 for some 30 miles between Quoddy Head and Machias Bay, passing along what's sometimes called the Bold Coast for its rugged terrain. Midway along, four-plus miles northeast of the town of Cutler, a parking area marks the trailhead for the five-mile loop hike through the 12,000-acre, state-owned **Cutler Coast Preserve.** Most of the trail runs right along very rugged waterfront cliffs, so watch your step. Primitive camping is available; call the state park department (207/287-3821) for details.

Route 191 to and from Cutler is one of Maine's great coastal drives, bouncing along over hills and dales with great views and almost no traffic.

The picturesque town of Cutler is a neat little port with colorful lobster boats bobbing offshore. Before or after a walk around the preserve, stop by the ever-pleasant **Cutler Country Store** (207/259-7122) on Route 191 and pick up a scallop burger, a sandwich, or a pizza—or just about anything else you might want. There's a pool table, pinball games, and a counter and booths, all usually full of locals talking away about anything and everything.

MACHIAS

The oldest town in Maine east of the Penobscot River, Machias (pronounced ma-CHAI-us; pop. 2,600) is proud of its history, especially its role in the Revolutionary War, when local patriots led by Jeremiah O'Brien took on the British Navy. To relive the era, head to the **Burnham Tavern** on Main Street, where the Daughters of the American Revolution give hour-long tours (Mon.–Fri. 9 AM–5 PM in summer only; $2) and hold discussions about the causes and tactics of the revolutionary efforts. A sign outside the circa-1770 building promises "Drink for the

Keeping up with the Jones's, Maine-style: for a great coastal detour off US-1, follow Route 187 on a lovely loop from Jonesboro to Jonesport. Hungry travelers have their choice of two great roadside haunts: **Sam's** (207/434-2300), a log cabin 400 yards south of US-1 in Jonesboro, serving biscuits and gravy from 5 AM every day but Monday; and **Tall Barney's** (207/497-2403) on Main Street in Jonesport, a lobsterman's favorite that's open year-round for breakfast, lunch, and early dinners. Jonesboro also has a super-cute roadside motor court, the **Blueberry Patch Motel and Cottages** (207/434-5411), right on US-1.

Outside Cherryfield along US-1, **Mill River Antique and Salvage** (207/483-4369) is one of the wildest and weirdest junk shops in a land of good junk shops.

Rural roads around Cherryfield, such as Route 193, run through the heart of Maine's substantial blueberry farms. The peak of the berry season is the middle of summer, when stands sell fresh berries— or you can pick your own, though most of the fields or "barrens" are run commercially, with gangs of workers using wooden rakes to do the plucking. If you're here in late August, head to the **Wild Blueberry Festival** in Machias. For details on anything to do with these little blue taste sensations, contact the Maine Blueberry Commission (207/581-1475).

Thirsty, Food for the Hungry, Lodging for the Weary"—but alas, it no longer delivers. For food and drink these days, head instead to pair of pizza places on Main Street. Lodging is available at the **Riverside Inn** (207/255-4134), a Victorian-era B&B right on US-1 (and the river!) in East Machias, and at a number of motels along US-1.

For further information on visiting this part of Maine, or to find out about the early-August Wild Blueberry Festival, contact the Machias Bay Area visitors bureau (207/255-4402), in the old Maine Central Railroad station at the junction of US-1 and Route 1A.

From Elm Street in central Machias, a must-do scenic drive follows Route 92 south along the coast past wonderful, rocky Jasper Beach to what's known as the Point of Maine, for a sweeping panorama highlighted by a clear-day view of Libby Island Lighthouse.

CHERRYFIELD

Roughly halfway between Machias and Ellsworth, US-1 passes through one of Maine's prime blueberry-growing districts, the fields ripening every August amid granite glacial moraines and many idyllic ponds. The many smaller back roads, like Route 182 that runs north of US-1, or even Route 1A, also make great fall foliage–viewing routes. Fortunately all roads hereabouts converge at Cherryfield (pop. 1,200), a small town with a wealth of architectural treasures. Historic Cherryfield is a museum of fine home building, with textbook examples of Greek Revival, Queen Anne, and most other gingerbread styles bearing witness to the town's history as a lumber and shipbuilding center. In fact, Cherryfield has more than 50 National Register properties dating from 1804 to 1940, many of which are in less-than-pristine condition, tucked in poorly maintained, rarely traveled roads.

ROUTE 186: SCHOODIC PENINSULA AND WINTER HARBOR

Looping off along the coast from US-1, Route 186 offers yet another incredibly scenic side trip along the Maine coastline. A full visit turns the five-mile trip between Gouldsboro and West Gouldsboro into a half-day odyssey, full of some of the most sublime scenes on the whole coast. Roughly 10 miles from either end and preserved as part of Acadia National Park, the Schoodic (SKOO-dik) Peninsula is a pink-tinged shelf of solid granite that juts out into the roiling Atlantic Ocean. The Schoodic Peninsula is ringed by a six-mile one-way loop drive that brings you close to many scenic vistas, all looking out from rugged cliffs that drop steeply down to the crashing surf.

There's no camping or admission fee in this part of Acadia National Park, but just outside the boundary you can set up camp at **Ocean Wood Campground** (207/963-7194).

From Ellsworth, alternate route Route 1A loops inland to Bangor, which is covered in the US-2 chapter on page 115.

ROUTE 3: ELLSWORTH AND TRENTON

Ellsworth, chartered in 1763, began as a lumber town but now is a thriving commercial center, located southeast of Bangor at the junction of Route 3 and US-1. Downtown is marked by lots of redbrick buildings but little excitement. Nevertheless, it's worth a visit if only for weekend brunch or a slice of pie at the **Riverside Cafe**, an upscale retro-diner at 42 Main Street (207/667-7220). The rest of Ellsworth is all malls (Wal-Mart, et al), car lots, chain motels, and gas stations—harsh reminders of the sprawling suburban America most visitors are trying to escape.

Between Ellsworth and Trenton, gateway to Mount Desert Island and Acadia National Park, there's a short but bittersweet six-mile parade of tacky roadside attractions along Route 3. If you've got kids with you or are in the mood to act like one, you can choose from such questionable pleasures as the **Great Maine Lumberjack Show** in Trenton, plus go-carts, trading posts, miniature golf courses—even a zoo. Just before the bridge, you pass many lobster pounds on this stretch of highway, the best of which is the **Trenton Bridge Lobster Pound** (207/667-2977), open daily (May to mid-Oct. only) since 1956; just look for the billowing clouds of steam.

Approaching Bar Harbor, Route 3 runs along Frenchman Bay, which borders the northeast corner of the island. Along with unique B&Bs including the **Inn at Canoe Point** (207/288-9511), many of the national motel chains, including Holiday Inn and Marriott, have outposts along this stretch.

BAR HARBOR

Once a semiprivate enclave of the very rich (can you say Rockefeller?), the town of Bar Harbor (pop. 4,400), the largest and busiest on Mount Desert Island, has turned to catering to the less well-heeled visitor as the old money has retreated to more discreet settlements to the west, such as Northeast Harbor—a.k.a. Philadelphia on the Rocks. Bar Harbor's principal thoroughfares, lined with gift shops, art galleries, bike rental stands, hotels, and restaurants, are Main Street, Cottage Street, and Mount Desert Street, the latter two intersecting at the lively and pleasant Village Green. West Street, which runs along the waterfront, is home to the **Lobster Hatchery** (daily 9 AM–5 PM in summer only), where you can see exhibits on the popular crustacean's life cycle.

Since most of Bar Harbor's old mansions were destroyed in a 1947 fire, there aren't all that many sights to search out,

Low tides leave excellent tide pools at Schoodic Point, but incoming waves can quickly drench (or drown) unsuspecting visitors. Be careful.

Bar Harbor is the U.S. terminus for the ferry to Yarmouth, Nova Scotia ($45–55; 888/249-7245), for a six-hour cruise that will save you hours of driving time if you are heading that way. A new addition is the superfast Cat, a catamaran ferry that makes the crossing (at speeds up to 55 mph) in under 3 hours, so you can go there and back in a day. (The boats also turn into casinos when they reach international waters.)

At 1,532 feet, Cadillac Mountain on Mount Desert Island is the highest point on the Eastern Seaboard of North America. It's named for the Frenchman Antoine de le Mothe Cadillac, who spent a summer on the island before heading west to found the city of Detroit.

MOUNT DESERT ISLAND

Mount Desert Island is an idyllic, 11- by 14-mile chunk of dense forests, barren peaks, and rocky inlets just off the coast of Maine. The island was first inhabited by the Penobscot people and was not explored by Europeans until 1609, when Samuel de Champlain named it Isle de Monts Déserts ("Isle of Bald Peaks") and claimed it for France. In 1844, Hudson River School artist Thomas Cole painted a stunning series of scenes featuring Mount Desert Island, which soon became a summer playground for elite Eastern families, many of whom built massive vacation "cottages" here, largely around Bar Harbor. In 1916, the Mount Desert colony, led by the Pulitzer and Rockefeller families, donated most of the island to the federal government to establish the first national park east of the Mississippi—Acadia National Park. The Great Depression and World War II effectively put an end to the Bar Harbor high life, and most traces of the summer colony were either torn down or destroyed by a huge fire that raged through Bar Harbor in 1947.

Today about half of Mount Desert Island remains in private hands, including the villages of Bass Harbor, Northeast Harbor, Seal Harbor, and Southwest Harbor, all of which are exclusive enclaves. These locales offer a much quieter version of island life than you'll get in Bar Harbor. Northeast Harbor is perhaps the most welcoming, with two public gardens, the genteel old **Asticou Inn** on Route 3 ($175–275; 207/276-3344), and some surprisingly affordable cafes like the **Docksider** on Sea Street (207/276-3965), where you can munch a crab sandwich while waiting for the ferry boats that shuttle across to the picturesque Cranberry Isles. For more on these less-visited corners of Mount Desert Island, contact the ever-friendly Northeast Harbor visitors bureau (207/276-5040).

Thunder Hole, Acadia National Park, Bar Harbor, Mt. Desert Island, Me.

although the Tiffany windows of lovely little **St. Saviour's Church,** on the west side of the Village Green, give some sense of the wealth that once lingered here. (As a sign of how much times have changed, the church hall is now a summer-only **Hostelling International youth hostel;** 207/288-5587.)

EAGLE LAKE FROM MOUNTAIN ROAD, ACADIA NATIONAL PARK, BAR HARBOR, MAINE

Lobsters are at the core of the island's cuisine, and two places to sample them are **Fishermen's Landing** at 35 West Street on the West Street Pier (207/288-4632), and the **Island Chowder House** at 38 Cottage Street (207/288-4905). There are dozens of generally good and relatively inexpensive restaurants clustered together in Bar Harbor's few short blocks, so wander around and take your pick. Many are clearly aimed at the tourist trade, none more so than the amiable **Freddie's Route 66 Restaurant,** 21 Cottage Street (207/288-3708), a pseudo-1950s diner that's absolutely packed with nostalgic memorabilia—jukeboxes, gas pumps, neon signs, you name it. It's got nothing to do with Down East Maine, but the food (from turkey dinners to veggie lasagnas) is plenty good.

If you are visiting during the summer high season, reserve your lodging well in advance. Despite the dozens of motels and B&Bs here, the town is often booked solid. Rates vary widely depending on the season; lodging in July and August may cost almost twice as much as in winter. With that said, Bar Harbor room rates actually tend to be lower than they are at places further south; rooms that would go for $100 a night in Ogunquit or Camden can be found for $60 a night here.

The classic place to stay is the **Bar Harbor Inn** ($80–280; 207/288-3351), right on the water next to the West Street pier. Other reasonable accommodations include the **Cadillac Motor Inn,** 336 Main Street (207/288-3831), and the **Wonder View Motor Lodge** (207/288-3358) on Route 3 northwest of town. **The Colony** (207/288-3383), on Route 3 just beyond Hulls Cove, is an austerely classic bungalow resort.

Besides the many bay-view bars, nighttime diversions in Bar Harbor include a pizza and movie at **Reel Pizza,** 33B Kennebec Place (207/288-3811), where you can enjoy an offbeat film while munching away. You can also watch movies as they were meant to be seen, in the gorgeously restored 1932 art deco **Criterion Theater,** 35 Cottage Street (207/288-3441).

ACADIA NATIONAL PARK

Mount Desert Island's natural glories are preserved in Acadia National Park, occupying 41,634 acres of the island's most scenic areas. Route 3 runs through the heart of the park, but the best way to appreciate Acadia is to track the 20-mile-long **Park Loop Road,** which circles the eastern side of the park. (Note that large campers and trailers are prohibited.) Midway along, the loop road pauses at Sand Beach, one of the few sandy beaches in Maine (get here early to find parking in summer), then passes the Thunder Hole tidal cavern before winding inland past Jordan Pond. If you want to get out and stretch your legs, the best way see the fantastic ocean views and breathe the fresh ocean air is to walk along the two-mile trail that links Sand Beach, the Thunder Hole, and the 110-foot-high Otter Cliffs. From Jordan Pond, the loop road continues past the turnoff (also accessible directly from Bar Harbor) for the drive to the top of Cadillac Mountain. Here, you'll experience a truly breathtaking panorama over all over Mount Desert

For local weather and good music, tune in to **WMDI 107.7FM** in Bar Harbor.

The upscale environs of Seal Harbor are home to one of the country's great car collections, on display inside the **Seal Cove Auto Museum,** on Route 102 (daily 10 AM–5 PM in summer only; $5; 207/244-9242).

A half-mile northeast of Bar Harbor, along Route 3 on the grounds of College of the Atlantic, you'll find the **Natural History Museum** (daily 9 AM–5 PM June–Aug., $2). Housed in a granite summer cottage, the museum offers exhibits and lectures on the region's flora, fauna, and geology, and has the hands-on Discovery Room designed specifically for kids.

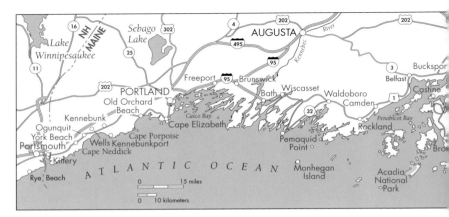

Island, the surrounding inlets and islands, and (on a fog-free day) miles and miles of the Maine coast.

In the summer and fall, when thousands clog the loop road and the streets of Bar Harbor, the most sensible visitors head to the park's hiking trails, which wind among the beautiful inland lakes and mountains. Approximately 57 miles of the unpaved, car-free "carriage roads" constructed (well, paid for) by Edsel Ford and John D. Rockefeller Jr. are open to walkers, bikers, wheelchairs, and baby strollers. Many of these roads leave directly from the main park visitor center, but some of the best (and least crowded) start from Jordan Pond, in the southwest corner of the park. Jordan Pond is also the site of the only restaurant within the park boundary, **Jordan Pond House** (207/276-3316), where you can reserve a table for an idyllic afternoon tea. In winter, when the park is virtually dormant, the carriage roads are kept open for cross-country skiing and snowshoeing, magical ways to get a feel for the place.

Acadia National Park also protects some exemplary places beyond Mount Desert Island, including the southern tip of Isle au Haut, tiny Baker Island (which you can visit on a ranger-guided tour), and the unforgettable Schoodic Peninsula across Frenchman Bay, accessible via US-1 just north of Ellsworth.

Along US-1 between Ellsworth and Bucksport, the **Big Chicken Barn Books and Antiques** store at 1768 Bucksport Road (207/667-7308) has an overwhelming variety of used books and magazines— more than 90,000 titles last time they counted—in a huge upstairs space.

Three miles north of Bar Harbor, on the edge of Hulls Cove, the main **Acadia National Park Visitors Center** (daily 8 AM–4:30 PM April–Oct., until 6 PM July–Aug.; 207/288-3338) is a good place to start a tour of the park or to find out about the very limited camping available (no hookups). To request information in advance of your trip, write to the visitor center at P. O. Box 177, Bar Harbor, Maine 04609.

BLUE HILL PENINSULA: BROOKLIN AND CASTINE

US-1 races fairly uneventfully between Ellsworth and Bucksport, bypassing the many artsy and upscale enclaves that fill the Blue Hill Peninsula. Winding back roads crisscross this area, linking the handful of small towns and providing miles of gorgeous vistas. The quaint, old town of Blue Hill (pop. 2,010) is the heart of the

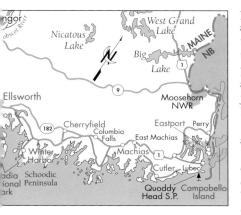

peninsula; after walking around to admire the historic homes, head south to **Blue Hill Falls,** which tumble down to the sea after a high tide. You can pick up pastries, eat breakfast or lunch, and maybe hear some good live folk or jazz music at the **Left Bank Bakery** on Route 172 (207/374-2201).

Perhaps the best destination hereabouts is the hamlet of Brooklin (pop. 785), on Route 175 near the southeast end of the peninsula. At the unmarked center of town, opposite the handy Brooklin General Store, sits one of coastal Maine's great little finds: **Morning Moon Cafe** (closed Mon.; 207/359-2373), offering great breakfasts (try the blueberry muffins!), a full lunch menu, and good coffee at low prices.

On the other (west) side of the peninsula, the stalwart town of **Castine** has survived attacks and occupation by French, British, Dutch, and finally American forces during various battles and skirmishes. Today, it enjoys peace from above its busy harbor. The lifeblood of Castine is the large Maine Maritime Academy, at the top of the hill, which teaches naval architecture and engineering and owns and operates nearly 100 different historic ships and training vessels. More interesting to visitors is the weird collection of ancient pottery, African and Polynesian masks, dioramas, and ships models crammed into the **Wilson Museum** on Perkins Street on the harborfront (Tues.–Sun. 2–5 PM; free; 207/326-8545). Next door, and part of the same complex of historical museums, is a fine old house, and behind is working blacksmith's foundry and, oddest of all, a pair of hearses.

South of Castine, on Cape Rosier, enjoy a taste of old Maine by spending a week at the 100-acre **Hiram Blake Camp** (207/326-4951), where you can rent a historic cottage for around $500 a week, plus an optional $150 or so for all your meals.

Writers, artists, and others in search of peace and quiet have long headed to the Blue Hill Peninsula. The town of Brooklin, for example, is where writers E. B. and Katherine White made their home after escaping from New York City. Now Brooklin is home to the editorial offices of *Wooden Boat* magazine and its optimistic sister publication, *Hope.*

Maine's only community radio station, East Orland's **WERU 89.9FM,** broadcasts eclectic music and left-leaning news and commentaries from Blue Hill to Bangor. They sometimes play requests (207/469-6600).

BUCKSPORT: FORT KNOX

Like most of Maine, burly, blue-collar Bucksport (pop. 4,825) preserves its historic places. Its most notable project is **Fort Knox.** This is not *that* Fort Knox, the one holding the nation's gold, but a granite fortress built in 1844 to protect the upper Penobscot River. It was never completed and never saw battle; nonetheless, it is fun to explore, with underground passageways and occasional Civil War–era living history re-enactments.

A different sort of fun-in-the-dark can be explored at the fascinating **Northeast Historic Film Center,** 379 Main Street (207/469-0924) in the historic Alamo Theater. (See "Going to the Movies" on page 60 for more details.)

GOING TO THE MOVIES

Think of movies and you think of Hollywood, not Maine. But strange as it may sound, one of the more interesting motion-picture museums has recently opened in an unlikely location: Bucksport, Maine, on US-1 at the head of Penobscot Bay. Under the auspices of an organization known as Northeast Historic Film, the old Alamo Theater in the heart of Bucksport is being restored into a study center for most everything to do with film—especially watching. Called **Going to the Movies,** the ongoing exhibition looks into the history of movies and movie theaters in the Northeast, with emphasis on what movie-going meant as a community activity—all those Saturday matinees were surely a ritual with long-term effects on America's hearts and minds. The center also serves as an archive for all sorts of home movies, saving those Super 8s and older films for posterity to study and enjoy. You can watch a sampling of these old home movies but be warned: viewing them may cause you to well up with nostalgic longing for the not-so-distant, pre-videotape past. The film association lacks the resources to fulfill its complete vision, so the museum is still pretty much in the realm of Coming Attractions but is definitely worth a quick visit for anyone who loves the magic of motion pictures—especially if your visit coincides with one of the screenings.

South of Bucksport, US-1 runs along the scenic shores of Penobscot Bay through the old shipbuilding town of Belfast, which has a quaint historic downtown; past the quaint cottages of Temple Heights, a historic Methodist summer camp; and Lincolnville, where you can catch ferries to Isleboro, just offshore. At the north end of this 50-odd-mile stretch, midway down US-1 between Bucksport and Belfast, much of the historic center of Searsport (pop. 2,600) has been preserved as Maine's oldest maritime museum, the **Penobscot Marine Museum** (daily 10 AM–5 PM; $5; 207/548-2529). The museum spans six buildings (including the old town hall) and showcases boat models, paintings, and historical exhibits. Also in Searsport, and handy for the Coastal Bike Path along the shores of Penobscot Bay, the **HI—Searsport Hostel,** 132 W. Main Street (207/548-2506), has dorm beds available in July and August.

Bucksport is home to one of coastal Maine's larger **paper mills.** Operated by Champion International, it's open for tours (hourly on Mon., Wed., and Fri.; free).

Searsport, at the south end of the mainline Bangor and Aroostook Railroad, is still a busy port, shipping out potatoes and paper pulp from all over inland Maine.

CAMDEN AND ROCKPORT

One of the best-looking larger towns on the Maine coast, Camden (pop. 5,100) has undergone a recent (and according to most locals, totally unnecessary) overhaul, thanks to the ongoing influx of cash from credit card company MBNA, which established a big office complex here in the 1990s. That said, Camden is still a delightful stop, climbing up densely forested hills from a deeply indented harbor. Frederick Law Olmsted designed much of the waterfront, taking advantage of the natural terrain to frame a wonderful series of views over the bay. At the center of the park are a large Civil War memorial commemorating Camden's fallen soldiers and a large open-air amphitheater where concerts and other performances are held.

The town itself climbs along steep streets to the west of US-1, which passes through Camden as Main Street. If you can time your visit for the Saturday before Father's Day, you see just how steep the streets really are when Camden hosts its annual **Soap Box Derby,** with homemade carts hurtling down Washington Street a block west of US-1. There's no real must-see museum or anything specific to search for, but wandering around between the town and harbor is a great way to while away an afternoon or two.

The same can be said of the neighboring town of Rockport, which separated from Camden in 1891. East of US-1 and hence much calmer and quieter than Camden, Rockport is another lovely historic harbor and a great place to get lost for a while. This pretty town is perhaps best known as the former summer home of Andre the Seal, a harbor seal (and fictionalized hero of children's books) whose statue stands on the picturesque waterfront. Rockport is also home to one of the premier photography schools on the East Coast: the **Maine Photography Workshops** (207/236-8581), which offers a wide range of classes and workshops throughout the summer.

Just north of Camden along US-1, **Camden Hills State Park** overlooks the southwestern shores of Penobscot Bay. Climb the road ($2 toll) to the top of 790-foot Mount Battie. Here, a rustic stone tower lets you look out over deep blue sea dotted with dozens of rocky islands and the sails of Maine's famous windjammer clipper ships puffed full by the constant breeze on Penobscot Bay. On a really clear day you can see Mount Cadillac in Acadia National Park, 40 or so miles down east.

For food, there's one place you have to try: **Marriner's,** the self-proclaimed Last Local Luncheonette, at 15 Main Street in Camden (207/236-2647), open since 1942 for hearty breakfasts and old-fashioned Maine-style lunches—fried shrimp or scallops, clam chowder, great BLTs, and of course lobster rolls. Another great place to eat and drink and get a feel for Camden is **Cappy's,** 1 Main Street (207/236-2254), which has good bar food, local-favorite seafood chowder, and a great selection of microbrewed beers.

For a place to stay in Camden, try the friendly **Whitehall Inn,** 52 High Street ($90–150; 207/236-3391), which has been in business for 101 years, offering guests use of rocking chairs on the porch and nightly jigsaw puzzle sessions instead of cable TV and phones in the spacious public rooms. The inn also has a nice dining room, where a complimentary breakfast featuring homemade blueberry muffins is served.

Along with neighboring Rockland, Camden is home port to most of Maine's famous windjammers, the colorful fleet of sailing vessels that carries passengers on week-long cruises around Penobscot Bay.

Tiny Lincolnville Beach is home to one of Maine's biggest restuarants, the **Lobster Pound** (207/789-5550), which stands right along US-1.

If you're here in the winter months, be sure to check out the community-owned **Camden Snow Bowl** (207/236-3438), three miles west of US-1 via John Street. Besides the usual ski lifts and a skating pond, it also holds the only wooden toboggan chute in the United States, which you can race down for $1 a time (half-price if you bring your own sled). Every February, weather willing, this is the site of international toboggan races.

A great place to stop and get clued in to life in Camden is the peaceful little **Meetingbrook Bookshop and Bakery,** downhill near the harbor at 50 Bayview Street (207/236-6808). With an excellent selection of books—everything from guides on Buddhist practice to Thomas Merton journals—and some very tasty cookies and brownies, this is a sort of community center for the folks who call Camden home.

Rockland calls itself the Lobster Capital of the World. Your town would, too, if it shipped out some 10 million pounds of the ruddy crustaceans every year, as Rockport does. For a quirky photo-op, visit the police station downtown and look for the lobster-shaped weathervane on the roof.

Just south of Rockland, along US-1 in Thomaston, the large **Maine State Prison** has a strangely fascinating gift shop selling artworks and handicrafts made by prisoners.

Moody's Diner is a great place to introduce yourself to yet another New England taste treat: the whoopie pie. A chocolate cake sandwich filled with creamy white frosting, Moody's whoopie pie is as big as a cheeseburger, so save room for one or take some on the road with you.

ROCKLAND

No one comes to Rockland (pop. 7,972) for the scenery, unless some people find fish-packing plants and Wal-Mart sprawl attractive. But travelers do come here for the **Farnsworth Art Museum,** the nationally respected art collection housed downtown at 352 Main Street (Tues.–Sat. 10 AM–5 PM, Sun. noon–5 PM; $5; 207/596-6457). Established in 1947, the Farnsworth primarily showcases pieces by artists who have worked in Maine, including such luminaries as Winslow Homer, Marsden Hartley, Rockwell Kent, Gilbert Stuart, and Fitz Hugh Lane. It is also a major repository of works by the Wyeth family.

Rockland also has some good places to eat. Have breakfast or grab a cup of chowder and a sandwich at **The Brown Bag,** 606 Main Street (207/596-6372); or next door, grab a chili-smothered hot dog from **Wasse's Hot Dogs** (207/594-7472). Or, for a real bang-up belly full, go down toward the water to **Conte's Fish Market,** in Harbor Park (207/596-5579), for huge portions of the freshest fish and shellfish available anywhere. The menus are hand-written every day, and most dishes are Italian influenced, with lots of garlicky pasta to wash down with flasks of Chianti.

On the coast south and east of Rockland via Route 73, another prime destination is the **Owl's Head Transportation Museum** (daily 10 AM–5 PM in summer, weekends only rest of year; $5; 207/594-4418), which has some truly classic cars, including a Stanley Steamer and a prototype Ford Mustang. There are also antique planes, including some World War I fighters à la Snoopy and the Red Baron. On some summer weekends the museum also invites classic-car collectors to show off their cars, and sometimes it sponsors air shows as well.

WALDOBORO

South from Rockland, US-1 swings inland away from the coast, reaching the water again at Waldoboro (pop. 4,800). This town boasts one of coastal Maine's culinary landmarks, **Moody's Diner** (207/832-7785), on US-1 at the Route 220 junction, whose neon sign has been blinking away since the early 1930s. It's not a classic stainless-steel prefabricated diner, but it's still a welcome sight, and the food (especially the fresh blueberry pie, rated among the best in a state that prides itself on those delicate little gems) is top drawer. Overlooking Waldoboro on the hill above the diner, Moody's also runs a nifty 1930s vintage motel, with

everything you could want: clean rooms, cable TV, and horseshoe courts. The motel is open mid-May to mid-October only, but rates are very reasonable ($30–45; 207/832-5362).

South and west from Waldoboro, US-1 crosses a series of scenic bays and rivers, running through the picturesque towns of Damariscotta (pronounced "dam-ris-COT-ta") and Wiscasset before hitting the postindustrial environs of Bath.

PEMAQUID POINT AND MONHEGAN ISLAND

The coast of Maine is among the most beautiful places on the planet, but the rush of visitors (and their cars) can often overwhelm the landscape and turn Maine into one giant parking lot. However, if you're willing to go a few miles off the beaten path, it's still quite possible to see Maine as nature intended it.

Pemaquid Point is one such out-of-the-way stunner. To get there, take US-1 to Waldoboro and go south on Route 32 approximately a dozen miles. You can also take Route 130 south from Damariscotta. At the far tip of the peninsula, photogenic **Pemaquid Lighthouse** guides ships around the state's most treacherous stretch of rocky shore. Also here is the small Fisherman's Museum, which focuses on the travails of life at sea. A little to the north, near the pretty fishing port of New Harbor, is the large **Colonial Pemaquid Museum** ($2), which examines life on the mainland. The reconstructed ramparts of Fort William Henry form the centerpiece of the museum.

Although Pemaquid Point is beautiful enough to justify a visit, the real draw of this part of Maine is the tiny, rugged, and breathtakingly wild **Monhegan Island,** 10 miles offshore. Monhegan Island is just over a mile long and less than a half-mile wide but its topography varies greatly. Along the eastern shore are some of Maine's highest headlands, but inland the landscape alternates between dense forest and wildflower meadows.

Approximately 75 people live full-time on Monhegan Island and a maximum of 200 travelers are permitted to visit daily. Cars are prohibited on the island; in fact, this gem of a place is practically road-free. Without the hassle of traffic, visitors are able to peacefully hike the trails crisscrossing the island, watch the colonies of birds (especially puffins) and seals congregating in the many hidden coves, listen to the roar of the surf, or simply relax in the island's few inns and restaurants. Another highlight is climbing the stairs to the top of the 1824 **Monhegan Island lighthouse,** from which you get a grand view of the quaint village of Monhegan and of Manana Island and the distant Camden Hills, both to the west. Adjacent to the lighthouse is a neat little museum full of gorgeous old black-and-white photos of Monhegan people and places.

Monhegan village contains a number of artists' studios and galleries and the island's few hotels and restaurants. The friendliest and most affordable restaurant-

Along Route 32 in Waldoboro, the historic **Lutheran Church** was built by German immigrants who in 1748 brought European civilization to what was then unsettled wilderness. The churchyard contains many fascinating old gravestones.

Wiscasset was once home to the **"World's Smallest Church."** Measuring just five by seven feet and sporting a golf ball atop its steeple, the church was built by Reverend Louis West in 1957 and open 24 hours a day, 7 days a week. It burned down in the mid-1980s.

Trailing Yew

Ferries to Monhegan village are available from three locations on the mainland and take from 90 to 50 minutes each way, depending on whether you depart from northern or southern mainland ports. **Monhegan Boat Line** (207/372-8848) runs mail boats three times to and from Monhegan from Port Clyde, south of Rockland on Route 131. **Hardy Boat Cruises** (207/677-2026) depart from New Harbor, near Pemaquid Point; **Balmy Days** (207/633-2284) ferries visitors to Monhegan from Boothbay Harbor, south of Wiscasset. Tickets for all lines cost $25–30 round-trip, over what can be fairly rough seas.

hotel is the *Trailing Yew* (207/596-0440 or 800/592-2520), which has a nice, family-style dining room serving fresh seafood for around $15 per person (add $9 if you want a lobster). The Trailing Yew was long owned and run by Josephine Day. She died in 1996 at the age of 99 but her quirky personality lives on in the establishment, especially in the rustic (and unheated) kerosene-lamp–lit rooms that fill a series of smaller outbuildings around a small meadow. Rooms here are a bargain at $60 per night per person, which includes a big breakfast and dinner. Cash and checks are accepted; no credit cards.

The **Island Inn,** overlooking the village harbor ($75–180; 207/596-0371), has the most comfortable and modern accommodations on the island. The inn also has a restaurant; credit cards accepted. All cafes and restaurants on the island are BYOB, so be sure to pick up a beverage at the Monhegan Store, at the center of the village, before dining out.

WISCASSET

Until recently, when you entered Wiscasset (pop. 3,500) from the north via US-1, you'd pass by the photogenically decaying hulks of two massive wooden schooners that used to sail from here. The boats have been removed, but there is still plenty to see in what was once the largest and busiest port north of Boston.

Today, Wiscasset is perhaps best known as the site of the now-defunct Maine Yankee, the state's first and last nuclear power plant. In the 1970s and 1980s, money from the power plant was used to clean up and renovate the town, prompting its residents to proclaim Wiscasset the prettiest village in Maine. Despite the cosmetic improvements, Wiscasset has managed to retain its genuine feel and not become just another tourist magnet.

Wiscasset is a great place to stop and walk around. Take a stroll down High Street to ogle at the magnificent homes. While you're here, be sure to check out at the **Musical Wonder House,** 18 High Street (daily 10 AM–5 PM in summer; 207/882-7163), where hundreds of music boxes, player pianos, gramophones, and other mechanized instruments can be seen on a $10 guided tour. Many of the music machines are amazing works of art. If you don't have much time, visit the small but fun gallery of music boxes, which you can play for just $1.

Another, even better reason to stop in Wiscasset is the food. Traffic often slows to a standstill on this section of US-1 (Main Street), and wherever there's traffic, there's bound to be great road food, as there is here. **Red's Eats** serves hot dogs, fried clams and oysters, fish 'n' chips, lobster rolls, and other goodies on Main

Street (207/882-6128), two blocks from the waterfront. Prices are a little on the high side ($10-plus for a lobster roll, for example), but the setting makes up for it. The food is take-out only.

BATH

With a big new bridge arching across the bay, and the towering cranes of a waterfront shipyard visible from almost everywhere in town, Bath (pop. 9,800) doesn't try to be pretty, and doesn't have to. One of the last remaining vestiges of Maine's

---

I-95 SURVIVAL GUIDE: ACROSS MAINE

MM298: Maine/Canada international border.

MM298: Exit 63 for US-2 through Houlton.

MM295: Exit 62 for US-1 through Houlton (see page 112).

MM269: Exit 59 for Island Falls (see page 112).

MM237: Penobscot River crossing, Exit 56 for Route 157 north to Millinocket, Baxter State Park and Mount Katahdin (see page 112).

MM190: Exit 52 for Route 43 south to US-1 and Old Town (see page 114).

MM177: Exit 46 for US-2 through downtown Bangor (see page 115).

MM150: Exit 39 for US-2 through Newport, the "Crossroads of Maine" (see page 116).

MM127.5: Kennebec River crossing, junction with US-201 south through Waterville and Augusta. I-95 joins briefly with the Maine Turnpike.

MM74.5: Androscoggin River crossing.

MM73: Exit 22 for US-1 through Brunswick, Bath, and Down East Maine (see pages 65–66).

MM67: Exit 20 for Freeport and L. L. Bean (see page 67).

MM55: Exit 15 for I-295 south through downtown Portland (see page 68).

MM42: Exit 6A for I-295 north through downtown Portland. Join Maine Turnpike southbound (nominal toll).

MM34: Exit 5 for I-195 east to Old Orchard Beach (see page 71).

MM24: Exit 3 for Route 35 east to the Kennebunks (see page 73).

MM18: Exit 2 for Route 109 to Wells and Ogunquit (see pages 73–74).

MM4: Junction with US-1 through the Yorks (see page 75).

MM2: Junction with US-1 through Kittery (see page 76).

MM0: Maine/New Hampshire state line.

Bath is home to the **Shelter Institute,** downtown at 38 Center Street (207/442-7938), which since the mid-1970s has been teaching individuals how to design and build energy-efficient, heavy-timber houses. Visitors can stop and learn a little or browse through the selection of books and tools, but the main offering is a series of short summer how-to courses.

once-thriving boat-building industry, the impressive Bath Iron Works ("BIW") is the state's largest employer but off-limits to casual visitors. The days when this shipyard launched massive cruisers and battleships on a regular basis may be ancient history, but BIW is still a significant enough presence in Bath to stop traffic when its 8,000 workers change shifts (weekdays around 3 or 4 PM).

About a mile down the Kennebec River from the heavy industrial environs of BIW, the exceptionally good **Maine Maritime Museum,** 243 Washington Street (daily 9:30 AM–5 PM; $7.50; 207/443-1316) occupies the site of another old shipyard, and among its many activities is a program that helps preserve the boat-building trade for future generations. In the museum building, ship models, paintings, various documents, and other displays explore the complex interactions of the many trades involved with the sea, from sailors to shipwrights. Along the waterfront, an old sail loft houses an exhibit on lobstering, while apprentice boatbuilders work to preserve and restore some of the museum's many historic vessels.

South from Bath, with the exception of a stretch through Brunswick where it joins up with I-95, US-1 is pretty much a freeway, so be sure to take time to travel the many slower side roads along the way.

If you want to get a good feel for Bath, the place to eat is **The Cabin,** a popular pizza place right across from BIW at 552 Washington Street (207/443-6224). There's also a great breakfast and bakery place called **Kristina's,** 160 Center Street downtown (207/442-8577).

BRUNSWICK

Just over five miles west of Bath, Brunswick is a world away in every possible way. The only real "college town" on the coast of Maine, Brunswick is home to prestigious **Bowdoin College,** which occupies 110 leafy acres on the south side of the main business district, a half-mile from US-1. Founded in 1794, Bowdoin (pronounced "BO-din") is a small, liberal-arts college that has turned out a stellar cast of graduates, including writers Nathaniel Hawthorne and Henry Wadsworth Longfellow, recent U.S. Senators George Mitchell and William Cohen, "Kinsey Report" author Alfred Kinsey, and Arctic explorers Robert Peary and Donald MacMillan, the first men to reach the North Pole back in 1909. Peary, MacMillan, and the native people of the Arctic region are the focus of an intriguing museum in Hubbard Hall on campus (207/725-3416). There's also a gorgeous 1890s art museum, designed by McKim, Mead, and White, that holds some phenomenal classical art and sculpture (207/725-3275). Both museums are free (open Tues.–Sat. 10 AM–5 PM, Sun. 2–5 PM).

The Chamberlain house, which previously belonged to the poet Longfellow, stands across from the historic First Parish Church, where Harriet Beecher Stowe is said to have been inspired to write *Uncle Tom's Cabin* while listening to an abolitionist sermon.

Along the main Maine Street in town, there are all the bookstores and cafes you could want (the **Bohemian Cafe** is a fave), plus a museum dedicated to former Bowdoin logic professor turned Civil War general, Joshua L. Chamberlain. Located in his former house at 226 Maine Street the **museum** (Tues.–Sat. 10 AM–4 PM; $3; 207/729-6606), traces Chamberlain's many important accomplishments. He led the Union forces at Gettysburg and Petersburg, and accepted Lee's surrender at

Appomattox, then went on to serve as governor of Maine and, finally, president of Bowdoin. Chamberlain died in 1914 at the age of 86 and is buried in Brunswick at Pine Grove cemetery.

BRUNSWICK PRACTICALITIES

Along with interesting places to look at and learn from, Brunswick also has at least two of Maine's most enjoyable places to eat. One of these is the all-American **Fat Boy Drive-In** (207/729-9431), on the US-1 frontage road between Bath and Brunswick, across from the runways of the Brunswick U.S. Navy Air Station. This thriving little drive-in, open since 1955, is the real deal; teenage carhops take your order and serve your meal in the comfort of your car—turn on your headlights if you want anything. Open mid-March to mid-October only, and generally just the right side of packed at lunch and dinner times, Fat Boy serves excellent burgers, BLTs, onion rings, and crinkle-cut fries, not to mention some of the best lobster rolls you'll taste anywhere. (And at less than $5, its lobster roll is about half the price of most places along the coast.)

Another nifty place is along US-1 on the west side of downtown: the **Brunswick Diner,** a bright red clapboard stand serving above-average breakfasts and other diner standards. West of the diner, alas, US-1 devolves into one of its periodic outbreaks of roadside sprawl, with a Wal-Mart and all the other usual suspects lined up between town and the I-95 junction. This where you'll find a nice, new **Comfort Inn,** 199 Pleasant Street (207/729-1129), and other accommodations.

If you can resist I-95, which rushes south from Brunswick, stay on the very quiet and pretty stretch of old US-1 that runs roughly parallel to the freeway and closer to the water. About midway between Freeport and Brunswick, you'll be rewarded with the sight of the **Maine Idyll** (cash only, $50–75; 207/865-4201), a lovely little white clapboard motor court and cabin complex set on 20 acres of peaceful Maine woods. Opened in 1932, the Maine Idyll contains the original main house and eight cottages, and 12 newer cabins, and offers all modern conveniences without sacrificing any of its charm.

FREEPORT: L. L. BEAN AND THE DESERT OF MAINE

Probably the single biggest tourist draw in the state of Maine is the round-the-clock megastore operated by outdoor-lifestyle supplier **L. L. Bean** (800/341-4341), which began selling hunting, fishing, and shooting gear long before anyone heard the words "factory outlet" or "sport utility vehicle." The business started here way back in 1912, when Leon Leonwood "L. L." Bean introduced his warm, waterproof hunting boots, but all of the other major retailers have opened outlets next to L. L. Bean, so many that the town of Freeport is little more than one huge (if comparatively tasteful) shopping center.

PORTLAND SURVIVAL GUIDE

The biggest city in Maine, Portland (pop. 65,000) offers visitors an ideal mix of urban sophistication packed into a compact and very picturesque setting on a peninsula in Casco Bay. Portland, as its name suggest, was a major port and its waterfront is still a center of activity, with burly old warehouses now converted into cafes, bijou restaurants, bars, and microbreweries. Portland also has many historic sites, a fine art museum, and New England's most popular minor-league baseball team; it's also the main departure point for boat trips out to the dozens of islands dotting Casco Bay.

The best place to start or finish a tour of Portland is the **Old Port** area, a harborside neighborhood of Victorian-era redbrick warehouses and commercial buildings decorated with exuberant and ornate cornices and carved keystones. This 20-block area was largely abandoned and left to decay during the 1960s but has been totally restored and revived—so much so that things can get decidedly rowdy here on summer weekend nights. During the day, art galleries and unique shops step up along cobblestoned streets from the stately **Customs House,** at 312 Fore Street. Two blocks west, more maritime wealth is visible in the Mariner's Church and the Seaman's Club, facing each other along Fore Street at the foot of Exchange Street.

Very little of Portland's once-busy shipping business comes into the Old Port these days, though you can still hop a ferry here for a tour of the offshore islands with **Casco Bay Lines** ($6–14; 207/774-7871). The country's oldest ferry company, Casco Bay Lines offers frequent trips out to the six inhabited islands, ideal spots for an afternoon picnic or bicycle ride. If you miss the boat, walk a half-mile south along the water and spend some time at the **Portland Fish Pier,** watching the trawlers and fishing boats come in laden down with tonight's (or more likely, tomorrow's) seafood dinners.

Downtown Portland follows Congress Street, which runs along a ridge one-quarter mile west of the waterfront, at the center of the peninsula. At the north end of Congress Street, the 1802 **Portland Observatory** is a maritime signal tower standing at the center of the Frederick Law Olmsted–designed Eastern Promenade, offering grand views over Portland Harbor (best seen after a climb up the tower's 100-plus steps). A mile south, at the other end of Congress Street, the **Portland Museum of Art** (daily 10 AM–5 PM, till 9 PM Thurs. and Fri.; $6; free Fri. evening; 207/775-6148) fills a striking modern building with a fine collection of made-in-Maine art by the likes of Winslow Homer, Andrew Wyeth, and Marsden Hartley. Besides Maine-inspired paintings at the museum, there is a also a fine array of French Impressionist work; top-quality touring exhibits frequently stop here. Next door, the hands-on **Children's Museum** (daily 10 AM–5 PM; $5; 207/828-1234) lets kids make believe they're lobster fishing or running a complex computer system—great for a rainy day.

Congress Street also holds the childhood home of poet Henry Wadsworth Longfellow (1807–1882), whose legendary poems "Hiawatha" and "The Midnight Ride of Paul Revere" earned him the honor of being the first American to be interred in the Poet's Corner of London's Westminster Abbey. The 1786 **Longfellow house,** at 485 Congress Street (daily 10 AM–4 PM; $4; 207/879-0427), is one of the oldest in the city and is filled with mementos of the poet and his family. Facing the house, **Monument Square** has a statue of Longfellow in pensively poetic mood.

Portland Practicalities

Surrounded on three sides by water (Back Cove in the north, Casco Bay on the east, and the Fore River to the south), peninsular Portland can be a hard place to get your bearings. The best thing to do is to make your way to downtown (take exit 6, 7, or 8 off I-295), park the car, then walk: almost everything you'll want to see is within a half-mile of the center.

Just off I-95 on the south side of the city, the Portland International Jetport is the biggest airport in Maine, served by Continental, Delta, United, USAir, and other major carriers. Frequent flights come here from JFK and Logan, and can save many hours on the road; most major rental car companies have offices here, making Portland a handy starting point for a New England tour.

By Maine standards, Portland is a very big city, with more than 200,000 people living in the metropolitan area and dozens of restaurants and lodging options. The best places to eat are based around the Old Port neighborhood, where you can sample international and American food that's as good as any in New England. Start the day with breakfast at bustling **Becky's Diner,** 390 Commercial Street (207/773-7070), which has great baked goods as well as the usual fried fare; they're open from 4 AM every day, 24 hours on weekends. Not surprisingly, fish is featured on many Portland menus, especially at what is generally rated the best seafood place in town: **Street and Company,** an informal but very popular (and fairly pricey, with entrees running $15–20) restaurant off Fore Street in the Old Port area at 33 Wharf Street (207/775-0887). Reservations are strongly recommended. Another solid bet is the **Seamen's Club Restaurant,** 375 Fore Street (207/772-7311), housed in the historic Gothic Revival space of the Seamen's Club. Before or after a meal, you can enjoy a pint or two of ale in the Old Port's busiest bar, **Gritty McDuff's,** 396 Fore Street (207/772-2739), which has its own microbrews as well as boutique beers from all over the world.

Hotels, motels, and B&Bs are available in all price ranges, starting with the summer-only dorm beds of the Hostelling International **Portland Hostel,** 645 Congress Street ($20; 207/874-3281), located right downtown a short walk from the Old Port area. The usual motels can be found along I-95 (there's a Howard Jones, a Holiday Inn, and a Motel 6 at exit 8), but even at these places prices range from around $50 to more than $100 in summer. The nicest place downtown may be the **Radisson Eastland,** 157 High Street ($125–250; 207/775-5411 or 800/333-3333), a midsized 1920s hotel located next to the Museum of Art. More homey is the **Inn on Carleton,** 46 Carleton Street ($90–150; 207/775-1910), a 17-room B&B in a quiet Victorian brownstone mansion.

For more information on Portland, contact the **visitors bureau** at 305 Commercial Street (207/772-5800).

After shopping, the next big attraction in the Freeport area is the so-called Desert of Maine, located west of I-95 exit 19 (daily 9 AM–5 PM; $6). This plot of land is really not a desert, but rather the result of careless farmers stripping away the natural vegetation, leaving the winds and rain to wash away topsoil and expose the sandy subsoils. Nevertheless, this privately owned attracted is falsely hyped as "Maine's Famous Natural Phenomenon," with images of camels playing up its supposed exotic status.

CAPE ELIZABETH

The Portland area effectively marks a major change in the landscape of coastal Maine. North of here are rugged, granite shores; to the south the seaside landscape is generally flatter and sandy, and formed of glacial moraines rather than solid rock. The softer geology south of Portland has created some of the state's most popular beaches, especially around Cape Elizabeth, which offers easy public access to some of Maine's most extensive stretches of undeveloped coastline. Scenic Route 77, which for most of the way has a decidedly unscenic name (Spurwink Road), loops around the cape, between South Portland and the town of Scarborough, home to Maine's main horseracing track.

Starting from Portland, the first of many highlights here is the landmark **Portland Head Lighthouse,** off Route 77 on Shore Road, which was built in 1791 and is among the most famous in the country. There's no access to the tower, but the adjacent lighthouse-keeper's house is the site of a small museum (daily 10 AM–4 PM in summer, weekends only rest of year; $2). There's also a nice park containing a small beach, a ruined mansion, wide lawns, and a band shell, where the Portland symphony performs on select summer evenings.

Back along Route 77 at the far-eastern tip of Cape Elizabeth, a pair of lighthouses (one working, one not) stands in the aptly named **Two Lights State Park,** where you can get a coastal panorama if you stand atop the concrete remains of an old artillery emplacement. The neighboring **Lobster Shack** (207/799-1677) owns the best parking spaces, so you may want to become a customer and enjoy a lobster roll while watching the sun go down.

From the tip of Cape Elizabeth, Route 77 hooks back west, running past Portland's largest and most popular beach, the wide strand of **Crescent Beach State Park.** Changing rooms and a small snack bar are on the premises, and a lifeguard is on duty. Parking costs $2.50.

Continuing south and west along Route 77 is **Higgins Beach,** where you'll find some of the Maine coast's best waves. The lack of public parking keeps the beach mostly locals-only, but you can walk to the beach if you stay at the friendly and affordable **Higgins Beach Inn** ($60–90; 207/883-6684), just across the

Forget about L. L. Bean or the Desert of Maine; the literally biggest attraction in town is the Big Indian that stands some 50 feet tall between US-1 and I-95 on the south edge of Freeport. This politically incorrect statue looms next to a now-closed gift shop.

Along northbound I-95, between Freeport and Portland, is the glass-walled world headquarters of cartography company **DeLorme** ("duh-LORM"). Inside you'll find a map store (daily 9 AM–5 PM; free; 207/846-7100), where you can peruse paper and digital maps and atlases. In the lobby is a globe, nicknamed Eartha, which at 42 feet in diameter is exactly one-millionth the size of the Earth; like the Earth, it also rotates on its axis once a day.

road. The inn has a nice restaurant, but you can also check out the food at the humble but popular **Spurwink Country Kitchen** (207/799-1177), also on Route 77.

OLD ORCHARD BEACH

Located about 10 miles south of Portland and three miles east of I-95 or US-1 via Route 9 or I-195, Old Orchard Beach ("OOB," pop. 7,000) is the biggest and most blue-collar beach resort in Maine. Don't be surprised to hear people shouting in French; this busy beach resort draws a large percentage of its 100,000 peak daily visitors from Quebec. It's a real throwback of a place, a northern Coney Island with all of the semi-disreputable activities that make beach towns so much fun. The best thing apart from the beach is the **Palace Playland**, 1 Old Orchard Street (207/934-2001), where's there's no admission fee if you just want to wander around and experience sensory overload from the flashing lights, whizzing thrill rides, screaming kids, and pumped-up music. If you want to hop on the old-fashioned Dodge 'Em bumper cars, the roller coaster, the vintage carousel with calliope, or the dozen or so other rides, it'll cost $1 or $2 a time; the batting cages are 10 balls for a buck. Rides are free for an hour on Thursday nights before the fireworks show.

At the edge of the Palace Playland is a 500-foot-long pier, filled with food stands, a few rides, tattoo artists, and body piercers. Inland from the pier a block or two from the beach, Old Orchard Street is a little depressing, as the touristy T-shirt shops thin out and are replaced by empty storefronts. One highlight here is **Danton's Family Restaurant**, 16 Old Orchard Street (207/934-7701), a simple, sit-down coffee shop offering one of the only alternatives to OOB's deep-fried anything and everything. Elsewhere in town, along the beach and on the pier, you can pig out on pizza, burgers, "tube steaks" (a.k.a. hot dogs), french fries, plus that perennial New England favorite: deep-fried dough coated with powdered sugar. Yum.

The Class AA **Portland Sea Dogs** (207/874-9300) play at Hadlock Field on Park Avenue, at the edge of downtown Portland right along old US-1. Games almost always sell out, so order tickets early; if you're turned away, games are broadcast on **WZAN 970AM.** The stadium is fairly new and has new-fangled food—fried fish sandwiches and broccoli- and cheese-stuffed bread—along with traditional hot dogs.

Portland Head Lighthouse is the oldest in Maine. Commissioned by George Washington, it was constructed in 1791.

On Route 207 at the southernmost tip of Cape Elizabeth, jutting out into the Atlantic and facing Old Orchard Beach, narrow **Prout's Neck** was the longtime home of artist Winslow Homer. His old studio is open to the public (hours vary; 207/883-2249) and is located just beyond the big sign reading Positively No Passing. The rest of the area is mostly owned by the pricey **Black Point Inn Resort** ($200–350; 800/258-0003). **Scarborough Beach,** a town-owned strand from where you can walk or cycle out to Prout's Neck, is about the only place at Prout's Neck where ordinary folks will feel welcome.

In between blue-collar Old Orchard Beach and blue-blood Kennebunkport, the twin towns of Biddeford and Saco offer a more moderate taste of coastal Maine. Old mills have been converted into shops and offices, and the downtown areas are full of artsy galleries and secondhand stores. The real highlight may be the run of roadside amusement parks lining old US-1, especially on the north side of Saco. Here's where you'll find the slightly scruffy but still thriving **Saco Drive-In Theater,** 969 Portland Road (207/284-1016), which shows Hollywood hits every night in summer.

Accommodations are available in the many motels that line beachfront Grand Avenue south from the pier. If you want a view of the roller coasters from your balcony, you'll love the 1960s **Mount Royal Motel,** 30 W. Grand Avenue (207/934-2926). Cheaper motels and campgrounds are inland; for more information, contact the local **visitor bureau** (207/934-2500 or 800/365-9386).

KENNEBUNKPORT

Kennebunkport is all but invisible from US-1, so its elite environs are best toured along Route 9, which winds along the coast between Biddeford and Kennebunk. Even if you have no presidential ambitions (or at least no desire to see the heavily publicized haunts of former President George H. W. Bush), Route 9 is a great drive. Stop first at the gleaming white sands of **Goose Rocks Beach,** poorly signed but just a half-mile east of Route 9 at the end of Goose Rocks Road. This mostly private community, with lines of vacation homes fronting the beach and bay, offers a little taste of Cape Cod. Parking is a pain, so if you like the sound or look of it, stay the night at the **Tides Inn,** 252 Goose Rocks Road ($90–250; 207/967-3757), which has a variety of rooms and cabins, plus a restaurant and a popular pub.

Next stop along Route 9, about midway between Goose Rocks Beach and Kennebunkport, is **Cape Porpoise.** On Pier Road at the entrance to the cape stands the ever-friendly **Bradbury Bros.** general store, deli, and post office, and at the end of the road, the upscale **Seascapes Restaurant** (207/967-8500) offers lovely views of lobster boats shuttling in and out of the harbor.

From the turnoff to Cape Porpoise, Route 9 veers inland toward the very quaint center of Kennebunkport, **Dock Square,** but most visitors opt to follow Ocean Avenue along the water, so they can get a panoramic view of the anything-but-private **Walker Estate,** which former President George Bush inherited from his father, and frequently shares with his sons Jeb and current President George W. During the 2000 presidential campaign, the estate (which is impossible to miss and has a special parking area set aside for gawkers) was heralded by a trio of flags: one for

Maine, one for Florida, and one for Texas, representing the states the Bushes call home.

Inland from the coast, Kennebunkport's other main draw is the expansive and enjoyable **Seashore Trolley Museum** (daily 10 AM–5 PM in summer; $8; 207/967-2800), well signed along Log Cabin Road, about midway between the main harbor area and US-1. The oldest mass transit museum in the

United States started as a preservation effort back in the 1930s, at a time when the widespread adoption of the automobile sparked the elimination of urban rail systems across the country. The extensive museum collection includes an entire late-Victorian station from Boston's MBTA, as well as more than 200 trolley cars from systems all over the world, even an original New Orleans streetcar named Desire. A few of the streetcars are used to conduct summertime sunset tours of a four-mile loop around the nearby area, with ice cream included in the fare.

KENNEBUNK

Right on US-1 and originally part of neighboring Wells, tidy Kennebunk is a prototypical coastal Maine town. The town was once a busy shipbuilding center, but its economy now relies mostly on tourists who stop here to appreciate the early American architecture on their way to the nearby beaches. The centerpiece of Kennebunk is the **Brick Store Museum,** which occupies a collection of restored 1820s buildings on US-1 at 117 Main Street (Tues.–Sat. 10 AM–4:30 PM; $3), and displays items on local history as well as more unusual subjects. Another sight to see is the impossibly ornate **Wedding Cake House,** which stands along Summer Street (Route 35), midway between Kennebunk and Kennebunkport.

WELLS

Stretching for miles along US-1, Wells isn't exactly postcard material but it is comparatively inexpensive, and best of all it has a sense of *fun,* something sorely lacking from many of Maine's tonier communities. The beach here, marked by a sign along US-1 pointing the way to Wells Beach, is long and wide and backed by vacation homes, but you can (usually) park in one of the big lots, which charge $7 a day or $25 for a whole week. (And yes, you can and must come and go; there's no overnight camping.)

Hidden away in what looks like a warehouse along US-1, north of the Wells Beach turnoff, is a fine collection of 80-odd early automobiles at the **Wells Antique Auto Museum** (daily 10 AM–5 PM; $5; 207/646-9064). You can take a ride in a real Model T for an extra $1.

The real reason to spend time in Wells is the food. Offerings here aren't as fancy as you might find elsewhere, but you won't find doughnuts as fresh as those cooked up at **Congdon's,** on US-1 across from the turnoff to Wells Beach. On the north edge of Wells, another great place is the **Maine Diner** (daily 7 AM–9:30 PM; 207/646-4441), which serves up good breakfasts, famous seafood, and tons of T-shirts spreading their memorable if not exactly original slogan: "Remember the Maine!" For the best local seafood, be sure to stop at **Billy's Chowder House**

Kennebunkport may still be most famous for its connections to the Presidents Bush (H. W. and W.), but neighboring Kennebunk is semifamous for the natural personal-care products manufactured at **Tom's of Maine,** on Railroad Avenue (207/985-2944). Take a free tour, get a free tube of toothpaste, but whatever you do, don't confuse this place with the very different Tom of Finland shop in nearby Ogunquit.

Most of the coastline around Wells and Kennebunk is protected under the **Rachel Carson National Wildlife Refuge,** which stretches all the way to New Hampshire but has its headquarters office on Route 9 midway between Wells and Kennebunkport (207/646-9226). From here a wheelchair-accessible nature trail crosses the tidal estuary, offering up-close views of the lush grasses and migrating birds. The refuge is named in memory of Rachel Carson (1907–64), whose book *Silent Spring* helped inspire the contemporary environmentalist movement.

(207/646-7558), a clapboard roadhouse on Mile Road, midway between Wells and Wells Beach, that's open for lunch and dinner every day.

For a place to stay, choose from any of the many quaint old cabins and motor courts along US-1, or head down to the beach, where the **Atlantic Motor Inn** at the foot of Mile Road (207/646-7061) has beachfront rooms from $60 per night in shoulder season, twice that in July and August.

OGUNQUIT

Ogunquit (pop. 930) is only about five miles south of Wells, but it couldn't be more different. The name roughly translates from a Native American dialect to "beautiful place by the sea," and it is indeed very pretty, especially if you can work your way past the art galleries, boutiques, and B&Bs along Shore Road to reach **Perkins Cove,** at the south end of town. The cove is a photogenic spit of land, jutting out to form a picture-perfect harbor complete with bobbing lobster boats and a narrow suspension drawbridge that opens up to allow sailboats to pass through. It is well worth the hassles you may have finding a place to park; to avoid this annoyance, leave the car in town and ride out here on the trolleys (50¢), which circle Ogunquit all day long.

Across the drawbridge is the excellent **Ogunquit Museum of American Art,** 183 Shore Road (Mon.–Sat. 10 AM–5 PM, Sun. 2–5 PM; $3; 207/646-4909). It has a fine collection of local seascapes painted by the many world-class artists, including Marsden Hartley, Rockwell Kent, and Thomas Hart Benton, who've spent time in and around Ogunquit. Along with the art, the museum also offers some stunning coastal views.

Back in Perkins Cove, in between watching the lobstermen unload their catch and perusing the galleries and bookstores, you can choose from a pair of places to eat. The plain but very pleasant **Lobster Shack** is open all day for breakfast, burgers, hot dogs, and beer, as well as the inevitable lobster rolls, boiled lobster, and grilled lobsters. Across the road, and near the other end of the culinary spectrum, **Hurricane** (207/646-6348) has a reputation for serving unforgettably good fresh seafood in inventive ways—lobster gazpacho, anyone?—with cinematic Atlantic Ocean views. If you'd prefer to dine al fresco, try the ever-popular **Barnacle Billy's** (207/646-5575), overlooking Perkins Cove and serving upwards of a half-ton of lobster each day in summer.

Accommodations in Ogunquit are relatively expensive and hard to find, since so many people return here summer after summer. One of many characterful places in town is the **Rockmere Lodge,** 40 Stearns Road ($80–180; 207/646-2985), where comfortable rooms in a quiet location within walking distance of the beaches and Perkins Cove fill a well-preserved 1899 house. For more information or help finding a room, visit or call the **visitors bureau** (207/646-2939 or 800/639-2442), on US-1 on the south edge of town.

Ogunquit's long and lovely beach stretches between the Ogunquit River and the Atlantic Ocean. The main parking lot ($2 per hour) is at the south end off Beach Street, but you can also get here by taking the footbridge over the river from the parking lot ($6 per day) at the end of Ocean Street. Trolleys also serve both beaches.

Along US-1 at the north edge of Ogunquit, **Brewster's Micron Mall** is a quirky old filling station stocked up with all roadside essentials, from maps and postcards to candies and chips.

Between Ogunquit and York, near Cape Neddick along US-1, a pair of roadside places offer inexpensive, unpretentious meals. If you like hot dogs, pull up a barstool at **Flo's Steamed Dogs** (11 AM–2 PM daily except Wed.), and try to figure out the secret recipe that makes their trademark sweet-sour hot sauce so addictive. For a health-conscious alternative, try the friendly **Frankie & Johnnie's Natural Foods** (207/363-1909), which has the biggest and best vegetarian menu on the coast.

YORK BEACH

Old Orchard Beach may be bigger and wilder, and other places prettier, but if you want an all-in-one combination of nice sands, beachfront amusement, and scenic views, there's nowhere better than York Beach (pop. 900). York Beach is two miles south of Ogunquit via scenic Shore Road, or two miles northeast on US-1 from I-95 exit 1. In the center of this lively, small beachfront resort off the broad Short Sands Beach, is the Fun-A-Rama arcade, an open-air wooden shed holding everything a quarter can buy, from pinball games to skeeball and air hockey. There's also a minigolf course and a small but fun candlepin bowling alley, which costs about $2 a line. Candlepin is fairly similar to regular bowling but uses small, wooden balls (you grab them and hurl them down the lanes, rather than sticking your fingers into holes).

York Beach faces north, so the surf is usually calm, and the clean sands make it ideal for families. Best of all, a block away stands one of southern Maine's sweetest spots, the ice cream parlor and candy factory doing business since 1896 as **The Goldenrod,** 2 Railroad Avenue (207/363-2621). Famous for their taffy, which you can watch being made through a plate glass window, the Goldenrod also makes milk shakes and other soda fountain specialties and has a full restaurant, too.

At the other end of York Beach, a short two blocks from the Fun-A-Rama, is the popular **Wild Kingdom,** where more than a dozen kid-friendly rides (spinning tea cups, a haunted house, etc.) are joined by fried-dough stands and a set of batting cages (10 balls for $1 token).

If you prefer picturesque lighthouses and rugged coastal scenery over old-time amusements, you'll want to head a half-mile east on Broadway from York Beach out to the unlikely named **Nubble Light,** a dainty Victorian-era wooden lighthouse that sits on a postcard-pretty island, 30 yards offshore from a rocky but very accessible park. On the way to the lighthouse, you drive past the ever-popular **Brown's Ice Cream Stand,** serving huge cones and great sundaes.

YORK VILLAGE

South from York Beach, Route 1A runs along the slender two-mile strand of Long Strands Beach, past motels, vacation homes, and a big RV park before bending west through the center of York Village (pop. 9,800). One of the largest and oldest communities in Maine, York was first settled way back in 1624, named Bristol in 1638, and renamed Gorgeana (after the founder, Mr. Gorges) in 1642, when it was the first city in the American colonies to receive a royal charter. Little remains from the very early days, but a complex of six historic buildings has been restored as **Old York,** off Route 1A and Lindsay Road (207/363-4974), and now serves as a great introduction to the town's history. Admission is $2–6, depending upon how many buildings you tour. All tours begin at the 1750 Jefferds' Tavern, which retains its Old World feel with heavy floorboards and a rough-hewn bar. Dozens of other well-preserved old buildings fill the small area between here and picturesque York Harbor, so take the time to stop and wander around.

West from the harbor, Route 103 runs along and across the York River; just north of the crossing, a wide pullout provides parking spaces for fishermen, dog walkers, and others bound for the delicate, green Whiggly Bridge and the **Steedman Woods,** a 16-acre nature preserve with well-maintained paths.

South from York, Route 103 offers the prettiest way to Portsmouth and New Hampshire. Stop at historic **Fort McClary,** an 18th-century fortress built to protect Portsmouth harbor, for a good view of the ocean before winding your way to Kittery.

KITTERY: PORTSMOUTH NAVAL SHIPYARD

Across the Piscataqua River from its New Hampshire namesake, the Portsmouth Naval Shipyard is the oldest in the New World, and it was here that many of the most important warships in American naval history were build. Wooden frigates (such as the *Ranger,* launched in 1777 under the command of John Paul Jones) and the first nuclear submarines came out of this once mighty, now slightly moribund shipyard. Some 20,000 people worked here in its heyday during World War I, but the shipyard now employs something more like a tenth of that.

Two miles south of downtown Portsmouth along US-1 you'll encounter perhaps the most famous (and certainly the biggest) seafood place in New Hampshire. **Yoken's** (603/436-8224) is a family-oriented restaurant selling fish, fish, and more fish to up to 700 diners at a time in a massive building fronted by a flashing sign of a spouting whale. Don't have dessert there; instead go to **Lagos Ice Cream,** two miles south of Yoken's at the edge of Rye.

Whaleback Lighthouse in Kittery is the southernmost of the 64 lighthouses in Maine.

The compact, 100-acre grounds, which takes up an large island near the mouth of the Piscataqua River, are redolent with the sense of history, although to experience it from inside the gates you'll have to make prior arrangements (207/438-3550) and take a guided tour.

Kittery, the small town that grew up around the shipyard, is a very pleasant place, but since it's just a quick hop across the river to Portsmouth, it's hard to recommend an extended visit. For a good first or last taste of Maine, just before you cross the bridge over the Piscataqua, stop at **Warren's Lobster House,** 11 Water Street (207/439-1630), a no-frills, family-friendly former diner open daily for lunch and dinner (and a very popular, all-you-can-eat Sunday Brunch).

Located at the mouth of the Piscataqua River, the historic and contemporary capital of New Hampshire's short coast, Portsmouth, is covered in the US-4 chapter on page 172.

ROUTE 1A: RYE AND THE BEACHES

Between Portsmouth and Hampton Beach, Route 1A cruises along the ocean, passing some serious-money enclaves and state park beaches. At the center of it all, a mile or so inland, the town of Rye is one of New Hampshire's oldest communities, dating back to the 1660s.

At the north end of this route is the **Odiorne State Park,**

300 acres of wild coastline at the mouth of Portsmouth's harbor. Site of the 1623 Pannaway Plantation, the first New Hampshire settlement, the land here was relatively unchanged for the next 300 years, until the U.S. military took control of it during World War II. Now there are excellent waterfront walking and cycling paths, a small science center ($1), and views of Portsmouth Harbor and the offshore Isles of Shoals, including the oddly named Smuttynose.

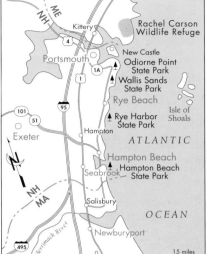

Running south, numerous small state parks offer beach access, and Route 1A winds past stately mansions on the inland side and some unpretentious seafood shacks. Parking at most of the beach areas is $5 per car weekdays, $8 at weekends, but there are a number of pullouts and other places where you can stop to decide if you want to stay a while. The first real beach area you come to is the largest, **Wallis Sands State Park,** a 150-foot-wide (at low tide) strand that curves around a large cove south of a rocky headland where scuba divers often dive. Between here and the marina at Rye Harbor, you'll pass **Petey's** lobster shack. South of Rye Harbor, the beaches are sandy and relatively uncrowded, backed by condos and vacation homes until the small parking area at Jenness State Park, roughly midway along the New Hampshire coast. The biggest and most ostentatious mansions are just south of here, but before you know it you're in the chaotic Coney Island sprawl of Hampton Beach.

HAMPTON BEACH

One of the biggest, brashest, tawdriest beach resorts this side of Coney Island, Hampton Beach stretches for three miles at the southern end of New Hampshire's short oceanfront. If you want to eat fried dough, fried clams, or french fried potatoes, you'll love it. If you want to relax, go somewhere else. During the peak summer season, Hampton Beach is abuzz with teenagers and twentysomethings strutting their stuff up and down the mile-long parade of T-shirt shops, video arcades, and fast-food shacks that line the main road, Route 1A. A central bandstand (known as the clamshell) frequently hosts free live music, and the larger **Hampton Beach Casino Ballroom** ($15–25; 603/929-4100) across the street, draws some pretty well-known pop music and comedy performers. Otherwise, the pleasures fade pretty quickly once the sun goes down.

Across New England, I-95 is the fastest and least interesting route, with the added insult of a $1 toll, while coastal Route 1A is much more leisurely and 100 times more interesting. In between the two, US-1 has some roadside fast-food and ice cream stands, funky junk shops, and one great little Italian place: **Ronaldo's** (4–9 PM Tues.–Sun.; 603/964-5064), in North Hampton at the junction with Route 111, catercorner to a parking lot full of golf carts. It doesn't look like much from outside, but inside a plywood cutout of Frank Sinatra welcomes you to a warmly lit dining room, where massive portions of food mean no one leaves hungry (and most people leave with a doggy bag or two).

Along Route 1A at the southern edge of Portsmouth, you pass **Brit Bits** (603/433-0001), which has to be one of the largest open-air collections of classic British cars anywhere. Although some of the MGs, Jaguars, and Triumphs are undergoing restoration, many of these wonderful old roadsters have been given over to the relentless rust machine that is New Hampshire weather. If this place doesn't have an original shift knob for your aging Spitfire, they'll find you a replica or have one made to order.

Midway along the New Hampshire coast, **Jenness Beach** is the place where the first transatlantic telegraph cable came aground in 1874. There's no plaque and nothing left to see; after all, it *was* an underwater cable.

Along Route 1A in the center of raucous Hampton Beach, the solemn **New Hampshire Marine War Memorial** features a young lady looking mournfully out to sea.

South of Hampton Beach, just shy of the Massachusetts border, is Seabrook, the last nuclear plant built in the United States. Opened in 1990, it produces as much as two-thirds of all the electricity used by New Hampshirites, who in turn pay the nation's highest electricity rates, thanks to Seabrook's $5 billion-plus in cost overruns.

Metered parking ($1 an hour, quarters only) is available up and down the main drag, and if you plan to stay a while, go to the large, less expensive lots further inland.

EXETER

Inland from Hampton and Hampton Beach via Route 101 is the gracious town of Exeter (pop. 13,250). Once the capital of New Hampshire, this town is now home to the prep school Phillips Exeter Academy. In 1775 wary colonists moved the capital here from loyalist Portsmouth and drew up a state constitution; when the constitution was signed here on January 5, 1776, New Hampshire became the first of the American colonies to declare independence from Great Britain. (Concord is now the capital.)

Five years later, John Phillips, whose brother had recently started a school at Andover across the border in Massachusetts, founded a school of his own here, which has since grown into one of the most expensive and best endowed in the country. The **Phillips Exeter Academy** now occupies the hill above the town; step inside the fortress-like main library building, designed in the late 1960s by Louis Kahn, to get a clear sense of the wealth of opportunity awaiting the fortunate few who attend. The atrium forms a four-story concrete cube etched with perfect circles—perhaps as a modernist reply to the Pantheon in Rome. It's a great place to surf the Internet, read a book, or lounge in a comfy chair and listen to a CD or two.

The town of Exeter stretches around the school along the banks of the Squamscott River, which flows into the Great Bay estuary navigable all the way to Portsmouth. Good bookshops, coffeehouses, and a nice old movie theater line Water and Front Streets. There are also two great bakery/sandwich shops: the earthy **Green Bean,** overlooking the river at 33 Water Street (603/778-7585), with a turkey-and-stuffing sandwich reminiscent of the day after Thanksgiving; and **Me & Ollie's Cafe,** 64 Water Street (603/772-4600), a branch of the popular Portsmouth bakery.

NEWBURYPORT

Set at the mouth of the Merrimack River, Newburyport (pop. 16,300) is a historic waterfront community that is rapidly becoming yet another trendy suburb of Boston. New live/work lofts and boutiques are being built around the compact center, which, for the moment at least, still retains its old-time ambiance. A fine example: **Taffy's Fountain Lunch,** at the top of State Street, a block east of Route 1A, is where you can hop on a stool at the counter and watch as the cook whips up a Coke or other soda the old-fashioned way, pouring in the syrup, splashing in some soda water, then whisking it all together. The food's plenty good (try the BLTs). Taffy's scores high on the Blue Highways scale—the walls are cov-

**I-95 SURVIVAL GUIDE: ACROSS NEW HAMPSHIRE
AND MASSACHUSETTS**

MM17: Maine state line.

MM16: Exit 7 to Portsmouth waterfront (see page 172).

MM14: Exit 5 to Portsmouth traffic circle, junction with US-1.

MM13.5: Exit 4 to US-4 west to Concord, and Route 16 (Spaulding Turnpike) north to the White Mountains.

MM6: Toll Plaza ($1 per car)

MM5.5: Exit 2 (toll 50¢), junction with Route 101 west to Exeter and Manchester, and east to Hampton Beach.

MM1: Exit 1 to Seabrook and US-1.

MM0.5: New Hampshire State Welcome Center and State Liquor Store.

MM0/89.5: New Hampshire/Massachusetts state line.

MM89: Exit 60 to Salisbury, US-1 and Route 1A (see page 80).

MM88: Exit 59 for I-495 southwest to Lowell (see page 158) and Worcester.

MM76: Exit 54 for Route 133, Rowley and the Agawam Diner (see page 82).

MM70: Exit 49 for US-1 and Route 62 east to Peabody and Salem.

MM66: Exit 45 for Route 128 east to Cape Ann (see page 82).

MM56: Exit 37 for I-93 north to Manchester, New Hampshire (see page 155).

MM46: Exit 30 for Route 2A to historic Lexington and Concord (see page 160).

MM45: Exit 29 for Cambridge and Route 2.

MM39: Exit 25 for I-90 (Massachusetts Turnpike) east to Boston and west to Springfield and Albany, New York.

MM29: Exit 15 for US-1, north to Brookline and south to Foxboro and Providence (see page 94).

MM11: Exit 6 for I-495, east to Cape Cod and north to Lowell and New Hampshire.

MM0: Rhode Island state line.

ered with at least three local calendars (all the current year), and most customers are longtime regulars.

The rest of the downtown area is very pedestrian friendly, full of 200-year-old buildings housing countless cafes and gadget shops, while the waterfront holds the

In mid-July, Exeter hosts reenactments of something New Hampshire never experienced firsthand: Revolutionary War battles, put on by hundreds of living history fans around the small **American Independence Museum** (Mon.–Fri. noon–5 PM in summer only; $4; 603/772-2622).

Just south of the New Hampshire border, the Massachusetts beach resort of **Salisbury** is a much smaller version of Hampton Beach, with a compact block of amusement arcades and fast-food stands running perpendicular to the beach. The rest of the border zone along US-1 and Route 1A is pretty squalid, with used car lots, bare-naked-lady bars, and fireworks stands all competing for your roadside attention.

Custom House, 25 Water Street (daily 10 AM–4 PM; $3; 978/462-8681), a maritime museum concentrating on local shipbuilding and goods trading with China. To get a sense of what the region looked like in days gone by, head east from Route 1A to Plum Island and the 4,500-acre **Parker River National Wildlife Refuge** ($5 per car; 978/465-5753), a barrier island that stretches south between the Parker River and the open Atlantic Ocean.

If you have an extra hour (or a day or two) to spare between here and Boston, the drive along Route 1A is many times more interesting than US-1, which itself is many times more interesting than I-95. Route 1A through the outskirts of Newburyport and its neighbor **Newbury** is lined with dozens of gorgeous old houses, a few fine churches, and many acres of green. In summer, the roadside scene is so lush that you'd be forgiven for thinking you were somewhere like the Sea Islands of South Carolina rather than the heart of New England.

IPSWICH: CLAM BOX AND CRANE BEACH

For a small town, Ipswich is hard to beat. Its long, sandy beaches are backed by pine forest and wildlife-rich marshes, and the village center is packed with a various restaurants and taverns. Ipswich also has a rich collection of old buildings; in fact, Ipswich claims to have more pre-1725 homes than any other town in the country.

Ancient history aside, the real draw of Ipswich is culinary, if that's not too grand a word for the delicious, fresh fried clams available at the roadside landmark **Clam Box** restaurant two miles north of town on Route 1A at 246 High Street (978/356-9707).

OLD CHAIN BRIDGE

If you're racing north from Boston along I-95, at the point where the freeway crosses the Merrimack River, look right and you'll get a great view of the **Old Chain Bridge,** a historic suspension span that connects the mainland to a small island in the middle of the river.

Shaped like a takeout food container, with sloping sides and an opening "flap" at the roof, the Clam Box is a true classic of a type of architecture sometimes called programmatic, because the building looks like what it sells. The food is excellent; *Gourmet Magazine's* roving road-food correspondents Jane and Michael Stern have rated the fried seafood here as they best they've tasted anywhere (and they've tasted everything everywhere).

East of Ipswich via Argilla Road, **Crane Beach** (parking fee $10–15 per car; half-price after 3 PM; 978/356-4354) is one of the finest beaches in mainland Massachusetts, and is usually big enough to accommodate the many people who come here on a warm summer day. Located less than one hour's drive from Boston, the beach stretches for four miles along broad sands, backed by pine forests and some swampy wetlands. A long (over a mile) walk through the woods will bring you to a huge house known as **Castle Hill,** the former home of plumbing-fixture magnate Richard Crane. The house is open for tours (Tues. only; 978/356-4351), but the 150-acre estate grounds are open daily.

To go along with the Clam Box and Crane Beach, Ipswich also has a handy old-style motel, the **Whittier Motel,** on Route 1A at the Route 133 junction (978/356-5205).

ESSEX: FRIED CLAM CAPITAL

Similar to neighboring Ipswich, only smaller and prettier, Essex (pop. 3,300) is a great place to getaway to—from wherever you're getting away. Spread out along the marshlands of the Essex River estuary, four miles east of Route 1A, Essex is green and peaceful, with numerous little roadside stands, restaurants, and historic sights along winding Route 133. The town was once a center for shipbuilding, which you can learn all about at the **Essex Shipbuilding Museum,** housed in an old schoolhouse at 66 Main Street (Tues.–Sun. 1–4 PM in summer, weekends only rest of year; $4; 978/768-7541), with displays detailing the adjacent 1668 shipyard, one of many formerly lining the waterfront.

Essex is now most famous for its fried clams, which, most experts agree, were first made here in 1916 by Lawrence "Chubby"

Woodman, whose legacy lives on at **Woodman's,** 121 Main Street (978/ 768-6451). Woodman's is a classic clam shack, and the clams are still deep-fried in lard for that deliciously rich, cholesterol-laden taste—so step up, place an order, and wait for your number to be called. Unlike most other clam shacks, Woodman's is open

Along US-1, at the Route 133 junction midway between Danvers and Newburyport on the edge of Rowley, the shiny steel **Agawam Diner** (508/948-7780) has been feeding locals and hungry travelers since the 1940s, and still draws raves for its melt-in-the-mouth banana and coconut cream pies. The Agawam is always full (unlike the McDonald's across the highway) but worth the wait.

Besides being rivals in the fried clam competition, Ipswich and Essex each has its own wild animal park along Route 133: Ipswich boasts **New England Alive!**, while Essex has **Wolf Hollow**.

Between Salem and Ipswich, Route 1A runs through some of the North Shore's most upscale, blue-blood communities. In Hamilton, for example, massive old-money estates sprawl behind stone walls and wooden fences, and the horsey set gets together on summer Sundays at 3 PM for afternoon **polo matches** at the Myopia Polo Club ($5, under 12s free; 978/468-7956), which well-behaved hoi polloi are welcome to attend. Bring a picnic and make a day of it.

year-round, and you can sample fish 'n' chips, fried calamari, and clam chowders, too.

A half-mile south of Woodman's along Route 133, **Farnham's Famous Fried Clams** (978/768-6643) has its fans. If you want to complete a tour of roadside frying, stop by the big red London Routemaster bus that's permanently parked another half-mile south along Route 133, outside the **Red Barrel Pub**, which does a fine line of fish 'n' chips.

For a place to stay in the area, it's hard to beat the **Essex River House** ($50–100; 978/768-6800), a nice little motel tucked away across from Woodman's, in between Route 133 and the riverfront.

CAPE ANN DETOUR: GLOUCESTER AND ROCKPORT

Cape Ann is a little taste of Maine off the coast of Massachusetts. Routes 127 and 127A encircle the cape, together making for some of finest scenic touring you want. Here you'll find dense forests inland with miles of rocky shoreline stretching between picturesque fishing ports that—in parts at least—don't appear to have changed for centuries. Gloucester (pop. 28,700), the largest town on Cape Ann and still a busy fishing port, is also the oldest, founded in 1623 by a hearty band of English who settled here intending to "praise God and catch Fish." (The original colony was located at Stage Fort Point, now home to Gloucester's main welcome center and a park-and-ride commuter lot.)

Unlike the many quaint, manicured lobster-fishing coves in Maine, Gloucester is the real deal, a heavy-duty harbor with dozens of rusty trawlers moored at docks backed by ice companies and packing plants. The downtown area, a block inland from the harbor, has some interesting museums as well as shops and cafes, but it's more a service center than a visitor destination. Rockport (pop. 7,500), on the other hand, is more attractive (and much more commercialized and tourist oriented), with a small-scale town center looking out over semicircular Sandy Bay to the Atlantic. On the south side of slender Bearskin Neck, Rockport also has a busy but small harbor, where the landmark red shed known as **Motif #1** is a favorite subject of tourists' photographs and artists' renderings. (Gloucester also has a reputation for attracting artists: Winslow Homer spent time in the town's Rocky Neck neighborhood, now packed with galleries and accessible by water shuttle from various points along the Gloucester harbor.)

The main road looping around Cape Ann is Route 127; this meandering road runs north from Gloucester, starting at the east end of the busy Route 128 freeway, the main link to and from US-1, I-95, and metropolitan Boston. Most of the cape is private property, but you can get some great views and learn a lot about its varied history by visiting **Halibut Point State Park** (daily sunrise–sunset; $2 per car;

WHALE-WATCHING IN NEW ENGLAND

A century ago, Yankee whaling ships circled the globe for months at a time in search of whales to kill for the mammals' valuable oils. These days, Yankee ships head out on half-day trips in search of whales so visitors can get a close encounter with one (and usually many more) of these massive yet graceful mammals. The two species of whales most often seen along the coast of New England are fleet finback whales and acrobatic humpback whales, which sometimes leap completely out of the water. Other important species are minke whales and the endangered right whales, though these (unlike the others) are increasingly rare. Besides whales, on any whale-watching trip you're also likely to see dolphins, harbor seals, and hundreds of seabirds.

One of the prime spout-spotting sites in New England are the fish-rich feeding areas of the **Stellwagen Bank National Marine Sanctuary.** A shallow underwater platform left behind by receding glaciers, the Stellwagen Bank covers nearly 850 square miles of open sea, stretching between Cape Ann and Cape Cod. Throughout the warmer months (early May through the end of October—the only times you'd want to be out on the north Atlantic Ocean anyway), commercial whale-watching tour boats leave daily from Gloucester Harbor and from Provincetown, usually heading out midmorning (around 10 AM) and returning midafternoon (around 3 PM). In July and August, you can also join whale-watching tours at points in southern Maine coast, at Boston and Plymouth, and at other harbors along the coast.

If you're planning your trip around a whale-watching cruise, try to start from Gloucester, which at 13 miles from Stellwagen Bank is the closest point to the best whale-watching spots. Reputable operators here include **Capt. Bill's Whale Watch,** 33 Harbor Loop ($28; 978/283-6995 or 800/33-WHALE) and the **Cape Ann Whale Watch,** 415 Main Street ($26; 978/283-5110). From Provincetown, **Dolphin Fleet** ($18; 508/349-1900 or 800/826-9300) offers three-hour trips departing every hour most mornings; **Provincetown Whale Watch** (508/487-3322 or 800/992-9333) and **Portuguese Princess** (508/487-2651 or 800/442-3188) also offer daily trips out to the whales' feeding grounds. All of these tours are guided by expert marine biologists, who will identify the different whales and describe their habits. These trips are very

popular, so try to make reservations as early as you can. Dress warmly, with a waterproof shell. Take some Dramamine if you're prone to seasickness, and take lots of film to capture the many Kodak moments.

To get a feel for life on the water in Gloucester, without spending your life at sea, take the frequent CATA ferry (hourly throughout the summer; $1; 978/283-7916) that links the downtown Seven Seas Wharf with picturesque **Ten-Pound Island** out in Gloucester Harbor. A former Coast Guard seaplane base, the island is home to a squat but photogenic, black-and-white lighthouse, which you can see from the Man at the Wheel statue on Gloucester's waterfront.

The Perfect Storm, the year 2000 release starring George Clooney and Mark Wahlberg, was set and filmed in and around Gloucester. One of the central settings, the **Crow's Nest** bar at 334 Main Street, has become something of a hot spot, despite being a dingy dive that bears no resemblance to its portrayal in the movie. A clapboard building was built on a wharf for the movie, but the real place is across the street from the water and has a redbrick front.

On a hill above Route 127, about a mile inland from Rockport's Pigeon Cove, the **Paper House** (daily 10 AM–5 PM; $1.50; 978/546-2629) is worth searching out if you like oddball Americana. It's a home completely thickly coated in varnished 1920s newspapers (hence the name); inside is a desk made entirely from newspapers detailing Charles Lindbergh's famous trans-Atlantic flight.

978/546-2997) at its northern tip. Located on the site of a huge granite quarry, the park is a miniature Acadia National Park, with rugged cliffs dropping down to the coast. The park's visitor center is housed in a World War II gun battery, built to look like a lighthouse. Alas, there's no swimming, but you do get great views across the water to the mountains of Maine, 30 miles away.

CAPE ANN PRACTICALITIES

Within easy reach of Boston, Gloucester and Rockport are popular enough to have a wide range of visitor services, but they're not *too* popular. Prices go up and traffic gets backed up on summer weekends, but most of the time this "other cape" is a very pleasant place to be. Cape Ann is linked to Beantown by the MBTA Commuter Rail's Gloucester-Rockport line (about $8 round-trip; 617/222-3200 or 800/392-6100), which comes into Boston's North Station, and helps make Cape Ann a convenient and generally less expensive base for exploring this historic corner of Massachusetts.

The differences in personality between the two Cape Ann towns is apparent in every aspect, especially their food and lodging options. Gloucester has motels and cafes, while Rockport has B&Bs and fancy seafood places. (Rockport is a "dry" town, so remember to bring your own beer, wine, or booze.) Just outside downtown Gloucester, on the waterfront midway between the harbor and the Man at the Wheel statue, the **Boulevard Oceanview,** 25 Western Avenue (978/281-2949) serves excellent Portugeuse-influenced seafood and fresh fish 'n' chips in a friendly, no-frills setting. Rockport's harbor is packed with good places like **Ellen's Harborside,** 1 Town Wharf (978/546-2512).

One of the many reasonable and characterful places to stay on Cape Ann is the **Manor Inn,** along Route 133 at 141 Essex Avenue ($60–115; 978/283-0614), an 1899 house with B&B rooms and a small motel annex; it's a rather long walk from Gloucester harbor, on the hill above the Annisquam River. If you mainly want to play on the beach, the best bet is the modern **Cape Ann Motor Inn** ($65–125; 978/281-2900 or 800/464-8439), overlooking Twin Lights island from Long Beach, off Route 127A. For a more peaceful escape, try the **Old Farm Inn** (978/546-3237), next to Halibut Point.

For more information about visiting Cape Ann, contact the **visitors bureau,** 33 Commercial Street (978/283-1601 or 800/321-0133) along the Gloucester waterfront, or stop by the summer-only **Welcoming Center** (978/281-8865) at historic Stage Fort Point west of downtown along the waterfront.

SALEM

If you've seen the movie *The Crucible* or had to read the Arthur Miller play in high school, you probably know this about Salem: in 1692, under the influence of West Indian slave Tituba, a handful of teenage girls from Salem Village (now the town of Danvers) accused more than 150 fellow residents of witchery. Within a year, 19 supposed witches were executed, and many more had their lives ruined (including a five-year-old boy who was imprisoned for over a year). You might think Salem would be ashamed of these Witch Trials, but no; commerce has won out over penitence, and the city capitalizes on its violent past with scores of tourist attractions re-creating some aspect or another of the supernatural.

Witchcraft aside, Salem (pop. 38,100) is a truly historic place. Founded in 1626, it was the original capital of the Massachusetts Bay Colony, a role assumed by Boston in 1630. Thanks to the immensely profitable maritime trade, Salem was the wealthiest city in the early years of post-colonial America, and by the middle of the 19th century it had evolved into a manufacturing center, with huge mills located in the hinterlands along the Essex and Merrimack Rivers.

The heart of Salem has always been the few blocks between the port and Salem Common. Along Derby Street, the **Salem Maritime National Historical Park** includes a pair of wharves and the re-created schooner *Friendship*. Across the street, you can also visit the **Derby House,** the preserved 1760s home of the ship owner who became Salem's first millionaire, and the 1819 **Customs House,** where Nathaniel Hawthorne worked before featuring it in his novel, *The Scarlet Letter.* Three blocks further east but not part of the National Park is another house Hawthorne made famous: **The House of Seven Gables** (daily 10 AM– 5 PM; $7; 978/744-0991).

Salem's one real "serious" museum was started by sea-

The two best sandy beaches on Cape Ann are Good Harbor Beach and Long Beach, next to each other along Thatcher Road (Route 127A) on the south side of the cape midway between Gloucester and Rockport.

Coming into Gloucester from Salem and the south, avoid Route 128 and opt for Route 127 instead, which winds along the bay past incredible mansions and quaint towns like Beverly Shores. This route, which dogs the MBTA Commuter Rail line almost all the way, will bring you in along the Gloucester waterfront past the landmark statue of the Man at the Wheel, a.k.a. the *Gloucester Fisherman,* erected in memory of sailors and fishermen lost at sea.

Although Salem gets all the witch-related tourist traffic, all of the supposed witchcraft actually happened in what used to be known as Salem Village, now the neighboring town of **Danvers,** where (unlike Salem) a number of actual sites still stand. Danvers doesn't advertise any of its connections to the events of 1692, but it does have the **Rebecca Nurse Homestead,** 149 Pine Street (Tues.–Sun 1–4:30 PM in summer only; $4; 978/774-8799), home of the old woman hanged alongside four other "witches."

Considering the violent intolerance that fueled the famous witch trials, it's ironic that the name "Salem" is derived from the Hebrew word shalom, meaning peace.

The House of Seven Gables

Witch-related amusements in Salem include the **Wax Museum of Witches and Seafarers,** ($5; 800/298-2929); the popular but disappointing **Witch Museum** ($6; 978/745-1692) on Salem Common, the pagan-run **Salem Witch Village** ($4.95; 978/740-9229), the entertaining **Witch Dungeon Museum** (978/741-3570), the **Witch History Museum** (978/741-7770), **Mass Hysteria Haunted Hearse Tours** (877/443-2773), and the play *Cry Innocent* ($6; 978/927-2300), a dramatic reenactment of one of the Salem trials. The only place with a direct tie to the events of 1692 is the **Witch House** ($5; 978/744-0180), home of Witch Trial judge Jonathan Corwin, who personally confiscated the land and property of people he convicted.

faring art lovers back in 1799, and is the oldest continuously operating museum in the USA: the **Peabody Essex Museum** (Mon.–Sat. 10 AM–5 PM, Sun. noon–5 PM, closed Mon. in winter; $10; 978/745-9500). Two blocks from the water at 132 Essex Street, this is one of New England's largest collections of fine art, with numerous portraits, seascapes, and other works by the likes of John Singer Sargent and Gloucester painter Fitz Hugh Lane. An adjacent building on Liberty Street, the **East India Hall** is filled to the gunwales with trade goods from around the world, including thousands of decorative pieces from China and Japan, plus fine furniture and intricately carved figureheads from Salem's world-beating fleet of ships. The museum also maintains some of Salem's finest old homes, open only on guided tours.

A change of pace from the hyper-tourism of central Salem, the small but very characterful (and free!) **Salem Willows Amusement Park**, with a block of ancient little fun fair rides, pizza places, ice cream stands, and all sorts of great arcade games, from skeeball to glow-in-the-dark air hockey. There's also a nice waterfront park with frequent free live music (such as Big Band swing every Tuesday night!). The park is about two miles north and east from Salem's historic waterfront at the mouth of Salem Harbor (drive out Derby Street past a power plant and a sewage treatment plant).

SALEM PRACTICALITIES

Salem is at its busiest during July, August, and Halloween, when hundreds of wanna-be witches descend upon the place, so you'll want to make advance arrangements during these peak times. Thanks to frequent MBTA Commuter Rail trains, Salem is also an easily manageable day trip to or from Boston, only 16 miles away. Places to stay aren't plentiful or especially cheap, however; apart from quaint old B&Bs like the **Amelia Payson House,** 16 Winter Street off Salem Common ($100–150; 978/744-8304), the best rooms are at the central and historic **Hawthorne Hotel,** facing the common from 18 Washington Square ($120–180; 978/744-4080).

Food options of all kinds—Italian, Thai, Mexican, and

more—are concentrated in the main tourist areas. **Salem Beer Works** just west of the waterfront at 278 Derby Street (978/741-7088) has wood-fired pizzas to go along with microbrewed beers. Down Derby Street, across from the House of Seven Gables, the pub **In a Pig's Eye** (978/741-4436) is a cozy place to unwind after a hard day with the witches. For a taste of real Salem, head south of downtown Salem toward Marblehead to **The Salem Diner** (daily 5:30 AM– 8 PM; 978/741-7918), off Route 1A at 70 Loring Avenue, down the hill from Salem State College. A fine example of a 1940s Sterling Streamliner and one of the most popular of the Boston area's many fine diners, the Salem Diner is usually packed with regulars enjoying their pancakes, eggs, coffee, and other diner staples. Dinner specials include such favorites as liver and onions and yummy lamb shanks. Come at sunset for a photo of the rooftop neon sign, its slanted lettering enhancing the sense of movement evoked by all those shiny curves on the roof.

For more information on Salem's rich and varied history, stop at the **Salem Maritime National Historical Park visitor center,** next to the Peabody Essex Museum at 2 New Liberty Street (daily 9 AM–5 PM; free; 978/740-1655), where you can watch a short film and pick up detailed information on the city's seafaring and manufacturing past. For help with the more practical present, contact the **Destination Salem visitor center,** 10 Liberty Street (978/744-3663).

MARBLEHEAD AND THE NORTH SHORE

The coastal areas north of Boston are relentlessly industrial and densely developed, but there are a few pockets where you can wander quiet streets and watch waterfowl migrating from wetland to wetland. The more distant places like Cape Ann and Salem are well-proven getaways from the urban melee, but the closest real escape from Boston is Marblehead (pop. 19,971), a yachting center set along a lovely harbor, east of Route 1A across the water from Salem.

In between Marblehead and Boston, there's almost no relief from the petrochemical tanks and car parts stores you'll pass by (usually at a snail's pace in sluggish traffic), although history buffs will want to make their ways to the **Saugus Iron Works National Historic Site** (781/233-0050), which preserves a 1646 iron foundry. Diner fans make a pilgrimage to **Capitol Diner,** 43 Union Street in Lynn (781/595-9314). Located across the street from a factory-turned–state park celebrating Lynn's heritage as shoe-making center, this 1920s Brill diner has a

If you want to pass for a knowing local, pronounce Peabody like this: "PEE-buh-dee."

Besides witches, Salem's most famous product was writer Nathaniel Hawthorne (1804–64), who was born in Salem and set many of his stories here. Much of the action in *The Scarlet Letter* takes place in and around the port and Custom House, and the real-life model for his *House of Seven Gables* stands a couple of blocks east.

Freelan O. Stanley, one of the twin brothers who invented the Stanley Steamer automobile, was killed in 1918 while driving his namesake creation down what's now US-1.

ROADRUNNER, ROADRUNNER

If you find yourself on the dysfunctional maze of highways and byways that snare drivers around the Hub, you may take some comfort from the words of Boston's world famous rock 'n' roll poet troubadour Jonathan Richman:

Roadrunner, roadrunner
Going faster miles an hour
Gonna drive past the Stop 'n' Shop
With the radio on
I'm in love with Massachusetts
And the neon when it's cold outside
And the highway when it's late at night
Got the radio on
I'm like the roadrunner

Alright
I'm in love with modern moonlight
128 when it's dark outside
I'm in love with Massachusetts
I'm in love with the radio on
It helps me from being alone late at night
It helps me from being lonely late at night
I don't feel so bad now in the car
Don't feel so alone, got the radio on
Like the roadrunner
That's right

colorful striped awning and some great cheap food: big breakfasts, burgers, turkey sandwiches, and more.

ACROSS BOSTON

The approach into Boston along US-1 from the north is one of those crazy strips of roadside Americana about which writers can't resist rhapsodizing. Like the Strip in Las Vegas, there's something charming about the chaos and cross-cultural craziness that abounds here in the otherwise unremarkable town of **Saugus**. Two examples: a five-story cactus stands in front of the **Hilltop Steak House,** while the pagoda-shaped roof of the "World's Largest Chinese Restaurant," **Weylu's,** is just down the road. Also here: the "Leaning Tower of Pizza," a one-quarter scale model of the Pisan landmark, stands in front of **Prince's Restaurant,** while on the other side of the highway you'll find the outrageous Polynesian facade of the **Kowloon Restaurant** and cocktail lounge. The best thing is, all of these places serve pretty good food.

Although Revere Beach doesn't compare favorably with Cape Cod or even Cape Ann, it does have a long, broad sandy strand (backed by disgustingly yucky water), some retro-Victorian beach pavilions, a pizza place, and best of all—free on-street parking! If you're coming from the north, drop your car here and take the T Blue Line subway into downtown Boston.

BOSTON SURVIVAL GUIDE

In the 360-plus years since its founding, Boston (pop. 558,400) has witnessed more historically significant events than any American city even twice its size. The youthful energy of the city's many college students certainly helps cloak the city's deeply entrenched parochialism, but the ghosts of Puritans past haven't entirely lost their grip on the place. So, while the club scene is vibrant, the coffee shops are bustling, and bookstores nearly outnumber video stores, don't expect to buy booze on Sundays or find many places open for dinner after 10 PM.

There are lots of places to start a Boston tour, but a personal favorite is the **Old North Church**, 193 Salem Street (daily 9 AM–5 PM, services Sunday at 9 AM, 11 AM, and 4 PM; free; 617/523-6676), a Boston landmark since colonial times, when the lantern signal set Paul Revere off on his midnight ride. The steeple has been rebuilt but almost everything else is original. Paul's house, the oldest in Boston, is a block away at 19 North Square. Best of all, the surrounding neighborhood, the predominantly Italian North End, is the city's oldest, most interesting, and most pedestrian-friendly quarter.

The other must-see place is **Fenway Park,** home of the Red Sox (tickets 617/267-1700). Located off Boylston Street at 4 Yawkey Way, this is the smallest and arguably most fascinating stadium in the nation. (The owners want to tear it down and replace it with a new ballpark, so come here while you can.) Before a game, you can improve your mind by whiling away a few hours at the nearby **Isabella Stuart Gardner Museum**, 280 The Fenway (Tues.–Sun. 11 AM–5 PM; $12; 617/566-1401). In the late 19th century "Mrs. Jack" Gardner built her home in the style of Venetian palazzo, crammed it with exquisite art, and then opened it as a museum. Her idiosyncratic taste is partially the charm
(continues)

of this place, along with the lushly landscaped interior courtyard. Boston's expansive **Museum of Fine Arts**, 465 Huntington Avenue (daily 10 AM–5 PM, with extended hours in summer; $12, free Wed. after 4 PM; 617/267-9300) is much bigger, with more than 200 galleries of just about every type and era of fine art from all over the world. The Japanese art collection is considered among the best in the United States, and there are also major works by such New England painters as Albert Pinkham Ryder, Winslow Homer, and Fitz Hugh Lane, among others.

Southwest of downtown Boston, behind 365 Huntington Avenue (US-1) along World Series Way and on the campus of Northeastern University, you'll find a slice of baseball history: the place where the Red Sox played before Fenway Park. Now a park, this is where the 1903 World Series was played, and where ace Cy Young pitched the first perfect game of the modern era, on May 5, 1904. A statue of Young stands in the park to commemorate the man and his accomplishments. Many thanks to Peggy Engel, author of the fine book *Baseball Vacations*, for providing this tip.

Atop the tallest building in New England, the **John Hancock Observatory**, 200 Clarendon Street at Copley Square (daily 9 AM–10 PM; $6; 617/572-6429), is simply the best place to get a view of Boston. The I. M. Pei–designed monolith made headlines early on, when its windows developed a tendency to pop out and shatter all over the sidewalks below. For a nice contrast of Boston landmarks new and old, step across the square to Trinity Church, designed by H. H. Richardson in his trademark Romanesque style.

Boston Practicalities

Boston sits spiderlike at the center of a web of major arterial highways (US-1, Route 2, US-3) and Interstates, including I-90, I-93, and I-95. Air travelers get to deal with the chaos and malfunction of Logan International Airport, the major gateway to New England for U.S. and foreign flights. Logan is very close to the center across Boston Harbor—just a seven-minute ride from downtown if you take the Water Shuttle to or from Rowes Wharf (every 15 minutes weekdays, 30 minutes on weekends; $10 o/w, $17 r/t). Logan is also connected to the city by the Blue Line Massachusetts Bay Transportation Authority subway (a.k.a. the T, which also refers to MBTA's network of buses, trolleys, ferries, and commuter trains); scheduled vans such as Back Bay Coach, which makes hourly rounds to a dozen downtown hotels; on-demand vans like U.S. Shuttle (800/449-4240; $7-13 depending on destination); taxis; and, of course, rental cars.

Boston's 21st-century traffic and 17th-century streets are not for the fainthearted. Narrow, often unidentified, poorly maintained, and laid out in irregular patterns conforming to long-buried topography, the city's avenues are also home to some of the most aggressive give-no-quarter, bumper-riding red-light-runners you'll ever meet. Since such conditions create a fundamental nightmare for out-of-town drivers, the best bet is to leave your car as far out of the city as you can (at the Revere Beach or Alewife T stations, or commuter rail stations further out in the suburbs), and either take public transit like nearly everyone else, or use your feet. All the hotels, restaurants, and attractions you might want are within walking distance of the T. Various passes are available for $5 a day, $18 a week, so you can get around everywhere for less than it costs to park; for help planning your route, call 617/722-3200.

Places to stay in Boston start with the budget **HI Boston Hostel,** 12 Hemenway Street, near the Green Line's Hynes/ICA station ($22; 617/536-9455). It's a standard urban hostel, which is to say that if the person in the next bunk snores, good luck catching a good night's rest. Book private rooms ($54 for two) a month in advance. Many steps up the comfort scale is the **Boston Park Plaza Hotel,** 64 Arlington Street, near the Green

swan boats in Boston Public Garden

Line's Arlington station ($149–229; 617/426-2000 or 800/225-2008). It is grand and enormous (966 rooms) yet not impersonal. For a B&B at the foot of historic Beacon Hill, try **John Jeffries House,** 14 Embankment Road, near the Red Line's Charles station ($125–175; 617/367-1866). Across from the Charles River Esplanade (where the Boston Pops Orchestra performs their 4th of July concert), this Victorian inn proves that you don't have to sacrifice comfort and convenience for savings.

Thanks no doubt to Boston's Puritan past, the city has never had much of a reputation for its food. That said, there are some fun places to eat, like **The Daily Catch,** 323 Hanover Street (617/523-8567), within walking distance from the Haymarket T. This North End joint is so tiny, if he wanted to, the cook could shake hands with half his customers without leaving his stove. Calamari (squid) is the house specialty, but the menu's mainstay is Sicilian seafood-over-linguine (with red or white sauce), served in saute pans instead of on plates. The restaurant takes cash only and no reservations, so expect a wait after 6 PM. A yuppie-free zone in the heart of the Back Bay, **The Other Side Cosmic Cafe,** 407 Newbury Street (617/536-9477), catercorner from the Green Line's Hynes/ICA station, is a popular place for people who want fruit and vegetable smoothies, wheat grass shots, and veggie lasagna to accompany that late-night espresso.

And if you really have to have one authentic Boston meal, go to **Durgin Park,** in Faneuil Hall at 340 N. Market Street (617/227-2038), for beef, seafood, and baked beans served up at shared tables to a mix of tourists and masochistic locals.

For further information, drop by the Boston Common Visitor Center on Tremont Street near the Park Street T station for all your little fan-folded flyer needs. Lists of attractions and accommodations are also available in advance from the **Greater Boston Convention and Visitors Bureau,** 2 Copley Place (617/536-4100 or 800/888-5515).

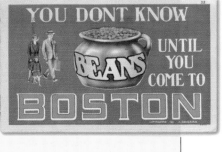

YOU DON'T KNOW UNTIL YOU COME TO BOSTON

US-1 becomes a freeway around Revere, about five miles north of downtown Boston. If you want to stay down on ground level, follow Route 60 and Route 1A (signs will say Logan or Airport) and detour east through Revere Beach, a historic resort area that's now home to petrochemical refineries and the Suffolk Downs horse racing track. If you want some up-close views of jets taking off from Logan, wind out to Winthrop, which sticks out into the bay right beneath the flight path.

If you take US-1/I-93, you'll cross the Charles River into downtown Boston on a nifty new cable-stayed bridge, designed by Swiss engineer Christian Menn; if you follow Route 1A, you come in via the Sumner Tunnel, entering downtown more or less underneath the Paul Revere House in the historic North End. The ongoing Big Dig construction, which is eventually going to replace the downtown I-93 expressway with a new tunnel, may send you along any number of detours, compounding Boston's traditional impossibilities for drivers. If you really want to see the city, park wherever you can and take public transportation.

To the south, US-1 starts off as Huntington Avenue past the Museum of Fine Arts and some nice parks, then hops on the VFW Parkway to the I-95/Route 128 beltway, and then runs parallel to the freeway for the rest of the way to Rhode Island.

Boston marks the junction of US-1 with our road-trip route along US-3, which runs north into New Hampshire and south along the coast through Plymouth towards Cape Cod. For more on this historic route, see pages 138–167.

BROOKLINE

Brookline (pop. 54,700) is very much a part of Boston but legally and in many ways socially separate from the Hub. Located off US-1 and well off the main tourist trail, the town has some little-known and truly fascinating historic sites and museums. Car-culture fans will want to visit America's oldest and most stylish collection in the **Museum of Transportation**, 15 Newton Street (Tues.–Sun. 10 AM–5 PM; $5; 617/522-6547), where some of the finest examples of early touring motor cars are housed on a sprawling 65-acre estate. Brookline is also the place where President John F. Kennedy was born in 1917; his family home at 83 Beals Street has been restored as the **JFK Birthplace National Historic Site** (Wed.–Sun. 11 AM–4 PM; $2; 617/566-7937).

The final pilgrimage place in Brookline's pantheon of history is in many ways the most significant: the home of landscape architect Frederick Law Olmsted, who did more than anyone else to shape the look of the American landscape. The idyllic suburban home where the designer of New York's Central Park lived and worked for the last 15 years of his life has been preserved as the **Frederick Law Olmsted National Historic Site**, at 99 Warren Street (Fri.–Sun. 10 AM–4:30 PM; donations; 617/566-1689).

On the south side of Boston, US-1 runs through the town of Dedham, where the notorious trial of **Sacco and Vanzetti** was held in 1921. Accused of murder during a robbery of a payroll truck, the two "anarchist bastards" (as the presiding judge described them) were executed after a trial most historians agree was a total miscarriage of justice.

PAWTUCKET

US-1 eases across the Rhode Island north and east of Providence at the blue-collar city of Pawtucket (pop. 72,644), which has played a vital role in American industrial history. Located in a waterfront park at the center of town and tiny by 19th-century factory standards, **Slater's Mill** (Tues.–Sat. 10 AM–5 PM, Sunday 1–5 PM in summer, weekends only March–May; $4; 401/725-8638) helped launch America's Industrial Revolution. Following the Revolutionary War, England banned exportation of goods to America. However, when English-born Samuel Slater, who apprenticed at Richard Arkwright's cotton mills in Derbyshire, moved to the United States, he brought with him the knowledge of the latest mechanized cotton-spinning technology. Slater also brought with him significant management skills, and in partnership with others, he transformed American manufacturing from handicrafts to mass production.

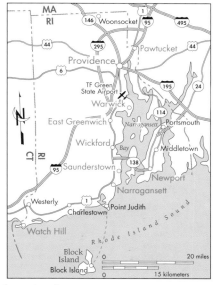

Numerous exhibits trace the historical context of Slater's efforts, but the real reason to visit is to watch and listen as the eight-ton water wheel creaks and groans around and around, powering the many belts and pulleys that still turn the machines as they did in Slater's day.

Pawtucket's other significant historic site is also well worth a visit, though it can be more difficult to find: the **Modern Diner,** 364 East Avenue (401/726-8390), just east of I-95. A classic streamlined Sterling diner, the Modern was the first diner to be registered as an official historic landmark. It's open every day from 7 AM–3 PM (from 8 AM on Sunday) for breakfast and lunch, with dinners available Tuesday–Friday until 8 PM. Check it out—the cranberry pancakes are great.

Boston has the Museum of Fine Arts; downtown Dedham has the **Museum of Bad Art** (Mon.–Fri. 6:30–10:30 PM, Sat. and Sun. 1:30–10:30 PM; free; 617/325-8224), a changing display of truly terrible paintings housed in the basement of the Dedham Community Theater, 580 High Street.

PROVIDENCE SURVIVAL GUIDE

Sitting at the north end of Narragansett Bay, Providence (pop. 160,728) was established in 1636 by Roger Williams, who had been exiled from neighboring Massachusetts for his religious views. A small, hilly city with a busy, partly industrial and partly recreational waterfront, Providence has done a good job of preserving its historic quarters. In fact, it boasts more colonial houses per square foot than any other American city. Capital of the nation's smallest state, Providence is also home to two premier colleges, Brown University and the Rhode Island School of Design.

US-1 comes into Providence as Main Street, while US-6 drops you at the center of town at a confusing ganglia of roads, canals, and freeways intertwining at the base of the landmark **State Capitol**, 82 Smith Street (daily 8:30 AM–4:30 PM; free). The building was completed by McKim, Mead, and White in 1904, and features a marble dome capped by a 12-foot-tall gilded bronze statue of the *Independent Man*. Two hundred yards east of the capitol, across the railroad tracks and the narrow Moshassuck River, the **Roger Williams National Memorial**, 282 N. Main Street (daily 8 AM–4:30 PM; free), recounts his life in a three-minute slide show. The memorial stands at the heart of historic Providence, and the surrounding streets, especially Benefit Street a block farther east, contain some of the finest intact colonial and early federal-era houses in the country. Walking tours are offered by the **Providence Preservation Society** (401/831-7440).

At the south end of the historic center, the small **Museum of Art** of the Rhode Island School of Design, 224 Benefit Street (Tues.–Sun. 10 AM–5 pm; $5; 401/454-6500), has an excellent survey of painting and sculpture from around the world. The marvelous **Providence Athenaeum**, 251 Benefit Street (Mon.–Fri. 10 AM–5 PM; free) exhibits selected items from its extensive collection of early American prints, maps, and books. Yet more culture is found on College Hill above, where the grounds of Brown University mix with a tree-lined neighborhood of stately 200-year-old homes.

A new testament to road-trip culture is on the menu in Providence. Walter Scott created the diner in 1872 when he started selling hot food from a converted horse-drawn freight wagon in Providence. The diner legacy will be explored in a new **American Diner Museum**, to be housed (probably starting in 2003) at the Heritage Harbor complex in the former Narragansett Electric Co. power plant, along the waterfront southeast of the I-95/I-195 interchange (401/331-8575).

One reason to drive I-95: the "World's Largest Bug," a bright blue, 50-foot-long termite nicknamed Nibbles Woodaway, stands atop the New England Pest Control building, a mile south of downtown Providence on I-95.

Providence Practicalities

There are good restaurants in and around the historic center. **Al Forno**, 577 S. Main Street (401/273-9760), is an Italian restaurant with a national reputation for inventive fine food. Many more of the best places to eat are in the predominantly Italian Federal Hill neighborhood, a half-mile west of the waterfront on the other side of the I-95 freeway. Try the very good **Grotta Azzura**, 210 Atwells Avenue, or any of a dozen other places packed along these few short blocks.

If you want to check out the city's many fine diners, start at the 1950s classic **Seaplane Diner**, 307 Allens Avenue, head back a generation to the 1930s **Wampanaug Diner**, 2800 Pawtucket Avenue, then go all the way back to the beginnings at the mobile **Haven Brothers Lunch Cart**, wheeled up to the steps of City Hall every afternoon.

Places to stay in Providence include the usual Interstate hotels and motels, plus a few pleasant B&Bs in and around the historic core; try the **Old Court**, 144 Benefit Street ($80–120; 401/751-2002).

For more complete listings and other information, contact the **Providence visitor center**, 1 W. Exchange Street (401/751-1177 or 800/233-1636). For the lowdown on who and what's playing in Providence's nightclubs and theaters, call the **club report** (401/455-8278) compiled by Brown University's alternative radio station, **WBRU-FM**.

At Providence, US-1 crosses our road trip along US-6, which runs east through New Bedford to the tip of Cape Cod, and west across the heart of Connecticut. For more, see pages 220–245.

EAST GREENWICH, WICKFORD, AND SAUNDERSTOWN

South of metropolitan Providence, US-1 runs briefly along the bay before reaching East Greenwich, a small town that's home to **Jigger's Diner**, 145 Main Street (daily 6 AM–2 PM; 401/884-5388), a lovingly restored Worcester diner serving homemade applesauce, tasty fish chowders, and award-winning Rhode Island jonnycakes (a kind of cornbread; three for $1.75). Fifteen miles south of Providence, US-1 next hits the water at Wickford, one of Rhode Island's (and some say New England's) most attractive little towns. First settled in 1709, Wickford has a number of 18th-century homes and other buildings along the waterfront Main Street, so be sure to stop the car and wander around. The **Old Narragansett Church,** at 55 Main Street, is one of the oldest Anglican-Episcopal churches in the nation, dating from 1707.

Gilbert Stuart Birthplace

South of Wickford, the most scenic route is along Route 1A through Saunderstown, where a snuff-maker's son grew up to become one of early America's premier artists. Ironically, considering the fact that his father was a Loyalist and he himself fled to London during the Revolutionary War, artist Gilbert Stuart created some of the new republic's most famous icons, including the famous portrait of George Washington that graces the $1 bill. His family home (and riverside snuff-mill) has been preserved as the **Gilbert Stuart Birthplace** (Thurs.–Mon. 11 AM–5 PM; $3; 401/294-3001), a mile east of US-1.

DETOUR: NEWPORT

North of Saunderstown, Route 138 runs east from US-1 and Route 1A, hopping across Narragansett Bay on a pair of islands and a pair of bridges ($2 toll) toward Newport, one of the East Coast's prime waterfront resorts. Although best known for the gigantic "cottages" built by the richest of the rich during the Gilded Age, Newport played a significant role throughout American history. For example, the beautiful **Touro Synagogue National Historic Site,** in the heart of town at 85 Touro Street (Sun.–Fri. 10 AM–5 PM; free; 401/847-4794) is the nation's oldest Jewish temple, built in 1763 by the substantial Jewish community attracted here by Rhode Island's religious tolerance. Touro Synagogue also has the distinction of being the nation's first historic restoration, having been preserved as a landmark way back in 1828. Newport also has the nation's oldest Quaker church, the **Friends Meeting House** (tours by appointment; $5; 401/846-0813), three blocks north at 29 Farewell Street.

Touro Synagogue

Unlike many historic ports, Newport was largely saved from wholesale devastation; instead of evolving into an industrial center, Newport became a summer home for the social elite, who during the last half of the 19th century built some of the most elaborate palaces you'll see anywhere. Dozens of these grand estates line Bellevue Avenue and the three-mile waterfront "Cliff Walk" south of town; most are open for tours 10 AM–5 PM daily, and charge $8–10 admission. The biggest house here is the Vanderbilt family's 70-room **The Breakers** (401/847-6544); the best known, thanks to its appearance in *The Great Gatsby* and other films, is probably **Rosecliff** (401/847-1000). At the end of the peninsula, the most interesting and enjoyable of all the Newport estates may be **Hammersmith Farm** (401/846-7346), its beautiful bayfront gardens designed by Frederick Law Olmsted. This was the summer home of Jackie Bouvier and was the site of her 1953 wedding to John F. Kennedy.

Newport has lots of fine restaurants, including the nation's oldest tavern—the very expensive **White Horse** on Farewell Street (401/849-3600)—and some more affordable, family-friendly seafood places on the piers, notably **Anthony's Shore Dinner Hall,** which has outdoor tables on Waite's Wharf (401/848-5058). It also has some prominent blue-collar landmarks, not least of which is **Bishop's 4th Street Diner** (401/847-2069), a 1950s O'Mahony parked at the traffic circle outside the gates of the Newport Navy Base. It's open daily from around 5 AM for breakfast and lunch, until 6 PM weekdays. Further north, along Route 114, Middletown has another old O'Mahony diner, **Tommy's Deluxe** at 159 E. Main Road (401/847-9834). Places to stay are all in the $150 range, so you may want to do Newport on a day trip from somewhere else. For more information, contact the huge waterfront **visitors center** (401/849-8048 or 800/326-6030).

.

The Breakers

Along the bay between East Greenwich and Wickford, the U.S. Navy Base at Quonset gave its name to those inexpensive and easily erected barrel-vaulted Quonset Huts, originally developed for wartime use.

Newport is best known for its connections to leisure pursuits like yachting, golf, and tennis (it hosted the first U.S. golf championships in 1894, and the historic casino, 194 Bellevue Avenue, is home to the International Tennis Hall of Fame), but it also has a delightful old baseball stadium, Cardines Field, right downtown across from the main visitors center.

Back when America used to win the America's Cup, the famous yachting races were always held here in Newport. If you want to learn more, visit the **Museum of Yachting** (daily 10 AM–5 PM; $4; 401/847-1018) near the tip of the peninsula at historic Fort Adams State Park.

NARRAGANSETT PIER AND WATCH HILL

US-1 and Route 1A rejoin north of Narragansett Pier (pronounced "nair-a-GAN-set"; pop. 3,700), a Victorian-era resort town that sits at the middle of a narrow peninsula. The "pier" in the name is about all that remains of a huge casino resort complex that burned down in 1900. These days, the peninsula is still a popular resort area, thanks to the many fine beaches that face onto the open Atlantic Ocean. At the tip of the peninsula is **Point Judith,** where a historic lighthouse stands watch over a rocky, wave-swept headland.

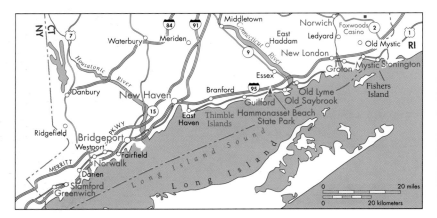

Along Kingstown Road (Route 1A) near its junction with US-1, keep an eye out for the **Narragansett Indian Monument,** a 25-foot-tall wooden statue carved in honor of local Native Americans.

Watch Hill is one of many Rhode Island beach towns where you can "Stop at the Sign of the Lemon" and enjoy the Slurpee-like frozen lemonade concoctions of **Del's.**

Fishers Island, offshore from Stonington, is legally part of New York.

West of Narragansett Pier, US-1 becomes a pretty fast freeway, on which you speed past some more great beaches, including East Matunuck State Park, two miles south of US-1 via Succotash Road, and Charlestown Beach, a Rhode Island version of Malibu midway along Block Island Sound.

Saving the best for last, Rhode Island's westernmost beach resort is picturesque Watch Hill, where the nation's oldest merry-go-round, the 1867 **Flying Horse Carousel** (50¢ a ride), sits between a private beach ($6 per person) and a waterfront resort area. East of the main resort area, **Misquamicut State Beach** ($5 per car) has an often-crowded half-mile strand, stretched between the ocean and an inland pond.

Among the waterfront restaurants here is the historic **Olympia Restaurant** (401/348-8211), serving chops and other meat and fish dishes since 1916 on white-linened tables. For a place to stay, try the **Ocean House** ($60–120; 401/348-8161).

STONINGTON

If you're coming into Connecticut from Rhode Island, your first taste of the state may prove to be the most memorable: Stonington, a small waterfront village that's regularly ranked among the prettiest in New England. Just five minutes from the crowds of Mystic Seaport via US-1 and Route 1A, and an equally quick detour off I-95 (exit 91), Stonington is one of those painfully quaint places that make you ask yourself if shopping malls and suburbia really *are* essential components of modern life. Here, along streets lined by mature trees and centuries-old homes, you catch glimpses of the Atlantic Ocean behind the state's oldest (circa 1823) lighthouse, which stands at 7 Water Street. Inside, the **Old Lighthouse Museum** (Tues.–Sun. 10 AM–5 PM; $4; 860/ 535-1440) has six rooms crammed with paintings, tools, scrimshaw, and model ships.

For all its beauty, Stonington is not an obviously touristy place, but it does have a couple of good places to eat: the small and eclectic **Water Street Café**, 142 Water Street (860/535-2122), and the nearby **Noah's**, 113 Water Street (860/535-3925), both serving breakfast, lunch, and dinner including excellent seafood and desserts.

It may not have the timeless charm of the rest of Stonington, but for a cheap place to sleep, the **Sea Breeze Motel**, on US-1 at 812 Stonington Road ($35–95; 860/535-2843), is hard to beat.

MYSTIC: MYSTIC SEAPORT

The small village of Mystic grew up along the water as a shipbuilding center and whaling port, and these days its lifeblood flows from a re-creation of its earlier self. Though you can get a feel for historic Mystic by wandering around past the houses of sea captains along High Street, eventually you'll be drawn down to Mystic Seaport, a 17-acre complex that claims to re-create a typical New England seaport of the mid-1800s. The largest and most popular maritime museum in the nation, Mystic Seaport has some 400 vessels, mostly dating from the 19th century, plus an entire town of shops, houses, and warehouses replicating the sorts of places that once stood all along the New England coast. If you want to get an idea what Mystic itself was like, spend some time studying the scale model of Mystic, circa 1860, which consists of some 250 finely crafted models of buildings and boats. Another don't-miss is the collection of carved wooden figureheads displayed in the Wendell Building, which itself is historic, having served the seaport's previous occupant, Mystic Manufacturing Company, a prominent shipbuilder.

In summer, Mystic Seaport is a main port of call for tall ships, two of which—the square-rigged *Joseph Conrad* and the only survivor of America's once mighty whaling fleet, the *Charles W. Morgan*, built in 1841 in New Bedford—can be boarded here year-round.

In summer, ferry boats ($15; 401/783-4613) run frequently from Providence, Newport, Narragansett, and New London to lovely **Block Island** (pop. 800), a nearly treeless island 12 miles off the Rhode Island shore. Twenty-five miles of hiking trails make walking the best way to explore, but you can also rent bikes or mopeds from stands near the ferry landing in Old Harbor. Block Island's many nice beaches, towering bluffs, and pair of picturesque lighthouses make it a popular destination. For more information, contact the visitors bureau (401/466-2982 or 800/383-2474).

Apart from ships, Mystic is also famous for pizza, thanks to the low-budget 1980s film *Mystic Pizza*, which turned Julia Roberts into a star. The original pizza parlor, also called **Mystic Pizza**, is more popular than ever, serving up pies from 10 AM to midnight every day; it's located west of the Mystic River along US-1 at 56 W. Main Street (860/536-3737). Another local food landmark is the tiny **Kitchen Little**, 135 Greenmanville Road (860/536-2122), between the Seaport and I-95.

DETOUR: FOXWOODS CASINO

One of the most controversial developments in recent years has been the phenomenal growth of gambling, especially on Indian reservations, and no place is bigger, brasher, and better at attracting gamblers than the Foxwoods Casino (800/PLAY-BIG), hidden away near rural Ledyard, seven miles north from I-95 exit 92 via Route 2. Open 24 hours with thousands of rooms and probably a million square feet of clattering slots, noisy craps tables, and swishing roulette wheels, Foxwoods is like a piece of Las Vegas dropped down in in the middle of the Connecticut nowhere. Appalling perhaps, profitable for sure. In 1998, the casino coffers enabled the tribe to open the $150 million **Mashantucket Pequot Museum and Research Center** (daily 10 AM–6 PM; $10; 800/411-9671), a spectacular, state-of-the-art educational center that re-creates the ways of the present tribe's ancestors.

I-95 SURVIVAL GUIDE: ACROSS RHODE ISLAND AND CONNECTICUT

MM43: Massachusetts/Rhode Island state line.

MM42: Exit 27 for downtown Pawtucket (see page 93).

MM38: Exit 22 for downtown Providence (see pages 94–95).

MM30: Exit 13 for Warwick and T. F. Green State Airport.

MM25: Exit 9 for Route 4 south to US-1.

MM7: Rhode Island Welcome Center.

MM0/112: Rhode Island/Connecticut state line.

MM103: Exit 91 for Main Street south to Stonington (see page 98).

MM100: Exit 90 for US-1 through downtown Mystic (see page 99).

MM97: Exit 87 for US-1 through Groton (see page 101).

MM94: Exit 84 for downtown New London (see page 101).

MM80: Exit 70 for US-1 through Old Lyme (see page 102).

MM75: Exit 66 for US-1 through Old Saybrook (see page 102).

MM67: Exit 62 for Hammonasset Beach (see page 103).

MM54: Exit 55 for US-1 through Branford, access south to Thimble Islands (see page 104).

MM48: Exit for I-91 north to Hartford and Canada.

MM47.5: Exit 47 for Route 34 north to downtown New Haven (see page 104).

MM38: Exit 38 for Route 15, the historic Merritt Parkway (see page 107).

MM30: Exit 28 for Main Street through Bridgeport.

MM26.5: Exit 24 for Fairfield, Black Rock Turnpike, and Super Duper Weenie hot dog stand (see page 107).

MM16: Exit 15 for US-7 north through Litchfield Hills and Berkshires to Canada (see pages 248–271).

MM5: Exit for US-1, the old "Boston Post Road" through Stamford and Greenwich (see page 107).

MM1: Connecticut/New York state line.

The other big Indian-run casino in Connecticut is a few miles west of Foxwoods: the **Mohegan Sun,** along the Thames River in Uncasville, north of New London and just east of I-395 (860/204-7163 or 888/226-7711).

Near Norm's Diner, the **U.S. Submarine Memorial** lists the names of all of the sailors and submarines lost at sea during World War II.

GROTON

Once a busy shipbuilding center on the east bank of the Thames ("Thaymz") River, Groton ("GRAW-ton") oozes old "salty dog" maritime brawn, but it has suffered mightily from the end of the Cold War. Groton is the homeport of the U.S. Navy submarine fleet and is where the world's first diesel-powered (1912) and nuclear-powered (1954) submarines were built by the

Electric Boat division of General Dynamics. There's not much to see here, but you can tour the now-decommissioned nuclear sub, **USS Nautilus,** (Wed.–Mon. 9 AM–5 PM; free; 860/449-3174) at a pier adjacent to the navy base. The museum next door traces the history of submarines, starting with a model of Jules Verne's *Nautilus* as commanded by Captain Nemo in *20,000 Leagues Beneath the Sea.*

For another taste of history, step into Groton's own **Norm's Diner,** right off US-1/I-95 at 171 Bridge Street (860/445-5026), a vintage 1954 Silk City that's open early (5 AM) until late (11 PM), 24 hours on Friday nights.

Fort Griswold State Park in Groton was the site of one of the most brutal acts of the Revolutionary War, when British soldiers massacred 84 American militiamen who had surrendered. This event was all the more significant because the former commander of Fort Griswold, Connecticut-born Benedict Arnold, was in charge of the attacking British forces.

NEW LONDON AND NORWICH

Built around one of the finest natural harbors in New England, the town of New London (pop. 28,540) still revolves around the sea. Colonial New London was a haven for privateers and smugglers, until Benedict Arnold and his British forces destroyed the town during the Revolutionary War battles at Fort Trumbull and Fort Griswold. During the 19th century, the town

The annual Harvard-Yale Regatta, in which hundreds of young men and women participate in rowing races, is held each June on the Thames River between Groton and New London.

became a prime whaling port, and new buildings sprang up, including the Greek Revival beauties along Huntington Street's "Whale Oil Row" and the H. H. Richardson–designed Union Railroad Station. New London also has a cemetery, "Ye Towne's Antientest Buriall Place," a block north of Whale Oil Row, and is home to the U.S. Coast Guard Academy, which stands across I-95 from the historic waterfront.

PARADE, NEW LONDON, CONN.

New London was also the boyhood home of playwright Eugene O'Neill (1888–1953), whose home, **Monte Cristo Cottage** ($3; 860/443-0051), has been preserved as a museum. O'Neill's father was an actor who made a career playing the Count of Monte Cristo; hence, the house's name. The house, which was the setting for O'Neill's autobiographical play *Long Day's Journey into Night,* is located off US-1 at the south end of town, at 325 Pequot Avenue.

North from New London via Route 32 and I-395 is the historic port city of Norwich (pop. 37,391), located at the head of the Thames River. One of the oldest cities in Connecticut, Norwich is best known as the birthplace of Revolutionary War traitor Benedict Arnold, but it also had colonial America's first paper mill (1766) and its first nail factory (1772).

If you've had enough history and just want to play on the sands, head about four miles south from central New London (two miles beyond the Monte Cristo Cottage) to **Ocean Beach,** where a wide sandy beach is backed by an old-fashioned amusement arcade and a boardwalk.

CONNECTICUT RIVER: OLD LYME AND OLD SAYBROOK

Between New London and New Haven, the Connecticut River finally reaches the ocean after a 400-mile journey from its start in the mountains of far-north New Hampshire. Its end is marked more by a whimper than a bang, and a profusion of quaint little waterfront towns lining its shores. On either side of the river, the pretty towns of Old Lyme and Old Saybrook face each other on the south side of the I-95 freeway.

Standing east of the river, Old Lyme (pop. 6,535) has a lovely triangular green, many fine homes, and the **Florence Griswold Museum,** 96 Lyme Street (Wed.–Sun. 1–5 PM, longer hours in summer; $5; 860/434-5542), which mainly displays works by members of Old Lyme's longstanding arts colony, which was based in this Georgian-style mansion. Old Lyme also boasts a very pleasant B&B, the **Bee and Thistle Inn,** 100 Lyme Street ($120–250; 203/434-1667), which offers a dozen different rooms in a 250-year-old home. The Bee and Thistle also has an excellent restaurant, rated among the best in this part of New England.

Across the Connecticut River, Old Saybrook (pop. 9,552) is a fraternal twin to Old Lyme, with two main claims to fame: the predecessor to today's Yale University was based here until its move to New Haven in 1716; and one of the first military-minded submarines, the *Turtle,* was built here in 1776 and briefly used in the Revolutionary War. (A model of the *Turtle* can be seen upriver at the Connecticut River Museum in Essex.)

CONNECTICUT RIVER TOUR

Upstream from Old Lyme and Old Saybrook but easily reachable from US-1 and I-95 are several quieter and quainter (if decidedly upper-crust) hamlets. Among them are **Essex,** which claims to be the "#1 Small Town in America," and **East Haddam,** where patriot Nathan Hale taught at the one-room schoolhouse next to St. Stephen's Church. Both can be reached by following Route 9 or Route 54. Essex in particular is a must-see, if only to spend some time wandering its sleepy streets or taking a tour (schedule varies; $10–16; 860/767-0103) on a historic steam train, riverboat, or both. It's also home to the excellent **Connecticut River Museum** (Tues.–Sun. 10 AM–5 PM; $4), appropriately situated along the riverfront at 67 Main Street. Here displays explore the importance of local ships and shipbuilders in the West Indies trade that started Connecticut on its prosperous way.

One of the many sightseeing highlights in this lovely region is **Gillette Castle State Park** ($4; 860/526-2336), a stone mansion with 190 acres of vista-packed grounds, and an interior to match the hand-wrought facades. Built by Broadway stage actor William Gillette, who made a career playing the role of Sherlock Holmes, the estate overlooks the river from the east bank, two miles south of East Haddam off Route 148.

For a place to eat or stay, the justly famous and truly historic **Griswold Inn**, 36 Main Street ($90–190; 860/767-1776) in Essex has two dozen rooms, a great restaurant, and a very cozy 208-year-old bar.

HAMMONASSET BEACH

Fronting onto Long Island Sound, Connecticut's beaches are generally peaceful and quiet, ideal for long walks if not so great for serious surfing. One of the largest and most user-friendly stretches of the state's 250-plus-mile shoreline is preserved for the public at Hammonasset Beach, a 1,000-acre state park ($6; 203/245-2785) with a long, lifeguard-protected strand, showers and changing rooms, a nature center, hiking/biking trails, plus a very large ($12 per night, 550-site) tent and RV **campground**.

Hammonasset Beach is easy to find, south of US-1 from the town of Clinton, and connected by its own semi-freeway from I-95 exit 62.

GUILFORD

Since the earliest colonial times, Guilford (pop. 19,800) has been one of the main stopping places along the Connecticut coast, yet unlike other colonial centers, Guilford hasn't really changed all that much. A handful of lovely 17th- and 18th-century houses still line its large, tranquil, green, and somnolent streets, including the 1660 Hyland House and the 1774 Griswold House on Boston Street; both are open for tours throughout summer. A half-mile down Whitfield Street from the town green is one of the oldest houses in the nation. The **Henry Whitfield House** was constructed in 1639 and has been converted into a small, state-run museum (Wed.–Sun. 10 AM–4:30 PM; $3; 203/453-2457), with period furnishings and a herb garden.

For a place to eat, it's hard to beat **The Place**, a summer-only stand on US-1 at east end of town. Run by local schoolteachers, The Place serves up fresh boiled lobster and corn-on-the-cob in a lovely garden setting.

Along with historic homes, Guilford also has the **Tower Motel**, on old US-1 at 320 Boston Post Road ($60–90; 203/453-9069), an inexpensive, family-friendly find amid Connecticut's national chains and upscale B&Bs. Many units have kitchens, and you can borrow equipment from the office if you want to play horseshoes or croquet on the lawn.

The best approach to Gillette Castle is to take the **Chester-Hadlyme Ferry,** which nips back and forth across the Connecticut River from April through November. The picturesque town of Chester is also home to the **National Theater of the Deaf,** 5 Main Street (860/526-4971 or TTY 860/526-4974), an enthusiastic company of hearing-impaired actors and actresses whose productions have to be seen to be believed.

East of Guilford, on US-1 at 1324 Boston Post Road near the Clinton/Madison town line, the **Clam Castle** (203/245-4911) has been serving up fried clams and french fries for generations. Madison also has some very nice (though strictly private) beaches like West Wharf Beach, where the historic **Madison Beach Hotel** ($90–175; 203/245-1404) has waterfront rooms with balconies.

ROUTE 146: THE THIMBLE ISLANDS

You see almost nothing of the Connecticut coast driving on I-95 and very little even from US-1, so if you want to get a sense of the country's wealthiest waterfront communities, you'll have to take a detour along one of the smaller roads that loop off to the south, along Long Island Sound. One of the prettiest of these scenic detours, Route 146, winds along the water between Guilford and New Haven, passing through a series of sleepy-looking hamlets and villages whose homespun charms belie their residents' bank balances. The rolling highway dips down across lush wetlands past rocky little coves like **Shell Beach**, giving occasional glimpses of the tiny offshore rocks known collectively as the Thimble Islands. Despite the fact that some of these "islands" are so small and low that they disappear at high tides, about two dozen of them are close enough to shore to have full water, power, and other connections to the modern world. Their scenic isolation has attracted a select few residents (often living one home per island), including such creative luminaries as *Doonesbury* artist Garry Trudeau who share them with colonies of seals and seabirds.

The best place to stop along these rarefied shores is the village of **Stony Creek,** sometimes known as Indian Head. To get there, follow Thimble Islands Road south from Route 146, east of the town of Branford. From Stony Creek, you can get a closer look at the Thimble Islands by joining one of the guided cruises offered by boats like the ***Sea Mist*** ($8; 203/488-8905).

NEW HAVEN

If you come to New Haven (pop. 131,000) expecting some idyllic hamlet surrounding the Ivy League walls of **Yale University,** you may be in for a disappointment. New Haven is a postindustrial city, with modern office towers and low-income

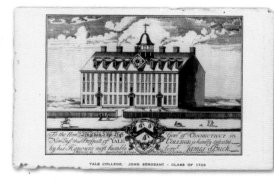

housing projects next to Yale's Gothic-style towers and faux-medieval cloistered courtyards. At the center of it all is the 16-acre Green, containing a trio of 19th-century churches (all built within a few years of 1812), with the Yale campus spreading to the north and west.

The Yale campus is the main draw in New Haven and has enough stuff tucked away in the

houses on the Thimble Islands

nooks and crannies of its many museums and libraries to keep you occupied for as long as you can afford to linger here. Artists, architects, and aesthetes will want to visit Yale's two fine art galleries, both designed by Louis Kahn, who taught here for many years. In 1953, at the beginning of his career, Kahn designed an addition to the **Yale Art Gallery,** 111 Chapel Street (Tues.–Sat. 10 AM–6 PM; Sun. 1–6 PM; free), which houses a full spectrum of painting and sculpture from around the world: ancient Greek vases, Chinese bronzes, Renaissance portraits, and more contemporary works by the likes of Manet, Picasso, and Winslow Homer. Across the street and keeping the same hours is Kahn's late masterpiece, the **Center for British Art,** which houses the personal collection of its benefactor (the late Paul Mellon, Yale Class of 1929, who died in 1999) in roughly chronological order. In the permanent collection, the art on display ranges from Elizabethan portraits to post–World War II paintings by Francis Bacon and Pop artist Peter Blake. The heart of the collection is the most comprehensive survey of British painting outside Britain, with important works by Gainesborough, Reynolds, Turner, and Constable.

If you prefer words to pictures, you'll want to spend some time at the **Beinecke Rare Books Library,** 121 Wall Street (Mon.–Fri. 8:30 AM–5 PM, Sat. 10 AM–5 PM; free), two blocks northeast at the heart of Yale campus, where a treasury of significant publications, including medieval manuscripts and a Gutenberg bible, is on display in a room with windows made of translucently thin slices of Vermont marble.

NEW HAVEN PRACTICALITIES

One place any carnivorous road-tripper must stop to eat is **Louis' Lunch,** 263 Crown Street (closed Sun. and Mon.; 203/562-5507), an unpretentious redbrick box just a block west from the Green. Although the birthplace debate still rages, Louis' makes a solid claim to having invented the hamburger, because it was the first cafe in the country to put hamburgers on the menu. It's been serving up steamed (not fried or grilled) burgers on toasted bread (not bun) with no ketchup, no mustard, and no end of insults from the surly staff since 1903 (or 1895, depending on whom you ask).

New Haven has another American culinary landmark: **Frank Pepe's Pizzeria,** 163 Wooster Street (closed Tues.; 203/865-5762), south of downtown in the heart of New Haven's fascinating Little Italy. One of the oldest, possibly *the* oldest (and many say the best) pizza place in the nation, Frank Pepe's is famous for its clam-topped white pizza, covered with chopped-up Rhode Island littlenecks. The spot serves no pasta, just pizza, and it's almost always crowded—expect a wait or eat early or late.

Back in the center of town, across from Louis' Lunch and next to the nifty Neon Garage (a multi-story parking lot decorated with neon signs), one of New Haven's more contemporary hot spots is the simply named **Bar,** 254 Crown Street (203/495-1111), a brewpub where you can get a good brick-oven pizza or a sophisticated salad and wash it down with microbrewed ales.

In contrast to its fairly plentiful good restaurants, places to stay in New Haven are rarer and rather expensive. Within walking distance of Yale, the old-fashioned

If New Haven's halls of academe ever lose their attraction, head south and east from the city along US-1 to East Haven, where the **Shore Line Trolley Museum,** 17 River Street (daily in summer 11 AM–5 PM; $6; 203/467-6927) runs a restored trolley along the water between Short Beach and the museum. The collection includes nearly 100 other restored trolleys, subway cars and train carriages.

Walking around downtown New Haven, don't be surprised to see crosswalks where the Walk/Don't Walk signs actually count down the time until the lights change.

The Class AA **New Haven Ravens** (203/782-1666 or 800/RAVENS1), affiliated with the Seattle Mariners, play ball at characterful Yale Field, 252 Derby Street across from the much larger Yale Bowl stadium. Yale Field, built in 1927, is where Babe Ruth and the young future President George H. W. Bush—who played ball for Yale—were photographed together. Ravens games are broadcast on **WAVZ 1300AM.**

Hotel Duncan, 1151 Chapel Street ($45–95; 203/787-1273) has about the only rooms under $100 a night; other budget options are a Motel 6 along I-91, and a pricier but more convenient **Holiday Inn,** 30 Whalley Avenue (203/777-6221).

Despite the lack of cheap beds, New Haven can make a reasonable base for day trips down to New York City, thanks to improvements in the commuter train service, that make it possible to get to Grand Central Terminal in around 90 minutes.

For more information, contact the New Haven **visitors bureau** on the Green (203/787-8822), or contact the Yale University **information center,** north of the Green at 149 Elm Street (203/432-8469).

New Haven marks the southern end of US-5, which runs north along the Connecticut River through Massachusetts and Vermont up to the Canadian border. For more, see pages 190–217.

BRIDGEPORT

Although it's not exactly a scenic delight, the busy, heavily industrialized city of Bridgeport (pop. 142,000) is worth a closer look, if only to catch a baseball game at one of the more enjoyable minor league baseball parks in the Northeast. The postindustrial Ballpark at Harbor Yard at 500 Main Street is where the 1999 Atlantic League champions **Bridgeport Bluefish** ($4–10; 203/345-4800) put on a show all summer long—right alongside I-95.

If you can't make it to a Bridgeport Bluefish game, you can often catch the action on **WICC 600AM.**

Baseball aside, Bridgeport is best known as the longtime home and base of operations for legendary showman P. T. Barnum (1810–1891), a statue of whom looks out over the harbor from the foot of Main Street. Nearby, at 820 Main Street, the ornate **Barnum House** (Tues.–Sun. 10 AM–4:30 PM; $5: 203/331-9881) is a suitably outlandish and eye-catching home for a fascinating collection of Barnum memorabilia. Here, you'll find circus posters and props as well as outfits worn by Barnum's star performer, General Tom Thumb, the Bridgeport native born Charles Stratton in 1838. A life-size **statue of Tom Thumb** stands (all of 40 inches tall) atop a 10-foot base on his grave in the Mountain Grove Cemetery, on North Avenue at Dewey Street.

Baseball and Barnum aside, Bridgeport is also famous for another pop culture icon: the **Frisbee.** The famous flying disc was inspired by and named local baker William Frisbee, whose pies were sold all over the northeastern United States in the 1930s. When the empty pie tins were tossed out, they flew, and a new pastime was created.

THE GOLD COAST: NORWALK, STAMFORD, AND GREENWICH

The communities of far-southwestern Connecticut are among the wealthiest in the country. Norwalk, Stamford, and Greenwich have long attracted stockbrokers and other highly paid professionals commuting to and from Manhattan. Surprisingly, you won't see many telltale signs of big money as you cruise through the so-called Gold Coast on US-1, the old Boston Post Road. Dunkin' Donuts, malls, and nondescript glass towers—not the stylish restaurants, boutiques, and mansions you might expect—dominate the landscape here. This is about as far from Rodeo Drive as you can possibly imagine.

There is one bright spot in the suburban tedium. Norwalk's 24-hour **Post Road Diner** is a welcoming place, serving just about any type of food you could want. The diner is at the southwest edge of town, a half-mile off I-95 exit 14, at 312 S. Connecticut Avenue (203/866-9777)—just look for the giant neon arrow.

At Norwalk, US-1 crosses the southernmost sections of our road trip along US-7, which runs north all the way to the Canadian border. For more on US-7, see pages 248–271.

ROUTE 15: THE MERRITT PARKWAY

If you want to take the most scenic route between Bridgeport and New York City, head north from I-95 onto the parallel Merritt Parkway (Route 15), one of the last classic 1930s parkways more or less in original condition. When it opened to traffic in 1938, the Merritt Parkway was the first fast, limited access highway across this part of the state, and was partly responsible for Connecticut becoming New York City's commuter suburb.

The Merritt Parkway's roads are narrower than those of the Interstate, and the entrance and exit ramps are more than a little dangerously tight. The highway has been designated a national historic site, which provides some protection from planners who want to widen, straighten, and generally "improve" the Merritt so it looks more like I-95. The old tollbooths were removed in the 1980s, and some of the tightest on- and off-ramps have been made safer, but the Merritt's charm remains intact, mostly because of the many fine bridges and dense roadside forests.

George Dunkleberger designed the more than 60 stone and/or steel bridges that carry cross-traffic over the 38-mile parkway. The bridges are some of the finest works of civil engineering you'll ever see. Not only functional, they are aesthetically pleasing as well, with arches and abutments embellished with friezes of neo-Classical urns and garlands, Pilgrim fathers, and even brawny workers in the Social Realist style. To truly enjoy these and other merits of the Merritt, take a leisurely Sunday drive in a classic cruiser. It'll make for a much more satisfying trip than you could have racing on I-95.

The Condé Nast publishing company headquarters straddles the Stamford/Greenwich boundary on US-1. On the grounds are art deco–era obelisks inscribed with the titles of the company's many magazines, including *Vogue, Glamour,* and *House and Garden.*

US-1 in Stamford has been dubbed Jackie Robinson Way, in memory of Major League Baseball's first black player. Robinson joined the Brooklyn Dodgers in 1947.

The town of Fairfield is home to one of the wonders of the roadside world: the **Super Duper Weenie,** off US-1 at 306 Black Rock Turnpike (Mon.–Sat. 11 AM–8 PM; 203/334-DOGS). Hot-dog meister Gary Zemola has said that he "took one look at a hot dog truck and suddenly realized his destiny in life." He likes to say that he's graduated from a truck to a sit-down restaurant, but he still makes everything from scratch, from the relishes to the french fries. If you stop and eat here, you'll be grateful Gary's found such a tasty calling.

The town of **New Canaan,** on Route 106 off the Merritt Parkway at exit 36, epitomizes the Gold Coast high life. Celebrites such as David Letterman and designers such as architect Philip Johnson (whose 1949 Glass House is a modernist icon) live on New Canaan's well-coifed streets. If you want a celluloid introduction to this ritzy town, check out the 1990s film *The Ice Storm,* starring Kevin Kline and Christina Ricci.

THE GREAT NORTH WOODS: US-2

THE GREAT NORTH WOODS: US-2

The main route across northern New England, US-2, winds its way through Maine before rolling up and down the mountains of New Hampshire and Vermont. Although busy and well traveled in places, US-2 is still comparatively quiet and peaceful. Since colonial times, most of the through traffic in New England has run north to south along the coasts or through the valleys, while only the brave or a foolhardy few have attempted cross-country travel in this mountainous region.

From the town of Houlton on the Canadian border, where the country's major artery, the I-95 freeway, comes to an end, US-2 takes a more scenic route through the Great Maine Woods running alongside rivers and passing through a number of logging and paper-mill towns cleared out of the dense forests. Its beauty is not as obvious as the road along the coast, but it does have its attractions, including the sublime peak of Mount Katahdin, the former shipbuilding city of Bangor, and a number of lakeside resorts.

US-2 leaves Maine following the Androscoggin River across the New Hampshire border and skirts White Mountain National Forest, whose peaks loom to the south and provide enticing sunsets. The mountains themselves are dealt with in the following chapters, but here on their fringes you get a sense of both the proud history of these former mill towns and the various "tourist attractions" that have sprung up in their wake.

From the Victorian-era city of St. Johnsbury, capital of Vermont's pastoral "Northeast Kingdom," the remaining stretch of US-2 across Vermont travels through one of the most scenic areas in New England. As it heads west, the road follows the winding Winooski River, through Montpelier, Vermont's capital, and its

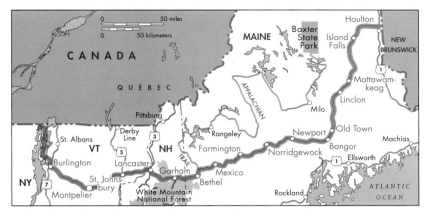

cultural capital, Burlington. When you see these two small, engaging cities, you understand that it's true what they say, Vermont is the most rural state. The rolling countryside that spreads in between these two "big cities" (which have a combined population well under 50,000 people) is proof in a picture that Vermont is still one big beautiful farm. Precocious from the beginning, Vermont's constitution was the first in the United States to prohibit slavery and establish public schools. Vermont is known for a strong liberal tradition. Even the state's Republicans are moderates, and you get a clear sense of this if you spend any time in towns like Plainfield, rural home of avant-garde Goddard College.

Although US-2 might seem to dead-end at the Canadian border, it actually picks up again a thousand miles away, at Sault Ste. Marie and continues west all the way to Seattle.

North and south of US-2, the lush Green Mountains contain millions of acres of amazing scenery and some of the best ski areas in the East (Mad River Glen and Stowe, to name two), all linked by scenic Route 100. Continuing west, toward the New York state border, US-2 has a last hurrah in the lovely Lake Champlain islands, where rolling pastures are bound by undeveloped shorelines and mountains rise along the distant horizons.

HOULTON

It may not look like much from a distance, especially if you're racing along on I-95, but there's more than enough of interest in Houlton (pop. 5,600) to make it worth getting out of the car and onto your feet. The main draw is the perfectly preserved downtown business district, now called the **Market Square Historic District**. Here, a block east of US-1 in a spacious plaza along the Meduxneag

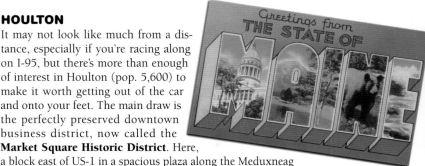

River, you'll find one or more of everything a county town could need. All seem unchanged since 1908 or maybe 1958: an appliance store, a beauty parlor, two bakeries, two bookstores, two banks, a clothing store, a florist, and best of all, a two-screen movie theater showing current hits for less than $5 on Tuesdays. (There's also an Internet cafe, if you feel the need to keep in touch with the modern world.)

Both US-2 and I-95 start and finish at the Canadian border, two miles east of downtown Houlton.

About half of the businesses in Houlton have the word Shiretown in their names, reflecting the town's status as seat of Aroostook County, the potato-growing region that covers the whole of far north Maine.

A block west of Market Square, on Bangor Road (US-2), grab a bite to eat at the **Elm Tree Diner** (207/532-3181), open for over 50 years and one of few alternatives to the national chains, all of which line up at the I-95 exits.

ISLAND FALLS: WEBB MUSEUM OF VINTAGE FASHION

Just off I-95 exit 59, 25 miles southwest of Houlton via US-2, one of the most odd attractions in northern Maine has to be the **Webb Museum of Vintage Fashion** (Mon.–Thurs. 10 AM–4 PM, June–Oct. only; $3; 207/862-3797), in the tiny town of Island Falls. Filling 17 rooms of a turn-of-the-20th-century house in the center of town, this "museum" is more like a guided tour through the closets of a succession of aged relatives, but it is captivating and engaging in a weirdly voyeuristic way. The "fashion" on display would never have graced the covers of *Vogue*; rather, the clothes you'll see here are what real people wore a century or more ago.

All along this stretch of US-2, the great mass of Mount Katahdin dominates the western horizon on a clear day.

MILLINOCKET: BAXTER STATE PARK

The paper mills of Millinocket produce as much as 20 percent of the nation's newsprint.

Between Houlton and Millinocket, the roadside landscape changes from the farmhouses and potato fields of Aroostook County to the mills and forests of the Great North Woods.

Between Houlton and Bangor, US-2 parallels the bigger and busier I-95, which despite its freeway scale is an official state Scenic Route. The main event along I-95 is a turnoff, roughly midway along, heading north to the logging and paper mill town of Millinocket, which serves as gateway to the wilds of Baxter State Park. Millinocket (pop. 6,600), northwest from I-95 via Route 11, is a typical backwoods Maine town and one of the state's prime outdoor sports centers. If you can be here for the annual 4th of July party or the End of the Trail festival in September, you'll get a good sense of the mix of people who call this area home.

The rest of the year, the best place to get a feel for Millinocket (and get fed as well) is the **Appalachian Trail Cafe,** 210 Penobscot Avenue (207/723-6720), open daily 5 AM–10 PM and usually full of locals. Another lively place, with a more adventurous range of meals (pizzas, calzones, steaks, seafood) is the **Scootic Inn,** 70 Penobscot Avenue (207/723-4566). Before or after your meal, head across the street to the North Maine Bowling Center.

The reason most people find themselves in Millinocket is to prepare for a trip to Baxter State Park, the 205,000 acres of dense Maine Woods surrounding the mile-high summit of Mount Katahdin, Maine's highest peak. About 20 miles northwest of Millinocket is a real wilderness with no paved roads but 175 miles of hiking trails. All trails are preserved thanks to the foresight of Maine Governor Percival Proctor Baxter (1879–1969), who during the 1930s bought the land himself and donated it to the people of Maine after failing to convince state legislators to ante up the cash. As a condition of the bequest, Baxter insisted that the land remain wild, so most signs of the modern world are prohibited, including radios, cell phones, even seeing-eye dogs. There's just one rough road around the park's perimeter, plus a few cabins, so to see Baxter properly you'll have to hike and camp. Day use fees are $8 per vehicle, free for Maine residents. Bring all your food, water purifiers, and plenty of insect repellent, and be prepared for any and all weather. Expect abundant wildlife, amazing wildflowers, powerful waterfalls, and breathtaking views. For details, or to make camping reservations (June–Oct. only—no refunds), write or visit the **Baxter State Park Authority,** 64 Balsam Drive in Millinocket, Maine 04462 (207/723-5140).

Midway along the road from Millinocket, the **Big Moose Inn** (207/723-8391) has handy, well-priced rooms, cabins, a campground, and a restaurant, the only taste of civilization near the park.

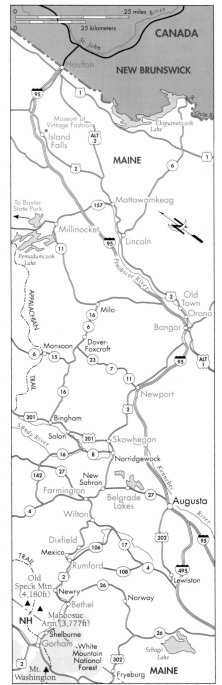

Beyond Baxter State Park, the intriguingly named **Golden Road** heads north and west through the forests to Moosehead Lake and the Canadian border. This privately owned, mostly unpaved 70-mile logging road (and a very busy one at that—remember to give way to trucks!) is open to private cars but not bikes. Drivers must check in at the gate and pay a daily fee (about $9).

At the heart of Baxter State Park stands Mount Katahdin, the highest point in Maine, which marks the start of our hiking and driving tour along the Appalachian Trail. See page 277 for more.

PENOBSCOT RIVER TOWNS: MATTAWAMKEAG AND LINCOLN

If you opt to follow US-2 rather than I-95 between Houlton and Bangor, you'll be repaid in spades around the time you reach the town of Mattawamkeag on the banks of the wild Penobscot River. The biggest attraction in this area is the town-owned Mattawamkeag Wilderness Park (207/736-4881), which offers all the comforts Baxter eschews (bathrooms and hot showers, for instance), plus a nice sandy beach, great riverside recreation, and 1,000 acres of trees. The entrance to the park is east from US-2, and the turnoff is marked by the handy **Keag Market and Cafe.**

A dozen miles southwest, following the Penobscot River the whole way, US-2 reaches the big mill town of Lincoln ("Land of Lakes and Leisure"), which, true to its motto, has lovely spring-fed Lake Mattanawcook at its center, not to mention a pair of war memorials at each end of town—one Civil War, the other World War I, both topped by a statue of a solitary soldier.

From here US-2 runs parallel to I-95, which is about two miles to the west. The drive along US-2 takes you through a series of sleepy little riverside towns before winding into Orono and the outskirts of Bangor, 50 miles away.

Because its incorporated area covers 78 square miles, Lincoln claims to be the largest town east of the Mississippi River.

Maine is the only state that sets aside a seat in the legislature for a representative of its Native American tribes.

OLD TOWN AND ORONO

After a leisurely 40-mile run along the wild Penobscot River from Lincoln, US-2 hits Old Town (pop. 8,300), where a steaming James River paper mill welcomes you back to modern times. Back in the 1830s, Old Town, one of Maine's earliest industrial centers, had an iron foundry and a large sawmill but the town hasn't much grown since then. The main business in town is the **Old Town Canoe Company,** 130 N. Main Street (207/827-5513), makers of high-quality canoes and kayaks since 1904. Next door, housed in an old church, the **Old Town Museum** (Wed.–Sun. 1–5 PM in summer only; donations) has the usual array of historical items plus a collection of paintings and sculptures by Bernard Langlais, who is perhaps best known as the creator of the massive **Skowhegan Indian** that looms over the town of Skowhegan.

For a better sense of local Native American culture, head north along Main Street from the heart of Old Town across the bridge to **Indian Island,** the down-at-heel home to some 500 descendents of the Penobscot Indians who once controlled much of modern-day Maine. (The remaining Penobscot reservation consists mainly of the many islands dotting the Penobscot River, from here north to Canada.) Examples of sweetgrass baskets, beadwork, drums, and birch bark canoes can be seen in the small **Penobscot Indian Museum** (daily 10 AM–4 PM, longer hours in summer; donations; 207/827-4153), 100 yards north of the bridge, across from the white-steepled Indian Faith Tabernacle.

In painful contrast to the general poverty of Indian Island, the neighboring town of Orono (pop. 9,800) is clearly thriving thanks to the 15,000 students and staff of the main University of Maine (UMO) campus (207/581-3740), located here since 1868. The university has all the usual libraries, concert halls, and other attractions you'd expect, plus one more: the independent **Bangor Blue Ox** baseball team who play their games ($4–6; 207/941-2337), throughout the summer at the university stadium off College Avenue.

Off the campus and across the river from the center of Orono, the main event is the **Maine Forest and Logging Museum** (daily dawn–dusk in summer only; free, except for special events; 207/581-2871). Often called Leonard's Mills, this is a 300-acre recreation of a Maine logging camp, and it is at its liveliest when the living history volunteers reenact the life and times of centuries past.

BANGOR

Built on the banks of the Penobscot River, Bangor (pop. 33,200, pronounced "BANG-gor") is the largest city in northern Maine. This site was an important rendezvous for local tribes, who called it Kendusbeag or "eel-catching place." In 1604 Samuel de Champlain sailed up the Penobscot River as far as Treats Falls here, but long-term settlement did not begin until 1769. Throughout the next century, Bangor was the most important lumber town of the eastern United States. It also developed into a shipbuilding center, and Bangor's lumber circled the globe. The people of Bangor were devoted to providing amusement for the loggers and sailors who would arrive in town with free time and fat wallets. In a riverside neighborhood called the Devil's Half Acre, dozens of bars, bordellos, and gambling dens competed to empty the men's pockets, but now the most prominent sign of life along the water is the **Sea Dog Brewery**, 26 Front Street (207/947-8004), one of Bangor's most popular bars and restaurants.

Nineteenth-century Bangor was as wide open as any town in the Wild West, but traces of rougher days have all but disappeared. Modern Bangor, once a supply center for the northern half of Maine, is still a center for the lumber industry. Coming into town across the Penobscot River, you'll turn right onto Main Street and see a 31-foot statue of a smirking **Paul Bunyan**, erected in 1959. The compact downtown area, mostly redbrick 19th-century buildings interspersed with church spires, lies a few blocks to the east of Paul Bunyan. Here you'll find some impressive 100-year-old buildings now housing a little of everything: an Internet cafe, two comic book shops, and at least four quality bookstores.

The small cemetery next to the Indian Island museum holds the grave of **Louis Sockalexis,** a Penobscot Indian and turn-of-the-century professional baseball player from whom the Cleveland Indians took their name. Sockalexis, who was born and raised here, was a phenomenally talented player whose success led to his early demise, apparently due to his drinking habits. His name lives on in the tribal bingo hall, home to some of the state's highest-stakes games.

Roughly midway between Orono and Bangor, along US-2 just east of Hogan Road, the lovely grounds of **Mount Hope Cemetery** are open daily from 8 AM to dusk for aimless walks, views over the river, and homage to prominent citizens of Maine, including Civil War–era Vice President Hannibal Hamlin, whose grave is right along State Street (US-2). The cemetery also has the oldest U.S. Civil War Memorial, erected in memory of Bangor's dead in 1864.

Bangor is home to best-selling horror writer **Stephen King,** who lives in a suitably Gothic and surprisingly visible mansion at 47 W. Broadway. If you want to write to him, you can, c/o P. O. Box 1186, Bangor, Maine 04402.

The **Bangor Historical Society** (Mon.–Fri. noon–4 PM; $2), housed in an 1836 Greek Revival mansion downtown at 159 Union Street, has the usual range of exhibits, furnishings, and paintings reflecting 19th-century life. Away from the center of Bangor, car, truck, and tractor fans flock to the **Cole Land Transportation Museum** (daily 9 AM–5 PM May–Nov.; $3), off I-95 and I-395 at 405 Perry Road, which displays more than 200 historic vehicles, from wooden wagons to modern 18-wheelers.

On the west edge of Bangor, off I-95 exit 44, soothe your white-line fever at the truckers' favorite stop, **Dysart's** (207/942-4878). This around-the-clock fuel stop and cafe offers a place to rest where you can dig in to the world's largest sundae, the 18-scoop "18-Wheeler."

Thanks to the nearby college, Bangor has a much wider variety of places to eat and drink than you'll find most anywhere else in inland Maine. Unexpectedly, there are a couple of inexpensive Indian and Pakistani places, including **Taste of India** at 68 Main Street (207/945-6865). For whiling away an evening, head down to the **Sea Dog Brewery** at 26 Front Street (207/947-8004), or cross the Penobscot River to **Stacey's,** 420 Wilson Street (207/989-4940), where you can drink beer and listen to country-western music 'til the early hours. For something a little more cerebral, the **Whig and Courier Pub** on Broad Street at the center of Bangor serves good food and even better beer.

The pick of area lodging is the **Phenix Inn** ($80–150; 207/947-0411), a restored 1873 hotel at 20 Broad Street downtown. The best local motel is the **Main Street Inn,** 480 Main Street ($50–65; 207/942-5282). The national chains (Motel 6, Rodeway, Super 8) have their motels out on US-2 near the airport and I-95 exit 45B, a mile or so west of town, which is where the fast food is, too.

For more information on Bangor, contact the **visitors bureau,** next to Paul Bunyan at 519 Main Street (207/947-0307).

NEWPORT

Midway across the state, at the point where two-lane US-2 joins the high-speed I-95 freeway, Newport (pop. 3,036) is known as the Hub of Maine. Like most other towns that play up their connections to the rest of the world, Newport is not really a place to linger, but it does have the **Log Cabin Restaurant** (207/368-4551) on US-2 three miles east of town, as well as a Wal-Mart and the usual array of fast food and cheap (-ish) motels.

Between Newport and Bangor, 20 miles to the east, there's no good reason to follow pot-holed old US-2. You may as well race across the state on I-95. Heading west between Newport and Skowhegan, US-2 runs across low rolling hills covered with pine and birch forests. The only signs of habitation here are a few mobile home trailers and scraggly farms.

If you're driving around Maine wondering what the many signs saying **Redemption Center** mean, the truth is disappointingly mundane. Rather than serving some higher purpose, these places are simply where you can return those returnable soda cans and bottles, for 5¢ a pop.

SKOWHEGAN

First settled in 1771 on an island in the Kennebec River, the mid-sized mill town of Skowhegan (pop. 8,725) was also the birthplace of the late Margaret Chase Smith, one of Maine's most renowned politicians and a 36-year veteran of the U.S. House and Senate. Her home is now the **Margaret Chase Smith Library Center** (207/474-7133; Mon.–Fri. 10 AM–4 PM;

donations) and it includes a museum depicting her life and a conference center. The **Skowhegan History House** (207/474-6632; Tues.–Fri. 1–5 PM in summer only; donations), 40 Elm Street, is a brick Greek Revival structure with exhibits on town history, and off US-201, just north of US-2, the **Skowhegan Indian**, a 62-foot statue sometimes billed as the Largest Wooden Indian in the World (and also known by the less flattering rubric, BFI), stands unloved and unmarked in the parking lot behind a gas station.

North from Skowhegan, US-201 runs along the Kennebec River, offering some of Maine's greatest fall foliage vistas. One of the prettiest stretches is around the town of Bingham, about 25 miles north of Skowhegan.

BELGRADE LAKES: ON GOLDEN POND

Between Skowhegan and Farmington, US-2 passes through a pair of quietly quaint places. **Norridgewock** is a historic hamlet, now home to a New Balance shoe factory and the popular Cradle of Dawn Cafe, and **New Sharon** has a rusty old bridge spanning the Sandy River. The region's real draw is south of US-2: the Belgrade Lakes, a chain of seven lakes circled by ageless vacation cabins and summer camps. It was this idyllic location that inspired author Ernest Thompson to write the book *On Golden Pond*, later made into that weepy Fonda family movie. The movie was filmed at New Hampshire's Squam Lake off US-3 in the White Mountains, but you can re-enact real-life scenes here in Maine by taking a ride on the **Great Pond Mailboat** (Mon.–Sat. at 10 AM; $10), which departs from the boat house in the village of Belgrade Lakes, along Route 27.

FARMINGTON

Like many other northern Maine towns, Farmington (pop. 4,200) was first settled by soldiers who fought in the Revolutionary War. The rolling hills that surround it still hold a few farms and orchards, but as elsewhere, the economy revolves around trees—both as tourist fodder during the fall color sweeps and as pulp for paper mills (there's a big pulp mill just south of town on US-201.) US-2 bypasses the center, but the downtown area has a few blocks of tidy brick buildings housing barber shops, bookstores, and cafes supported in large part by the presence of the large Farmington campus of the University of Maine. The university runs the small **art gallery** (207/778-7000; Sun.–Thurs. noon–4 PM; free) at 102 Main Street downtown showing local artists.

On the south edge of downtown, at the US-2/Route 4 junction, a pair of neighboring places offer the local culinary treats. Although it began as a classic streamlined prefab, the smoke-free **Farmington Diner** (207/778-4151) has become a bit

During the second week of August, Skowhegan is home to the **Maine State Fair** (207/474-2947). Celebrated annually since 1818, it is one of the oldest state fairs in the country. On weekend nights all summer long, you can catch an alfresco movie at the **Skowhegan Drive-In** (207/474-9277) on East Front Street.

In 1976, the Kennebec River at Skowhegan was the site of the last log drive in Maine.

Farmington's main claim to fame is that way back in 1873 a local teenager, Chester Greenwood, rigged up a pair of beaver-skin pads on a piece of bent wire to create the world's first earmuffs.

In the town of Rangeley, an hour northwest of Farmington via Route 4, the **Wilhelm Reich Museum** (Tues.–Sun. 1–5 PM in July and August; $5; 207/864-3443) preserves the flat-roofed final home and tomb of the iconoclastic psychoanalyst who died in 1957. See the Appalachian Trail chapter on page 283 for more.

shabby, but it is still open dawn to dusk for the usual greasy spoon delights. Across the road, **Gifford's Ice Cream** (207/778-3617) serves cones and foot-long hot dogs all summer long.

WILTON

Midway between Dixfield and Farmington, the town of Wilton was the longtime home of famous shoemaker **G. H. Bass Company,** makers of those leather "Weejuns" so loved by preppies. The Bass company recently abandoned Wilton for some low-paying-labor-cost place like Puerto Rico, but their old mill is still in use. Next to the mill, an old boarding house holds the **Wilton Farm and Home Museum** at 10 Canal Street (Sat. and Sun. 1–4 PM in summer only; donations; 207/645-2843). This is a fascinating little museum with exhibits on everything from old bottles to the life of the Wilton-born "Maine Giantess," Sylvia Hardy, an 8-foot-tall, 400-pound woman who was a star of P. T. Barnum's famous freak shows. The museum tells the story of G. H. Bass and their shoe-making operations. Across the street from the mill and museum is the nice little **Curiosity Book Shop**, with a wide selection of books about Maine.

Wilton is also home to a large windmill marking the **Dutch Treat** restaurant and ice cream stand right on US-2 east of town.

DIXFIELD

Heading west from Farmington, US-2 passes through wilder country, with excellent views of the tree-covered White Mountains rising over the New Hampshire border to the west. Five miles east of Rumford, in the heart of the Androscoggin River's broad valley, Dixfield (pop. 2,574) is a small town with a slight aura of the 1960s. The **Village Restaurant and Bakery** on US-2 at the west end of town is the main meeting place, and you can also eat at the **Old Opera House Restaurant,** housed inside—what else—an old opera house. Just east of Dixfield along US-2, a big blue house holds the **Mainely Critters Museum** (hours vary; free; 207/562-8231), where displays show off the native Maine habitats of an array of "flattened fauna," a.k.a. road kill.

At a junction in Dixfield, a single sign points the way toward Peru and Mexico. Paris, Leeds, Canton, Madrid, Belgrade, and Rome are also within 30 miles—only in America!

Just northwest of Rumford, **Black Mountain** (207/364-8977), is a nonprofit ski area owned by the Greater Rumford Community Center and subsidized by area towns. It offers skiing, snowboarding, and other winter amusements at much lower prices than you'd pay at mainstream resorts.

RUMFORD

The biggest and brawniest place along otherwise rural US-2, Rumford (pop. 7,078) is a grungy-looking mill town with low brick buildings and a downscale downtown along Waldo Street, above the winding Androscoggin River. At the west end of downtown, just upstream from all the heavy industry, you'll find the Androscoggin Falls, which provided the hydropower that led to the original settlement of the town. Now, enormous steam-puffing smokestacks loom large at the Mead Publishing Paper Division, New England's largest paper mill, surrounded by huge piles of logs, chips, and wood residue, all pushed around incessantly by anxious machinery. (Tours are offered Tues. and Thurs. afternoons; 207/369-2045.)

The ugly reality of Rumford (and its next-door-neighbor, Mexico, where the mill is located) is in many ways what makes it remarkable. While most cities try, if unsuccessfully, to hide their industry, Rumford and Mexico literally embrace it. The enormous Mead paper mill sits smack in the heart of Rumford, while US-2 winds up and around the valley that shapes the town, with the mill's huge smokestacks always at the center of what can seem a frighteningly post-apocalyptic landscape. Clearly this isn't a town designed for tourists, but if you're interested in how Americans live, work, and amuse themselves in places where industry still rules, Rumford is worth investigating.

For food and drink around Rumford, the stretch of US-2 east of town has a pair of great little hole-in-the-wall places. Furthest out is **Rowe's Afternoon Delight**, midway between Rumford and Dixfield, with really great lobster rolls served on hamburger buns. Another popular roadside haunt, the **Mexico Chicken Coop**, in the mill town of Mexico offers this slogan, "No Brag, Just Fact. Good Eating, That's Our Greeting." To start the day off right, have breakfast at the 1930s **Freddie's Restaurant** off US-2 on Congress Street (207/364-3069), where gruff guys in Carhartt caps and union jackets will clue you in to what's going on in town.

If you want an up-close view of the goings-on in Rumford, walk across to the mill on the narrow footbridge suspended above the river, but if you're after country scenery instead of rumbling machinery, you may wish to leave town as quickly as possible. The route along US-2 road winds around the valley as the Androscoggin makes an oxbow, and an even nicer route heads north following Route 17 and the Swift River toward the Rangeley Lakes. (See the Appalachian Trail chapter on pages 274–308 for more.)

BETHEL

At the far west end of its run across Maine, US-2 winds along the south bank of the Androscoggin River through the dense pine and birch forests of the White Mountain National Forest. Ten miles east of the New Hampshire border, along a placid stretch of the Androscoggin, Bethel (pop. 2,329) was first settled in 1774. At the tail end of the Revolutionary War, the town, then named Sudbury, suffered the last Indian raid inflicted on New England. In 1836, Gould Academy, one of Maine's oldest prep schools, was established at the west end of town near historic Main Street. Information on Bethel's many other well-preserved old buildings can be found in the 1813 **Moses Mason House**, 15 Broad Street, which doubles as a small museum (Mon.–Fri. 10 AM–4 PM; $2).

Rumford's main claim to national fame is as the birthplace of Edmund Muskie, governor, U.S. senator, secretary of state, and vice-presidential and presidential candidate in 1968 and 1972 respectively. Rumford celebrated the new millennium by unveiling a statue of Muskie but made national headlines when it turned out there was a typo. They spelled "presidential" as "presidental." Other big news in Rumford: Wal-Mart plans to open their only store in this neck of the Great North Woods, a 100,000-square-footer along US-2 just east of town.

For a more tongue-in-cheek taste of Maine, stop by the **Maine Line Products** store in Bethel at 23 Main Street (207/824-2522), and pick up a pair of "moose-drop" earrings and other jewelry made from lobster parts. The shop has some serious stuff, too, all made in Maine. They may carry postcards depicting Angus, King of the Mountain; he's the **world's largest snowman**, built in Bethel in 1999.

After the railroads came through, Bethel quickly became a center for White Mountain area tourism. The **Bethel Inn and Country Club** (207/824-2175 or 800/654-0125), founded in 1913, was one of New England's early health and fitness resorts, and it continues that tradition today. The club is surrounded by an 18-hole golf course, and if you're looking for upscale lodging and dining, this is the place to go. The **Red Top Restaurant** right downtown on US-2 is the polar opposite; try the hash. The **Norseman Motel** (207/824-2002) and the **River View Resort** (207/824-2808), both about two miles east of Bethel near the junction of US-2 and Route 26, are the moderate lodging choices.

For outdoor enthusiasts, the **Sunday River Ski Area** (207/824-3000 or 800/543-2SKI), six miles northeast of town, draws thousands of visitors to the area

the Shaker Museum at Sabbathday Lake

for skiing in winter and hiking and mountain biking in summer. Near the well-marked turnoff to Sunday River, there's a nice picnic area with a covered bridge, along US-2 and the Androscoggin River. If you head north from here a mile or so past the ski area another sign will point you toward the intricately constructed **Artist's Covered Bridge**, which spans the Sunday River.

From US-2 at Bethel, Route 26 runs southeast toward Portland and the coast, passing through the spa town of Poland Spring and the world's last-remaining intact Shaker community at **Sabbathday Lake**, where a small museum gives tours (Mon.–Sat. 10 AM–4 PM in summer; $5; 207/926-4597).

Just east of the New Hampshire border, 10 miles west of Bethel, a sign marks a turn south from US-2 onto Route 113 toward **Evans Notch**. This narrow winding road, which is marked "Not Maintained for Winter Travel," runs along the Wild and Cold Rivers up to a stunningly scenic mountain pass.

GORHAM, NEW HAMPSHIRE

Gorham (pop. 3,173), incorporated in 1836, was another early tourist town. Its boom began after the railroad came through in 1851. Tourism is still the main industry, from the summer tourists to the autumn "leaf-peepers" to the winter skiers. (Nobody visits much during the early spring mud season when motel rates are at their lowest.) There is a **visitor center** on Main Street (US-2; 603/752-6060), and the **Gorham Historical Society** (Mon., Wed., and Fri. 1–5 PM; donations) stands in an old depot at 25 Railroad Street, a half-block off Main Street.

For lunch and dinner try **Wilfred's**, 117 Main Street (603/466-2380), specializing in bounteous and inexpensive turkey dinners; **Welsh's Restaurant**, 88 Main Street (603/466-2206), serves the most popular breakfast. The **Royalty Inn**, 130 Main Street, (603/466-3312), is a good full-service motel with a large health club next door.

Just east of Gorham, the road passes through a famous grove of birch trees, the "world-renowned Shelburne Birches." Here you find the big but pleasant **Town & Country Motor Inn** ($45–75; 603/466-3315) with some spa and resort facilities, such as saunas, a golf course, and a good restaurant. This is also where the **Appalachian Trail**, which runs from Maine's Mount Katahdin to northern Georgia, crosses US-2.

West of Gorham, right off US-2, the summer-only **Moose Brook State Park** (603/466-3860) has basic campsites and a swimming hole built back in the 1930s by the New Deal CCC.

The sign welcoming you to New Hampshire reads, Brake for Moose, referring to the more than 200 car-moose collisions to date. Apparently moose are hard to see at night because headlights shine through the legs, rather than on the body of this towering beast.

If you want to unwind after a day on the trails, sit down and enjoy a free concert in Gorham's central park every summer Tuesday at 7 PM.

East of Gorham, US-2 crosses the Appalachian Trail, winding between Grafton Notch in Maine and the summit of Mount Washington. The section heading north from here is considered among the most demanding in the whole 2,158-mile trail. There's no real driving equivalent, but the closest approximation—and the very popular driving route up Mount Washington and south through Pinkham Notch—is covered on pages 274–308.

JEFFERSON

High above the Israel River on the slopes of the White Mountains, the small resort town of Jefferson (pop. 1,003) is home to two big tourist draws. For the truly masochistic parent, about a mile west of Jefferson is **Santa's Village** (603/586-4445; daily 9:30 AM–7 PM, summer only; $15, under age 4 free), with candy canes looming threateningly at the entrance, a Ferris wheel, a roller coaster, the Yule Log Flume and, of course, Santa himself. Just east of town is **Six Gun City** (603/586-4592; daily 9 AM–6 PM, summer only; $11.95), an ersatz Wild West town featuring cowboy skits ("Come on out, you varmints!"), frontier shows, a carriage museum, and a pair of water slides.

Outside the town, along US-2 on a crest between Gorham and Jefferson, the **Grand View Lodge** (603/466-5715) has nice rooms and truly grand views. Two accommodations in Jefferson deserve mention. The friendly **Applebrook B&B** (800/545-6504; $45–60 for a double or $20 per person in the seven-bed dorm) offers full Victorian splendor gilded with summer raspberries and a hot tub under the stars. **Jefferson Inn** (800/729-7908; $44–70 for a double, suites from $65) has a Dutch- and German-speaking innkeeper, panoramic views, and a swimming pond.

LANCASTER

Across the Connecticut River from Vermont, Lancaster (pop. 3,550) is a market town that was first settled in 1764. US-2 becomes Main Street through Lancaster, lined with dozens of attractive old homes and churches, a cemetery on a knoll to the north, and on the south side, a heroic redbrick courthouse that dates from 1887. At the junction of US-2 and US-3 at the west side of town stands the **Lancaster Historical Society**.

Two miles south of Lancaster via US-3, the mountaintop estate of the man who saved New Hampshire's forests from the lumber industry has been preserved as **John Wingate Weeks Historic Site** (Wed.–Sun. 10 AM–6 PM in summer only; $2.50), complete with a tourable mansion and an observation tower giving grand views of Mount Washington and Vermont's Green Mountains.

Just west of Lancaster, the broad **Connecticut River** flows south all the way to Long Island Sound. To the north of Lancaster, the same river is a well-known fishing stream; smallmouth bass and brown trout are abundant here. If you weren't thrilled by the modern bridge that carries US-2 just upstream from Lancaster, head five miles south of downtown on Route 135 to an impressive old **covered bridge**

that spans the Connecticut River and meets US-2 in the Vermont town of Lunenburg.

There are moderately priced motels on US-2 east of town. Downtown you'll find the **S&S Lancaster Diner**, serving Chinese and American food (with pool tables upstairs) at 60 Main Street (603/788-2802), and the **Lancaster Motor Inn**, 112 Main Street (603/788-4921).

CONCORD AND LUNENBURG, VERMONT

Crossing the New Hampshire border, US-2 heads across rocky rolling hills covered with pine and birch forests interspersed with a few scattered farms. This corner of the state, a recreational paradise of hills and lakes and few year-round residents, is known as the Northeast Kingdom. Along the banks of the broad Connecticut River, Lunenburg is a perfect New England village of white clapboard houses clustered around a church; Vermont specializes in this species of quaintness.

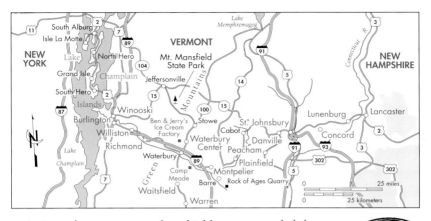

At Lunenburg, you can take a highly recommended detour across the Connecticut River on a historic covered bridge. Fifteen miles west of Lunenburg you reach Concord, which features a country store and a small historical society. Concord was the home of the **First Normal School**, America's first teachers' academy, founded in 1823.

ST. JOHNSBURY

In the 19th century, the economy of St. Johnsbury (pop. 7,600) was based on maple products and the manufacture of platform scales. Fairbanks Scales, founded by the inventor of platform scales, still operates a plant here. Today it is the pleasantly peaceful commercial center of Vermont's Northeast Kingdom, at the junction of the US-2 and US-5 highways, the I-91 and I-93 freeways, and the Maine Central and Canadian Pacific railroad tracks. The economy has never regained its Victorian-era prosperity, meaning the town's extensive stock of historic landmark architecture has been preserved almost totally unchanged. Elegant (and often empty) four- and five-story brick buildings line the riverfront and railroad line along US-2 and US-5. On the hill above the riverfront, a more genteel commercial district surrounded by massive trees and dozens of grand Victorian homes is highlighted by two of the most fascinating institutions in the state, both funded by the largess of the Fairbanks family.

At the center of town, at 30 Main Street, stands the **St. Johnsbury Athenaeum, Art Gallery and Public Library** (Mon.–Fri. 10 AM–5:30 PM; free) in a red brick 1871 building. The building houses a surprising collection of 19th-century paintings, the jewel of which is Albert Bierstadt's monumental *Domes of Yosemite*.

A block east down Main Street, you'll find my very favorite museum in all New England: the **Fairbanks Museum** (Mon.–Sat. 10 AM–6 PM, Sun. 1–5 PM; $5), a charmingly quirky Victorian-

MUSEUM & PLANETARIUM

era center of knowledge established by Franklin Fairbanks in 1889. A pair of menacing stuffed bears greet visitors inside the entrance, followed by a seemingly endless display of taxidermied wildlife—a veritable Noah's Ark of North American fauna. Climb the spiral stairs to the mezzanine of the main gallery, a grand Richardsonian Romanesque space topped by a coffered barrel vault and furnished with fireplaces and other homey touches. You'll find more fascinating oddities: arrowheads and other anthropological artifacts, rocks and fossils, and art made out of bugs (including a portrait of General Pershing made out of flies and moths!). View exhibits on local history, a set of dollhouse furniture made by author Mark Twain, and a very funny letter written by Robert Louis Stevenson in which he wills his birthday (which he said he was too old to need anymore) to Fairbanks' daughter (whose own birth fell on Christmas, meaning she effectively missed out).

St. Johnsbury has some fine bookshops: **Northern Lights** at 79 Railroad Street (802/748-4463), great for digging deeper into local lore. But before you dig, you may want to improve your luck by consulting the experts at the **American Society of Dowsers** bookstore, nearly next door at 99 Railroad Street (802/748-8565). For out-of-print books and general ephemera, try **That Book Store**, 443 Railroad Street. Finally, try the **Moose River Lake and Lodge Store**, at 69 Railroad Street (802/748-2423), where you can pick up books on how to design and decorate your backwoods cabin and maybe some Vermont essentials, everything from maple syrup to taxidermied wildlife, up to and including a real dead **moose head** mounted on a plaque and priced at $1,650.

St. Johnsbury's eating options include **Hilltopper Restaurant**, 1214 Main Street (802/748-2241), across the street from the Athenaeum, and **Anthony's Diner** (802/748-3613), on Railroad Street at the US-5/US-2 junction. For motels, try the **Fairbanks Motor Inn**, on US-2 at 32 Western Avenue ($50–75; 802/748-5666), or the peaceful and quiet creekside cabins of **Aime's Motel** ($40–65; 802/748-3194), on US-2 about five miles east of town, a half-mile north of I-93, exit 1.

Taking a scenic alternative to the I-93 freeway east from St. Johnsbury, US-2 passes over the Memorial Bridge (1943) spanning the Passumpsic River. One mile east of the bridge you'll find the **Maple Grove Farms** complex based around an old mill building. Highlights include the maple museum (and tasting room), and the so-called world's largest maple candy factory (tours Mon.–Fri. 8 AM–4 PM; $1; 802/748-5141). Vermont is in the heart of maple sugaring territory, which runs all the way from Maine to Michigan, and up into Canada. Maple Grove Farms has been in business here since 1915, and it is the largest packager of maple syrup in the United States. In front of the store, you can have your picture taken in front of the World's Largest Can of Maple Syrup (which is, alas, empty).

North of US-2, three miles from Marshfield via Route 215, the hamlet of Cabot is home to Vermont's main cheese producers, the cooperatively run **Cabot Creamery** (daily 9 AM–5 PM; 800/837-4261). Most days you can watch slabs of cheese being processed, and there are always free samples of cheddars (mild to extra sharp), smoked cheddars, even bacon-flavored cheddars.

DANVILLE: AMERICAN SOCIETY OF DOWSERS

Danville, yet another picture-postcard Vermont village, is set on a hill surrounded by farms. The center of Danville is a classic New England village green with a general store and the customary churches. On Brainerd Street just off the green, you'll find the headquarters of the **American Society of Dowsers** (Mon.–Fri. 9 AM–4:30 PM; 802/684-3417), whose members have refined their talents for finding water or mineral deposits using a wooden dowsing rod. The building houses a small exhibit on the history and practice of the art and a shop where you can buy dowsing books and dowsing rods; they also have a bookshop in St. Johnsbury.

PEACHAM

South of US-2 from the center of Danville, enjoy the main road and a lovely pastoral drive toward Peacham, a perennial contender for the title "prettiest village in Vermont." During the fall color sweeps, the mountaintop village is likely to be crowded with sightseeing tourists, but most of the time it's a somnolent little place. In fact, Peacham is so timeless that the producers of the movie version of Edith Wharton's Victorian fable **Ethan Fromme** filmed it here (without having to remove any streetlights or other signs of modern life). Along with the white-steepled church and the hilltop cemetery, Peacham is centered around the wonderful **Peacham Store** (802/592-3310), where you can buy aromatic soups and hearty sandwiches or admire the sundry crafts on display. The surrounding countryside is packed with images of rural Vermont—hay fields, red barns, country stores—and distant views are dominated by the towering White Mountains of New Hampshire looming over the horizon to the east.

From Peacham, you can come back the way you went or wind your way east to another postcard-pretty Vermont village, **Barnet**, which retains its central charms despite being bordered by US-5 and the I-91 freeway. Barnet and the rest of the Connecticut River corridor are covered in the US-5 chapter.

WEST DANVILLE: JOE'S POND

West Danville, a summer community on the edge of Joe's Pond, is ringed by old vacation cabins. The pond, which at sunset in summer is one of the more idyllic spots imaginable, was originally called Indian Joe's Pond, which explains the presence of Indian Joe Court, a set of roadside cabins dating from the pre–politically correct era. At the center of town and at the junction of US-2 and Route 15, you'll see a micro-sized covered bridge and the **Hastings Store** (802/684-3630), the local "if we ain't got it, you don't need it" emporium, selling cheddar cheese, maple syrup, fishing supplies, and other Vermont essentials.

At the hilltop cabins of **Indian Joe Court** ($45–60; 802/684-3430), guests can borrow pedalboats or canoes from a 300-foot beach and hang out on the water. You can also stay at the one- or two-bedroom cabins of **Point Comfort** ($55–65; 802/684-3379). Both establishments have weekly rates if you're lucky enough to linger here a while. Indian Joe has a few RV sites, too.

Heading west toward Plainfield, US-2 drops down into the valley of the **Winooski River**, a prime trout-fishing river, which it follows all the way to Lake Champlain.

PLAINFIELD

Plainfield is where the 1960s live. This tiny town boasts a bookstore, a pair of huge barns, a fly-fishing shop, and the **Maple Valley Country Store**, a combo deli-cafe-pizzeria that's the local hangout (tie-dye welcome; 802/454-8626). The soups are fantastic, as are the veggie burgers. The store's parking area is built on a foundation of recycled granite, leftovers from the nearby quarries and stonecutters. Plainfield also has a great place to eat breakfast: the **River Run** at 3 Main Street (802/454-1246), where you can get a great heap of pancakes studded with fresh blueberries for around $5.

Just west of Plainfield is the campus of **Goddard College**, one of the nation's most renowned counter-cultural institutes of higher learning, where you can sometimes get a cheap room in summer (802/454-8311). Hitchhikers are common on US-2 between Plainfield and Montpelier. To stay a while, consider a night on the farm: at **Hollister Hill Farm**, 2193 Hollister Hill Road east of town ($50-65; 802/454-7725), they make their own maple syrup (and serve it over pancakes at breakfast) and raise all sorts of organic produce (from vegetables to "beefalo" hybrids).

I-89 SURVIVAL GUIDE: ACROSS VERMONT

MM130: U.S./Canada border.

MM 129: Exit 22 for US-7 (at latitude 45 North, this is midway between Equator and North Pole).

MM118: Exit 20 for St. Albans and US-7 (see page 250).

MM111: Rest Areas (both directions).

MM98: Exit 17 junction with US-2 west toward Lake Champlain Islands.

MM92: Exit 16 junction with joint US-2/US-7 north to Colchester and south through Winooski (see page 135).

MM89: Exit 14 for downtown Burlington.

MM79: Exit 11 for Richmond (see page 132).

MM64: Exit 10 for US-2 through Waterbury and scenic Route 100, north past Ben & Jerry's to Stowe (see page 130) and south toward Granville Gulf State Preserve (see page 184.)

MM59: Exit 9 for US-2 past Camp Meade.

MM53: Exit 8 for US-2 through Montpelier (see page 127).

MM50: Exit 7 for US-302 to Barre.

MM41: Highest elevation on I-89, 1,752 feet.

MM13: Exit 2 for Route 14 and Appalachian Trail route to Pomfret and Woodstock (see page 179).

MM4: Exit 1 for White River Junction (see page 200) and US-4 west to Woodstock and Killington (see page 182).

MM1: Junction with I-91, north to St. Johnsbury and south to Brattleboro (see page 206)

MM0: Vermont/New Hampshire state line, on a bridge across Connecticut River. I-89 continues south across New Hampshire, running parallel to the our road trip route along US-4.

MONTPELIER

The smallest capital in the country, Vermont's Montpelier (pop. 8,200) was settled in 1787 and designated the state capital in 1805. Today Montpelier's economy is based on government, insurance, and tourism.

Following the US-2 Business route into town, the gold dome of the capitol building hovering over the valley ahead signals your arrival in Montpelier. Constrained by the Winooski River on one side and the narrow valley on the other, Montpelier is so compact that you can park your car and find all the sights within a 10-minute walk. (Thankfully, the I-89 freeway and the main US-2 bypass are well away from downtown.) A quick poll of shops along State and Main Streets reveals the cosmopolitan nature of the town: bookstores (including Bear Pond Books, at 77 Main Street (802/229-0774), coffee bars, and wine merchants, as well as multiple combinations of the same.

Pedestrians rule in Vermont, so be sure to stop for anyone using a crosswalk or risk a big ticket. Vermont police also enforce the state law that requires drivers to use turn signals when changing lanes.

In the Danbury/Montpelier region, alternative music fans will want to tune their car radios to the **"The Point,"** broadcasting Phish, Everclear, Lucinda Williams, Neil Young, and other rowdy rockers on two frequencies: **95.7FM** and **104.7FM.**

The north side of State Street opens up into a broad lawn fronting the **State Capitol**, the focal point of the Republic of Vermont (like Texas, the state takes some pride in the fact that it was an independent "country" before joining the rest of the United States). The original capitol building was opened in 1808 but soon burned down; a replacement was built in 1836 and it too burned down. In 1859, the current, more heroic struc-

State Capitol, Montpelier, Vt.

ture was erected from local Barre granite. The statue on the dome represents Ceres, the goddess of agriculture. Doric columns hide a Revolutionary War cannon and a statue of Ethan Allen. The state legislature is only in session from January to April —being a Vermont politician is a part-time job. The rest of the year they go about being farmers, businesswomen, and so on, but you can tour the building year-round (Mon.–Fri. 8 AM–4 PM; guided tours available).

Above the capitol rises **Hubbard Park**, a 100-year-old, 154-acre green space, with seven miles of hiking trails and a 54-foot observation tower atop the summit, the highest point in Montpelier.

Just west of the capitol is the **Vermont Historical Society Museum** (Tues.–Sat. 9 AM–4:30 PM, Sun. noon–4 PM; $3), where permanent and temporary displays illustrate different aspects of Vermont's history, and you can also find lots of 19th-century furniture and a small bookstore and gift shop.

MONTPELIER PRACTICALITIES

Montpelier residents take their eating seriously. Very good and very inexpensive food is readily available thanks to the local presence of the New England Culinary Institute, a cooking

Rising up a hill along State Street (US-2) a few blocks west of the capitol, the **Green Mount Cemetery** is filled with impressive granite monuments. Many of these were carved by the immigrant stonecutters of nearby Barre for their own family plots, and the well-groomed grounds make ideal picnic spots, especially on a summer afternoon.

Near Montpelier, watch sap being turned into delicious maple syrup at the **Morse Farm and Sugarhouse**, three miles northeast from the capitol along Main Street.

school that operates the **Main Street Bar and Grill** (802/223-3188) and **Chef's Table** (802/229-9202), both at 118 Main Street. Montpelier fast food means bagels, Ben & Jerry's ice cream, and breads from **Manghis' Bread** at 28 School Street (802/223-3676), just east of Main Street. A full range of healthy deli food and drink is available at the **State Street Market**, 20 State Street (802/229-9353), and the nearby **Coffee Corner** (802/229-9060), on the corner of State and Main Streets offers breakfast with atmosphere you'll appreciate.

For upscale lodgings in period surroundings, go to **The Inn at Montpelier** ($80-140; 802/223-2727), two renovated 19th-century homes that have been joined into one hotel. The best moderate choice is the **Econo Lodge** ($45-75; 802/223-5258) on Route 12 south of the river.

BARRE: ROCK OF AGES

Montpelier thrived off the granite quarries of nearby Barre (pop. 9,482), which stretch along US-302 southeast of the state capital. Downtown Barre (pronounced "Barry," as in Manilow or Bonds) is well worth a wander and full of funky local shops, but the real draw is the nation's largest granite producer, the **Rock of Ages quarry** (daily 8:30 AM–5 PM in summer; $4; 802/476-3119), four miles southeast of Barre off South Main Street (Route 14). The quarry can also be reached from I-89 exit 6.

One of the world's largest, the main quarry is an awesome sight. Stand at the edge of the quarry, amid heavy-duty cranes and derricks, and gaze straight down for nearly 500 feet, the equivalent of a 40-story building. If you stayed long enough, you could watch the entire process, from the cutting of huge slabs through the final sculpting and polishing, which has largely been automated. The finishing touches are exacted at the Craftsman Center, where skilled workers shape the stone into statues and tombstones.

Head up Quarry Hill, midway between downtown and the Rock of Ages quarries, to see **Thunder Road International Speedway** (Thurs at 7 PM, Sun. at 6 PM in summer only; $7; 802/244-6963), which hosts loud and lively stock car races on its high-banked quarter-mile track.

Between Montpelier and Barre, the **Wayside Restaurant** on US-302 (802/223-6611) has tasty fruit pies and inexpensive down-home meals.

CAMP MEADE

Back on US-2, midway between Montpelier and Waterbury just west of Middlesex, stands Camp Meade, a Depression-era Civilian Conservation Corps camp that once housed workers building dams and flood control projects and since has been turned into a popular restaurant and motel ($45; 802/223-5537). It is also a shrine to America in the 1930s and 1940s, from the New Deal to D-Day, mostly the latter: a fighter plane, a tank, and military trucks adorn the grounds. A gift store sells army surplus goods, the restaurant sports camouflage tablecloths and a bomb

Riverside
Cemetery,
Route 100B

suspended from the rafters, and the cabins are named after luminaries such as General Patton and Colonel Oliver North. Primarily Camp Meade draws a nostalgic crowd of retired folk reliving their past and swapping war stories, but it's a fascinating and definitely unique place to stop.

ROUTE 100: WAITSFIELD AND WARREN

Running south from Waterbury, Route 100 travels through the heart of the Green Mountains all the way south to Massachusetts, and is one of the state's most popular leaf-peeping routes. The scenic route north from Waterbury, described above, runs through Stowe all the way to Canada, while the section south of Waterbury through the Mad River Valley has legions of fans as well.

Winding south from Middlesex along the banks of the Mad River, Route 100B is a beautiful drive (with wide, bike-friendly shoulders!) passing through the village of **Moreton** with its post office, church, central green, and photogenic cemetery before linking up with Route 100. The rugged river is dotted with swimming holes and at least one very deep gorge, marked by tiny signs saying simply Canoe Portage.

Leaving US-2 east of Waterbury, Route 100 runs south for some 20 miles before reaching **Waitsfield**, a pretty town with a lovely covered bridge set deep in a narrow canyon carved by the Mad River. South of Waitsfield, Route 100 winds through the short but sickening mini-mall sprawl of Irasville, toward **Warren**, where beneath the shiny surface you can still see a few remnants of its historic lumber mills. Although overrun by Sugarbush-bound skiers in peak winter months, most of the time these low-key villages are calm and cool, looking more like simple, old-fashioned farming communities than the semi-trendy tourist hotspots they really are. For proof of their popularity with well-heeled city-dwellers, you need only peruse the menus at the **Pitcher Inn**, a block east of Route 100 at 275 Main Street in Warren ($200–425; 802/496-6350), where fresh local produce, wild game, and one of the state's finest wine lists draws epicures from all over the world. This small historic inn was totally rebuilt after a 1993 fire, and now is one of New England's most romantic (and expensive) getaways. A more affordable option is the **Mad River Inn**, a B&B at 243 Tremblay Road ($80–120; 802/496-7900).

Although prices at its restaurants and inns can be a bit steep (as can the nearby ski slopes), the innumerable hiking and biking trails (like the six-mile trip along

East Warren Road, a country lane linking Waitsfield and Warren) make this area one of the most popular in Vermont for outdoor recreation. One of the nicest spots is four miles south of Warren, 24 miles south of US-2, where Route 100 enters the lovely **Granville Gulf State Park**, sometimes called the Granville Gulf Reservation, which the boundary sign describes as "six miles of natural beauty to be preserved forever." A real highlight of Granville Gulf is **Moss River Falls** near the park's southern boundary.

The areas along Route 100 south from Granville Gulf to Killington and beyond are described in the US-4 chapter on page 183; the sections of Route 100 further south are described in the Appalachian Trail chapter on pages 299–300.

Like Stowe to the north and Killington further south, the mountainous region along Route 100 to the south of Montpelier is home to two more of Vermont's popular ski areas. The larger and more developed of these is **Sugarbush**, west of Warren (802/583-2381 or 800/537-8427), which has full snowmaking, slopeside condos, and over 100 trails cut into 2,400 vertical feet over two mountains. Much calmer and quieter, **Mad River Glen** (802/496-3551 or 800/850-6742) is along scenic Route 17 east of the Appalachian Gap and has no snowmaking or slopeside condos—just 2,000 very steep vertical feet, nearly half of which are rated "expert."

The term "gulf," in Vermontese, describes a short valley set between mountain passes. Usually a gulf is defined by two separate streams that flow in opposite directions; Granville Gulf marks the division between the Mad River and White River watersheds.

Don't confuse Waterbury Junction, birthplace of Ben & Jerry's, with Waterbury, a satellite community of Montpelier with some large state government office buildings, located just *south* of the I-89 freeway. Waterbury Junction is about 1.5 miles north of Waterbury.

WATERBURY JUNCTION: BEN & JERRY'S

Although Vermont is known for beautiful mountains and the brilliant fall color of its hardwood forests, its number one tourist attraction is none other than **Ben & Jerry's Ice Cream Factory**, a kind of hippie Disneyland in Waterbury Junction, on the hillside above Route 100, a mile or so north of I-89. On the grounds of the brightly painted factory you'll see a number of large cartoonish artifacts you and your kids can play on: weird vehicles, whimsical picnic tables, and the like. Ben & Jerry began making its ultra-rich ice cream in 1978; today the company sells its products across the country and abroad. The company is also famous for its activism, donating a percentage of its profits to philanthropies supporting "progressive social change."

You can tour the factory (daily 9 AM–5 PM; $2; 802/244-TOUR or 800/244-8687 for information), although production is halted on Sundays, holidays, and company celebration days (call before visiting). Check out the factory gift shop and the Scoop Shop, featuring all of Ben & Jerry's ice cream, frozen yogurt, and sorbet flavors. Outside are many picnic tables where you can enjoy the ice cream and a view over the valley.

ROUTE 100: STOWE AND SMUGGLERS NOTCH

The first and most famous mountain resort in the Green Mountain state, Stowe has a unique history and a very attractive setting at the foot of 4,393-foot Mount Mansfield, Vermont's highest peak. Although best known for its skiing, the town itself is more attractive than most winter resorts and draws a year-round clientele of well-heeled types from all over the East. People come here to relax, play tennis, ride horses, or take scenic country drives, but the popularity of the place can cause clogged traffic on the winding roads that meet at Stowe's still-quaint village green.

Stowe was put on the tourist map thanks to the famous von Trapp family (of *Sound of Music* fame), who came here after fleeing the Nazis in their native Austria at the start of World War II. The family built a mountainside lodge, which burned down and has been replaced by the sprawling **Trapp Family Lodge** outside town via Luce Hill Road ($120–250; 802/253-8511 or 800/826-7000). The Alpine Chalet-style design of the Trapp Family Lodge

the Trapp family

has been replicated in myriad ways in most of Stowe's other hotels and resorts. Stowe is definitely not for the budget-challenged, but if you're hungry you can join the occasional celebrity slumming-it at the **Backyard Tavern** at 395 Mountain Road (Route 108; 802/253-9204), where cheeseburgers, a great jukebox, and $2 pints draw a regular crowd of locals, too. The main ski (and mountain bike) area is west of Stowe proper along Route 108 on the slopes of Mount Mansfield. On a clear summer day, you may want to take the **drive** ($14 per car) to the top of Mount Mansfield. The price is as steep as the road itself (which is to say, very!), but the panoramic view from the summit is breathtaking. If you don't want to drive, you can also ride a **gondola** ($11) to the summit, slide down the **alpine slide** on a plastic toboggan ($8 or 5 rides for $28), or rent a mountain bike and ride down the slopes, returning uphill on the ski lifts ($15/half-day; $25 all day). For details or for more information on skiing, contact **Stowe Mountain Resort** (802/253-3000 or 800/253-4754).

Beyond the Stowe Mountain ski area, Route 108 is closed in winter, but when open, it's one of the state's most twisting highways, squeezed down to a single lane in places between precipitous cliffs. One of the most memorable mountain drives in all New England, the road over Smugglers Notch also provides access to the legendary Long Trail, which actually follows the road for a mile near the 2,170-foot crest.

West of the notch, Route 108 drops down into the Lamoille Valley (which is pronounced "la-MOY-el," as in the Jewish man or moyel who performs circumcisions) and ends up at the historic hamlet of Jeffersonville, packed full of dainty late Victorian homes and buildings. North from Stowe to the Canadian border, Route 100 runs through a gentler but still rugged, picturesque region, passing through broader valleys largely given over to farmland.

An excellent source of **hiking information** is the Green Mountain Club. Its *Day Hiker's Guide to Vermont* and *Guide Book of the Long Trail* are both available direct from the GMC, which is on Route 100, 10 miles north of the Ben & Jerry's Ice Cream Factory. Order direct by phone or mail (RR 1 Box 650, Route 100, Waterbury Center, Vermont 05677; 802/244-7037), or buy a copy from one of Vermont's many great local bookshops.

From the center of Stowe, a great way to stretch your legs is to follow the **Stowe Recreation Path**, a five-plus-mile pathway that stretches from Main Street along the West Branch River to a photogenic covered bridge.

On a clear day, the 3,861-foot summit of Jay Peak, which marks the northern end of the Long Trail, offers a 360-degree panorama view stretching as much as 100 miles in every direction. From the top, you can sometimes see Montreal to the north, the Presidential Range and White Mountains to the east, and the Adirondacks to the west.

RICHMOND AND WILLISTON

Between Montpelier and Burlington, US-2 follows the Winooski River valley lined with dairy farms. For most of the way, the road parallels the less-than-attractive concrete expanse of I-89, but a few sights along the "old road" make the two-lane route preferable.

The country town of Richmond is home of the unique **Old Round Church**. Turn at the town's only stoplight and drive a half-mile south, where this 16-sided, two-story white clapboard structure stands just east of the road. The church was built in 1813 and is the communal effort of five different Protestant denominations. They eventually feuded, of course, and the structure lapsed into civic use becoming the town hall. Today it is used as a meeting house, and on summer weekends the local historical society (802/434-6070) gives guided tours.

Williston (pop. 4,887) sits roughly 10 miles east of Burlington and less than a mile north of the freeway. Although large by local standards, Williston is a classic northern New England town, its streets lined by towering maple trees and white clapboard houses.

THE PEOPLE'S REPUBLIC OF VERMONT

Known in tourist circles for its fall color, excellent skiing, and rambling pastoral landscapes, the Green Mountains State of Vermont is also notable for its fiercely independent politics. Vermont's nonconformist politics date back to the state's foundation as an independent republic before it joined the United States as the first addition to the original 13 colonies. The state's progressive ideological nature has been highlighted more recently by the activities of its most famous company, Ben & Jerry's Ice Cream, which was founded by recovering hippies. The company went on to trumpet "socially responsible" capitalism while naming its flavors after Grateful Dead guitarist Jerry Garcia and other notorious free thinkers. The year 2000 may have seen Ben & Jerry's get bought out by a huge conglomerate, but the year also saw at least one progressive move, the adoption of Vermont's Civil Union law, which is intended to provide the legal benefits of marriage (with regard to insurance in particular) to same-sex couples, including people not residing in the state.

These days, Vermont is represented in Congress by the only alternative politician in Congress, the staunchly independent Bernie Sanders, who has represented the state since 1990. Before coming to Congress, Bernie (as he is always referred to) taught at Harvard, worked as director of the American People's History Society, and served as Mayor of Burlington, Vermont's largest city, for 10 years. His accomplishments in Burlington included building affordable housing; revitalizing the city's waterfront; and initiating arts, youth, and women's programs, all of which helped earn Burlington recognition as one of the most livable cities in America.

BURLINGTON

After the original French settlers were ejected from the Lake Champlain region in 1760 at the end of the French and Indian Wars, English settlers soon arrived, and Burlington (pop. 39,150) was chartered in 1763. The area was abandoned during the Revolutionary War. Afterward, Ethan Allen, leader of the famous Green Mountain Boys band of guerrillas, and his brothers were granted huge tracts of land along the eastern shore of Lake Champlain. The Allen brothers were ambitious. Not only did they encourage settlement and industry in Burlington, but in 1791 they founded the University of Vermont here. The town boomed, aided by its strategic position on Lake Champlain, the quickest route between New York's Hudson River and Montreal. Burlington quickly became the center of Vermont industry, finance, education, and culture—a position it has held ever since.

US-2/US-7 passes right through the center of Burlington, following Winooski Avenue to the north, then along Main Street, lined by motels and restaurants on the outskirts but eventually crossing the lively, sprawling campus of the **University of Vermont** (UVM), which stands on a shallow hill on the east side of town, a mile west on Main Street from I-89, exit 14. Along Colchester Avenue on the north edge of campus, the **Robert Hull Fleming Museum** (Tues.–Fri. 9 AM–4 PM, Sat. and Sun. 1–5 PM; $3; 802/656-0750) is the main visitor attraction, with a small but varied collection of fine and applied arts from ancient Egypt to the present. A less rarefied campus sight is the anarchic **W.H.A.M.K.A.**, the Williams Hall Art Museum of Kitsch Art, which fills a display case in the main hallway of the art school with Pez dispensers and other pop icons. It's free and open whenever the buildings are (usually 7 AM–11 PM).

Burlington was the home of Dr. Nelson Jackson, who in 1902 (along with his chauffeur and a stray dog they picked up along the way) became the first to cross the country by automobile.

In 1981, the people of Burlington elected one of America's few socialist mayors, Bernie Sanders. He was reelected three times and has since served as U.S. Congressman from the "People's Republic" of Vermont. During election years (which is every other year) signs and stickers saying Bernie can be seen all over the state, and Bernie himself makes frequent appearances at county fairs, parades, VFW meetings, and the like all over Vermont.

Midway between Lake Champlain and the UVM campus, downtown Burlington is anchored by the **Church Street Mall**, a pedestrianized and increasingly chain-dominated shopping district that lies perpendicular to Main Street, north from Burlington's stately old City Hall. From City Hall, Main Street continues west to Lake Champlain, where the **Burlington Waterfront Park** has a strollable boardwalk linking up with **Battery Park**, home to a collection of cannons pointing menacingly across the lake. In 1812, these cannons were used against British warships that bombarded the town. Bands frequently play here on summer evenings, and a bike path runs along the water. If you feel like getting out on the water, you can rent a boat from the **Community Boathouse** (802/865-3377), or take a $9 sunset cruise on board the *Spirit of Ethan Allen* (802/862-8300). (Keep an eye out for Champ, Vermont's version of the Loch Ness Monster, who dwells deep in the waters of Lake Champlain.)

Through Burlington and Winooski, US-2 is joined by north-south US-7, which runs between Canada and Long Island Sound. The drive along US-7, from the foot of the Green Mountains down through the Berkshires and Litchfield Hills, is covered in full detail. One place you ought to see is the wonderful Shelburne Museum, just three miles south of downtown Burlington (see the US-7 chapter on page 250 for more).

BURLINGTON PRACTICALITIES

Downtown Burlington offers all the delights of a typical college town: bookstores, bars, ethnic food, and trendy but generally inexpensive shopping. (If you like thrift stores, you'll want to visit Battery Street Jeans, at 182 Battery, down by the waterfront.) For food, two local favorites, the all-Asian **Five Spice Cafe**, 175 Church Street (802/864-4045), and the **Daily Planet**, behind Church Street at 15 Center Street (802/862-9647), feature international fusion food, from pastas to Latin American dishes. Also nearby are the mid-1950s stainless-steel **Oasis Diner**, 189 Bank Street (802/864-5308), and the tasty **Ali-Baba's Kabob Shop**, 163 Main Street (802/862-5752).

Thanks to the many students and Vermonters' general love of live music, Burlington has some great nightclubs, ranging from the retro-Rat Pack ambience of **Nectar's**, 188 Main Street (802/658-4771), where the band Phish was born and bred, to the high-style art deco of the **Flynn Theater**, 153 Main Street (802/863-5966), across from City Hall, where bigger name bands perform.

Places to stay, alas, don't come particularly cheap, unless you opt for the dorm beds at the very friendly **Mrs. Farrell's HI Home Hostel**, 27 Arlington Court ($20; 802/865-3730), three miles northwest of town near the Ethan Allen Homestead. A couple of steps up is the **Burlington B&B** on the north side of downtown at 38 Converse Court ($50–80; 802/862-3646). There are also many $50-to-80-a-night roadside motels along US-7 south of downtown Burlington, including chains like Howard Johnson's and Travelodge, and locally owned ones like the **Town and Country Motel**, 490 Shelburne Road ($40-75; 802/862-5786).

For additional information on the Burlington area, contact the **visitors bureau**, 60 Main Street (802/863-3489).

CENTENNIAL FIELD: VERMONT EXPOS BASEBALL

The Vermont Expos mascot, Champ, was inspired by the Loch Ness Monster–like creature who is thought to live in the depths of Lake Champlain.

Tucked away in a residential neighborhood, just north of Burlington along Colchester Avenue, Winooski's historic Centennial Field is one of America's great old minor-league ballparks. The small green wood-and-concrete stadium, which opened in 1922, is home to the Class A **Vermont Expos** ($1–6; 802/655-6611), who play in the New York-Penn League against teams like the Pittsfield Astros and the Lowell Spinners. On a sunny summer Sunday afternoon, with the Green Mountains rising over the outfield fences, Centennial Field is a delightful spot to watch a game, whether or not you're a big fan of baseball. Between innings, local kids compete for silly prizes (rolling old tires through a slalom of plastic cones to win a free oil change, for example) and the team mascot Champ dances around trying to rouse the crowd. If nothing else, the price is right: standing-room-only tickets cost $1, which let you hang out along the left field line between the opposing team bullpen and the very popular beer tent (Long Trail Ale on tap!).

Games, which start Sundays at 5 PM and weekdays at 7 PM, are broadcast on **WKDR 1390AM**.

WINOOSKI

If you have a little time or an abiding interest in America's industrial heritage, get off I-89 at exit 15, or follow Riverside Street (old US-2) north from Burlington to the center of Winooski, an old mill town now focusing on the totally restored Champlain Mill, downtown at 1 Main Street. This former woolen mill now houses more than 20 cafes and specialty shops, including the **Book Rack** (802/655-0231), and the rest of town provides a blue-collar balance to Burlington's somewhat up-scale airs. The town green is marred by a bank and large parking lot, but the surrounding buildings hold some interesting spots, including **Sneakers Bistro**, 36 Main Street (802/655-9081), which serves great breakfasts and lunches. For burgers, beers, and Red Sox memorabilia, stop by **Champlains** next door.

Another popular spot for "homecooked food and friendly, upbeat service" is **Libby's Blue Line Diner** north of Winooski on Main Street in Colchester, just off I-89, exit 16 (802/655-0343). With the usual diner menu of breakfasts and burgers enhanced by the addition of grilled eggplant and fresh fish, it's a cut or two above average. The frequent lines out the door—especially on weekend mornings—are proof of this.

LAKE CHAMPLAIN ISLANDS

In its scenic jaunt toward New York and the Canadian border, US-2 winds north and west from Winooski across the sleepy Lake Champlain Islands. Pancake flat and covered with cows, orchards, and pick-your-own fruit farms, this trio of islands is beautiful to drive across, with the Adirondacks rising to the west and the Green Mountains to the south and east, but there's not a lot to do.

One of the more unlikely institutions located on the Lake Champlain Islands is the summer home of the world-famous **Royal Lippazaner Stallions** (802/372-5683), Austrian dressage horses that perform in an arena along US-7 near North Hero.

Just before US-2 leaves the mainland, you'll see **Sand Bar State Park** (802/241-3655) set in a forest with picnic tables and bathing beaches, surrounded by sprawling, wildfowl-rich marshes on either side. At the other side of a short causeway, South Hero is another quaint little place; it and North Hero were named after those famous Vermont Revolutionary War heroes, the Green Mountain Boys, Ira and Ethan Allen. Because it's the county seat, it looks big on the map, but tiny **North Hero** (pop. 502) is little more than a gas station, a stone courthouse, a number of quiet luxurious vacation homes dating from the early decades of the 20th century, and the very handy **Hero's Welcome**, a cafe and gift shop at the center of the two-block-long town. A mile south of North Hero along US-2, **Shore Acres Resort** ($80–125; 802/372-8722) offers tennis courts, boating and swimming, moderately priced lakeside rooms, and a restaurant famed for its chocolate pie, served at dinner only.

On US-2, in between the two Heros, the town of **Grand Isle** (pop. 1,642) ambitiously claims to be the Beauty Spot of Vermont. A well-marked turn east off US-2 leads to tiny **Grand Isle State Park** on the shores of the lake, where there's a nice campground. A mile north of the town of Grand Isle, along US-2 next to a school, the **Hyde Log Cabin** is considered by many to be the country's oldest log cabin, dating from 1783. The interior (Wed.–Sun. 11 AM–5 PM in July and Aug.; $1) contains period furnishings and exhibits on frontier life.

WHITE MOUNTAINS TO PLYMOUTH ROCK: US-3

WHITE MOUNTAINS TO PLYMOUTH ROCK: US-3

Running through some of the most stunning scenery in New England, US-3 is one of those older roads that keeps the pleasures of driving alive. Pretty much bypassed by the modern I-93 freeway, this road is definitely "less traveled by," to borrow a phrase from Robert Frost, who wrote much of his finest poetry within a stone's throw of US-3.

More than three-quarters of this route passes through New Hampshire, where it has long been known as the Daniel Webster Highway, after the state's favorite son.

In the early part of the 19th century, the far-northern fringe of New Hampshire was simultaneously claimed by Canada and the USA, leading to one of the odder examples of Yankee self-determinism. In 1832, a few dozen land speculators and local residents declared the region to be the independent Indian Stream Republic. They maintained their own separate legislature, currency, and court system until 1836, when the New Hampshire militia arrived to bring back them back into the fold.

In its long ride south from the Canadian border, US-3 makes a full survey of New England. Starting at the Connecticut Lakes, the semiwild headwaters of the Connecticut River, the road soon reaches Franconia Notch, where the famous stone-faced Old Man of the Mountain looks out over one of the region's quintessential views. Besides having some of New England's most breathtaking natural beauty and most intense fall color, this section of the road is also lined with engaging survivors of early American roadside tourism. At Clark's Trading Post, for instance, you can "See Live Bears," ride a steam train, and generally do all sorts of silly things against a backdrop of incredible mountain splendor.

South of here, at the heart of New Hampshire, is another feature-packed region. Dozens of gorgeous lakes range from absolutely idyllic (as at Squam Lake, where the movie *On Golden Pond* was filmed) to the funfair shores of Lake Winnepesaukee, lined by old resorts and more pinball machines than you could play in a lifetime of summer vacations.

Approaching the Massachusetts line, the character of US-3 changes yet again, as it runs along the historic Merrimack River through the state capital, Concord, and some of the largest mill towns in America, like Manchester and Nashua, both now better known for tax-free shopping than for producing very much. Across the Massachusetts line, the burly, multiethnic city of

Lowell was another important mill town, so important that its mills have been preserved as a national park. Lowell was also the birthplace of *On the Road* author Jack Kerouac, and its classic diners, lively baseball stadium, and sundry other attractions make it worth a stop. Another very different stop before US-3 reaches Boston is historic Concord, where the war for American independence first broke out in earnest.

South of Boston, US-3 changes its name to Route 3, and changes scene yet again, running along Cape Cod Bay near a series of lovely beaches, bound for that icon of America, Plymouth Rock.

THE CONNECTICUT LAKES

Equally popular with hunters, anglers, and autumn leaf-peepers, the narrow, northernmost neck of New Hampshire is known as the Connecticut Lakes region which holds the source of the Connecticut River. From the Canadian border, US-3 runs right past the Third, Second, and First Connecticut Lakes, which you can see behind the dense hardwood forests that border the roadway. (The actual headwaters of the Connecticut River are at Fourth Lake, over the Canadian border.) The three

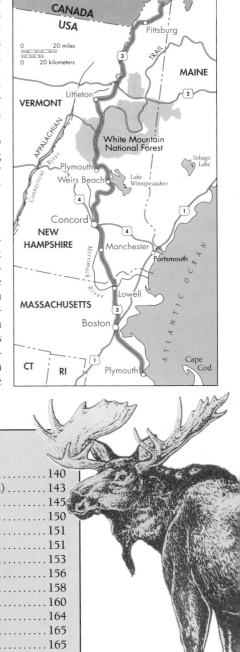

US-3 HIGHLIGHTS

North of the border, in the Quebec village of Chartierville, a much-discussed roadside phenomenon seems to make water (or your car!) roll uphill. A brown marker, about a mile and a half north of the border crossing, explains the mystery (but in French, so the phenomenon may remain a mystery to non-francophones).

If you're driving a Winnebago and want to be assured of the best of future good fortune, come to Colebrook in mid-September for the **Blessing of the RVs,** held at the Shrine of Our Lady of Grace along US-3 at the south edge of town. For the two-wheeler crowd, a similar service is held the weekend after Father's Day. Call 603/752-3142 for details.

Even rural New Hampshire catches voting fever during presidential primaries. Dixville locals are famous for casting their ballots just after midnight on election day, so they can be the first to announce results in what has traditionally been the first primary in the country.

lakes are all great for canoeing, bird-watching, and trout-fishing. Although most of the surrounding land is owned by timber companies, access by car or mountain bike to the many unpaved roads that head off into the nearby wilds is free and easy—just remember that logging trucks have the right of way.

At the southern end of the Connecticut Lakes, near Pittsburg, is Lake Francis, a man-made reservoir managed by the New England Power Company but open to boaters and sightseers as a state park. Rough-hewn **Pittsburg** (pop. 910), the state's northernmost town, was described in the 1930s WPA *Guide to New Hampshire* as "a frontier town of little pretense," and little has changed since then. This backwoods town is a *long* way from Boston (in fact, it's much closer to Montreal), and the few services cater more to anglers and snowmobilers than to casual visitors. Prices are generally low: hearty breakfasts and lunchtime soups and sandwiches at **Moriah's Restaurant** on Pittsburg's Main Street are a great deal, and the **Spruce Cone Cabins** (603/538-6361), overlooking Lake Francis, charge a bargain $50 a night.

South of Pittsburg, US-3 continues on its diagonal course, hitting the mutual border of New Hampshire, Vermont, and Quebec at Stewartstown. Across the river is Beecher Falls, Vermont, the birthplace of the Ethan Allen furniture company. From Stewartstown the road follows the ever-widening Connecticut River south to **Colebrook,** another North Woods mill town with a small but essential array of services.

ROUTE 26 DETOUR: DIXVILLE NOTCH

East of Colebrook, high up in the northern fringe of the White Mountains, Dixville Notch is a rugged, densely forested gorge far away from anything resembling civilization. Or so you might think, until you catch a glimpse of the magical-looking **Balsams Hotel** ($205–280; 603/255-3400 or 800/255-0600), which is a true oasis of style and comfort way out in the wilderness. Built just after the Civil War (at the same time as the more prominent Mount Washington Hotel), this grand, red-roofed palace is one of only two survivors from the early heyday of White Mountains

tourism. The utter luxury of the place, combined with unlimited golfing (in summer) and downhill or cross-country skiing (in winter, when you can also skate out onto lovely Lake Gloriette), helps it draw the upscale clientele who can afford the all-inclusive nightly rates. Mere mortals are also welcome to dine, drink, or quietly gape. All meals and activities (biking, golfing, swimming, nightly movies, etc.) are included in the rates.

East of the Balsams Hotel, Route 26 climbs up through the heart of Dixville Notch, the only east-west gap in the northern Appalachian chain. Best appreciated by scrambling up on to **Table Rock,** a short but steep quarter-mile climb up from Route 26 across from the Balsams, Dixville Notch is an 800-foot-deep gash barely wide enough for the roadway to squeeze through. If you continue east, Route 26 will bring you along the Clear Stream into the town of **Errol,** a hunting-fishing-rafting center on Route 16, which runs south near the Maine border, joining US-2 at Gorham.

STARK

Between Colebrook and Lancaster, paper mills and other industrial outposts detract a little from the roadside scenery, but there are still many highlights. From **North Stratford,** for instance, the bridge across the river to Bloomfield, Vermont, has a set of war memorials made of stacks of cannonballs. The main stop in these parts, however, is just east of the river, US-3, and the mill town environs of Groveton: the tiny hamlet of Stark (pop. 527). The town lies six miles east of US-3 by way of Route 110, an official Scenic and Cultural Byway that runs along the northern edge of the White Mountain National Forest. Stark is a photogenic little place, with a delicate covered bridge leading to a church, a schoolhouse, and a well-maintained green, all between the highway and the banks of the Upper Ammonoosuc River.

Across the river from the green, the **Stark Village B&B** (603/636-2644) welcomes weary travelers, and also hosts the annual **Stark Fiddlers' Contest** the last Sunday in June.

If want your drive to be accompanied by the finest in rowdy folk and rock music (Lucinda Williams, Neil Young, Phish, et al.), tune in to Littleton's "The Point," **WDOT 95.7 FM.**

Running parallel to US-3 across the Vermont border, scenic Route 102 winds along the Connecticut River. Along the way, there's the one-lane **Columbia Covered Bridge** between Route 102 in Leamington, Vermont, and US-3 in Columbia, New Hampshire. Further south, Route 102 passes through the Greek Revival heart of historic Guildhall, Vermont, just a few miles north of US-2.

Between Littleton and Twin Mountain on US-302, the **World's Largest 3/16 Scale Model Railroad That's On Public Exhibit** forms the centerpiece of the Crossroads of America (Tues.–Sun. 9 AM–6 PM in summer only; $4; 603/869-3919), in a private house two miles east of Bethlehem.

US-3 crosses US-2 at the historic town of Lancaster, which is described on page 122.

US-3 crosses US-2 at the historic town of Lancaster, which is described on page 122.

DETOUR: LITTLETON

Between Lancaster and Franconia Notch, US-3 takes a direct but rather uninteresting trip through Whitefield and Twin Mountain. If you have time, veer to the west along one of two more scenic roads, Route 136 along the Connecticut River, or Route 116, which winds along the Ammonoosuc River. Both roads bring you to a very enjoyable little New Hampshire town, Littleton, which retains its individuality despite sitting in the shadows of I-93.

Littleton (pop. 6,081) is a real throwback to the 1950s, with dime-an-hour parking meters on Main Street (US-302) and not a minimall to be seen. Littleton has one unique attraction: an exhibit focusing on the stereoscopic view card, the town's contribution to tourism. Once produced by the millions by Kilburn Brothers, a Littleton company, the cards can now be seen at the local historical society, itself housed in an historic **Opera House** at 1 Cottage Street. (For aficionados, the former Kilburn Brothers factory has been converted into an apartment building along US-302 just east of downtown.) Littleton has a classic diner— the **Littleton Diner** at 145 Main Street (6 AM–9 PM; 603/444-3994), serving breakfast all day, plus the usual diner staples like roast turkey dinners, in a lovely 1940 Sterling. (And no, the shingled mansard roof is not original.) Next to the diner stands a truly historic hotel, **Thayer's Inn,** 136 Main Street (rooms $40–75; 603/444-6469), which has been welcoming travelers since 1843. One room has been preserved in original condition, while the rest of them feel old and full of character, but they offer all the modern essentials (some share bathrooms). At the top of the hotel is a dainty cupola, offering a 360-degree view of the town and the nearby mountains.

FRANCONIA

Between Twin Mountain (at the junction of US-302 and US-3) and where US-3 merges with I-93, you'll find the aging face of the area's long association with tourism: a variety of motel courts and "housekeeping cottages" at least as old as you are. Despite their outward dowdiness, several make a virtue of the

rustic, but given their prime location most are hardly the bargains you might hope for, with rates running as high as $80 a night. More interesting and historic lodging may be had on a 200-acre working farm in Franconia (pop. 811), where since 1899 the friendly Sherburn family's **Pinestead Farm Lodge,** on Route 116 south of town, has offered simple rooms and warm hospitality at reasonable rates ($35–40 with shared bath and kitchen; 603/823-8121).

Dating back to the same era is **The Homestead** ($50–90 double; 800/823-5564), a country inn just west of Franconia on Route 117 in **Sugar Hill.** The township is aptly named: the sugarbush (a grove of sugar maples) on Hildex Maple Sugar Farm, also on Route 117, contributes its unforgettable essence to breakfasts at the very popular **Polly's Pancake Parlor.** Polly's is located in the farm's thrice-expanded 1830 carriage shed (open weekends only April to mid-May and late Oct., daily otherwise; 603/823-5575). Warning: after trying real maple syrup, you may never be able to go back to Aunt Jemima's or Mrs. Butterworth's again.

The most famous farm in the vicinity is certainly **The Frost Place** (Sat.–Sun. 1–5 PM Memorial Day–June, Wed.–Mon. 1–5 PM July–Columbus Day; $3; 603/823-5510) on Route 116 south of the Franconia village intersection. Besides the 1.5-mile Poetry Trail and the displays of Robert Frost memorabilia from his 11-year residency here, there's a regular program of readings by the current poet-in-residence.

FRANCONIA NOTCH

Franconia Notch is the tourist Grand Central of the White Mountains. I-93 offers easy access, and the Old Man of the Mountain, the state's mascot, is found here in the granite cliffs of the Notch. There are also a host of other attractions—an aerial tram, the state's own "little Grand Canyon," covered bridges, a powerful waterfall called the Flume, even a trading post with trained bears. The combined admission fees to these attractions will sorely test budgetary restraint, but if you include the time to hike around or sit still by a mountain stream you could easily spend a week or more enjoying it all. Weaving under the Interstate like the opposite strand of a DNA double helix is US-3, the old route through the Notch, lined with stores and motels whose tackiness belongs to such a bygone era, it's almost historic. Of course, nature upstages all the gift shops and water parks, and requires no admission fee.

The main draws in Franconia Notch start with the most famous: the **Old Man of the Mountain,** a series of five granite ledges, 1,200 feet above the valley, that viewed from certain angles seem to resemble an old man's profile. A series of pullouts signed as Old Man Viewing Area

NEW ENGLAND SKI MUSEUM

Franconia, New Hampshire

Cannon Mountain, site of the first aerial tram for skiers in the nation, is also home to the **New England Ski Museum** (daily noon–5 PM; free; 603/823-7177), which has a well-presented history of the sport plus an array of posters, ski fashions, and skiing videos. One of the original aerial tram cars has been preserved among the many attractions at Clark's Trading Post, near Lincoln at the south end of Franconia Notch.

For some reason (to aid unmarried couples traveling Dutch? a ploy to fool the computationally illiterate comparison shopper?), most lodgings in the White Mountains advertise rates on a per-person rather than per-room basis, even though the minimum rates are almost always for two people.

Take those moose-crossing signs seriously. Dozens of collisions occur annually, and you can bet your car won't fare too well if it hits an animal that weighs well over a half-ton.

lines I-93, with the clearest view available from above Profile Lake, near the trout-rich headwaters of the Pemigawasset River. If you're having trouble finding him, the Old Man is high up on a ridge, west of the highway.

The other well-known feature of Franconia Notch is at the south end, five miles south of the Old Man. **The Flume** is a granite gorge, 15 feet wide and nearly 100 high, carved by roaring waters. To get there, head to the large **visitor center** (603/745-8391), pay the admission fee ($8), and take a short bus ride to near the start of the wooden boardwalk, which runs the length of the 800-foot-long gorge and ends up at the ear-pounding rumble of Avalanche Falls.

Though less famous than the Old Man and the Flume, another favorite Franconia Notch stop sits in between the two: **The Basin,** where a lovely waterfall in the thundering Pemigawassett River has polished a 25-foot-round pothole. Thoreau visited it in the 1820s and thought it was remarkable; it's still a peaceful place to sit and picnic and be soothed by the natural white noise.

Cyclists will appreciate the nine-mile paved bike path through Franconia Notch, from just north of Cannon Mountain south to the Flume Visitor Center. Basically downhill all the way (north to south), the path is free of both pedestrians (the hiker's Pemi Trail is parallel but totally separate) and bladers (discouraged, as the grade has too many steep spots to be safe for most skaters). Check ahead for bike availability if staying at a local inn, or rent from the folks at the Cannon Mountain aerial tram (about $8 an hour or $25–29 a day, depending on style rented; rate includes helmet and lock). For **trail information** consult with the AMC staffer on duty at the Franconia Notch State Park's **Lafayette Campground,** near exit 2 of the Parkway; the campground has 97 sites (no RV hook-ups), showers, and a general store (mid-May to mid-Oct.; $14; 603/823-9513).

A short walk from the Lafayette Campground, the AMC operates the only indoor accommodations in Franconia Notch: the **Lonesome Lake Hut** ($65; 603/466-2727), a very popular, family-friendly octagonal bunkhouse located about a mile (and 1,200 vertical feet!) west of Lafayette Campground.

FRANCONIA RIDGE

If walking around the Flume or the Basin down in Franconia Notch has whetted your appetite for the great outdoors, you're in luck: some of the wildest and most breathtaking backcountry in New Hampshire rises east of I-93, along the knife-edge Franconia Ridge. From the parking area at Lafayette

THE BASIN, FRANCONIA NOTCH, WHITE MTS., N. H.

Aug. 19, 1921.

Campground, a paved connector heads under I-93 to the **Falling Waters Trail,** which heads fairly gradually uphill to the east, past a 40-foot waterfall, then gets increasingly steep as it climbs toward a junction with the hikers' famous Appalachian Trail, (or AT) Just over 3,000 feet above and three miles east of the start, the Falling Waters Trail reaches the AT atop 4,760-foot Little Haystack Mountain. From there the AT follows the narrow Franconia Ridge north for another mile, climbing up and over Mount Lincoln to the 5,249-foot summit of Mount Lafayette. This is a challenging climb for experienced hikers only, and the exposed ridge is definitely *not* a good place to be in anything approaching inclement weather (summer thunderstorms are a potentially fatal hazard). On a clear day, though, you'll be rewarded with truly breathtaking 100-mile views in all directions, which is why this stretch is regularly rated among the top sections of the entire 2,000-plus-mile Appalachian Trail system.

The Appalachian Trail crosses the Franconia Notch Parkway and Pemi Trail at Whitehouse Bridge, in between the Basin and the Flume.

Technically speaking, the six-mile stretch of I-93 that passes through the narrowest part of Franconia Notch isn't Interstate at all but the so-called Franconia Notch Parkway, finally completed in 1988, after years of squabbling. Although divided and with limited access, it's only a single lane in each direction, with a speed limit of 45 mph.

To park a car at any trailhead in the White Mountains National Forest, you'll need to buy a pass from one of the information centers; these passes cost about $5 and are good for seven days. You can also pay a $3 fee each time you park, or take a chance that no park ranger will come along and discover your disobedience. The fees all go toward the WMNF budget, not to some big national pool in D.C., and are used to help pay for local trail improvements, road maintenance, and other essential upkeep needed to deal with the 7 million people who come to the forest every year. Also note that because the wilderness is one big toilet for all creatures great and small, you'll need to purify any water that doesn't come out of a tap. Finally, dogs are not allowed on any of the 1,000-plus miles of trails within the WMNF. For additional information on anything to do with the WMNF, contact the main **ranger station** (603/528-8721).

On the shoulder of Mount Lafayette, 1,000 vertical feet from the summit, the AMC operates the summer-only **Greenleaf Hut,** where you can get hot food or a cool drink, or even stay the night. At peak times, make reservations (bunks and two meals cost about $65; 603/466-2727) as early as you can. To do the whole Franconia Ridge hike in a day, you may want to descend back to Franconia Notch via the steeper but quicker Old Bridle Path, which will return you to Lafayette Campground, giving good views of Cannon Mountain much of the way.

CLARK'S TRADING POST

Just south of Franconia Notch along US-3, a barrage of deliciously tacky tourist attractions and old-fashioned roadside Americana awaits you. Well-maintained 1930s motor courts line the highway. Try the very comfortable **Franconia Notch Motel** ($55–75; 603/745-2229), which has quaint cabins along the banks of the Pemigawasset River. (The beds have "Magic Fingers" massagers—25¢ for 15 blissful minutes!) Not far down the road is Clark's Trading Post (daily 10 AM–6 PM; $9, $3 under 5, free under 3; 603/745-8913), where you can enjoy a slice of good ol' cornpone kitsch. At Clark's, you can ride on a real old wood-burn-

ing railroad over an authentic 1904 covered bridge (and be chased all the way by a hairy, hilarious Wolfman); admire an immaculate 1931 LaSalle in a vintage gas station; tour a haunted mansion; take a wet ride on a bumper boat; or explore the endless cases of museum-quality stuff the Clark family has collected over the 75-odd years this roadside landmark has been in business here. Everything from board games and oil cans to historic photos and postcards fills display cases in every corner of the property, so there's never a dull moment. (They'd make a mint selling this stuff on eBay!)

For the past 50 or so years, the main draw at Clark's has been the chance, according to the sign, to See Live Bears. House-trained black bears perform a series of entertaining tricks—rolling barrels, shooting basketballs through hoops, and riding scooters—and they clearly seem to enjoy their work (not to mention the ice cream cones they're rewarded with). The trainers and caretakers crack jokes and make wry comments about "bear facts" and how the animals are "bearly" able to behave themselves, but they smile and beam every time the bears do what they're supposed to, giving the performances a feel more akin to a school play than to a professional circus. Many of the bears are born and reared here at Clark's, and although they're captive, they have a much longer life expectancy than wild bears. Across from the enclosure where they perform you can pay respects to the graves of favorite bears who've performed here over the years. Spend any time at Clark's and you'll begin to realize that the bears are regarded as family members (albeit seven-foot-tall, 500-pound family members).

Clark's has been in business since 1928, when it was known as Ed Clark's Eskimo Dog Ranch, and everything about it is very much a family affair. More than a dozen Clarks and close relatives work here throughout the summer, doing everything from training and caring for the bears to making milk shakes. The bear shows at Clark's Trading Post start every two hours or so (roughly at noon, 2, and 4 PM), and you could happily spend most of a day here, making it well worth the price of admission. If you're just racing through, be sure to at least visit the gift shop, which is stocked with all the wonderfully tacky stuff (wind-up toys, funky postcards, snow domes, and the like) retro-minded road-trippers drive miles to find.

LINCOLN AND NORTH WOODSTOCK

Three miles south of Franconia Notch, tiny North Woodstock (pop. 700) is a good example of what White Mountains towns used to look like before vacation condos popped up like prairie dog colonies; neighboring Lincoln (pop. 1,229) is the portrait of "after." North Woodstock is a handful of mostly unpretentious businesses at the junction of US-3 and Route 112, while Lincoln seems to be nothing but a strip of ski-clothing stores, malls, and motels east of I-93 at the base of the Loon Mountain ski resort. When Loon's condo-covered foothills fill to capacity during fall and winter holidays, the weekend population can mushroom more than twentyfold to more than 30,000.

As a rule, the Granite State isn't known for offering outstanding dining, and the Lincoln area is a typical example, with its choice of après-ski pub grub, local pizza-

and-grinder parlors (submarine sandwiches are called grinders in this state), and family dining on "Yankee soul food" like turkey, prime rib, and spaghetti with meatballs. Lincoln's **Country Mile** (closed Wed.) opposite the Millfront Marketplace serves a fine breakfast, with from-scratch pancakes and breads. **Peg's Restaurant,** on the main drag in North Woodstock, also offers a decent breakfast and lunch (daily 5:30

AM–4 PM; 603/745-2740), while **Frannie's Place** (603/745-6041), on US-3 seven miles south of Route 112, is worth a detour, particularly on nights when they feature the All-U-Can-Eat fish fry. Other dining options are easily found all along Route 112, from North Woodstock to the Loon Mountain base lodge.

Accommodations also line Route 112 (the western end of the scenic Kancamagus Highway) in Lincoln, and there are hundreds of rooms along US-3, just south of exit 1 off the I-93 Franconia Notch Parkway. The rates remind you that, fast food aside, the area is first and foremost a resort destination; even the oldest, most rustic motel courts charge around $50, and during the busiest holidays rates typically double. The **information center** next to the I-93 overpass on the west side of Lincoln offers plenty of brochures for area motels and B&Bs, and the chamber of commerce operates a free phone **reservation service** (800/227-4191).

On the west side of I-93, a mere half-mile from the resorty environs of Lincoln and Loon Mountain, North Woodstock is a friendly, undeveloped antidote to all that rampant tourism. Stretching along US-3, North Woodstock presents a kinder, gentler version of the White Mountains. The town features the ancient Fadden's General Store and a roadside trailer called **Theda's,** which sells freshly made hot dogs and grilled-cheese sandwiches. The **Woodstock Inn** ($60–100; 603/745-3951) is a handsomely restored historic lodge with a popular pub and dining room. North Woodstock also has one of the region's only year-round bargains (for singletons especially): **The Cascade Lodge** (603/745-2722). Next to the Woodstock Inn and resembling an old rooming house with its simple bedrooms and small shared baths down the hall, the Cascade becomes most like a hostel in summer when single thru-hikers coming down off the Appalachian Trail stop for a hot shower and dry bed. During the summer they're "stacked like cordwood" in the doubles and triples of the old house by the cheerful, chatty, and chain-smoking owner, Bill Robinson. Rates are about $20 a night per person.

If you spot some beefy guys in skirts heaving telephone poles around at the base of Loon Mountain, you've probably stumbled across Lincoln's annual **Highland Games,** held the third weekend of September. Fortunately, you don't have to toss a caber or know how to skirl to take part in the festivities. For information or advance tickets, call 800/227-4191.

In case you're wondering what North Woodstock is north of, there is a much smaller hamlet called Woodstock, little more than a collection of cabins, about three miles south of North Woodstock along US-3.

Diner fans will want to check out the **Sunny Day Diner** at the north edge of North Woodstock on US-3 (Wed.–Mon. 7 AM–2 PM; 603/745-4833), a stainless-steel Master diner that, as if to show off how far from a greasy spoon a diner can be, features a CIA-trained cook. (That's the Culinary Institute of America, not the other one.) Using its own homemade breads, the Sunny Day makes some fine french toast (including a deeply flavored banana variation that goes great with local maple syrup); it's also open for early dinners 5–8 PM Friday and Saturday. The Sunny Day, which is just south of Clark's Trading Post, moved here in 1987, after a long life as Stoney's Diner in Dover, New Hampshire.

And if you've gotten tired of all that sublime Mother Nature the White Mountains are famous for, North Woodstock also offers the high-octane thrills of the **White Mountains Motorsports Park** ($9), where at least five different classes of stock cars race around a half-mile, high-banked oval at 6 PM every Saturday night, all summer long. The track is at the south edge of North Woodstock, hidden away behind the US-3 frontage next to a gravel pit.

Lincoln sits at the west end of Route 112, the amazing Kancamagus Highway, which is described in full in the Appalachian Trail chapter on pages 274–308.

I-93 SURVIVAL GUIDE: ACROSS NEW ENGLAND

MM11: Junction with I-91 (north end of I-93).

MM8: Exit 1 junction with US-2 west to St. Johnsbury and east to Lancaster, New Hampshire (see page 122).

MM1: Vermont Welcome Center (northbound only).

MM131: Vermont/New Hampshire state line.

MM130: Exit 44, New Hampshire Welcome Center with scenic views of the nearby dam.

MM124: Exit 42 junction with US-302 to Littleton (see page 142).

MM121: Exit 41 junction with US-302 to Bethlehem.

MM115: Exit 37 junction with US-3 through Franconia (see page 142).

MM112: Boundary of Franconia Notch State Park, freeway slows to 45 mph and narrows to two lanes. (This is the only two-lane Interstate in the world. Wow!)

MM110: Old Man of the Mountain (scenic viewpoints), and Lafayette Campground (see pages 143–44).

MM107: The Basin (see page 144).

MM106: Exit for the Flume and US-3 southbound.

MM104: Boundary of Franconia Notch State Park.

MM102: Exit 33 for North Woodstock (see page 146).

MM101: Exit 32 junction with Route 112, east past Loon Mountain ski area to scenic Kancamagus Highway (see page 290).

MM95: Exit 30 to Woodstock, junction with US-3 and Route 112 west to Lost River Gorge (see page 293).

PLYMOUTH: POLAR CAVES PARK

One of the bigger towns in northern New Hampshire, Plymouth (pop. 5,800) is the southern gateway to Franconia Notch and home to the large campus of Plymouth State College. Just across the river from I-93, Plymouth is a fairly serene place, with an old-fashioned general store (**Louis Samaha's**, selling everything from sliced ham to harmonicas) and a movie theater with a 1950s marquee on the block-long Main Street. But it's best known for one of the most hyped tourist attractions in the state: Polar Caves Park (daily 9 AM–5 PM in summer only; $9.50; 603/536-1888). Five miles west of Plymouth via Route 25, this natural talus slope has long been one of New Hampshire's tackier tourist traps, offering visitors a chance to wander along a well-marked path through a series of

Plymouth has long been a popular tourist stop: the stately **Pemigawassett House** hotel was one of many identically named Plymouth Inns that catered to travelers during the heyday of railroad tourism. Writer Nathaniel Hawthorne (born 1806) was an early visitor, and died there on May 18, 1864.

MM81: Exit 25 to Plymouth and Polar Caves Park.

MM76: Exit 24 to Ashland, junction with US-3 (see page 151).

MM57: Exit 20 to Tilton, home of world-famous Tilt'n Diner and junction with US-3 north to Lake Winnipesaukee (see page 154).

MM49: Exit 18 east to Canterbury Shaker Village (see page 153).

MM46: Exit 17 to Boscawen, junction with US-3 and westbound US-4.

MM40: Exit 15 to downtown Concord (see page 154), junction with US-4 east to Portsmouth.

MM24: Exit 9 to Manchester (see page 155).

MM15: Exit 5 to Route 28 through Derry (see page 156).

MM1: Exit to Route 28 for America's Stonehenge and Canobie Lake Park (see page 156).

MM0.5 New Hampshire Welcome Center and State Liquor Store.

MMO/47: New Hampshire/Massachusetts state line.

MM40: Exit 44, junction with I-495 west to Lowell and Lawrence, east to I-95.

MM29: Exit 37, junction with I-95 and Route 128.

MM18.5: Exit 26 to Storrow Drive along the Charles River, access to Cambridge and downtown Boston.

MM18: Exit 24 to Logan Airport via Callahan Tunnel.

MM16: Exit 20 to I-90 (Massachusetts Turnpike or "Mass Pike").

MM12: Exit 12 to Route 3A to Quincy and Nantasket Beach (see page 165).

MM7: Exit 7 to US-3 toward Cape Cod.

MM0: Exit 1 for I-95 south toward Providence (see page 94).

cool caves formed by stacks of giant boulders deposited here by receding Ice Age glaciers. Since 1922, the natural oddity has been enhanced by a maze of wooden boardwalks that take away most of the sense of adventure, and if the caves begin to pall you can also tour a maple syrup museum or feed the deer or the ducks in the minizoo. There's a gift shop, too.

Back in Plymouth, there's a great place to eat, a block east of downtown toward I-93: the **Bridgeside Diner** (603/536-5560) on Route 175A just east of its namesake bridge over the Pemigawassett River. Open daily for breakfast and lunch, the Bridgeside is a very popular place, worth the occasional wait for its heapin' helpings of fried chicken, meatloaf, soups, and sandwiches. Thanks to I-93, Plymouth also has one of the biggest selections of motels in the region, mainly national chains (including a fairly reasonable **Best Western White Mountains**).

ROUTE 3A DETOUR: NEWFOUND LAKE TO FRANKLIN

Off Route 3A on the southeastern shore of Newfound Lake, Bridgewater is home to the landmark **Inn at Newfound Lake** ($80–120; 603/744-9111), a Victorian gem set on spacious lakefront grounds. This is also the place to take a relaxing ride on the *Moonlight Miss,* which offers hour-long cruises out onto the lake.

Whether or not you go to the Polar Caves Park, the drive along Route 3A south from there makes a much quieter alternative to US-3, which bends east through the popular Lake Winnipesaukee region. (In between Route 3A and US-3 runs the I-93 freeway.) Just five miles west of I-93, Route 3A is a world away, passing along the shores of Newfound Lake, fourth largest in the state and nestled in a ring of mountains. The present Route 3A runs along the lake's eastern shore, but the older and more interesting alignment follows the western shore, starting at the hamlet of **Hebron** (pop. 385), which has all you could ask of a New England village—an 1803 church with a steeple, a central green with dainty gazebo, a general store, and a handful of historic homes, all clad in gleaming white clapboard.

South from Hebron, the drive bends away from the privately owned lakeshore before reaching the water again at **Wellington State Park** ($2.50, day use only), where a half-mile of uncrowded sandy beach, backed by groves of pine

BIRTHPLACE OF DANIEL WEBSTER, BUILT 1780, FRANKLIN, N. H.

Near the crossroads town of Franklin, where Route 3A rejoins US-3 five miles west of I-93, the main event is the **Daniel Webster Birthplace State Historic Site,** the two-room cabin where Daniel Webster (1782–1852) was born and spent his first year.

trees, offers lovely sunset views over lofty Mount Cardigan.

From Wellington, the road winds slowly (30 mph max—lots of kids playing) along the lakeshore toward the quaint town of **Bristol** at the south end of the lake. Bristol has its own small beach (complete with Adirondack chairs), above which sits the friendly **Cliff Lodge** ($90–120; 603/744-8660), one of the few accommodation options for those unlucky enough *not* to have access to a vacation cabin here. Bristol also has the best food for miles; in the town center a mile or so south of the lake, you'll find the early-rising **Riverside Diner,** 9 S. Main Street (603/744-7877) behind the more elaborate **Peddler's Round,** 19 Central Square (603/744-5911).

ASHLAND, HOLDERNESS, AND SQUAM LAKE

In between famous Franconia Notch and wild Weirs Beach, US-3 passes through a quieter stretch of small towns and serene lakes. East of I-93, the first place you reach is sleepy Ashland, worth a stop for a pair of places to eat. Toward the upper end of the dining spectrum, the original **Common Man** on Main Street (603/968-7030) still serves its trademark New England specialties (like a roast duck with maple cider glaze); it also has live music on weekends. At the other extreme, the equally popular (and much more affordable) **Riverside Dairy Joy** on US-3 is a roadside stand (with picnic tables) serving fried chicken, fresh seafood, and ice cream.

From Ashland, US-3 bends north and east along the shores of Little Squam Lake, passing a pretty covered bridge that leads to the small but lovely **Ashland Town Beach,** where peak-season visitors are asked to pay a $3 parking fee. Further along, five miles from Ashland, you reach Holderness, where US-3 bends south again along gorgeous Big Squam Lake, the state's second-biggest inland body of water, best known as the location for the movie *On Golden Pond.* From a boat dock east of town, **Original Golden Pond Tours** (603/279-4405) will take you out on the water, pointing out locations from the film. In between Ashland and Holderness, the quaint lakeside cabins of **Little Holland Court** ($55–115; 603/968-4434) are a nice place to stay.

LAKE WINNIPESAUKEE: WEIRS BEACH AND MERIDETH

With a White Mountains backdrop and a 300-mile shoreline packed with beaches, vacation homes, and amusement arcades, Lake Winnipesaukee has long been one of New Hampshire's most popular getaways. There are towns and hamlets and tourist draws all around the lake, but if you want to have some fun in the sun, the biggest and best of all is **Weirs Beach,** along US-3 on the lake's western shore. The compact center of Weirs Beach stretches along a curving strand, south of an ancient-looking amusement pier. Vacation cabins climb the hill above the sands, and in between is a short but sweet barrage of fried dough stands, skeeball arcades, and—best of all—bumper cars, ideal for working off the road rage that can build up in Winnipesaukee's summertime traffic jams.

Discussing Lake Winnipesaukee, the 1930s WPA *Guide to New Hampshire* says that although there are 132 different spellings on record, the present spelling was established by an act of the New Hampshire legislature in 1932. According to some, the name means "Smile of the Great Spirit."

After dark, cruise along US-3 to yet another retro attraction in Weirs Beach: the **Weirs Drive-in** (603/366-4723), a very popular alfresco movie theater, right across from Endicott Park and that flashing Weirs Beach sign.

From the center of Weirs Beach, you can hop aboard the huge (1,200-person capacity) ship **Mount Washington** ($15; 888/843-6686) for a scenic tour of the lake, or take a ride on the historic **Winnipesaukee Railroad** ($7.50; 603/745-2135),

At the southern end of Weirs Beach, across from the neon Weirs Beach sign on the beach in Endicott Park, the 12- by 6-foot granite boulder known as **Endicott Rock** once marked the northern border of Massachusetts Bay Colony. In 1652 it was chiseled with the initials of Governor John Endicott and four surveyors.

On the east shore of Lake Winnipesaukee, the sedate town of Wolfeboro calls itself the oldest summer resort in America, because Governor Wentworth vacationed there in colonial times.

which heads north to the more serene lakefront town of Merideth, four miles from Weirs Beach along US-3. Along with a wealth of historic architecture, Merideth also has a great place to eat: **Hart's Turkey Dinners** (603/279-6212), a giant roadhouse along US-3 at the Route 104 junction, has been serving (you guessed it) delicious roast turkey for lunch and dinner since 1954. West of Merideth in the town of New Hampton, on Route 104 a mile east of I-93 exit 23, **Bobby's Girl Diner** (603/ 744-8112) was the last Worcester diner ever built (in 1957). The well-maintained original (now in use as the smoking section of a much larger restaurant) previously lived as Lloyd's Diner in John-

ston, Rhode Island, and later sat on blocks on Long Island before being moved here in 1994. Now it's a retro wonderland serving good food three meals a day, seven days a week (Mon.–Sat. 5 AM–9 PM, Sun. 6 AM–8 PM). If you order the lighter-than-air pancakes, be sure to pony up the $1 extra for pure maple syrup.

Places to stay along this part of Lake Winnipesaukee are plentiful but often very pricey in the peak summer season. The are lots of quaint old-fashioned cabins and motor courts, including the centrally located and characterful **Half Moon Motel and Cottages** ($60–90; 603/366-4494) and the more peaceful **Grand View Motel** ($55–80; 603/366-4973), off US-3 just north of the beach area. Probably the most down-to-earth place to settle down at is **Three Mile Island**; no, it's not the site of

the nation's nearest nuclear disaster but a very pleasant 43-acre island. Run by the Appalachian Mountain Club and open late June through August only, it offers about 40 very peaceful cabins with three full meals at reasonable rates (roughly $350 per person per week; 603/279-7626). A boat ($1.25) links the island with Merideth three times a day, so you can come and go (although most people stay put). There's no real beach, but canoes and kayaks can be rented for nominal fees ($2–5 a day), and it's a definite escape from the 9-to-5 grind. Reserve as soon as you can after April 1, or ask about cancellations or other openings.

LACONIA

Commercial center of the Lakes region, Laconia is not exactly quaint, but it's not all bad, either. It's a good place to pick up essential supplies (Wal-Mart and all the other usual offenders are here, in all their mega-mall glory). Laconia also merits a mention here because of the annual invasion of Harley-Davidson riders, who converge on Laconia's blue-collar bars during the mid-June **Loudon Classic** motorcycle races. The races, a.k.a. Speed Week or the Nationals, are held at the New Hampshire International Speedway, midway between Laconia and Concord on Route 106. In midwinter, a different sort of crowd shows up for Laconia's annual **dogsled races.** The dog races are said to be world-class; for dates and details, call the visitor bureau (603/524-5531) or the race organizers (603/524-3064).

East of Laconia, one of the few places where casual visitors can get access to the lakeshore is at **Ellacoya State Park** (603/293-7821) along Route 11 about five miles east from US-3. There's a nice beach and a pricey but very pleasant **campground** ($30 a night).

A half-dozen miles south of Laconia via Route 107, the small town of Gilmanton isn't just another Peyton Place, as the song "Harper Valley PTA" would have it. No, sir—this is the original Peyton Place, the admittedly fictional setting of the sexually explicit 1956 novel that became an instant bestseller (and later a movie and TV show) for Gilmanton writer Grace Metalious.

Besides the annual Speed Week motorcycle races in mid-June ($25–50; 603/783-4931), New Hampshire International Speedway 10 miles from Laconia or Concord along Route 106, also hosts a series of NASCAR and Winston Cup races, plus some low-key vintage car races in midsummer.

CANTERBURY SHAKER VILLAGE

For a soothing antidote to Laconia and the often-busy Lakes region, head south along Route 106 and detour west to the serenity of Canterbury Shaker Village (daily 10 AM–5 PM in summer, weekends only Oct., Nov., and Apr., closed in winter; $9; 603/783-9511). Although it's under a mile west of the throbbing engines racing around New Hampshire International Speedway, the 690-acre village feels untouched by internal combustion or most other features of the modern world. Many of the late-18th-century buildings still stand, some in original condition, such as the schoolhouse, where celibate Shakers taught local children; and the

1792 Meeting House, which now displays examples of Shaker products, from boxes and brooms to simple but refined furnishings. Other buildings have been quietly converted to house a gift shop selling high quality handicrafts and a very fine Shaker-style restaurant, **The Creamery** (lunch only, great pies!).

The blue-collar town of Tilton, on US-3 at I-93 exit 20 (the main gateway to Laconia and Lake Winnipesaukee), has a nice riverside park in its historic center. Out by the freeway there's the ever-popular, shocking-pink **Tilt'n Diner,** a 1950s O'Mahony with great food, real people, and a classic car cruise every summer Monday night.

Between Boscowen and Concord, US-3 doubles up with US-4, which runs east to Portsmouth and west toward the New York border. The US-4 route is covered in the next chapter.

CONCORD

Capital of New Hampshire since 1808, Concord (pop. 38,000) is a surprisingly small and manageable city. The main landmark here is the gold-domed **State House,** which is both the oldest state capitol still in regular use and home to the largest legisla-

ture in the nation—424 representatives. The State House is the visual and actual center of the city, standing off Main Street across Eagle Square. Nearby is Concord's main visitor attraction, the **Museum of New Hampshire History** (Mon.–Sat. 9:30 AM–5 PM, Sun. noon–5 PM; $5; 603/226-3189). Inside the museum, displays include everything from the Victorian paintings that helped make the White Mountains such a popular tourist destination, to an example of Concord's most significant product,

the **Concord Coach.** First made in 1827 by Abbot, Downing, and Company, the Concord stagecoaches were famed for their durability and quality craftsmanship. Wells Fargo and most other stage lines used these coaches, so today the Concord Coach is credited with helping open up the Wild West in the days before railroads and superhighways.

BEAR BROOK STATE PARK: THE MUSEUM OF FAMILY CAMPING

The drive into Concord from the north along US-3 takes you past some signature Granite State sights: the main state forest nursery, where tiny saplings line the highway; a trio of cemeteries, all crowded with granite monuments; a masonry supplier, with acres of granite and marble slabs; and finally a huge prison, with a small shop across the highway selling prisoner-made furniture and crafts.

It may not be everyone's idea of a perfect day out, but a quick detour east along Route 28 from US-3 between Concord and Manchester will take you up into the forests of Bear Brook State Park, where various small museums look into some unlikely corners of American life. The setting is peaceful and quiet, appropriately near the park campground, but the Museum of Family Camping (daily 10 AM–4 PM in summer only; donations; 603/239-4768) is much more than the name implies. Yes, there are lots of camp stoves, trailers, cots, and lanterns, some dating to the early years of the 19th century, but what's unexpected is

the detailed display tracing the history of the New Deal–era **Civilian Conservation Corps,** usually known as the CCC. The CCC put more than a half-million men to work planting trees and building parks, campgrounds, and trails during the Great Depression. The whole museum complex, which also includes a **Snowmobile Museum** and a nature center, is housed in one of the few CCC camps still standing, the Bear Brook Camp, which has been added to the National Register of Historic Places.

MANCHESTER

Like its English namesake, Manchester (pop. 99,000) was one of the most important mill towns of the 19th century, and the massive brick remnants of once-bustling factories still line the banks of the Merrimack River through the city. The most impressive of these is the old **Amoskeag Mills,** a mile-long battery of some 70 stalwart cotton mills on both banks of the river. The world's largest factory during its heyday, the Amoskeag Mills made Manchester into a company town, employing more than 15,000 people (including many French Canadians, who still make up a large portion of Manchester's population), before finally collapsing during the Great Depression. Some efforts have been made to convert the old buildings to more contemporary uses, but there's still a long way to go.

A cerebral and serene contrast to Manchester's mills and malls is the lovely **Currier Gallery of Art,** 201 Myrtle Way (Wed.–Mon. 11 AM–5 PM; $5, free on Sat. mornings; 603/669-6144), housed in a recently renovated 1929 Beaux Arts palace just east of the downtown business district. Like a mini Metropolitan Museum of Art, the Currier contains a little of everything, but rather than being divided up by schools and style, the works are mixed together in and around the museum galleries, much as they would be in a private home. The Currier Gallery also owns the **Zimmerman House,** a Usonian house designed by Frank Lloyd Wright in 1950 and unchanged in the years since. Open only to guided tours ($7), the house epitomizes the architect's efforts to design affordable, attractive, upper-middle-class houses that would enhance and interact with their natural settings. It's the only Wright house in New England open to the public, and it's full of original furnishings and other trademark touches.

Off I-93 near the US-4 junction, you'll see signs for the **Christa McAuliffe Planetarium,** built in memory of the Concord schoolteacher who died in the *Challenger* space shuttle disaster.

Trying to attract shoppers from Massachusetts to New Hampshire's sales-tax–free shops, the southern edge of Manchester, along I-93 especially, is packed with massive malls, including the Mall of New England.

While most of Manchester's mills are closed or used for other purposes, the Queen City is still home to at least one fabric-oriented company: Velcro, whose U.S. headquarters are here.

Amoskeag Mills

In between the mills of Manchester and Nashua, where US-3 rolls alongside the Merrimack River, the grounds of the massive Budweiser brewery hold a scene right out of their advertising: those proud-looking Clydesdale horses, trotting along through a picturesque hamlet. The famous white-footed horses have been raised and trained here since the 1930s, when the company bought its first team to celebrate the end of Prohibition. You can meet the horses, and sample the beer, if you take a free guided tour (Wed.–Sun. 10 AM–4 PM; 603/595-1202).

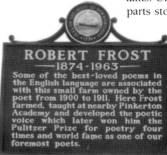

ROBERT FROST
— 1874-1963 —
Some of the best-loved poems in the English language are associated with this small farm owned by the poet from 1900 to 1911. Here Frost farmed, taught at nearby Pinkerton Academy and developed the poetic voice which later won him the Pulitzer Prize for poetry four times and world fame as one of our foremost poets.

Along Route 28 in North Salem, keep your eyes out for the 1940 Sterling diner known as the **28 Bar 'n' Grill,** 282 N. Broadway (daily 6 AM–2 PM; 603/898-2828). And if you follow Route 28 south into Massachusetts, there's another great old diner in the burly heart of Lawrence. A well-restored 1930s Worcester diner, brought back to its original condition after years of use and a 1999 fire, **Al's Diner** (978/687-9678) is alive and well at 297 S. Broadway.

Like Concord, Manchester is not really a destination in itself, but it does have one spot to draw any weary traveler in search of a good meal: the **Red Arrow Diner,** a brick-and-mortar diner with a great neon sign, a block east of Elm Street downtown at 61 Lowell Avenue (603/626-1118). Opened back when the Amoskeag Mills was still churning out bolts of cotton, the smokefree Red Arrow has been serving up hearty meals (and great pies) around the clock ever since.

ROUTE 28: DERRY AND SALEM

South from Manchester, US-3 continues along the banks of the Merrimack River, through the sprawling Boston suburb of Nashua and across the state line into Lowell, Massachusetts, another historic mill town. It's not a particularly pretty drive, and there's nothing much of interest to stop for. A much better option is to follow alongside the I-93 corridor on Route 28, one of the oldest main roads between Boston and the White Mountains. Unless your definition of scenic stretches to include auto parts stores, wrecking yards, and gas stations, it's not exactly a pretty drive, either, but if you look closely along the roadside, you'll find some truly neat places to visit.

First and foremost of these has to be the **Robert Frost Farm** (daily 9 AM–5 PM; $2) on Route 28 a mile and a half south of Derry. Restored by the state to its appearance between 1900 and 1911, when the poet lived and worked here as a young man, it's a wonderful change of pace from the hurly-burly of the highway. New England's most popular poet, Robert Frost (1874–1963) wrote many of his best-known poems while living here, farming and occasionally teaching at a school in Derry. His poem "Mending Wall," for example, explores the deeper significance of the mundane annual repair of the stone wall that runs along the south border of the property. You can walk along the very same wall if you take the pleasant, half-mile nature trail that circles round the farm, passing through the woods and along a colonial-era footpath before returning to the homestead. The barn behind the house has a small bookshop and a theater where a video on Frost's life and times, narrated in part by poet Seamus Heaney, is shown throughout the day.

Further south along Route 28 are a pair of more-hyped attractions. First and worst of these, about four miles by road from the Frost Farm, south of Route 111 two miles east of Route 28, is **America's Stonehenge.** It might be worthwhile if the proprietors (appropriately enough, the Stone family) had a better sense of humor. Instead, the eroded hilltop rocks are presented in a totally tendentious fashion, aimed at making you believe that maybe, just maybe, some adventurous

THE ROAD LESS TRAVELED

Robert Frost is celebrated as New England's favorite poet. In fact, his line about the road less traveled has been adopted as the slogan for New Hampshire's tourism promotion efforts. However, while his roots here run deep, he was actually born in San Francisco. While living on a farm outside Derry, New Hampshire, Frost wrote some of his first and most enduring poems, including "Mending Wall" and "The Wood Pile." Frost had his first success while living in England in the years before World War I, when at age 40 he found an unlikely admirer in imagist poet Ezra Pound. Frost's first books, *A Boy's Will* and *North of Boston,* were published in London in 1913 and 1914, respectively, then he returned to New England to become, in his own words, "Yankier and Yankier." Two years after giving a memorable reading at John F. Kennedy's inauguration, Frost died and was buried in Bennington, Vermont.

Here is one of many memorable poems:

The Road Not Taken

Two roads diverged in a yellow wood,
And sorry I could not travel both
And be one traveler, long I stood
And looked down one as far as I could
To where it bent in the undergrowth;

Then took the other, as just as fair,
And having perhaps the better claim,
Because it was grassy and wanted wear;
Though as for that the passing there
Had worn them really about the same,

And both that morning equally lay
In leaves no step had trodden black.
Oh, I kept the first for another day!
Yet knowing how way leads on to way,
I doubted if I should ever come back.

I shall be telling this with a sigh
Somewhere ages and ages hence:
Two roads diverged in a wood, and I—
I took the one less traveled by,
And that has made all the difference.

Celts came across the ocean and built an astronomical observatory here some 4,000 years ago. If only Leonard Nimoy had narrated the video, it might be OK; as it is, save your money.

Much more fun, west of Route 28 on the outskirts of Salem, **Canobie Lake Park** (daily noon–10 PM in summer, weekends only in spring and fall; $19 adults, $12 kids; 603/893-3506) is a cheery, old-fashioned amusement park, with a big Ferris wheel, a Victorian merry-go-round, Dodge 'Em bumper cars, lots of arcade games, plus a few modern thrill rides (including a flume ride called The Boston Tea Party). Open since 1902, when intercity electric trolleys came here from all over southern New England, Canobie Lake Park has a nice setting on Canobie Lake and that always-welcome rarity, free parking.

LOWELL

Lowell, Massachusetts, America's first planned industrial city, saw its best days over a century ago, and it's those days people have spent millions of dollars trying to recapture. Most of the money has been spent by and for the fairly new **Lowell National Historical Park,** (978/970-5000), keepers of the redbrick remains of Lowell's massive textile mills. The park service runs a **visitor center** at 246 Market Street Street (daily 8:30 AM–5 PM; free; 978/970-5000), across from the photogenic neon mule of Haffner's gas station (illustrating the slogan, It Kicks!). However, the focus of the park is the **Boott Cotton Mill** ($4), towering over town at

Lowell is the birthplace of not only Jack Kerouac but also screen actress Bette Davis and Victorian painter James Abbott McNeil Whistler. **Whistler's birthplace** is preserved as a museum at 243 Worthen Street (Wed.– Sat. 11 AM–4 PM, Sun. 1–4 PM; $3; 978/452-7641), a block from the Lowell National Historical Park visitor center.

If you're here in summer and want to get a feel for life in Lowell, check out a Class A baseball game at modern LeLacheur Park along the Merrimack River, where the Red Sox–affiliated **Lowell Spinners** (978/459-2255) play July through September. Home and away games are broadcast on **WCCM 800AM.**

the foot of John Street, between the Merrimack River and a section of the canal network that diverted water from Pawtucket Falls to power Lowell's machines. This mill and most of the rest of surviving Lowell date not from Lowell's earliest, most interesting days in the 1830s—when thousands of young women, going to work for the first time outside the home, were proud to call themselves "mill girls"—but from the late 1920s, when Lowell's largely immigrant workforce suffered long hours for low pay. The city's era of industrial success was cut short by the onset of the Great Depression.

Lowell is a very confusing place to drive, so park your car near the national park visitor center and walk or ride on one of the reproduction 1901 **electric trolleys** ($4) to explore the city.

Club Diner (978/452-1679) on Dutton Street and the **Paradise Diner** on Bridge Street, are very near the main historic mills. The best is a bit further afield: the **Four Sisters Owl Diner,** at 244 Appleton Street (daily 6 AM–2 PM; 978/453-8321). Once you get inside, the ambiance is perfect, as is the food.

JACK KEROUAC

At "five o'clock of a red-all-over suppertime" on March 12, 1922, Jack Kerouac (baptized John L. [Jean-Louis] Kerouac by his French Canadian parents) was born in Lowell, a city sincerely regarded as one of the wonders of the world back when the Industrial Revolution was as fascinating as the Internet is now. Although this original dharma bum is more widely remembered for hanging out with Ferlinghetti in San Francisco and with Ginsberg in New York, and for pasting the beat generation firmly across the map of American culture, Kerouac also wrote five novels based on friends and familiar places in his native city. His fictional work, from *On the Road* on, is that much more interesting when read in the context of his real life, here, along the Merrimack River.

Reciprocating Kerouac's lifelong love for Lowell, the National Park Service publishes a walking-tour brochure on Jack and his life in Lowell. They also help sponsor the annual **Lowell Celebrates Kerouac!** festival the first full weekend in October. Maps and guides to the man and the town are available from the **visitor center,** 246 Market Street (daily 8:30 AM–5 PM; free; 978/970-5000).

If you want to pay your respects to Kerouac, who died in Florida in 1969, he is buried in Edsom Cemetery, two miles south of downtown Lowell via Gorham Street. Fans by the hundreds beat a path to his grave, which is on Lincoln Avenue between 7th and 8th Streets, marked by a pile of beer cans and other ritual offerings.

CONCORD: THE SHOT HEARD ROUND THE WORLD

US-3 south of Lowell has either been turned into freeway or absorbed entirely by I-95 and its siblings, but there are a few things in the neighborhood you may want to check out if you're not in a hurry to hit Boston. A good example is lovely little Concord, the destination of British Redcoats that fabled day in April 1775, when the war for American independence began. A reconstructed **Old North Bridge**, site of the "shot heard round the world," still arches over the placid Concord River next to open fields and drystone walls. The superb setting draws artists and picnickers as well as history buffs, and if the crowds aren't too bad the scene ranks among the most evocative in New England. The **Minute Man National Historical Park** maintains a free year-round visitor center (978/369-6993) on the hillside overlooking the famous battlefield. Stop in and pick up a guide to the rest of the park's

PATRIOTS AND POETS

One of the more enjoyable rites of spring in and around Boston is the annual celebration of the events leading up to the American Revolution. Now held on the third Monday in April, but originally occurring on April 18, the state holiday known as **Patriot's Day** sees all kinds of special events. Most famous is the Boston Marathon, which since 1897 has been run from Hopkinton southwest of the city through Newton to its finish at Copley Square. Although the marathon follows a very different route, it is held on the anniversary of another famous race, the one between British soldiers and patriot Paul Revere, who made his legendary ride on the night of April 18, 1775, to warn his fellow minutemen of the British march on Lexington and Concord. In the words of poet Henry Wadsworth Longfellow, whose poem "The Midnight Ride of Paul Revere" used to be force-fed to all American school kids, here's an account of that night.

*Listen my children and you shall hear
Of the midnight ride of Paul Revere,
On the eighteenth of April, in Seventy-five;
Hardly a man is now alive
Who remembers that famous day and year.*

*He said to his friend, "If the British march
By land or sea from the town to-night,
Hang a lantern aloft in the belfry arch
Of the North Church tower as a signal light,—
One if by land, and two if by sea;
And I on the opposite shore will be,
Ready to ride and spread the alarm
Through every Middlesex village and farm,
For the country folk to be up and to arm."*

Concord, Mass., Minute Man Statue

holdings along the "Battle Road" (a.k.a. Lexington Road and Route 2A) between Concord and Lexington.

Although it often seems as if you can't toss a stick anywhere in eastern Massachusetts without hitting something of historic significance, this is especially true in Concord, where some of the most influential American writers—Ralph Waldo Emerson, Nathaniel Hawthorne, Henry David Thoreau, Louisa May Alcott, to name the most famous four—either lived and/or worked. To get a sense of the lives of these influential and interconnected writers, head to that ancient-looking parsonage alongside the famous Old North Bridge, **The Old Manse** (daily 10 AM–5 PM, April–Oct.; $5.50; 978/369-3909), whose study-window views are not so very different as they were when Ralph Waldo Emerson and Nathaniel Hawthorne lived here. And if the mood strikes you, you can visit the final resting place of these

the reconstructed Old North Bridge

At the end of his ride, on the morning of April 19, Paul Revere reached the Buckman Tavern in Lexington, where fellow revolutionaries John Hancock and Samuel Adams (he of boutique beer fame) were asleep, awaiting word of the British advance. Revere woke them (and some 70 others), and at 5:30 AM they assembled to meet the Redcoats. Although the minutemen backed off, shots were fired and eight Americans were killed. Three hours later, when the British moved on to Concord, they were met by a much larger and better organized force of minutemen, who fired back and started what we now know as the Revolutionary War. This battle, which raged all day and followed the overwhelmed British all the way back to Boston, was remembered in another oft-recited patriotic poem, by Concord writer Ralph Waldo Emerson, words from which are inscribed on the base of Concord's minuteman statue.

By the rude bridge that arched the flood,
Their flag to April's breeze unfurled,
Here once the embattled farmers stood,
And fired the shot heard round the world.

These events and many related ones are all reenacted each year, either on their actual anniversary or on Patriot's Day, and usually at the historically accurate crack of dawn.

Henry Wadsworth Longfellow

Not far from Thoreau's reconstructed cabin at Walden Pond, a very different philosophy of simplicity may be found in the design of the **Gropius House,** on Baker Bridge Road in Lincoln. Built between 1937 and 1938 by and for Bauhaus founder Walter Gropius at the start of his tenure at Harvard University, this small showcase blends Bauhaus form-is-function precepts with traditional New England simplicity. Extremely knowledgeable guides give hourly **tours** (Fri.–Sun. noon–4 PM in summer; $5; 781/259-8098).

Perhaps you haven't got a week—like Thoreau did—to row down the Concord River. You can still make your own, albeit abbreviated, journey with a summer or fall canoe rental from **South Bridge Boat House,** 496–502 Main Street in Concord (978/369-9438).

literary lions along Author's Ridge in **Sleepy Hollow Cemetery,** off Bedford Street northeast of the town center.

Visitors may be struck by the quantity of No Parking signs lining the streets of Concord, but the reason for this barrage of apparent inhospitality may be seen on any sun-drenched summer weekend, when long columns of cars bound for the beach at nearby **Walden Pond** jam the streets. Serious fans of Henry David Thoreau and his little experiment of simple living may be able to overlook its overstressed condition, but more than likely you'll be taken aback by the erosion, the kamikaze mountain bikers, the crowds, and the racket of passing commuter trains. Of course, there is still some magic to the place, although it usually takes a near-dawn in late spring or near-dusk in late fall to find any hint of transcendence along the pond's well-worn peripheral path.

For a quick introduction to all this and more, stop by the **Concord Museum** (daily 9 AM–5 PM; $6; 978/369-9763), just east of the town green, where the collection contains everything from the lantern used in Paul Revere's famous ride to dozens of household objects (beds, chairs, desks, etc.) belonging to Emerson and Thoreau.

CONCORD PRACTICALITIES

If you want to linger in Concord long enough to have some transcendent moments of your own, stay the night at one of many nice B&Bs like the **Hawthorne Inn,** 462 Lexington Road ($160–220; 978/369-5610) across from Hawthorne's home, the Wayside.

For more information about the Concord area, contact the historic Wright Tavern **visitor center,** 2 Lexington Road (978/369-3120), by the east end of the town common.

CAMBRIDGE

One last stop before you hit Boston proper is erudite Cambridge (pop. 95,802), an inseparable sibling to the big city but very much a place in its own right. Best known for its top colleges, Harvard and Massachusetts Institute of Technology, Cambridge is very much what Berkeley, California, is to San Francisco: a liberal-minded, earthy, and open-minded foil to the big money and social pretension that so often characterizes its big brother across the water.

The two colleges and their many fine museums (especially Harvard, which boasts world-class collections in the Fogg Art Museum, the Sackler Gallery of Far Eastern Art, and the Peabody Museum of Archaeology) are the main draws for visi-

tors, but the "town" away from the "gown" is equally worth exploring, despite the recent outbreak of chain-store disease around Harvard Square. For an antidote, head two stops north on the T subway to Davis Square in neighboring Somerville, where a classic 1940s Worcester diner, **The Rosebud,** off Elm Street at 381 Summer Street

CAR TALK

Ever tuned in to your local national public radio station and instead of hearing breaking news and informed commentary, you got two guys laughing their heads off and making jokes about cars and mechanics? Well, you probably tuned in to Car Talk, the Cambridge-based call-in show featuring a pair of MIT-trained auto mechanics, Click and Clack, the Tappet Brothers, otherwise known as Tom and Ray Magliozzi. From its humble beginnings back around 1977, Car Talk has become the most popular program at the left edge of the radio dial, reaching more than 2 million listeners every week. In between bouts of sarcasm and scandal-mongering, Tom and Ray do actually give advice about cars—advice that occasionally helps people—so if you're having trouble with your car, give them a call at 1-888-CAR-TALK, or send a message through their website, www.cartalk.car.com. Either way, it's free. And you're safe from the public humiliation for a while at least. The show is not broadcast live but cunningly edited together in a darkened room off Harvard Square (look for a sign saying Dewey, Cheatham and Howe), with the help of sophisticated technology and an ever-expanding team of contributors with names like Zbigniew Chrysler, Orson Buggy, Rusty Steele, Denton Fender, Alan Greasepan, and Francis Ford Cupholda.

If you're in Cambridge ("Our Fair City") and happen to need some car repair, Car Talk's Ray Magliozzi runs the **Good News Garage,** 75 Hamilton Street (617/354-5383), off Brookline Street midway between Central Square and the BU Bridge over the Charles River.

(617/666-6015), serves up the highest quality breakfasts and lunches (cash only), with nary a Starbucks in sight. With all the college-age kids in town, it's no surprise that Cambridge also has a lively live-music scene; check out the **Middle East Club,** 472 Massachusetts Avenue (617/864-EAST), which gets the best local and national indie bands.

Harvard University

DRIVING ACROSS BOSTON

From Concord, the remaining dozen miles to Boston are most quickly devoured along US-2, although you can take slower Route 2A if you wish to follow the footsteps of those retreating British Redcoats. Either way will bring you to the same gateway for the metropolitan area. Following US-3 will bring you in through wealthy Winchester and eventually onto Memorial Drive along the Charles River, past the campuses of Harvard and MIT. But unless it's 3 AM and the roads are all clear, you would be well advised to leave your car in the gigantic Alewife T subway station commuter parking garage (about $8 a day) at the US-2/US-3/Route 16 junction in Arlington, and use the subway to get around the city. (Cyclists note: from the Alewife T, the very nice **Minuteman Bikeway** follows the bed of the old Boston & Lowell Railroad between Cambridge and the edge of Concord, for 11 idyllic, car-free miles.)

Driving directions across downtown Boston are basically a waste of paper, since signs are few and traffic is chaotic—especially with all the Big Dig construction—so you'll need to keep your eyes firmly on the road. But if you fear getting lost, head for I-93 and follow that unfortunate freeway south out of town, turning onto Route 3A to continue our road trip tour.

The sights and sounds of Boston are covered in the Boston Survival Guide on pages 89–90, as part of our US-1 road trip tour.

QUINCY: THE ADAMS FAMILY

South of Boston, Route 3 reemerges from the I-93 freeway at Quincy (pop. 84,985), home of the Adams family, the political dynasty that helped shape the early republic. John Adams (1735–1826) signed the Declaration of Independence, served as a diplomat during the Revolutionary War, helped negotiate the Treaty of Paris, then returned home to become George Washington's vice president and successor. His son, John Quincy Adams (1767–1848), served as president from 1825 to 1829. Rather than quit politics after losing the election in 1828, he returned to Washington, serving in the House of Representatives for the next 16 years. The rather modest houses where both men were born, plus a nice garden and a historic church, are preserved as part of the **Adams National Historic Site,** which covers 13 downtown acres starting at a visitor center at 1250 Hancock Street (daily 9 AM–5 PM; $2; 617/770-1175).

More recently, Quincy has been home to granite quarries and the truly huge Fore River Shipyard, on Route 3A at the south edge of town, where the massive battleship **USS Salem** (Mon.–Sat. 10 AM–4 PM; $6; 617/479-7900) is berthed as part of a nascent shipbuilding museum. This dense forest of cranes,

---

If you happen to be around Boston before Christmas rather than in mid-April, you may want to take part in another historical reenactment: the **Boston Tea Party.** Every year, on the Sunday nearest to the anniversary of the original event (December 16, 1773), volunteers dress up as Indians (mimicking the colonists who disguised themselves as Native Americans) and throw bales of tea into the harbor from the decks of the Boston Tea Party Ship (617/338-1773).

The roadside scene along Route 3 south of Boston includes the **World's Largest Padlock,** hanging from the side of a storage center along Route 3/I-93 near the John F. Kennedy Library.

If you manage to avoid rush hour, the drive along Route 3A through Quincy can be surprisingly scenic. The road winds along the bay past Wollaston Beach, where a three mile strand offers few waves but plenty of lifeguards. There are views of the offshore islands, and good food can be found at **Tony's Clam Shop,** at the south end of the beach.

Although the South Shore region from Quincy to Plymouth looks rather suburban and spread out, it is very densely populated (or "thickly settled" as the road signs say). This accounts for the horrific rush hour traffic, as too many people try to drive to and from work in Boston.

derricks, and scaffolding rises along the south side of the 1930s Fore River Bridge, along Route 3A at the south edge of town.

Paragon Park,
Nantasket Beach, Mass.

NANTASKET BEACH

Due east and across the water from Quincy, Nantasket Beach is a long, thin strand that juts north into Massachusetts Bay. Twenty miles by road from Boston (but less than three miles by boat), and reached from Route 3 or Route 3A along Route 228, Nantasket Beach is both enormously popular and seemingly forgotten. Lined with old-fashioned amusement arcades, a 1920s carousel, and some old-fashioned beach pavilions where free concerts and senior-citizen dance lessons are held, Nantasket draws thousands of people on hot summer weekends. However, it's big enough to hold them all with sand to spare. If you just want to relax in the sun rather than sit in traffic trying to get to Cape Cod, Nantasket is a better (and much cheaper) bet. Beach parking is a bargain $3, and the five miles of sandy ocean beach means you won't have to fight for space.

At the northern tip of Route 228, the peninsula ends up at hilly **Hull,** a residential community of low-rise businesses and 100-year-old houses where you can see the Boston skyline yet feel light years away from the hustle and bustle of the city. Where the road dead-ends in the bay you'll find **Pemberton Bait and Tackle** (617/925-0239), which has a snack bar and boat rental. It's an ideal spot to start some on-the-water exploration.

South of Nantasket Beach, Route 3A winds inland from the shore, running through some fairly upscale suburbs, almost all of which (like Scituate and Marshfield) have their own beaches.

PLYMOUTH:
CRANBERRY WORLD

Whether or not the Pilgrims ever set foot on Plymouth Rock, one thing is for sure: at the first Thanksgiving, they ate cranberries. This is one of many lessons you'll learn if you visit Plymouth's second-biggest attraction, **Cranberry World,** just off the harbor at 158 Water Street (daily 9 AM–5 PM; free; 508/747-2350). Run by cranberry-producer Ocean Spray as part of its unceasing promotional efforts, the museum also has cooking demos all day long, and displays include a scale model of a cranberry bog and some old harvesting rakes. The gift shop is great, too; where else can you pick up those ever-essential cranberry-colored Frisbees and yo-yos? Cranberry World is located east of Route 3A, a half-mile north of Plymouth Rock.

All around Plymouth County and Cape Cod, low-lying square plots of land are filled with short, dark-leafed shrubs and divided by narrow irrigation channels. These are cranberry bogs. The bogs are best seen during the October harvest, when cranberries carpet the flooded fields.

Across the road from Cranberry World, a small factory store sells the products of another American consumer icon, **Pepperidge Farm.** The shelves are stacked high with yummy cookies and Goldfish crackers.

PLYMOUTH ROCK AND PLIMOUTH PLANTATION

What witches and the witch trials are to Salem at the north end of Massachusetts Bay, the Pilgrims and their tribulations are to Plymouth (pop. 45,600). This historic spot, where Boston Harbor merges into Cape Cod Bay, is among the more rhapsodized and memorialized in America, and at least a quick visit is all but essential to any full New England tour. The main pilgrimage point has to be Plymouth Rock, the supposed landing site of those weary *Mayflower* passengers back in 1620. There's little evidence to back up the choice of this particular rock as *the* place, but like the Liberty Bell and Mount Rushmore, it's something every red-blooded American tourist has to see.

Now protected by a neoclassical granite portico and inscribed with the date 1620, Plymouth Rock is right on the waterfront, off Water Street at the south end of North Street. The rock is part of a pleasant park, which also includes the ***Mayflower II,*** a replica of the Pilgrim's ship (daily 9 AM–5 PM; $6.50), where an on-board exhibit describes the Pilgrims' two-month transatlantic journey. On a hill across the street from Plymouth Rock is the **Plymouth National Wax Museum** (daily 9 AM–9 PM in summer, until 5 PM rest of year; $6; 508/746-6468), where the light-and-sound show depicting the landing at Plymouth Rock is *almost* worth the price of admission. The wax museum

Although the Pilgrims are often given credit for establishing the first permanent white settlement in what later became the United States, they arrived a dozen years after other English settlers established Jamestown, Virginia. (In fact, the Pilgrims themselves had wanted to go to Virginia as well, but they ended up in Massachusetts only because they were blown off course.) And of course, when the *Mayflower* landed, the native Wampanoag people had already been here for thousands of years.

PLYMOUTH ROCK. PLYMOUTH, MASS.

Plimoth Plantation

is the only sign of Plymouth being such a potential tourist trap; the whole place is actually fairly low-key, with a couple of gift shops and snack bars across from the Rock. Two blocks inland, downtown Plymouth looks like any other very pleasant New England suburb, with no tacky T-shirt shops to be found.

Further south, two miles from Plymouth Rock along Route 3A, or off the Route 3 freeway at exit 5, Plimoth Plantation (daily 9 AM–5 PM; $16; 508/746-1622) is a living history re-creation of the original Pilgrim colony and features costumed interpreters taking part in planting, harvesting, and other daily chores.

Playing on the common perception of the Pilgrims as thrifty, reliable and steadfast, the automobile company Chrysler named its new line of low-priced cars "Plymouth" In 1928.

From Plymouth Rock, it's only about 15 miles to Cape Cod. If you want to tour the cape and maybe see where the Pilgrims *really* landed (at Provincetown, the far tip of Cape Cod), have a look at our road-trip tour along US-6, which begins on page 220.

OCEAN, LAKES, AND MOUNTAINS: US-4

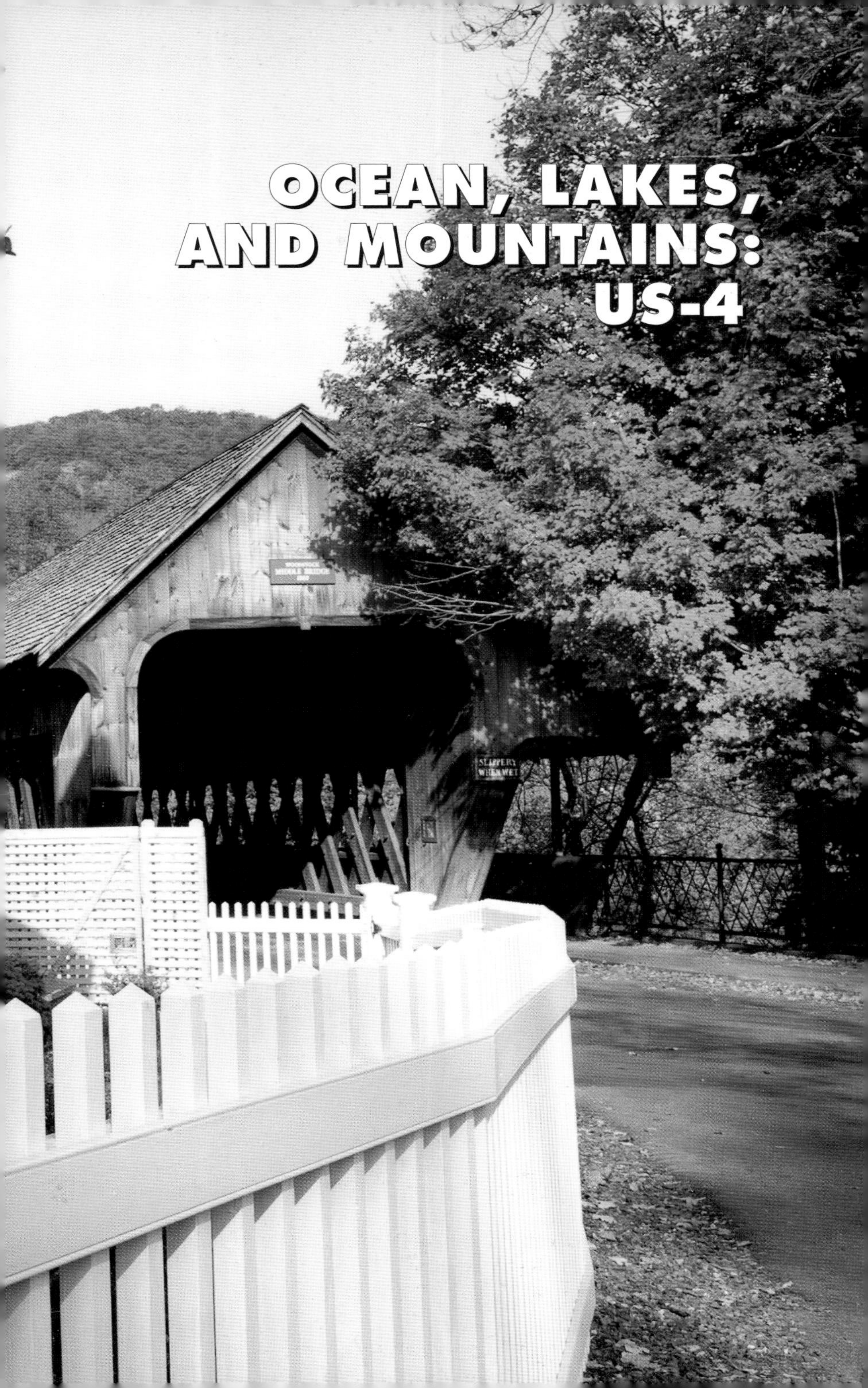

OCEAN, LAKES, AND MOUNTAINS: US-4

Starting along the New Hampshire coast at the old town of Portsmouth, US-4 winds inland across the heart of New England, passing by idyllic lakefront resorts, across majestic mountains, and through dense hardwood forests. Its first leg, from the coast to New Hampshire's capital, Concord, is one of the oldest roads in the region; during the colonial period, this stretch of road connected Portsmouth, one of the colonies' busiest maritime ports with the state's political center further inland. Now it's a quiet drive, passing through small rural towns like Durham, home of the main University of New Hampshire campus.

"Live Free or Die" is the feisty motto of tiny New Hampshire, the state that hits the national limelight every four years when its political primaries launch the horse race for the White House. During the campaign's opening stretch, with photo ops on their minds, presidential candidates occupy all of the best seats at New Hampshire's many great diners, and locals have to run for cover to avoid having their votes solicited by every candidate and their opinions polled by every reporter. And it's not so hard to escape the madding crowd in New Hampshire's rugged landscape. Veering north from Concord, US-4 passes by the lovely waterfront resorts of Lake Sunapee, as well as Enfield, one of the larger Shaker village communities, now converted into a luxury resort. West of here, the road drops down into the valley of the Connecticut River, nipping past the Dartmouth College town of Hanover before entering Vermont.

The drive across Vermont on US-4 offers a pretty complete portrait of the Green Mountain State, starting off at the burly old railroad town of White River Junction, and then following that river up into the mountains to the tony resort of Woodstock, vacation home of the Rockefeller clan and many other moneyed New Yorkers. Quaint beyond measure, Woodstock is also a good staging area for tours of the surrounding mountains. Take one of the many country roads that run off from US-4, or

If you want to start or finish your trans–New England US-4 tour as close to the Atlantic as you can, head east from Portsmouth proper, taking Route 1B on a loop through the upscale island environs of New Castle, first settled back in 1623. Follow the road out to oceanfront **Fort Constitution,** previously known as colonial-era Fort William and Mary, which was the site of one of the first uprisings of the American Revolution. Along the way, keep an eye out for the shell of the stately old **Wentworth-by-the-Sea** hotel, now surrounded by chain-link fences and stranded amid country-club estates.

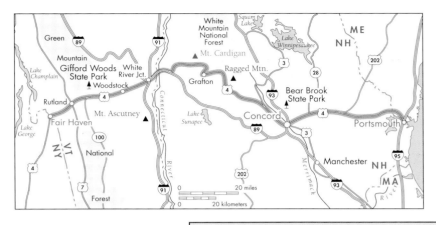

famous Route 100, which crosses US-4 at the crest and runs through the heart of mountains, lined by B&B inns, small farms, and endless forests all the way.

Besides pretty towns and panoramic mountain scenes, this part of Vermont is best known for skiing, with the mighty resort at Killington covering entire mountainsides. At its western end, US-4 makes a quick run

through the former marble-cutting city of Rutland before heading toward the New York border, passing through the rolling countryside of the lower Lake Champlain valley.

Once you've made your way through the complicated systems of one-way streets and unsigned detours to the center of Portsmouth, parking the car can be difficult. However, the town is small enough that you can park on the outskirts and walk anywhere within a few minutes.

PORTSMOUTH

Having undergone a complete makeover from rowdy naval port to bijou shopping and tourism center, Portsmouth is among the most popular stops on the New England coast. One of the most successful and prosperous of the early colonial settlements, thanks in large part to shipbuilding, Portsmouth benefited from quick access to inland forests and their nearly endless supplies of timber. This early prosperity explains the number of impressive colonial-era homes that still dominate the townscape.

As Massachusetts ports like Salem, Boston, and New Bedford expanded and took over international trade, Portsmouth faded to second-tier status and became increasingly dependent on the large U.S. Navy shipyard that still functions in the harbor, across the water in Maine. Apart from a thriving red-light district and other less-than-salubrious activities, Portsmouth remained somewhat of a backwater, and it wasn't until the threat of urban redevelopment arose in the 1950s that locals really started to take pride in their town's past. The first and still most important sign of this preservationist mentality was the revitalization of the colonial-era buildings of **Strawbery Banke**, Portsmouth's original center and now one of the country's premier living history museums (daily 10 AM–5 PM in summer only; $12; 603/433-1100). Spreading inland from the waterfront a few blocks south of the downtown business district, this neighborhood, also known as Puddle Dock, consists of 10 acres and 40 buildings, including nine houses, plus gardens and workshops. It's a complete time machine, re-creating the past as it was lived, day by day, from the 1600s up through World War II. Strawbery

STRAWBERY BANKE PORTSMOUTH New Hampshire

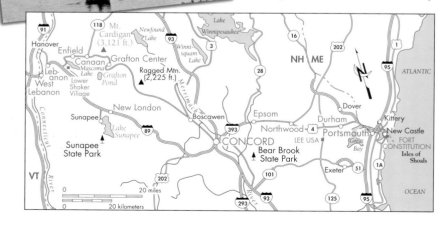

Hotel Wentworth, New Castle, N. H.

Banke is worth planning a whole day around, since it's the sort of place that sinks in slowly rather than overwhelms with high-tech displays. Fortunately, the admission tickets are good for two days, so you can come and go as you please.

After Strawberry Banke, the main attraction of Portsmouth is in the overall fabric of the town, rather than in specific sights. Walk along the waterfront, past dozens of historic homes and some colonial-era warehouses. Then head to the business district, where, along a tangled web of streets, local shops inhabit 200-year-old warehouses and business premises. (It's still pretty much chain-store-free, apart from a Gap, a Banana Republic, and a Starbucks.) Market Square is the center of it all, with Congress, Market, and Pleasant Streets angling off in different directions from the landmark spire of the North Church.

Across from Strawberry Banke, **Prescott Park** stretches along the Piscataqua River, providing grand views across to Badger's Island and the naval shipyard in Kittery, which you can walk to via the US-1 Memorial Bridge. Prescott Park also hosts a summer-long festival of free concerts and open-air theater, and preserves a colonial-era warehouse, once used by Captain John Paul Jones to outfit the *Ranger,* as a folk art museum displaying figureheads and model ships.

US-4 starts at Portsmouth, at the junction with our coastal road trip along US-1, which begins on page 46. The two roads cross at the Portsmouth Rotary, one of the more insane intersections in New England, as close to a demolition derby as most drivers care to be.

PORTSMOUTH PRACTICALITIES

If you like to eat, drink, and have fun, you'll like Portsmouth. With many good restaurants in just about every price range and culinary style this lively young city is among the better places to wine and dine in New England. No, it's not Boston, or even Portland, but for its small size there are a lot of possibilities. Don't forget, the colonial settlers who established Portsmouth came here not only for the protected harbor but also for the plentiful strawberries they found growing along the historic Strawberry Banke, so you know they value good food here.

Right at the center of Portsmouth, facing the front of the North Church, start (or re-start) your engines with a cappuccino at **Café Brioche,** 14 Market Square (603/430-9225), with sidewalk tables looking up at the landmark Portsmouth Atheneum, a private library that's open only rarely. Around the corner is the excellent, Turkish-run **Cafe Kilim,** and behind the church is something every hungry traveler dreams of, a great little bakery/deli: **Me & Ollie's,** 10 Pleasant Street (603/436-7777), serving thick sandwiches piled high on delicious wholemeal bread freshly baked that morning. Another great place: **Gilley's,** 75 Fleet Street (no phone), an original 1930s Worcester lunch cart serving burgers, perfectly crispy golden fries, and hot coffee from around 11 AM until well after 2 AM every day and night. Watch Red Sox and Patriots games here on a tiny screen above the grill, if you don't mind being

Fans of West Coast microbrewed beers may be surprised to find the very large, state-of-the-art **Redhook Brewery** along US-4/Route 16 just west of I-95 in the Pease Tradeport, formerly Pease AFB (which former President George H. W. Bush used to commute between Washington and his family estate at Kennebunkport, Maine). This is the East Coast branch of the famed Seattle brewery, and hour-long tours are available (daily 1–5 PM; $1; 603/430-8600); to taste the hoppy, "well-built" ales you have be 21 or older.

Leaving US-1 and I-95 at Portsmouth's busy main rotary, US-4 starts life doubled up with Route 16, the freeway-scale Spaulding Turnpike that runs north to the New Hampshire Lakes area. US-4 is sometimes referred to as the First New Hampshire Turnpike, because of its historic role linking the coast with the capital.

forced to support the home team. Gilley's has been in business since 1919 and the cart used to be hauled up to Market Square every lunch hour, but now it's parked semi-permanently a few blocks away, just west of Congress Street.

For something more substantial, try **Cafe Mediteraneo**, across the street from Gilley's at 152 Fleet Street (603/427-5563), one of the Seacoast region's most popular Italian restaurants. Probably the nicest place in Portsmouth, **Lindbergh's Crossing** is tucked away in the bottom of a dockside warehouse at 29 Ceres Street (603/431-0887), serving the freshest available seafood with nouvelle cuisine flair. Another great fish place is five blocks from the water but well worth the walk: **Jumpin' Jay's Fish Cafe,** off Congress at 1 Middle Street (603/766-3474), where you can have all kinds of fish any which way but fried.

For more traditional fried seafood, a number of places line the waterfront in and among the taverns and docks. For fish 'n' chips, scallops 'n' chips, or shrimp 'n' chips, make your way to **The Old Ferry Landing**, overlooking tugboats, bridges, and the Piscataqua River from an old wharf behind Ceres and Bow streets. The most famous (and certainly the biggest) seafood place in Portsmouth is two miles south of downtown along US-1: **Yoken's** (603/436-8224), a huge, family-oriented restaurant sells fish, fish, and more fish to upwards of 700 diners at a time. Cynics will say the best thing about the place is the giant flashing sign of a giant blue ("Thar She Blows") whale along the road, but Yoken's has been in business for more than 56 years and is still going strong, so they must be doing something right.

In contrast to the abundance of food, finding reasonable accommodations can be tricky. There are a number of motels around the I-95/US-1/US-4 Portsmouth Rotary junction outside downtown, but these centrally located rooms usually go for upwards of $100 a night. One nice old and not *too* expensive a place is the **Sise Inn**, 40 Court Street (603/433-1200).

If you need help finding a bed or anything else in Portsmouth, contact the **visitors bureau,** 500 Market Street (603/436-1118).

DURHAM AND LEE USA

Fewer than 10 miles upstream from Portsmouth and home to the main University of New Hampshire campus, tranquil Durham (pop. 11,800) is not what you might expect from a college town. The requisite lineup of bookstores, coffeehouses, and pizza places here is severely limited—there's one of each—and they occupy little more than a short strip that stretches barely a full city block.

For a total (and literal) change of pace from sleepy Durham, head a little way west on US-4, then a mile south and west along Route 125 to Lee USA (7 PM Fri. only; $12 adults, under–12 free; 978/462-4252), a very popular short-track automobile race course that's open all summer long. Rated the "#1 Friday Night Track in New England," the short, asphalt-paved three-eighths-mile high-banked oval roars to life with a series of quick but furious stock-car races. If you've never been a fan of auto racing, or have only experienced it on TV or at the Indy/Daytona level, the action here may seem shockingly loud and terrifyingly up-close and personal, but it's guaranteed to get your heart beating at an accelerated rate.

NORTHWOOD AND EPSOM: ANTIQUE ALLEY

The stretch of US-4 between Portsmouth and Concord is among the oldest in the state, but the roadside scene along New Hampshire's first turnpike is surprisingly quiet, with only a few outbreaks of minimalls and fast-food franchises to spoil the rural views. You won't find major attractions or significant historic sites here, but the dozens of small antique shops lining the middle 10 miles or so, between the outskirts of Northwood and Epsom, make this road a Mecca for shoppers and collectors.

Midway along US-4, a large and inviting lake spreads at the center of 600-acre Northwood Meadows State Park (day use only), and just west of here stands a popular roadside restaurant, **Johnson's,** serving family-friendly fare, including excellent, thick-cut onion rings, creamy frappes and milk shakes, and all-you-can-eat fish 'n' chips.

Approaching Concord, US-4 briefly turns in to a freeway before linking up with US-3 around the northern fringes of New Hampshire's capital city.

The University of New Hampshire at Durham is the base for one of northeast New England's more interesting college radio stations, **WUNH 91.3 FM.** For requests, complaints, questions, or prize-winning answers to quizzes, call them at 603/862-2222. The Durham area is also home to **Great Bay Area Radio 1610 AM,** a public service natural history station that broadcasts intimate details of the Great Bay estuary that covers much of the New Hampshire coast. If you want to learn about horseshoe crabs or other denizens of the wetlands, tune in.

The small but engaging capital city of Concord, New Hampshire is covered in the US-3 chapter on pages 138–167.

I-89 DETOUR: NEW LONDON AND LAKE SUNAPEE

If you don't have the time or the inclination to follow winding US-4 between Concord and Lebanon, at least take a quick look at New London (pop. 3,180), a postcard-pretty village just off the I-89 freeway from exit 11 or 12. A prototypical New England village, with the campus of Colby-Sawyer College, a historic inn, and a landmark meetinghouse lining Main Street (Route 114), New London's hilltop setting makes it a favorite stop for leaf-peepers and photographers during the fall color season. To get the full New London experience, stay a night or two at the historic **New London Inn,** 140 Main Street ($80–120; 603/526-2791 or 800/526-2791), which has been welcoming travelers since 1792. The inn also has a fine restaurant, **Zeke's,** where overnight guests get a full complimentary breakfast.

On the south side of I-89, Lake Sunapee is another New Hampshire classic, a historic vacation spot spreading at the foot of 2,743-foot Mount Sunapee. The lake, one of the prettiest in New England, features a trio of lighthouses, a mile-long state beach, and a relatively low level of tourism development. To get a feel for the town, drive around the lake or hop on board one of the historic steamboats offering cruis-

---

I-89 SURVIVAL GUIDE: ACROSS NEW HAMPSHIRE

MM 61: Connecticut River/Vermont state line.

MM 60: Exit 20, West Lebanon's fast-food, shopping malls.

MM58: Exit 19, junction with US-4 toward White River Junction and with Route 10, north to Hanover.

MM54: Exit 17, junction with US-4 east to Enfield and Lower Shaker Village (see page 177).

MM37: Exit 12A to Lake Sunapee and Mount Sunapee State Park.

MM34: Exit 12 to New London.

MM0: Start/finish of I-89, south of Concord at junction with I-93.

The Sunapee area was home to one of the first cars in the country. In 1869, a local man named Enos Clough fabricated a horseless carriage that so terrified local horses it was banned from public use.

es, like the MV *Kearsarge* ($10; 603/763-5477). Cruises depart from Sunapee Harbor in the main tourist center of **Sunapee** (pop. 2,638) at the midpoint of the western shore, along Route 111. The main beach is in **Mount Sunapee State Park** (603/763-2356), at the southern end of the lake, above which hiking trails and a summer chairlift ($6) climb up to a mountaintop cafe. The summit is often crowded, but if you hike a little way down the backside of the mountain you can find some peace at lovely Lake Solitude, a mile or so southeast from the summit via a well-signed, semi-steep, and fantastically rewarding trail.

Back down by the lake, the beach at Mount Sunapee State Park is home to the state's largest arts and crafts fair the second week of every August, when the **League of New Hampshire Craftsmen** holds its annual nine-day showcase here ($8; 603/224-3375).

Grafton Pond, one of the best places in New Hampshire for wildlife watching, lies southwest of the Ruggles Mine, and is accessible via Riddle Hill Road, a long gravel road winding between Grafton Center and Canaan. Bring your canoe or kayak, and push off from a landing on the western shore to view the moose, deer, and bears common to the area.

GRAFTON CENTER: RUGGLES MINE

Heading northwest from Concord, away from I-93 and the Merrimack Valley and into the mountains, US-4 passes by the birthplace of New Hampshire icon Daniel Webster, just north of the hamlet of Salisbury. Further west, deep into the southern fringes of the White Mountains, the village of Grafton Center (pop. 925) is home to the oldest mine in the state. Here, at the Ruggles Mine (daily 9 AM–5 PM in summer only; $9), locals quarried mica—so pure it came out of the ground in transparent six-inch squares—for making window panes. Visitors are encouraged to take away samples of the unusual mineral deposits, which also include feldspar, amethyst, quartz, and garnets; however, unless you're a real rockhound, you may find the admission charge a little steep. That said, the setting is terrific, surrounded by a trio of peaks, and the mine workings give a vivid sense of the brutal manual labor involved in hauling the material out of the ground and onto wagons for the long ride to Portsmouth.

CANAAN AND MOUNT CARDIGAN

Canaan (pop. 3,279) is a tidy little colonial-era village that has been here since it was founded in 1761 by settlers from the Connecticut town of the same name. US-4 follows Broad Street through the heart of this mountain town, lined by stately trees and an array of semi-stately homes, and with views of neighboring peaks and the distant Green Mountains of Vermont.

North and east from Canaan via Route 118, the 3,121-foot peak of Mount Cardigan stands alone, its bald granite top capped by a fire lookout tower. Although the mountain looks a little desolate from below, the views from the summit are among the broadest and best in New England. From here you can see the Green Mountains of Vermont looming above many meandering miles of the Connecticut River valley to the west. To the east you'll see lovely Newfound, Squam, and Winnipesaukee lakes. The popular **West Ridge Trail** to the top starts at the parking area, 3.5 miles beyond where Route 118 turns from pavement to dirt. The hike is under two miles each way, with a elevation gain of over 1,300 feet. If you're feeling hearty, you can turn the day hike into an overnight adventure by heading east from the summit down the Mowglis and Manning trails to the remote, AMC-operated **Cardigan Mountain Lodge** (603/744-8011), which offers meals, reasonably priced bunkhouse accommodations, and tent campsites.

Along US-4 on the west side of Canaan, you can see the workings of one of New Hampshire's last remaining granite quarries, the **Enfield Granite Company,** which has a small gift shop selling portable products made from the state rock.

ENFIELD: LOWER SHAKER VILLAGE

A dozen miles east of Hanover and the Connecticut River, south on Route 4A from the town of Enfield, one of the largest and most unusual of the former Shaker villages has been resurrected as a combination museum and resort complex. Now housing the plush **Shaker Inn** ($105–155; 603/632-7810 or 888/707-4257), the massive stone-built former Shaker dormitory retains many of its original Shaker-style features as well as some novelties, like the world's only Shaker cocktail bar. Among the many Shaker communities that existed all over New England in the 1800s, this one, known as the Lower Shaker Village, was always unusual. At its peak in the 1850s, more than 300 celibate Shakers lived and worked here, producing handcrafted home furnishings while living in the massive Great Stone Dwelling, the largest and most monumental Shaker structure anywhere.

During the late 19th century, Enfield's Shakers, in pursuit of spiritual peace, produced simple homespun goods, while other residents were busy producing parts for the Enfield Rifle.

Surrounding buildings have been preserved as a **museum** (daily 10 AM–5 PM in summer, weekends only rest of year; $5; 603/632-4346), which serves as a good introduction. However, it is most worthwhile if you haven't visited other Shaker communities, such as the one near Concord at Canterbury (see page 153).

After the demise of the Shakers in the mid-1920s, the compound was used as a Catholic seminary. The LaSallette order still has a monastery here, which explains the presence of the large shrine and the hillside of seasonal Christmas lights.

LEBANON AND WEST LEBANON

Sitting rather quietly a couple of miles east of the Connecticut River, near the point where US-4 gets submerged beneath the I-89 freeway, historic Lebanon (pop. 12,183) has a town green so spacious it seems more like the outskirts of a city park than the center of a town. Near the northwest corner is the main commercial area, or what's left since the malls arrived, kept alive in part by a pair of establishments. **Sweet Tomatoes,** facing Coburn Park (lunch weekdays until 2 PM, dinner nightly from 5 PM; 603/448-1711), is an ever-popular trattoria whose gourmet pasta and wood-fired pizzas pull in crowds from miles around, and across from it you'll find **The Bean Gallery,** a very shiny, black, smoke free temple to art and espresso, open from very early to very late every day but Sunday (603/448-7302).

Right along the bonny banks of the Connecticut River, three miles south of patrician Hanover, the commercial busybody of West Lebanon has everything you probably try hard to avoid: shopping plazas, traffic tie-ups, and familiar fast-*everything,* all clustered around I-89's two local exits. Amid all of the commercial mayhem are two more restaurants of note: the **Bangkok Garden** Thai restaurant in the K-Mart Plaza on Route 12A (lunch daily to 3 PM, dinner Mon.–Sat. from 5 PM; 603/298-6553); and **The Seven Barrels** (603/298-5566) on the south side of the I-89 overpass. One of the brewpubs on the region's growing list, the "Seven Bs" has a good line of beers and a liberal sampling of English pub grub: bubble and squeak, toad-in-the-hole, and fish 'n' chips.

Harder to find but worth a visit is the **Four Aces Diner,** north of I-89 on US-4, just uphill from the old bridge to Vermont, with very good from-scratch diner fare at down-to-earth prices (Sun.–Mon. to 3 PM, Tues.–Wed. to 8 PM, Thurs.–Sat. to 9 PM; 603/298-6827). This classic 1950s Worcester diner, built into the side of a red clapboard mill, does all its own baking and has a soda fountain, too.

With I-89 passing through the town and I-91 just across the river in Vermont, there are several budget and chain **motels** on both sides of the Connecticut River. Take your pick of Radisson, Super 8, HoJo's, Comfort, Days, Holiday Inn, and many more.

In the Lebanon area, a pair of great drives cross US-4. Running north–south along the west bank of the Connecticut River, US-5 (including the town of White River Junction) is covered on pages 190–217, while the famous Appalachian Trail, which parallels US-4 between Lebanon and Killington, is covered on pages 274–308.

QUECHEE AND QUECHEE GORGE

West from White River Junction, US-4 climbs upstream into the valley of the Ottauquechee River (auto-KWEE-chee) near Quechee, a second-home community to country-clubbing executives from Connecticut and Boston. You cross Quechee Gorge almost without warning, but adjacent parking on both sides of the gorge gives you a chance to take a longer look at the dramatic little canyon or to stretch your legs along the rimside hiking trails. East of the gorge there's a tacky Quechee Village souvenir shop, which boasts a tiny train and the well-preserved **Yankee Diner,** a streamline-style 1946 Worcester diner that's been incorporated into the **Farina Family Diner** (802/296-7911), a retro–all-American roadhouse serving up the usual standards.

interior of Yankee Diner

West of the gorge, you can turn north into old Quechee, a quaint old town with a lumber mill-cum-art gallery selling Simon Pearce glassware. A Norman Rockwell–esque rope swing hangs under a covered bridge, and on lazy summer afternoons local youths drop from it into the river below.

East of the gorge, **Quechee State Park** (802/295-2990) provides access to the Ottauquechee River, and also has camping with hot showers.

WOODSTOCK

"The good people of Woodstock have less incentive than others to yearn for heaven," said a 19th-century resident. It's a sentiment readily echoed today. Originally settled in the 1760s, Woodstock (pop. 3,212) remains an exceedingly well-preserved example of small-town New England—tidy federal-style homes, built by wealthy professionals of the newborn American republic,

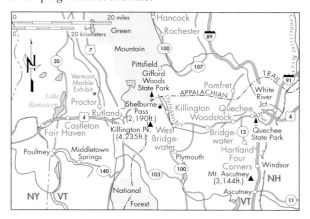

still ring the classic village green. Now the historic village is home to wealthy retirees and their fortunate sons and daughters. You'll see the signs of this old money throughout the town: well-stocked wine racks at the general store, shady basketball courts along the river, excellent performing arts at the Town Hall Theater, and, most importantly, the wherewithal to refuse any compromising commercial development. Having financially generous, conservation-minded residents like Laurance Rockefeller around hasn't hurt, either. To put it mildly, expansion of the tax base is *not* a pressing issue for this community.

During summer and fall, walking tours are an excellent way to take stock of the town's history and architecture. Call or visit the **information booth** (802/457-1042) on the Green for a schedule. Hiking trails lead up both the summits overlooking the town. A community blackboard, a.k.a. the **Town Crier,** at the corner of Central and Elm, lists local events and activities all year. Even if you're racing through Woodstock, bound for the mountains, be sure to stop in Woodstock long enough to enjoy this quick tour: from the oblong Green, cross the Middle Covered Bridge, and follow the Ottauquechee downstream along River Street. Then work your way back via Elm Street past F. H. Gillingham & Sons, Vermont's oldest country store.

If you've admired the rolling fields and weathered wooden fences, savored the local apples and sharp cheddar, enjoyed the scent of mown hay or boiling maple sap, you'll appreciate an even closer look at New England's farms with a visit to the **Billings Farm & Museum,** on Route 12 north of the village (daily 10 AM–5 PM May–Oct., weekends 10 AM–4 PM Nov.–Dec., and Dec. 26–31; 802/457-2355; $7). Frederick Billings, better known as the builder of the Northern Pacific Railroad (Billings, Montana is named for him), began this working dairy farm in the late 19th century. Its restored farmhouse and huge barns illustrate the rural life in galleries, demonstrations, and hands-on activities.

If you continue north on Route 12 past the Billings Farm, then veer to the right before you reach the Suicide Six ski area, you can take a lovely pastoral tour of the various Pomfrets—South Pomfret, Pomfret, and North Pomfret—plus the equally tiny hamlets of Hewitts Corner and Millbrook, before suddenly returning to the busy modern world via I-89 at West Hartford.

Across the road, another historic farm has recently been opened to the public as the **Marsh-Billings National Historical Park** (tours daily; $5; 802/457-3368), Vermont's only national park. The property, which includes the former home of Laurance Rockefeller (who married Billings's granddaughter), is a study in conservation practice, its dense woodlands living proof of the merits of sustainable agriculture.

If you prefer your nature undomesticated and "red in tooth and claw," head up Church Hill Road from the west side of the Green to the **Vermont Institute of Natural Science** (daily 10 AM–4 PM except Sun. Nov.–April; 802/457-2779; $6). The institute devotes itself to environmental education and wildlife rehabilitation, but for casual visitors the highlight of the 77-acre nature preserve is the self-guided trail through the **Raptor Center,** a set of 26 outdoor habitats for hawks, eagles, owls, and other birds of prey, all permanent convalescents from hunting or accidental injuries.

WOODSTOCK PRACTICALITIES

Notice, as you approach Woodstock Village Green that there are no overhead power lines on the two main downtown streets, Central and Elm. Laurance Rockefeller paid to have the lines buried back in 1973.

Hungry travelers will find plenty of choices around town, although some eateries assume you have a private endowment. The burgers at **Bentley's,** across from the Town Crier at 3 Elm Street (802/457-3232), are a tad high priced, but consider the accompaniments: Vermont microbrews, oriental carpets, Victorian sofas, and a casual, cheerful, talkative crowd. If you'd pay as much for good vibes as you'd tip for good service, it's worth a visit. Another agreeable and not-too-pricey place is the **Village Inn,** 41 Pleasant Street (802/457-1255), which is semifamous for its roast turkey dinners.

For simple or not-so-simple deli items, try Central Street's natural foods market **18 Carrots,** offering veggie burritos and softball-sized muffins, or **The Village Butcher,** 18 Elm Street (802/457-2756) across from Bentley's, which has very good deli sandwiches (and 25¢ dill pickles), a fine selection of wines and microbrewed beers, and all the Made in Vermont maple syrups and aged cheddars you could ever want.

There are also two bare-bones road-food haunts bookending the town along US-4. At the east of town, you'll find the white shack housing **WASP's Snack Bar,** 57 Pleasant Street (802/457-9805), and on US-4 a half-mile west of the Green, is the open-air **White Cottage Snack Bar** (802/457-2968). Next to the White Cottage is a healthier alternative, the **Woodstock Farmer's Market,** with top-quality produce and full meals available.

Accommodations run the gamut from $60 motels to $100 B&Bs to $200-a-night inns. Expect stiff increases during high season, which in Woodstock is most of summer and fall, along with the winter holidays. The main place right in town, the 144-room, Rockefeller-built **Woodstock Inn** (802/457-1000) on the Green, will set you back $200 a night or more, and for that kind of money you might expect something more appealing than its suburban country-club ambiance. (Although it tries hard to look like a stately old place, the hotel was actually built from scratch in 1969.) More reasonable lodgings can be found outside the village or in neighboring towns. Around the huge Killington ski area about 20 miles west on US-4, for example, summer is considered off-season, so prices are set accordingly. Otherwise, the modest **Braeside Motel** ($70–120; 802/457-1366 or 800/303-1366 inside Vermont) along US-4 on the eastern outskirts of town is about as budget-friendly as you're going to get.

The local **chamber of commerce** (802/457-3555) can supply a directory of area lodgings in advance or in summer from their booth on the Green.

For a long-distance leaf-peepers update on the progress of Vermont foliage, call the state's **fall foliage hotline** (24-hour recording, Sept. and Oct. only) at 802/828-3239.

Vermont holds more than a hundred **covered bridges,** several good examples of which are to be seen between Quechee and Bridgewater. Look for the 1836 Taftsville Bridge west of Quechee, the Middle Bridge in Woodstock (which was totally rebuilt way back in 1969), and the 1877 Lincoln Bridge four miles west of Woodstock. The nation's longest covered bridge crosses the Connecticut River at Windsor, about 15 miles southeast of Woodstock, with a 460-foot span built in 1866.

If you're in the area around mid-June, check out the **Quechee Hot Air Balloon Festival,** held during Father's Day weekend.

BRIDGEWATER

The tiny town of Bridgewater (pop. 895), stretching along the banks of the Ottauquechee, seems well on the way to the middle of nowhere. But that's what lures many visitors to this region—the fact that so much of it seems to have contentedly hung back with Rip Van Winkle. That said, Bridgewater is a gateway to one of the state most important somewheres: the ski resorts of central Vermont. The large woolen mill in Bridgewater (pop. 895) has been

converted into the Old Mill Marketplace, its water-powered turbines and textile machines replaced by small shops selling a typically Vermont mix of antiques, ski apparel, New Age books, and gift-packaged Vermont foods to visitors heading for the mountains.

A jot further west on US-4 at **Bridgewater Corners,** the Appalachian Trail route turns south on Route 100A toward Ludlow. The junction is just beside **Long Trail Brewers,** whose taproom (lunch available, open daily until 6 PM) is worth a visit if you haven't yet tried the state's most popular microbrew. Their flagship Long Trail Ale is named after the route that inspired the Appalachian Trail: the 85-year-old Long Trail, a 255-mile footpath running along the spine of the Green Mountains from Massachusetts to Canada.

Since the demise of the friendly old Bridgewater Village Diner (due to nonpayment of taxes), the best local road-food place is **Blanche and Bill's Pancake House** (Wed.–Sun. 7 AM–2 PM; 802/422-3816), on US-4 four miles west of the Route 100A junction, just east of Route 100. The ruddy brown shed that houses the restaurant doesn't raise great expectations, but once you're inside, Blanche, who lives next door, will most likely be on hand to welcome you and help you order from the 40-odd specials plastered to the wall. (Other walls are packed with Boston Red Sox pennants and memorabilia. To be safe, remove any Yankees caps before entering.) Offering almost every imaginable combination of eggs, pancakes, waffles, bacon slices, and sausage links, each of the hand-lettered specials is listed in alphabetical order, and prices are all in the $4–6 range.

During November and December hikers should be especially alert, as these months are hunting season throughout New England. Most hunters know to stay away from the most popular hiking areas and are ready to head home by the time you finish breakfast, anyway, but it doesn't hurt to wear bright clothing and avoid practicing your bushwhacking skills during these months.

KILLINGTON

Through the Bridgewater area, US-4 is generously wide shouldered and level, making it a popular cycling route, especially during the fall color season, when the dense hardwood forests that climb the slopes above the roadway are blazing with autumn hues. When the leaves have fallen and been replaced by snows, this scenic stretch changes character completely, becoming one of the East Coast's most prominent ski resorts, Killington. The permanent population of Killington is maybe 50 people, but on winter weekends as many as 10,000 skiers flock to its seven different mountains and many miles of trails (lift tickets around $50; snow info 800/621-6867). The skiers also support a plethora of real estate agencies, restaurants, and bars, especially off US-4 on the main road to the slopes, Killington Road.

Compared to the rest of Vermont, Killington is not an especially attractive place to be in summer, when the parking lots of the time-share condo complexes are empty and the hills are scarred by clear-cut ski trails, but the lack of crowds also means lower prices for accommodations. Everywhere from roadside motels to upscale resorts like the **Inn at Six Mountains** ($70–250) offer their lowest rates when the temperatures are highest.

In the Killington area, tune to "The Mountain," **WEBK 105.3 FM** for the best in alternative pop music—everything from the Grateful Dead to Beck and Bela Fleck.

GIFFORD WOODS STATE PARK

Sitting in the scenic heart of the Green Mountains, at the junction of US-4 and Route 100 and very near the junction of the Long Trail and the Appalachian Trail, Gifford Woods State Park (802/775-5354) protects one of the few virgin stands of sugar maples left in New England, with 16 acres of these massive trees, including some that are up to 300 years old. There's a nice **campground,** with hot showers, and access to many fine trails, including the Appalachian Trail and the Long Trail, which run together across US-4 just west of 2,190-foot Shelburne Pass.

Next to Gifford Woods is another, larger stand of never-cut woodland, protected as an undeveloped natural area, with yet more sugar maples as well as birches and hemlocks, which all make for marvelous fall color.

ROUTE 100: ROCHESTER, HANCOCK, AND GRANVILLE GULF

Route 100 runs north–south through the geographical and spiritual heart of Vermont, winding from curve to curve past cornfields and fat cows lazing in impossibly green pastures, alongside gurgling streams, up and down switchbacking passes, and generally setting the standard for what scenic roads ought to be. Route 100 runs right at the edge of the Green Mountains National Forest, parallel to Vermont's beloved crestline Long Trail, and every so often passes by a picturesque gas station–cum–general store, selling everything you'll need to keep you on the road, from gas to maple-syrup milk shakes. Up and down the whole state of Vermont, Route 100 is a wonderful drive, as are just about all of the roads that intersect it.

North of US-4, the first place you come to along Route 100 is **Pittsfield,** an all-in-white hamlet set in a pastoral valley and surrounded by hayfields and acres of corn. From here Route 100 edges east into the White River Valley, passing through Stockbridge, which centers on an ancient-looking Ford dealership, and a couple more places that seem to exist solely on maps. The next stop is Rochester, at the junction with Route 73, which heads west over scenic Brandon Gap. Rochester is a proper Vermont town, with a village green and a bandstand. A mile north of town is the main **ranger station** (802/767-4261) for this part of the Green Mountains National Forest, where the friendly staff will tell you all about the best day hikes, campgrounds, and historic sites in the area. Two miles south of Rochester, across the river and away from Route 100, the **Liberty Hill Farm B&B** ($70–140; 802/767-3926) is a family-friendly farmstay B&B and has a working 100-plus-acre dairy where you can hike, bike, fish, or help feed the cows (and the ducks and chickens and cats).

The biggest town in these parts, **Hancock** is a lumber town with a small hardwood mill and a showroom for White River Timber Frames home builders and designers. Stop for a vegetarian meal at the **Sweet Onion** (802/767-3734), which also has B&B rooms. Or go inside the old **Hubbard's General Store** at the Route 125 junction, pick up some aged cheddar and a soda or a beer, and watch the world go by. North of Hancock, Route 100 passes through what is still a working landscape, with ski club cabins sharing the roadside scene with a few barns and remnants of historic sheep pens.

The one don't-miss highlight of this middle section of Route 100 is **Granville Gulf State Preserve,** five miles north of Hancock and about 30 beautiful miles north from US-4. The Green Mountains rise steeply to either side of the road, and just off the west side of the road, delicate **Moss Glen Falls** tumble down through craggy cliffs to a gurgling stream. A short boardwalk, built using recycled wood products, as well as supermarket plastic bags, leads to the foot of the falls from a small parking turnout.

The more northerly stretches of Route 100, from Granville Gulf north through Warren, Waitsfield, and Waterbury to Stowe and beyond, are covered in the US-2 chapter on page 130. The scenic drives west from Route 100, over the Green Mountain crest via Appalachian Gap, Middlebury Gap, and Brandon Gap, are described in the US-7 chapter, on pages 252–253.

NORMAN ROCKWELL MUSEUM

West of the crest, in the few miles between Killington and Rutland, US-4 drops down from the mountains and into the broad valley at the foot of Lake Champlain. The Adirondacks loom large along the western horizon, and in the foreground US-4 passes yet another museum, this one dedicated to the art of Norman Rockwell. Almost all the works displayed here are reproductions, presented with some historical context but much less connection to their creator than you'll get from the other Rockwell museums, like at Arlington (see page 256) or the big one at Stockbridge (see page 264). To see for yourself, the museum (daily 9 AM–6 PM; $4; 802/ 773-6095) is inside a big brown barn right on US-4, two miles east of the US-7 junction and downtown Rutland.

RUTLAND

Rutland (pop. 18,200) is a study in contrasts, sometimes sneeringly described as "a little bit of New Hampshire dropped down in the Green Mountain State." One of the few fairly big cities in otherwise rural Vermont, Rutland has struggled to establish a new identity for itself following the collapse of its former economic mainstay, the marble industry. In Rutland's downtown area, bistros, coffee bars, and the **Book King** bookstore now fill the lower levels of once-busy industrial premises. These new businesses are now contending with a massive new megamall, containing a Wal-Mart and a multiplex movie theater, right on its doorstep. Whether downtown Rutland will retain its personality in the face of franchises, only time will tell; As of 2001, Starbucks still hadn't ventured in.

For eats, visit the old downtown area, a far cry from the franchises that line the highways. Try the central **Coffee Exchange,** on the corner of Center Street and Merchants Row, and the slightly upscale **Bistro Cafe,** next door at 103 Merchants Row (802/747-7199) serving very tasty food.

Most of Rutland's abundant **motels** line the US-7 stretch north and south from downtown, with prices that are generally a lot lower than in the rest of Vermont. You'll find a Howard Johnson's and a Holiday Inn south of town near the fairgrounds where flea markets and monster truck rallies frequently are held.

It's hard to imagine now, but a hundred years or so ago the Green Mountains were almost completely bare and treeless, used primarily for grazing sheep. If you hike in the mountains these days, you're likely to come across old stone walls and cabins all but buried beneath the dense hardwood growth that now covers the mountains and provides all that famous fall color.

Rutland marks the place where US-4 crosses scenic US-7, which runs along the western foot of the Green Mountains from Canada across Connecticut.
US-7 is covered beginning on page 248.

downtown Rutland

PROCTOR: VERMONT MARBLE

Northwest of Rutland, the quarries that provided the raw stone for most of Vermont's marble industry are centered upon the town of Proctor, where nearly everything that could be made of marble is made of marble—even the sidewalks. The entire manufacturing process, from the ancient geological metamorphosis to quarrying and finishing of the stone, is covered in intimate detail at the enormous **Vermont Marble Exhibit,** at 62 Main Street (daily 9 AM–5:30 PM; $5; 802/459-2300). There's also a Hall of Presidents, featuring a bust of every man to hold the nation's top job as well as various displays of sculptors at work.

TOWARD NEW YORK: CASTLETON AND FAIR HAVEN

The landscape west of Rutland is far less dramatic than the Green Mountains to the east. Rolling hills covered with apple orchards are more the rule here, though marble and slate quarries have earned the region the name Slate Valley. To best experience the area, stay off the US-4 freeway and follow the older, slower route, now signed as Route 4A, which winds past red barns and stands of fresh-picked raspberries all the way to the state line. The main town hereabouts, Castleton (pop. 4,300) has roots that go back to the Revolutionary War. Ethan Allen and the Green Mountain Boys planned their attack on Fort Ticonderoga at a tavern here, and many fine buildings date from the late 18th and early 19th centuries. Castleton also houses the oldest campus of Vermont's state college system, and, best of all, the center of town has the shiny **Birdseye Diner** (802/468-5817), a 1940 Silk City in near-mint condition, open 7 AM–9 PM every day.

West of Castleton, Route 4A and US-4 cross the north–south Route 30, a scenic route that runs along the shores of lovely **Lake Bomoseen.** Route 30 is covered in greater detail in the US-7 chapter.

Fair Haven, the first or last town in Vermont, depending on your direction, has a pretty redbrick downtown area fringed by cottages and churches. Fair Haven was also home to early American politician Matthew Lyon, the only man to be elected to the U.S. House of Representatives by three different states. During his tenure in Vermont, Lyon was a bitter foe of President John Adams, and, while in jail serving time for supposedly treasonous remarks printed in a newspaper, he was re-elected by an overwhelming majority. In 1801 he cast the deciding vote that made Thomas Jefferson president, and he later was elected to Congress to represent both Kentucky and Arkansas.

From this part of Vermont, a quick drive north to Larabee's Point and a ferry ride across the southern tip of Lake Champlain will bring you to Fort Ticonderoga and the attractions of Lake George, New York.

CONNECTICUT RIVER VALLEY: US-5

CONNECTICUT RIVER VALLEY: US-5

Traveling along US-5, the Canada–New Haven, Connecticut alternative to I-91, you will come across a museum showcasing 30-foot puppets, small towns full of history and scenery, homes of well-known writers and poets, and a roadside motel where you can enjoy a drive-in movie from the comfort of your room. This great old road passes through some of New England's most stunning places with little or no traffic, and lets you set your own pace without fear of some huge truck appearing in your rear-view mirror.

US-5 starts off high up in the heart of Vermont's Northeast Kingdom, the most rural and peaceful corner of the nation's most rural state. This area is famous for its intense fall color and for being what Vermont *ought* to be. Locals like to say that this remote part of the state is what the rest of Vermont was like before vacation homes, freeways, and ski areas arrived in the years after World War II. Besides taking you to two very different but equally unique attractions—the border-defying Haskell Opera House and the boundary-breaking Bread and Puppet Theater—the northernmost section of US-5 offers a look at two of New England's most distinctive lakes, massive Lake Memphremagog and sublime Lake Willoughby, and endless acres of rural Americana. This part of Vermont is quintessential New England: picturesque villages still served by cluttered country stores, small farms nestled among the ridges of the mountains, and needle-sharp white church spires rising above forests ablaze with autumn colors.

After linking up with I-91 and the Connecticut River near the hilltop Victorian city of St. Johnsbury, US-5 follows the river south along Vermont's eastern border, passing through numerous small towns often linked by historic covered bridges. Though rarely more than a few miles from the I-91 freeway, this long stretch of US-5 feels as far away from the modern world as you can imagine. Even a quick drive along it through such evocative places as Fairlee or Bellows Falls will make you glad you left the fast lane behind.

The same can be said of US-5's trek through the mostly rural Pioneer Valley of Massachusetts, where historic frontier towns such as Deerfield have been preserved alongside the lively college towns of Amherst and Northampton. US-5 runs along the river most of the way, and for more adventurous driving there are numerous side trips, including the amazing Mohawk Trail, one of the first and still among the finest scenic routes in the country. Southern Massachusetts is dominated by burly mill towns, especially Springfield, and the industrial landscape continues most of the way through Connecticut as well, making US-5 less enthralling here than it is in the north. That said, the city of Hartford is worth a stop, especially for fans of Mark Twain, who lived here for most of his adult life, and its southern suburb of Wethersfield is full of historic homes and buildings, offering a taste of old-fashioned charm amid the modern highway sprawl.

US-5 HIGHLIGHTS

DERBY LINE

The town of Derby Line (pop. 900) sits not alongside the Canada-U.S. border, but directly on it. The border passes right through this pretty little town, and the international boundary is usually marked only by a change in street signs. (If they start speaking French, you've crossed over.) Despite Derby Line's undulating topography and meandering riverside layout, the line runs straight along the 45th Parallel, without regard to the lay of the land or to property lines.

The most prominent example of this disregard of international boundaries is the 1901 **Haskell Opera House** (Mon.–Sat. 10 AM–5 PM, longer hours in summer; free; 802/873-3022), on the top floor of the stately granite-and-brick Haskell Free Library, on Caswell Avenue between the I-91 border crossing (at the east edge of town) and the US-5 crossing (right downtown). The border runs right through the building, and it's the only place I know of where you can cross back and forth without facing a shakedown from the ever-vigilant customs officers. Check in at the circulation desk and ask about a tour (May–Oct.; $2 donation), and your guide, most often a French-Canadian student, will walk you upstairs to the ornate opera house, which reeks of frontier excess—all gilt and ornate plaster-

work. Most of the seating is on the U.S. side, but the stage is in Canada, so popular performers here used to become international favorites overnight. During Prohibition, stories were frequently told about U.S. officials sitting in the audience, watching performers they wanted, but legally weren't able, to arrest for bootlegging liquor.

The acoustically perfect opera house is still used for live shows, usually held on weekend evenings in the summer; shows cost US$6–15, and if you're lucky they'll start with a look at the lovely old curtain, painted with a picture of Venice.

NEWPORT

Sitting on the south shore of beautiful Lake Memphremagog, which stretches north into Canada, Newport (pop. 4,400) is a fairly busy place, catering to visitors from both sides of the border. The liveliest time to visit is late July, when the town hosts the **International Marathon Swim**—32 miles across the length of the lake. Main Street has some quaint old brick buildings dating from Newport's Victorian heyday as a summer resort, and also has the classic **Miss Newport Diner,** 985 E. Main Street (802/334-7742).

South of Newport, US-5 makes a long lazy loop west from I-91, reconnecting with the freeway at Orleans, home to a big Ethan Allen furniture factory.

GLOVER: BREAD AND PUPPET MUSEUM

Some of Vermont's prettiest places are in the Northeast Kingdom, east of I-91 and US-5, but one of the state's most fascinating stops is west of the freeway, outside the rural hamlet of Glover. A huge barn alongside Route 122 (four miles south of I-91 exit 25; go through Glover, then turn left at the cemetery) houses the **Bread and Puppet Theater and Museum** (daily 10 AM–5 PM June–Oct.; donations; 802/525-3031) and its incredible collection of puppets and props. The puppets are all hand made and come in various shapes and sizes, some towering over 30 feet tall. The museum also displays posters, masks, and banners belonging to the theater company, which was originally formed in New York City's Lower East Side in 1963. The company became famous first for its puppet shows and later for staging huge agitprop public pageants featuring some of the massive heads you can see at the museum.

While American and Canadian visitors are allowed to step over the border in the Haskell Opera House, if you cross over outside those hallowed halls (which is very easy to do inadvertently, considering that many crossings are unmarked and unmanned), by law you must check in with the nearest border guards. This is especially important if you happen to cross the border late at night. Big Brother is always watching, and if the authorities think you might be up to something, they will pounce, taking apart your car and dumping your gear on the ground in their search for contraband.

In the movie *Northwest Passage,* Spencer Tracy played the part of Robert Rogers, who led "Rogers's Rangers" during the French and Indian Wars in 1759. The movie dramatized the escape of this not-entirely heroic band of soldiers, who attacked and slaughtered a village of 200 "unfriendly" natives in St. Francis, Canada, then fled south to the relative safety of the Connecticut River Valley.

BREAD AND PUPPETS

It's hard to know where to begin describing the magic and intensity that manifests itself at the Bread and Puppet Museum, which fills two floors of an old barn on the rural outskirts of Glover, Vermont. As the museum brochure puts it, the museum "is full to the brim; its population density an expression not only of the accumulations of time but of the urgencies, which inspired the making of so much stuff: the poverty of the poor, the arrogance of the war-

mongers, the despair of the victims, and maybe even stronger than all that, the glory of this whole god-given world." All these words ring true, and more; nothing can prepare you for the physical presence of the brightly colored, passionately sculpted giant and not-so-giant figures that fill the place, hanging from the walls and rafters.

If you want to see the Bread and Puppet Theater in action, time your visit for a Sunday afternoon, when the group gives shows (dubbed the Basic Needs Theater) and hosts concerts; they also make appearances in various Fourth of July parades and other summer festivals in nearby towns like Cabot, Barton, and Lyndonville. Any of these is a sight you won't soon forget, so make the effort if you can.

ROUTE 14: CRAFTSBURY COMMON

In the Green Mountain foothills west of Glover, a series of villages all with variations on the name "Craftsbury" makes for lovely countryside tours, especially during the fall color season. Accessible by following Route 14, which runs south of US-5 from Newport and continues south to the fringes of Montpelier, Vermont's capital, the drive through these villages is a delight at almost any time of year. The highlight of Route 14 is the hamlet of **Craftsbury Common,** where a hilltop green common is fringed by the white clapboard buildings of the upscale (but photogenic) **Inn on the Common** ($120–180; 802/586-9619), at which you can enjoy a multi-course dinner or stay the night in antique-filled rooms. Outside the village, more active pleasures can be pursued at the **Craftsbury Outdoor Center** (802/586-7767), a cross-country ski center and summertime biking and canoe resort with moderately priced rooms and equipment rentals.

BROWNINGTON VILLAGE

From the town of Orleans, you can travel east two miles away from I-91 and experience what Vermont was like some 200 years ago by visiting the Brownington Village Historic District. Follow the few signs along Village Road (heading northeast and uphill) until you come upon the impressive **Old Stone House,** which was built in 1836 as a schoolhouse by Alexander Twilight, America's first African-American college graduate (Middlebury College, Class of 1835). Now a historical museum (daily 10 AM–5 PM; $5), it contains items of interest from Brownington and a number of other similar Vermont villages that have been all but abandoned for the past century or more.

the Old Stone House

LAKE WILLOUGHBY

"The vision of Willoughby comes with a sudden and breath-taking wonder, an unforgettable picture marked with a grandeur that is rare in the usually serene landscape of Vermont." So says the 1930s WPA *Guide to Vermont,* and for once the prose is not overwrought.

Long, deep, narrow, and hemmed by silver cliffs that rise up hundreds of feet, Lake Willoughby looks like it belongs among the Norwegian fjords or lochs of the Scottish Highlands. Though small (maybe one-tenth the size of Newport's Lake Memphremagog, and one-hundredth the size of New Hampshire's Lake Winnipesaukee), Willoughby is a beautiful spot and definitely worth planning a day or more around.

Located about five miles east of Barton, leaving I-91 from the same exit 25 that takes you south to the Bread and Puppet Museum, Lake Willoughby spreads alongside Route 5A, which at one time was the main US-5 alignment, reflecting the steely gray sides of 2,751-foot Mount Pisgah and the slightly smaller Mount Hor, facing each other across the deep waters. It's a fine sight at any time of year and is especially lovely during the fall color sweeps, when the surrounding forests are ablaze with reds and golds.

North of Lyndonville, I-91 reaches its highest point (1,856 feet) near MM150.5.

The four or so miles of Route 5A that swing along Lake Willoughby's eastern shore are only slightly developed, dotted with quaint little dockside vacation cabins and a few motels and cabin courts, like lovely **Perkins Hilltop Cottages** ($45–60; 802/525-6988) at the north end of the lakeshore. Another, plusher lodging option in this quiet corner of the world is the **Willoughvale Inn** ($90–150; 802/525-4123), with eight rooms, four cabins, and a fine-dining restaurant.

For a long-distance leaf-peepers' update on the progress of Vermont foliage, call the state's **fall foliage hotline** (24-hour recording, Sept. and Oct. only): 802/828-3239.

At the south end of the lake, a small gravel beach along Route 5A offers a sublime view north across the water, framing sunset views between the fjord-like gray cliffs and forested peaks.

THE BURKES

South of Lake Willoughby, some dozen miles north of St. Johnsbury, a collection of rural hamlets known as the Burkes (East Burke, Burke Hollow, West Burke) is the most upmarket part of the usually low-key Northeast Kingdom, thanks to the nearby presence of the Burke Mountain ski area. It's a beautiful region, with nearly

One of Vermont's hidden ski resorts, **Burke Mountain** (802/626-3305 or 800/541-5480) with its slopeside condos and 2,000-foot vertical drop, may help account for the surrounding area's upscale, leisure-class airs. Though not as big as most, it's among the best, and the high percentage of expert runs attracts top-level skiers, including some proto-Olympic downhillers, and anyone who hates lift lines.

For more information on Vermont's lovely northeast corner, contact the **Northeast Kingdom Chamber of Commerce,** in St. Johnsbury at 30 Western Avenue (802/748-3678 or 800/639-6379).

every turn in the road worthy of a postcard or snapshot. You can't go wrong touring the area's winding country lanes in search of pastoral charm.

If breathing in all that fresh country air works up an appetite, head to East Burke, on Route 114 at the foot of the ski area, and choose from a pair of places to eat: **Bailey's & Burke's** (802/626-1188), a country store with a pub out back serving burgers and gourmet pizzas, or the lovely little **River Garden Cafe** (802/626-3514) across the street, serving a variety of meat and fish dishes in a lovely garden setting. If you want to stay the night, check in to **The Village Inn** ($75; 802/626-3161).

US-5 crosses US-2 at the fascinating crossroads town of St. Johnsbury, unofficial capital of Vermont's Northeast Kingdom. One of the most historic places in the state, St. Johnsbury is described in detail on page 123.

FALL COLOR TOUR: BARNET AND PEACHAM

Between St. Johnsbury and Barnet, US-5 follows along the banks of the beautiful Passumpsic River, but by the time it reaches Barnet the old road runs right in the literal shadow of the superslab. But worry not: just west of US-5 (and I-91 exit 18), Barnet Center Road brings you to the heart of historic Barnet Center (pop. 1,415), settled by Scots and centered on a Presbyterian Church with an adjacent cemetery. Further west, Peacham (pop. 627) is a perennial candidate for the title of "Vermont's most photographed village," and it's many a fall color fan's favorite Vermont town. Stretching along the crest of a hill, the pretty, ultra-tidy village is one continuous Kodak moment.

South of Barnet, US-5 bows east away from I-91, passing through many miles of pastoral riverside scenery. Apart from a few barns (including at least one round one, housing a dairy), acres of corn, and a few hundred cows, there's not a lot to stop for. However, a brief detour from the town of Wells River, heading west onto US-302 to its junction with I-91 exit 17, will bring you a great road-food haunt: the **P&H Truck Stop Café** (802/429-2141), where you can enjoy fine seafood chowder, charbroiled cheeseburgers, and great pies, not to mention the marvelous Peterbilt/Kenworth/Mack Truck wallpaper, 24 hours a day. If you've been on the road too long, take a shower which costs $5, free with purchase of 75 gallons or more.

BRADFORD

Like most of the towns along the I-91 corridor, Bradford takes little notice of the hulking freeway that passes right by it. Instead, it stays focused on its traditional downtown area, which has a lively and thriving array of clothing stores, hardware stores, a busy bakery, the even busier Bliss Village Store, plus the **Perfect Pear Cafe,** (802/222-5912) all lined up along a block or two of US-5. North of downtown Bradford, US-5 passes through a stately residential district, with a mix of brick and wooden homes and some delicate church spires.

The town is fun to wander around, and one of the many interesting places to eat in the upper Connecticut Valley is hidden away here in tiny Bradford, behind US-5 overlooking the river from the basement of the local post office. Sound unlikely? Check it out: **Peyton Place** (dinner only, Wed.–Sun. only; 802/222-5462), run by a husband and wife team, Jim and Heidi Peyton.

FAIRLEE

Spreading out along US-5 at a bend in the Connecticut River, Fairlee is dominated by the landmark palisades, near-vertical cliffs that tower over 100 feet above the town. The natural cliff face had been blown away to make room for I-91, so the rocks are held in place behind chain-link fencing. They're still pretty impressive and the wall of rock makes a memorable gateway to the town.

Coming from the north, or heading north from Fairlee's I-91 exit 15, all road-trippers will want to stop and pay a visit to the **Fairlee Motel and Drive-In Theater** run by the Herb family (rooms $50–70; 802/333-9192). The motel may look like a standard motor court, but it has one totally unique feature: the back walls of each of the dozen or so rooms is a plate-glass picture window, giving overnight guests a clear view out at a full-sized drive-in movie screen. Cars and drivers ($5.50 per person) are welcome, too, and can listen from the original sound system, which you hook on the car windows, or tune your car stereo to 590AM.

Another roadside landmark: the **Fairlee Diner** (802/333-2569), between the river and US-5 at the center of town, serving breakfast and lunch from 5 AM–2 PM daily. It's not a classic prefab and does have dropped acoustic ceilings and fluorescent lights, but nonetheless it hums with local chatter and the food is great. Try the turkey sandwich with crispy fries and finish off with a slice of lemon meringue pie.

North of Wells River, East Ryegate looks like a textbook example of a company town. It was built years ago but is still dependent upon the large Kimberly-Clark paper mill.

North of Bradford, along US-5 in the hamlet of Newbury, the roadside **Four Corners Farm** grows and sells the very freshest fruits and vegetables, from delicate lettuces to baskets of blueberries.

Bradford calls itself Home of the First Globe because James Wilson produced the first American-made geographic globes here as early as 1812.

From the center of Fairlee, near the diner, a very cool and very rusty, old rainbow-**arched bridge** crosses the river over to Orford, New Hampshire, which is covered in our Appalachian Trail chapter.

Fairlee likes to claim that the world's first steamboat was operated here on the Connecticut River by lumberman Samuel Morey as early as 1793, 14 years before Robert Fulton launched the *Clermont*.

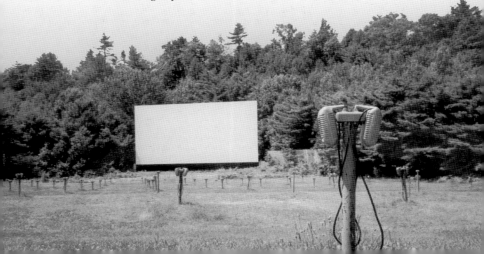

And if the two places above aren't reason enough to make you want to visit, the next two will be: Fairlee has the irresistible **Whippi-Dip Ice Cream** stand, on US-5 at the south end of town, and the picture-perfect **Silver Maple Lodge**, 520 S. US-5 ($50–80; 802/333-4326), which has a gorgeous set of 1920s cabins set back from the highway.

NORWICH

Across the river from Hanover and Dartmouth, Norwich (pop. 3,100) is smaller, and in many ways more enjoyable. With loads of old houses and white picket

---

I-91 SURVIVAL GUIDE: ACROSS NEW ENGLAND

MM178: Canada/Vermont international border.

MM177: Exit 29, junction with US-5 through Derby Line (see page 192).

MM176.5: Vermont Welcome Center, located at 45th Parallel, the midpoint between North Pole and the Equator.

MM170: Exit 28, junction with US-5 to Newport. U.S. Border Patrol office, in case you cross Canadian border after hours.

MM156: Exit 25 for Barton, Glover, and the Bread and Puppet Theater and Museum (see page 193).

MM150.5: Highest point on I-91, 1,856 feet.

MM131: Exit 21, junction with US-2 westbound to Joe's Pond and Montpelier (see page 127) and US-5 through St. Johnsbury.

MM128: Exit 19, junction with I-93 (southbound only).

MM122–112: Beautiful views of Connecticut River Valley.

MM121: Exit 18, junction with US-5 through Barnet and the scenic route west to Peacham (see page 196).

MM110: Exit 17, junction with US-5 and US-302 near Wells River; junction is home to 24-hour P&H Truck Stop (see page 196).

MM98: Exit 16 for US-5 through Bradford (see page 196).

MM92: Exit 15 for US-5 through Fairlee, home to the Fairlee Diner and the Fairlee Motel & Drive-In Theater (see page 197).

MM75: Exit 13 for Appalachian Trail crossing to Hanover, New Hampshire (see page 295).

MM71: Exit 11 for US-4 and US-5 through White River Junction (see page 200).

MM70: Junction with I-89, northwest to Montpelier and Burlington, southeast to Concord, New Hampshire.

fences surrounding a town green and a 25 mph speed limit that forces you to slow down and enjoy the roses, Norwich has the bookstores and bakeries of Hanover, but without the preppy stuffiness. It also has a wonderful version of that Vermont icon, the country store (**Dan and Wit's**), and a pretty country inn: the **Norwich Inn,** on Main Street a block west of US-5 ($70–120; 802/649-1143).

East of town, just before you cross the river into Hanover, New Hampshire, visit the **Montshire Museum of Science** (daily 10 AM–5 PM; $5; 802/649-2200), a hands-on exploration of science and technology that has everything from ant farms to wind tunnels.

MM60: Exit 9 for US-5 south to historic Windsor, a massive covered bridge, and the Saint-Gaudens National Historic Site (see page 201).

MM34: Exit 6 junction with scenic Route 103 through Rockingham and Chester (see page 203).

MM29: Exit 5 junction with US-5 through Bellows Falls (see page 203).

MM18: Exit 4 for US-5 through Putney (see page 204).

MM9: Exit 2 for Brattleboro (see page 206).

MM0.5: Vermont Welcome Center.

MM0/55: Vermont/Massachusetts state line.

MM43: Exit 26 for Greenfield and US-5 south through Historic Deerfield; junction with the Mohawk Trail (Route 2) east and west across the mountains (see page 207).

MM36: Exit 25 for US-5 north through Historic Deerfield (see page 209).

MM26: Exit 20 for US-5 through Northampton and Route 9 east to Amherst (see page 210).

MM11: Exit 14 for Massachusetts Turnpike (I-90).

MM9: Exit 13 for US-5 through West Springfield, bridges across river to downtown Springfield.

MM6: Exit 7 for downtown Springfield and Basketball Hall of Fame (see page 211).

MM0/58: Massachusetts/Connecticut state line.

MM53: Exit 46 to Enfield.

MM37: exit 29 for downtown Hartford (see page 214).

MM33.5: Exit 26 for historic Wethersfield (see page 216).

MM3: Exit 1 for downtown New Haven (see page 104).

MM0: I-91 junction with I-95, at Exit 48.

Between Norwich, Vermont and Hanover, New Hampshire, a broad new, neoclassical bridge carries cars and the Appalachian Trail (AT) over the Connecticut River. For more on this section of the 2,100-mile AT, the longest hiking trail in the USA, see pages 297–98. Just south, at White River Junction, US-5 crosses east–west US-4, which runs up through serene Woodstock and the Green Mountains ski areas around Killington. See pages 179–82 for more.

In the mid-1930s, the *WPA Guide to Vermont* had this to say about White River Junction: "The diners along Main Street are usually crowded with red-faced railroad men in blue overalls and husky truck drivers in leather jackets, while just across the way the hotel and restaurants are frequently thronged with Dartmouth undergraduates wearing casually their tailored sports clothes." White River has another claim to fame: it was here in 1844 that nitrous oxide (laughing gas) was first used as an anaesthetic.

About 20 miles up the White River Valley on I-89 or Route 14 is the township of South Royalton, birthplace in 1805 of Mormon founder **Joseph Smith.** A huge solid granite monument and visitor center (daily 9 AM–5 PM) mark the spot, along with about 80,000 lights between Thanksgiving and Christmas.

WHITE RIVER JUNCTION

Turn-of-the-20th-century White River Junction (pop. 2,582) used to echo with the sounds of some 50 trains a day traveling over six separate rail lines. The demise of the railroads and arrival of the Interstate cloverleaf on the outskirts of town effectively mothballed the downtown area, but like good vintage clothing, the historic center has been rediscovered by an art-smart crowd that doesn't mind the holes and missing buttons. Exclusive galleries and expensive boutiques aren't invading the old brick storefronts around the tracks; on the contrary, the town looks like it's still expecting the New Deal to come pay a visit. There are a couple of exceptionally interesting little places, like the magical **Lampscapes** gallery at 77 Gates Street, where artist Kenneth Blaisdell hand paints and sells all shapes and sizes of colorful lampshades, or the expansive **Vermont Surplus,** next to the railroad tracks, where you can take home a souvenir door frame, kitchen table, or a kitchen sink.

New England Central trains still rumble through White River Junction a few times a day, and Amtrak stops here on its mainline Vermonter route along the Connecticut River between New York City and Montreal. Apart from the trains, the main signs of life here are at breakfast and lunch, when the ancient-looking **Polka Dot Restaurant,** 7 N. Main Street (daily 5 AM–7 PM; 802/295-9722) serves the usual unpretentious, inexpensive grilled and fried foods. For a healthier start to the day, try the delicious fresh pastries and croissants that come out of the **Bakers' Studio,** (9 AM–5 PM; 802/296-7201), a 30-second walk away from the Polka Dot at 7 S. Main Street. In between the two, and adding some rare spice to the culinary mix, is the lively **Karibu Tule** (802/296-3756), serving Afro-Caribbean specialties at dinner (Wed.–Sun. 5–9 PM).

If you're looking for lodging with more character than the chain motels (Super 8, etc.) along the Interstates, consider downtown's **Hotel Coolidge** ($55 a night, $225 a week; 800/622-1124). Despite a passing resemblance to something from *Barton Fink,* it's very clean, very friendly, and definitely a good value. Even better value are their HI-hostel bunks, which go for around $20.

FRESH BEER HERE

Living in the Upper Valley of the Connecticut River must be thirsty work, or folks up here have a particularly well-developed appreciation for the finer beers in life. Whatever the reason, several microbreweries and brewpubs flourish within a very small radius of White River Junction.

Across the river, **The Seven Barrels** (11:30 AM–1 AM; 603/298-5566) lies on Route 12A beside the I-89 overpass in the megamall sprawl of West Lebanon, New Hampshire. Despite the unlikely setting, this brewpub offers a good line of beers—British bitter, India Pale Ale, oatmeal stout, various seasonals—a liberal sampling of English pub grub—bubble and squeak, toad-in-the-hole, fish 'n' chips—and some concessions to modern American palates—veggie burgers, buffalo wings, pasta specials.

Though the brewery started out right in White River Junction, it's a quick trip down US-5 to reach the current home of the **Catamount Brewing Company,** which offers free tours (daily at 11 AM, 1 and 3 PM; 800/540-2248) and tastings of their English-style ales and seasonal brews in their modern brewery on the north side of Windsor, hidden away in an industrial park a mile south of the I-91 exit. And up in nearby mountains along US-4, the **Long Trail Brewing Company** has a taproom (daily 10 AM–6 PM; 802/672-5011) at the junction of US-4 and Route 100A, west of Woodstock, Vermont, where you can try the state's most popular microbrew, Long Trail Ale. Their flagship ale is named after the route that inspired the Appalachian Trail: the 85-year-old Long Trail, a 255-mile footpath running along the spine of the Green Mountains from Massachusetts to Canada. They also have seasonals, stout, even a kölsch—a light, wheaty ale, perfect for quenching summer thirst.

WINDSOR

With a number of crafts and antique shops mixed in among church spires and historic industrial premises, Windsor (pop. 3,700; elev. 321) is lovely to look at, and its attractions are way more than skin deep. The first capital of Vermont, Windsor centers on the so-called **Constitution House** at 16 N. Main Street (Wed.–Sun. 11 AM–5 PM; $2), the former tavern, moved here from the outskirts of Windsor, where on July 8, 1777, Vermont declared itself a free and independent republic. Vermonters were the first in America to adopt a constitution that outlawed slavery and granted universal male voting rights without property requirements. Displays in the museum include some very rare newspapers dating from the short-lived Republic of Vermont, which eventually joined the rest of the United States in 1791.

CRACKER BARREL BAZAAR

JULY

FIDDLERS - 21
BAZAAR - 22

The **Windsor-Cornish Covered Bridge,** the longest in New England at 460 feet, was built in 1866. Walk Your Horses or Pay $2 Fine, says the warning emblazoned over the entrance on the New Hampshire side.

At the south end of Windsor, next to a waterfall, the 1846 Robbins and Lawrence Armory has been preserved as the **American Precision Museum,** 196 Main Street (daily 10 AM–5 PM; $5; 802/674-5781), which traces America's early moves into the Industrial Age. For historians of industrial development, this is a significant place. Back in the 1840s, gun makers here developed the precision machining processes that enabled them to produce identical, interchangeable parts, which in turn made possible the "American System" and eventually the assembly line. The changes that started here were new and novel enough that this distant Windsor factory was able to sell 25,000 rifles to the British Army at the Crystal Palace exposition of 1851. The dozens of tools, dies, lathes, metal presses, and other machines, including machines that make machines you can see on display here today were the first real harbingers of the international Machine Age that powered the late 19th and early 20th centuries.

North of Windsor, west of I-91 and US-5 via Route 12 in Hartland Four Corners, the popular **Skunk Hollow Tavern** on Brownsville Road (Wed.–Sun. 5 PM–midnight; 802/436-2139) is a lively, mostly local place for food, drink, and frequent live music.

The connection is never made explicit, but in some cruelly ironic twist of fate, the former manufacturing powerhouse of Windsor has become a Luddite-leaning center for handcrafts. In the lobby of the former Windsor House Hotel at 54 Main Street, the **Vermont State Craft Center** (9 AM–5 PM; 802/674-6729) is a high-quality gift shop featuring the work of more than 100 Vermont-based artists and craftspeople, selling everything from pottery to weavings. The hand-made wooden household utensils are especially coveted.

Across Main Street from the Vermont State Craft Center stands the oldest continuous-use post office in the United States. Another Windsor landmark is the oldest state prison in the United States, though this has been converted into a housing complex.

South of Windsor and west of US-5, **Ascutney State Park** (802/674-2060) has hiking, hot showers, and camping. Further south, along the river east of US-5, **Wilgus State Park** (802/674-5422) has swimming, hot showers, and camping.

CORNISH, NEW HAMPSHIRE: SAINT-GAUDENS NATIONAL HISTORIC SITE

Across the Connecticut River from Windsor, about two miles north of the covered bridge, the Saint-Gaudens National Historic Site (daily 9 AM–4:30 PM; $4; 603/675-2175) preserves the hillside home and studio of turn-of-the-20th-century artist and sculptor Augustus Saint-Gaudens. Born in Ireland to French and Irish parents, the artist came to New York as a six-month-old baby, and at age 13 he was apprenticed as a commercial artist, cutting cameos and taking classes at the Cooper Union. Twenty years later, in 1881 he had his first major success with a commission to create a monument to Civil War Admiral Farragut, on which he worked with noted architect Stanford White. Saint-Gaudens quickly became an eminent artist, summering here in Cornish while creating such important public monuments as the "Sherman's March to the Sea" statue that stands in Central Park, Boston's deep-relief Shaw Memorial, and a series of coins for the U.S. Mint (from a one cent penny to a $10 and a $20 gold piece).

Copies of all of these works and many more are on display around the lushly landscaped grounds, which give grand views across the river to Ascutney and the Green Mountains. Saint-Gaudens died of cancer in 1907 at age 59 and is buried on the estate beneath a marble tomb of his own design.

CHESTER AND GRAFTON

North of Bellows Falls, west from US-5 and I-91 exit 6, Route 103 runs up into the Green Mountains, passing through the pretty town of Chester (pop. 2,850) on its way to Ludlow and the Green Mountains ski resorts. Chester has some old Victorian hotels, the classic prefab stainless-steel **Country Girl Diner** on Route 103 (802/875-2650), and since 1912, the world headquarters for the cartographic National Survey (802/875-2121). Chester is a lovely spot in the fall, and all summer long is the destination of the **Green Mountain Flyer** scenic railroad from Bellows Falls. One of Vermont's most popular old hotels, the former Inn at Long Last, has been resurrected as the **Fullerton Inn,** 40 Common Street ($110–150; 802/875-2444) facing the town green off the main road.

South of Chester along Route 35, the village of Grafton (pop. 600) looks picture-perfect and tries hard to keep things that way. Like much of the Green Mountains region before the Civil War, Grafton was a wool-growing community, running thousands of sheep over what were then mostly

The **Grafton Village Cheese Factory,** a half-mile south of the Old Tavern at 533 Townshend Road (802/843-2221), makes some of the smoothest cheddar cheeses you'll ever taste from traditional raw (unpasteurized) milk and available in many different flavors and intensities. If you don't need tidy blocks that are easy to gift wrap, ask in the historic Grafton Village Store, 16 Main Street (802/843-2348) for their "random cuts," irregular chunks sold for a steep discount.

deforested hills. The sheep are long gone, the surrounding forests have recovered, and Grafton lives on, thanks to local preservationists. Supported by the nonprofit Windham Foundation, which since the early 1960s has overseen the resurrection of Grafton, the white-columned **Old Tavern** ($125–225; 802/843-2231) at the center of Grafton has become one of central Vermont's most popular old hotels, offering a dozen luxurious rooms and a great restaurant, serving contemporary versions of traditional New England favorites. There's also an amiable bar, so be sure to stop.

Grafton also has some fine art galleries, like the **North Star** on Townshend Road south of the Old Tavern. The whole ensemble of Grafton, from inn to green to white-steepled church, makes it many visitors' favorite Vermont village.

BELLOWS FALLS

Squeezed between hills and the river, with industrial quarters starting down by the river and stair-stepping up the hillside in a series of terraces through the business district to residential neighborhoods, Bellows Falls' is one of the most photogenic little cities in New England. Bellows Falls' impressive natural waterfalls add to the scenery, and the first canal in the United States was built in 1792 to bypass them. The town has been settled as long as anywhere and it has managed to remain an authentic place, with local shops, a movie theater, an excellent diner, and only the

Vermont's oldest highway, known as the King's Highway, ran near today's US-5 south of Bellows Falls between Westminster and Westminster Station, two miles to the north.

slightest trace of tourist dependency. If you think the Bellows Falls townscape looks and sounds like an ideal movie location, you're right; many films, including the recent *Cider House Rules,* have featured local streets and the historic railroad as backdrops to celluloid fantasy.

Eat at the **Miss Bellows Falls Diner,** a lovingly maintained 1941 vintage Worcester located downtown at 90 Rockingham Street (802/463-9800). The exterior preserves the original barrel roof and all the hand-painted enamel panels advertising "Booth Service," but it's the inside that's really fine: oak booths with chrome-trimmed tables, a marble counter, red-white-and-black tile floor, and warm incandescent light fixtures aplenty. The food's very good too, so stop in when you can.

Running right along the Connecticut and Williams Rivers between Bellows Falls and Chester, the **Green Mountain Flyer** (11 AM and 2 PM; $12; 802/463-3069 or 800/707-3530) offers two-hour trips on restored 1930s railroad rolling stock along the Williams River up to the mountain town of Chester—an excellent way to enjoy the fall foliage without worrying about keeping your car on the road. On the other side of the mountains, the same company offers trips between Bennington and Manchester.

PUTNEY

These days Putney (pop. 2,400) is a friendly, fairly sleepy place, but 150 years ago it was a swingin' little town, thanks to the presence of John Humphries Noyes and his fellow Perfectionists, who quietly established a free love community here in 1838. After quietly practicing a sort of communal (or Complex) marriage for years, the group left swiftly after Noyes was arrested here in 1847 and fled west to Oneida, New York.

While there is no plaque or marker remembering Noyes anywhere in Putney, the town does have one attraction for a certain sort of sensualist. What is perhaps the best and certainly the most unlikely barbecue stand in all New England, **Curti's All American BarBQ,** smokes away (in summer only) in an old school bus parked next to a Mobil station just above I-91 (right across US-5 from the Putney Food Co-op). Calling itself the Ninth Wonder of the World, and serving heavenly ribs cooked just right (smoked, not steamed into oblivion), Curti's is a great place to stop for a mouthwateringly meaty treat on a sunny afternoon. Breathe deep and say "aaaah."

If the time's not quite right for alfresco ribs, Putney is also home to the homey **Putney Diner** (802/387-5433) on Main Street; open daily

6 AM–8 PM (until 9 PM on weekends) for the usual grilled breakfasts and burgers. The Putney Diner may not have the period charm of a stainless steel or prefab classic, but it attracts a solid, local crowd—always a good sign for judging a diner's real quality.

To stay the night, look into the historic **Putney Inn,** along the river on Depot Road ($80–150; 802/387-5517), which has fireplaces in the lobby, Victorian-style furniture in the bedrooms, a friendly pub, and a fine restaurant.

About five miles north of Putney along US-5, **Santa's Land** (daily 10 AM–5 PM; $9.75; 802/387-5550) is a Christmas-themed amusement park with a tiny train ride, a carousel, and the essential deer corral. Kids 3–12 get a not-exactly-generous 50¢ discount on admission, so think twice before you bring the whole family.

DETOUR: MOUNT MONADNOCK LOOP

A short and very scenic detour east from the Brattleboro area can bring you to one of the most famous mountains in a region famous for its mountains: Mount Monadnock, the 3,165-foot peak that has given its name to a geographical class of mountains that stands alone. Rising up from the rolling farmlands of southern New Hampshire, the summit of Mount Monadnock gives views over all six New England states—the only place where this is true—with binocular-enhanced clear-day vistas stretching from the Boston skyline to Mount Washington. The views from the top are unobstructed by trees, due in part to the tough weather but also to the fact that back in 1810 pioneer farmers set fires that destroyed all the soil within 500 feet of the summit.

Putney is the national headquarters for the **Basketville** stores (802/387-5509), which advertise themselves from here to Florida and feature stacks of wicker baskets and a wide range of toys and domestic goodies. At time of writing, they were offering a free back scratcher to anyone who stepped in the door—something worth stopping for.

Mount Monadnock State Park (daily 8 AM–dusk; 603/532-8862) surrounds the summit. To reach the park and the peak, follow Route 124 southeast from Keene to the visitor center west of Jaffrey; the nicest, most popular, and most direct route to the top is the White Dot Trail, which takes about two hours up, less coming back.

North of Mount Monadnock, the pretty village of **Harrisville** isn't what you might expect from a mill town, but this tidy little place was one of the earliest mill towns in a state that grew to have the world's largest. Now quiet, the old mill buildings are reflected in the watery expanse of a glassy millpond, which from other sides reflects back a church steeple, stately trees, and finely kept clapboard houses. Ten miles to the northeast, Hancock, on scenic Route 123, is centered upon the state's oldest hotel, the **John Hancock Inn** ($120–230; 603/525-3318), which has a dozen rooms and a fine, early American-style restaurant.

Facing Mount Monadnock from the southeast, off scenic US-202 south of Jaffrey, the **Cathedral of the Pines** (May–Oct. daily 9 AM–5 PM; donations; 603/899-3300) is an outdoor memorial to all Americans killed in battle. Built by a couple in memory of their son who was killed in World War II, the memorial is set amid a peaceful pine forest and features plaques designed by Norman Rockwell.

Along with the New Hampshire peak that bears the Monadnock moniker, other well-known monadnocks in New England include Mount Katahdin in northern Maine and Mount Greylock in western Massachusetts; both these peaks are described in the Appalachian Trail chapter.

About a dozen miles north of Brattleboro, off Route 30 on a secluded hillside overlooking the Connecticut River Valley from the south side of Dummerston township, the British writer Rudyard Kipling lived and worked between 1892 and 1896 in a house he designed, known as Naulakha. Kipling came here after marrying a Brattleboro girl, Caroline Balestier, and during his short stay he wrote some of his most famous works, including parts of the *Jungle Book* and *Captains Courageous*. Kipling's house, owned by the British-based Landmark Trust, is generally not open to visitors' but it can be rented for $750–1,200/week (from the United States dial 011-44-1628-825-925).

BRATTLEBORO

Despite having a population smaller than most metropolitan suburbs, by Vermont standards Brattleboro (pop. 8,600) is a big city, with a busy downtown business district covering some steep hills at the confluence of the West and Connecticut Rivers. Located at the far southeastern corner of the state, Brattleboro has adopted the slogan "Where Vermont Begins," but the city more accurately marks the place where the mill towns of Massachusetts merge into the rural realms of the Green Mountain State. The first permanent settlement in Vermont, Brattleboro was founded in 1724 and boomed as an industrial center, but these days it has a dual personality: part politically lively, left-leaning community, part tourism center, catering to the visitors bound for the ski slopes to the west.

The compact downtown boasts a number of handsome brick and terra-cotta buildings dating from Brattleboro's turn-of-the-20th-century heyday, with department stores and hotels lining Main Street (US-5) around its junction with Eliot Street. Perhaps the most distinctive building is the 1930s art deco **Latchis Hotel,** 50 Main Street ($40–75; 802/254-6300), still run by the Latchis family, who also run the adjoining and even more exuberantly art deco movie theater, where you can enjoy mainstream films under a stylized zodiac sky.

For a taste of Brattleboro's left-leaning, nature-loving character, stop by **Common Ground,** 25 Eliot Street (Thurs.–Sun. only; 802/257-0855) for a vegetarian dinner or a delicious (and refined sugar–free) dessert. If you can imagine paying upwards of $25 a plate to eat in a diner, you may want to make your way to Brattleboro's famous destination diner, **T. J. Buckley's Uptown Diner,** two blocks west of Main Street (US-5) at 132 Eliot

Just west of Brattleboro along semiscenic Route 9, about two miles west of I-91, the **Chelsea Royal Diner** (daily 6 AM–9 PM; 802/254-8399) is a lovely 1938 Worcester diner that's been incorporated into a larger restaurant. The neon sign alone makes it worth a visit.

Street (802/257-4922). This authentic-looking 1920s Worcester diner, wrapped in a 1950s shell, is the stage for one of the state's best restaurants. With dishes like truffle-stuffed chicken and broiled scallops replacing the more standard diner fare, you won't find fried eggs or turkey dinners on the menu here.

DETOUR: HINSDALE, NEW HAMPSHIRE— BIRTHPLACE OF THE AUTOMOBILE?

Perhaps best known for its large greyhound racing track, tiny Hinsdale is a rough little place worth a visit, at least for aficionados of automobile history. Way back in 1875, a local mechanic named George Long built a four-wheeled vehicle that was powered by a charcoal-burning steam engine and could reach speeds of 30 mph. Long later built a gasoline-powered machine as well, which is now in the Smithsonian collection, but his initial efforts have never been popularly acknowledged. Hinsdale remembers, however, with a plaque along Route 119 at the edge of town, about five miles southeast from Brattleboro.

GREENFIELD: GATEWAY TO THE MOHAWK TRAIL

As I-91 speeds down into the Massachusetts parts of the Connecticut River valley, the freeway veers west around the Franklin County seat of Greenfield, a place once known for its cutlery, tap-and-die, and other metals-related manufacturing. The proximity of the Interstate has endowed Greenfield with some of the only chain motels in western Massachusetts. If you prefer a Howard Johnson's or Super 8 to a B&B or campground, you'll find them beside the rotary at the junction of Route 2 and I-91. It's not a place to linger, but Greenfield can make an affordable base to explore some of the many great roads that wind through this region, particularly the famed Mohawk Trail, Route 2, which runs west from town. This was the first official scenic route in America and still holds a number of fascinating little throwbacks to the early years of automobile-based tourism.

Under a mile west from town, the first of many great old-fashioned Mohawk Trail roadside attractions is the historic **Long View Tower,** which looks like a forest-fire lookout tower and offers a three state view as well as a small petting zoo and a miniature golf course. West from here, the Mohawk Trail climbs deeper into the mountains, and if you're in the market for a classic souvenir, drive a few more miles to the **Big Indian Shop,** three miles east of Charlemont, marked by a giant Native American figure and full of all the moccasins, rubber tomahawks, paperweights, and postcards you could want.

For one of the area's least expensive rooms, take the Interstate for two exits south of Greenfield to the Motel 6 outside Deerfield. Be aware that, even here, peak season rates run $50 a night or more.

For more on the Mohawk Trail, which runs west to the Berkshire towns of North Adams and Williamstown, see the Appalachian Trail chapter on pages 303–04.

ROUTE 2 DETOURS: SHELBURNE FALLS AND COLRAIN

Travelers in search of variety should head west from Greenfield along the historic Mohawk Trail, Route 2, and take a turn at the signs for the lively, artsy little town of Shelburne Falls, which is actually two towns, Shelburne and Buckland, facing one another across the Deerfield River. The two are linked by the **Bridge of Flowers,** a former electric-trolley bridge that was converted to a linear display garden after the trolleys closed down in the 1920s. Four score and a few

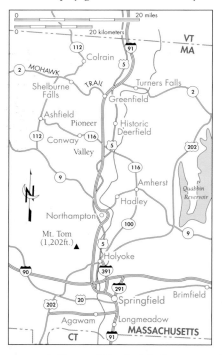

years later, there are mature trees growing out of the concrete arches, and every spring local gardeners add rich displays of annual color. The story of the trolleys is told in a small new museum, walking distance south of the bridge, and rides on restored trolleys are sometimes offered.

Another oft-touted wonder is the sculptured riverbed below Salmon Falls, just east of Bridge Street. Here, beside the spillway of diminutive Deerfield Dam and Powerhouse #3, the **Glacial Potholes** are popular for picnics, geological ruminations, hanging out with schoolmates, and boulder-hopping. Just don't fall asleep with your hearing aid turned down; the dam makes frequent releases of water, especially during the summer whitewater-rafting season.

Nearby food and beverage options include: espresso concoctions from Bridge Street's **Shelburne Falls Coffee Roasters,** or the vegetarian-friendly deli selections at the rear of **McCusker's Market,** facing the south end of the iron bridge. The best cheap grub in town is served up at the homey **Fox Town Coffee and Sandwich Shop** on Bridge Street, where you can feast on a short stack of pancakes with real maple syrup ($2), or enjoy a fresh BLT with a packet of potato chips and a pickle on the side for $2.55. For organic salads and richly sauced, red-meat-free entrees (including a famously yummy roast chicken with garlic mashed potatoes), try the **Copper Angel Cafe,** 2 State Street (413/625-2727) on the Buckland side of the bridge.

A short six miles north of Shelburne Falls along scenic Route 112, the town of **Colrain** holds another great place: the charming and whimsical **Green Emporium** (413/624-5122). Here you can enjoy creative dinners (Thurs.–Sun.) and a nice Sunday brunch in a former Methodist church. To contemplate the pastoral landscape with the eye and tempo of a true country rambler it would be best to make a local farm stay or B&B the base for your perambulations. Friendly **Penfrydd Farm** in Colrain (413/624-5516) is a fine example, with unpretentious $65-a-night rooms in an attractively renovated 19th-century farmhouse, a small herd of llamas, wonderful hilltop views across pastures and forest, and night skies thick with stars citydwellers would never see from their roof decks.

SCENIC ROUTE 116: ASHFIELD AND CONWAY

Come fall, the sugar maples in the surrounding mixed hardwood forest add a blaze of brilliant orange to the landscape, making Route 2 a favorite of leaf-peepers between the end of September and Columbus Day weekend. But if sharing the two-lane road with thousands of rubbernecking drivers becomes wearisome, consider taking a road less traveled. Almost any road will do, but a loop along Route 116 through Ashfield and Conway, a few miles south of Route 2, passes over several historic covered bridges and offers enough pastoral beauty to more than compensate for the detours.

Shunning the main highway doesn't require skipping meals, either. For instance, there are thin-crust whole pizzas and slices at the **Countrypie Pizza Company** (open daily 11:30 AM–9 PM; 413/628-4488), 343 Main Street across from Ashfield's public library. Given the fresh fancy toppings available, the prices are a real steal. Or coast down Route 116 to **Baker's Country Store** (413/369-4936), just east of Conway's old water tower, and sit down to a simple soup or sandwich amid the fishing tackle and canned goods. If you like your pastry crusts short and white, be sure to sample the fresh pies, particularly in the summer during berry season.

HISTORIC DEERFIELD

Back in the valley, a world away from the modern Interstate aesthetic but just three miles south of Greenfield along US-5, Historic Deerfield (daily 9:30 AM–4:30 PM; $12; 413/774-5581) is an immaculately preserved architectural ensemble dating from the early 1700s to around 1850. Over a dozen clapboard buildings, shaded by a canopy of stately old elm trees, form a mile-long reminder of the time when this part of Massachusetts formed the frontier of western civilization, and when English settlers waged bloody war against the native Pocumtuck Indians. The surrounding town of Deerfield and the famous Deerfield Academy prep school hardly intrude, leaving Historic Deerfield to stand as it was, fanlight windows, wrought iron, well-worn stones, and all. Inside each house, guides

Although early spring is aptly known as mud season throughout New England's back country, it's also when the sugar maple sap starts to flow. Boil away nearly 98 percent of the sap and you have genuine maple syrup delicious enough to make muddy, frost-heaved farm roads positively inviting. Call the **Sugar Season Hotline** (413/628-3912) to obtain a list of maple producers you can visit.

discuss the lives, belongings, and historical contexts of the former inhabitants, often with such parental intimacy that you half expect these long-dead Ebenezers, Jonathans, and Marys to be napping upstairs. One of the finest surviving colonial townscapes in America, Historic Deerfield is well worth a visit, no matter how brief, especially since there's no admission charge if you just want to stop and walk around.

The only real new addition to Historic Deerfield is the **Flynt Center of Early New England Life** (daily 9:30 AM–4:30 PM; adults $6, students $3; 413/774-5581), which opened in late 1998 at the edge of a field, behind Main Street. The 27,000-square-foot museum, designed to look like a colonial tobacco barn, displays thousands of fancy goods and other consumer treasures—pewter teapots, silk waistcoats, and the like—that were keys to civilized life here on the edge of wilderness.

PIONEER VALLEY: AMHERST AND NORTHAMPTON

South of Historic Deerfield, the so-called Pioneer Valley swaps its ancient airs for some youthful vitality in a pair of college towns that between them boast five major colleges and more than 50,000 students. The smaller of the two towns, Amherst (pop. 35,200) is best known for its namesake college and for being the longtime home of poet **Emily Dickinson,** whose house at 280 Main Street (Wed.–Sat. only; $4; 413/542-8161) near the center of town belies her legendary hermetic personality. Between her house and the town green, a pair of metal sculptures imagines a poetic conversation between Emily Dickinson and Amherst's other famous poet, Robert Frost, who taught here for many years.

The main NPR radio station in the five college area is **WFCR 88.5FM,** but there are many others worth listening to, including **WMUA 91.1FM,** broadcasting from UMass at Amherst. Hit seek and ye shall find something you like.

Another unique book-related attraction near Amherst is the new **National Yiddish Book Center** (Sun.–Fri. 10 AM–3:30 PM, closed Sat.; free; 800/535-3595), where more than a million Yiddish books are collected on the campus of Hampshire College, in a series of buildings designed to resemble an Eastern European village or *shtetl.*

Northampton is also known in some circles as the place where Vermont native Calvin Coolidge got his start, serving as mayor here before going on to become president.

Between Amherst and Northampton, the nine-mile stretch of Route 9 linking the two college towns is surprisingly ugly, lined much of the way by megamalls and suffering from frequent traffic jams. But once you're over the Connecticut River, any hassle will seem worth it when you arrive in the center of Northampton (pop. 29,300), one of New England's liveliest college towns. Energized by the presence of Smith College, the country's largest and richest women's college, Northampton has all the usual college-town attractions—cafes, bookstores, gardens, and art galleries—plus the unique **Words and Pictures Museum,** 140 Main Street (Tues.–Sun. noon–5 PM; $3; 413/586-8545), established by the creators of those lovable Teenage Mutant Ninja Turtles. If you think comic books are just for kids, you owe it to yourself to visit.

The center of Northampton is right on US-5, just west of the I-91 freeway, where you'll find lots of nice cafes, bars, and restaurants, including **Sylvester's,** 111 Pleasant Street (413/586-5343), a health-conscious breakfast and lunch place inspired by the writings of Sylvester Graham, creator of the graham cracker, who lived in Northampton in the 1830s. For a change of pace, head out to the northwest edge of Northampton along Route 9, where the **Miss Florence Diner,** at 99 Main Street in the hamlet of Florence, has a great jukebox and equally great corned beef hash and other diner standards, served up inside a lovingly preserved 1940s Worcester diner. Northampton, though no Greenwich Village, has evolved into one of New England's best places to hear live music, whether at summer music festivals or at intimate clubs like the excellent **Iron Horse**, 20 Center Street (413/584-0610).

If you're a fan of the NPR radio program *This American Life,* you may have heard about **Chad's Trading Post,** on Route 10 at 164 College Highway in Southampton (413/529-9338). This roadside diner is operated as a living memorial to the owners' teenage son Chad, who was shot and killed.

SPRINGFIELD

A hundred miles west of Boston, sitting on the east bank of the Connecticut River, from which it is effectively cut off by the raging torrent of cars and trucks on the I-91 freeway, Springfield (pop. 157,000) is a historic industrial center at the southern edge of the rural Pioneer Valley. Famous first for the Springfield Rifle, the gun that won the Wild West, and for the other weapons produced at the Springfield Armory (1779–1968), the city later saw the first automobile factory in the country (Duryea Brothers, who produced the first of their "Power Wagons" here in 1896). Springfield is also now home to the Basketball Hall of Fame, which traces the history of the game that Dr. James Naismith, a Canadian-born P.E. teacher at Springfield College, invented here in 1891.

If you're a hoops fan, the **Basketball Hall of Fame** (daily 9 AM–6 PM; $8; 413/781-6500) is a definite must. Founded by Naismith himself in the 1930s, soon after basketball became an Olympic sport, the Hall of Fame traces the sport from its beginnings (using peach baskets, from which the ball had to be removed by hand every time a basket was scored) through its rise to international prominence, highlighting players like Bob Cousy and Wilt Chamberlain as well as the antics of the Harlem Globetrotters. Besides admiring other people's athletic abilities, you can explore you own by shooting baskets from a moving walkway or measuring the height of your vertical jump. Refreshingly, the Hall of Fame has little connection with the NBA, even less with NBA-style hype. Although the Hall of Fame is isolated from the rest of Springfield, marooned between the river and I-91, a mile south of downtown, it's worth the detour to visit.

Two other specialized museums can be found in and around Springfield. First of these, at least in the minds of motorcyclists, is the **Indian Motorcycle Museum,** off St. James Avenue at 33 Hendee Street (daily 10 AM–4 PM; $3; 413/737-2624), where some of America's oldest and coolest bikes are crammed into the legendary company's factory, east of downtown off I-291's St. James Avenue exit. Indian was the largest and most successful motorcycle maker in the world in the years before WWI but went bankrupt in 1950. Further away, off old US-20 or I-90 exit 7, in the northeastern Springfield suburb of Indian Orchards, a collection of everything imaginable related to the ill-fated ocean liner is packed away along in the back room of Henry's Jewelry Store, along Route 141 at 208 Main Street (10 AM–4 PM; donations; 413/543-4770). Yessirree, it's the **Titanic Museum,** and a more unlikely location you cannot imagine. The collection, maintained by the Titanic Historical Society, was here long before the movie came out, although visitor traffic increased dramatically in its wake.

BRIDGE STREET, SPRINGFIELD, MASS.

New England's largest amusement park, **Six Flags New England** has all the thrill rides you could want, more than 130 in all, ranging from historic merry-go-rounds and roller-coasters (Cyclone, Thunderbolt, and the Mind Eraser) to the Hellevator, which ends with a 20-story free fall. Originally known as Riverside Park, Six Flags New England is southwest of Springfield, off Route 57 and Route 159 at 1623 Main Street in the town of Agawam (daily 11 AM–6 PM in summer, weekends only spring and fall, closed winter; $28; 413/786-9300 or 800/370-7488).

Fans of the writer Theodore S. Geisel (1904–91), better known as Dr. Seuss, will be interested to know that he was born and grew up in Springfield.

SPRINGFIELD PRACTICALITIES

US-5, running along the west bank of the river, bypasses the center of Springfield, but you can enter the city by a pair of bridges. The postindustrial downtown has a few skyscrapers amid the many Victorian relics and some classic old restaurants, like the **Student Prince and Fort,** off Main Street at 8 Fort Street (413/734-7475), which has been serving bratwurst and other hearty German treats for lunch and dinner since around 1935. The area around Springfield is rich in All-American diners. North of Springfield, the town of Chicopee holds the classic **Al's Diner,** 14 Yelle Street next to the Willamansett Bridge (413/534-3607). To the east, in between Springfield and Brimfield, just off I-90 exit 8, the **Day & Night Diner,** at 456 Main Street in Palmer, makes a great alternative to franchised fast food, serving up hearty fare in a classic old diner.

Another real draw of the Springfield area is the availability of inexpensive rooms, a rare thing in much of New England. The best range of motels is concentrated around the Mass Pike at the I-90/I-91/US-5 junction in West Springfield, where most of the major chains have properties. Rates vary tremendously depending upon seasonal demand, but you can usually find something for under $60 a night at the large **Red Roof Inn,** on US-5 at 1254 N. Riverdale ($48–95; 413/731-1010). Within a short radius there's also a Best Western, a Comfort Inn, a Hampton Inn, and a Quality Inn.

For more information or help, contact the Springfield **visitors bureau,** 1441 Main Street (413/787-1548 or 800/723-1548).

Just south of the Massachusetts border, US-5 passes through the sleepy suburban town of Enfield, which during the 1940s was the home of the great African-American actor, writer, and political activist Paul Robeson.

US-20 DETOUR: BRIMFIELD AND OLD STURBRIDGE VILLAGE

East of Springfield along old US-20, which before the I-90 Turn-pike came through was the main east–west highway across Massachusetts, you'll find two very different approaches to antiquity. First up is Brimfield, an unpretentious stretch of high-way commerce that, come summer, explodes into action as one of the biggest antique and collectible markets in the world. Thousands of dealers and thousands more buyers converge upon Brimfield for a set of weeklong fests known as the **Brimfield Fleas** (usually early May, mid July, and early September), setting up shop all along the highway, in parking lots, pastures, and everywhere in between. The flea markets account for most of the business the tiny town of Brimfield sees all year. For more information, dates, and even a place to stay at the chaotic heart of it all, contact the **New England Motel and Antique Market** (508/ 347-2179).

Further east along US-20, 25 miles from Springfield near the junction of I-90 and I-84, Old Sturbridge Village (daily 9 AM–5 PM April–Oct.; $15; 508/347-3362 or 800/733-1830) is a 200-acre re-creation of merry old postcolonial America, circa 1830. Costumed interpreters practice old-fashioned arts and crafts, from herb gardening to sheep-shearing, in a community that includes replicas or restorations of 40 different buildings. A bank, a general store, a shoe shop, and a meeting house surround the Village Common, while water-powered grist and sawmills stand at the fringes of the complex.

Although very little is known about his youth, John Chapman, the man most of us know as the near-mythic Johnny Appleseed, was born outside Boston on September 26, 1774. Son of a farmer who fought against the British at Concord, Johnny Appleseed grew up in Longmeadow before heading west around 1797. A level-headed nurseryman and farmer, rather than the dreamy wanderer he's sometime characterized as being, Chapman was a deeply religious Swedenborgian Christian minister who planted extensive apple orchards across Ohio and Indiana on what was then the western frontier. Chapman lived to the ripe old age of 74 before dying in Fort Wayne.

SUFFIELD AND WINDSOR LOCKS

Before US-5 crosses into Connecticut, the fairly industrial environs of Springfield give way to the leafy suburbs of Longmeadow, but once you're in Connecticut the scene along US-5 exposes its true role as a frontage road for the I-91 freeway. Further north, in Vermont and most of Massachusetts, US-5 is still a rather rural cruise, but across densely settled Connecticut the few high points are pretty much drowned out by a lot of lows. Especially on the west bank of the river, dairies and tobacco farms still outnumber office parks and auto parts stores, but this stretch of US-5 is nothing like the scenic pleasure you've experienced to the north.

That said, there are a few reasons you may find yourself here. South of Suffield, just west of the town of Windsor Locks and a mere 14 miles north of Hartford, the **New England Air Museum** (daily 10 AM–5 PM; $6.50; 860/623-3305) occupies a pair of buildings on the grounds of Hartford's busy Bradley International Airport. This is one of the largest collections of antique aircraft on display anywhere in the world, with well over 100 planes and

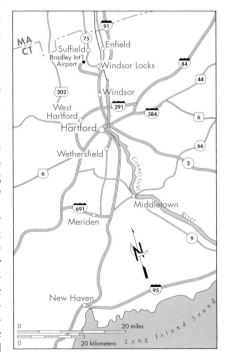

HARTFORD SURVIVAL GUIDE

Hartford (pop. 139,739) is a likeable city. Likeable, that is, if you appreciate Connecticut's capital for was it was—a handsome, cultured town—not what it is—a generic modern city. A century ago it could have been said that Hartford was a pillar of the nation's civilizing forces: literature and guns. Epitomizing the shift to a service economy, Tom Sawyer and Colt .45s have been superseded by actuarial tables and death benefits. Hartford is an insurance company town now, which may explain why the downtown sensibly rolls up its sidewalks and turns out the lights after the office towers empty out at 5 PM.

While mergers, downsizing, recession, defense conversion, and other euphemisms for bad times at the home office have bruised modern Hartford repeatedly in recent years, local history offers several excellent distractions, most famously in the form of the **Mark Twain House** (Mon., Wed.–Sat. 9:30 AM– 4 PM, Sunday noon–4 PM; $6.50) at 351 Farmington Avenue, two right turns and under a mile from I-84 exit 46. Samuel Clemens (the pseudonymous Twain) built this grand Victorian mansion with Tiffany interiors and a shipload of fine furnishings in order to be close to his publisher. After 17 years of a lavish lifestyle—and the completion of some of his most famous novels—Clemens and his family gave up their Hartford life and moved to Europe to escape financial hardship. Besides guided tours, this restored National Historic Landmark hosts regular lectures, readings, "Conversations with American Humorists," and a summer "Twain at Twilight" concert series, which always includes some great gospel music—Twain's favorite.

The distinction of being the oldest public art museum in the nation belongs to the **Wadsworth Atheneum,** an institution that hasn't rested on its 150-year-old laurels behind its prodigious stone facade at 600 Main Street in downtown Hartford (Tues.–Sun. 11 AM–5 PM; $7, free first Thursday of each month; 860/278-2670). Permanent collections from around the globe and across the ages are leavened with major traveling exhibitions, films, and gallery programs. The state's premier showcase for contemporary artists is another of Hartford's crown jewels: **Real Art Ways** (Tues.–Sat. till 5 PM; galleries free; 860/232-1006), across from Pope Park on Arbor

Trinity College, on Summit Street near the center of Hartford, offers free Wednesday evening concerts in June and August. Call 860/297-2139 for more info.

The best source of arts and entertainment listings in the region is the free weekly *Hartford Advocate,* available in newspaper boxes around town. Another source: *The Hartford Courant,* published since 1764 and thus the oldest newspaper in the United States.

If you ever wondered where Katharine Hepburn acquired her accent, look no further than the affluent, liberal, old Connecticut Yankee enclave of West Hartford. Another significant West Hartford resident was lexicographer Noah Webster, creator of the first American (as opposed to English) dictionary, first published back in 1828.

Street. Its recently expanded galleries and auditoriums host an eclectic film, video, music, and performance series (Sept.–May; various admission fees), along with such annual special events as the January Gender Bender Ball, October Halloween party, and summer jazz festival.

Hartford Practicalities

Dining in downtown Hartford is a choice between your average convention-hotel restaurant and the sort of watering hole that draws tie-loosening office workers more concerned with rinsing the taste of the office out of their mouths than with the complexity and freshness of the soup du jour. More interesting than either is a trip to the **Hog River Grill**, on Farmington Avenue, walking distance east of the Twain House and open daily until midnight except Sunday, when it shuts earlier. It's an unusual double-wide stainless-sided 1949 Paramount diner, its excellent condition complemented by the retro-American menu, with new upscale touches like ricotta-stuffed french toast, veggie selections, Southwestern stylings, and Elm City Stout (from New Haven) on draft. While the Hog River Grill fits the streamlined stereotype of the neon-reflecting jukebox-and-soda haven, neighboring West Hartford's **Quaker Diner**, 319 Park Road (off I-84 exit 43, then right; 860/232-5523), sheathed in boxy redbrick, captures dinerdom's pre–Raymond Loewy roots right down to the Moxie soda and other staples as familiar to its first customers as Herbert Hoover's campaign promises. Prices are anachronisms, too, even on items like oat bran pancakes and spinach omelets; open for breakfast and lunch only.

Hartford also has a great Little Italy section. Along a few blocks of Franklin Street, you'll find such classics as **Carbone's**, 588 Franklin Street (860/296-9646), and **Chef Eugene's**, 428 Franklin Street (860/296-4540). Ethnic Americana doesn't stop there, either: *Gourmet Magazine's* Connecticut-based road-food correspondents, Jane and Michael Stern, love the amazing **Polish National Home**, 60 Charter Oak Avenue (860/247-1784), where you can feast on kielbasas and potato pancakes while swigging mugs of beer.

If you plan upon spending the night around Hartford, you'll find a handful of familiar names in both Hartford proper (Sheraton, Holiday Inn, Super 8, Suisse Chalet) and off I-84 in adjacent East Hartford (Ramada, Holiday Inn), as well as a dozen miles north of the city along I-91 near Bradley International Airport (Motel 6, Fairfield Inn, Holiday Inn). For something special, consider the historic **Goodwin Hotel**, a fully modernized hunk of Victorian confectionary downtown at 1 Haynes Street ($99–229; 860/246-7500 or 800/922-5006). For the price of a night there, you could stay a week at the **Mark Twain Hostel**, 131 Tremont Street ($18; 860/523-7255).

For more comprehensive information, contact the **Greater Hartford Convention and Visitors Bureau**, 1 Civic Center Plaza (860/728-6789 or 800/446-7811).

For ad-free soul, hip-hop, and reggae music in the Hartford area, tune to **WRTC 89.3FM.**

whole hangars full of related artifacts. Just west of the airport on US-20, the **Old New-Gate Prison and Copper Mine** (Wed. –Sun. 10 AM–4 PM, May–Oct. only; $3; 860/653-3563) preserves the damp tunnels of a colonial-era copper mine that also served as Connecticut's first prison. Mining began here as early as 1707 and during the Revolutionary War, Tory sympathizers and British POWs were held in these cold, cavernous cells.

> The little notch that cuts into northern Connecticut around the town of Gillette Corner, Massachusetts, 10 miles west of US-5, is the result of a colonial-era mistake that set the border a half-dozen miles further south than it should have been.

WETHERSFIELD

A world or two away from the suburban sprawl of car parts and fast food that lines old US-5 south of Hartford, the very pleasant and very picturesque former shipbuilding community of Wethersfield has dozens of colonial-era buildings and a real feel for earlier times. Founded in 1634 as one of the original three towns in Connecticut (Windsor and Hartford were the others), Wethersfield was spared the industrialization of other early centers. Although this undoubtedly caused economic hardship, it also made the town into a handy, undistorted window back into earlier times. With more than 200 well-maintained pre-1850 buildings lining its streets, Wethersfield is sort of a lived-in version of Massachusetts's Historic Deerfield—if real people still worked and played in Historic Deerfield.

Running through the heart of Wethersfield, Main Street holds a trio of Georgian houses jointly preserved as the **Webb-Deane-Stevens Museum**, at 211 Main Street (daily 10 AM–4 PM, closed Tuesday; $5; 860/529-0612). Two of the homes show off the home life of the prosperous colonial classes and contain many elaborate furnishings, including a bedroom set specially made for George Washington who slept here in May 1781 while planning the Yorktown Campaign with the French military leaders during the height of the Revolutionary War. The Stevens House, by contrast, shows the more modest and comfortable home of a leather craftsman.

WALLACE STEVENS'S HARTFORD

While Vermont and New Hampshire battle over the right to claim poet Robert Frost as a native son (and, by the way, Frost was born in San Francisco), Hartford stakes primary claim to the works of Pulitzer Prize–winning poet **Wallace Stevens** (1879–1955), who lived here for most of his adult life. Now considered one of the major American poets of the 20th century, Stevens received little recognition until the eve of his death, and lived a quiet life here in Hartford. Working as a lawyer for an insurance company, Stevens would compose his whimsical, impressionistic poems (like "Emperor of Ice Cream") while walking to and from his office. The two-mile route he followed, mainly west of downtown along Asylum Avenue, is in the process of being marked with excerpts from his poem "Thirteen Ways of Looking at a Blackbird," which reads in part:

I do not know which to prefer,
The beauty of inflexions
Or the beauty of innuendos,
The blackbird whistling
Or just after.

Wethersfield also offers some handy lodging options, at both ends of the price spectrum. There's a Motel 6 along Route 99, and the down-to-earth **Terra Motel**, on US-5 and Route 15 at 1809 Berlin Turnpike (860/529-6804), has rooms from around $35. For twice that, you could stay at the 1830s Greek Revival–style **Chester Bulkley House**, 184 Main Street ($70–150; 860/563-4236), now a nice B&B at the center of town. To complete ye olde New England experience, treat yourself to a meal at the **Standish House**, 222 Main Street (860/257-1151), a gourmet restaurant housed in a 1780s mansion.

South of Wethersfield US-5 edges west, away from the Connecticut River, and runs in the shadow of the I-91 freeway all the way to New Haven. If you want a more enjoyable drive, follow the historic river to its southern end in Long Island Sound, taking busy Route 9 down to smaller, more scenic country roads like Route 154. Some of the more interesting places near the coast, like Essex and East Haddam, are covered in the US-1 chapter.

East of US-5, the town of Middletown is home to Wesleyan College and also has a landmark diner: **O'Rourke's** at 728 Main Street (860/346-6101), a 1946 Mountain View with trademark "cow catcher" corners playing up the historic connection with railroad dining cars.

At the north end of Wethersfield's Main Street, the Town Cove has a pretty marina full of bobbing boats and a historic warehouse that reminds us car-borne travelers how waterways used to be the primary mode of transportation.

At the end of its long run south from Canada, US-5 disappears into I-91 in downtown New Haven, near the junction with US-1. New Haven and this stretch of US-1, including the lovely Thimble Islands offshore, are covered on page 104.

CAPE COD AND CENTRAL CONNECTICUT: US-6

CAPE COD AND CENTRAL CONNECTICUT: US-6

US-6 is one of the most schizophrenic highways in New England, changing character more often than comedian Jim Carrey. Long stretches pass by some of the most beautiful scenery in the country. Others make you wonder whether you were somehow transported to the Rust Belt. The route's physical qualities embody these contradictions, switching back and forth between two-lane country roads and modern four-lane freeways. On US-6, old and new merge with each other but not always seamlessly.

For example, at the tip of Cape Cod, US-6 and its previous incarnation, Route 6A, take you to some of the most desirable destinations in New England. With so many historic towns and miles of sandy beaches, you may find it hard to decide where to linger. If you avoid the summer-weekend crowds, Provincetown can be one of the most enjoyable places to visit in New England.

Cape Cod's topography is constantly shifting. Each year the Atlantic Ocean deposits up to 10 feet of the Outer Cape's cliffs each year on Provincetown and Monomoy Island beaches, and erodes more than 30 acres of ground throughout the Cape.

Nearby hamlets such as Wellfleet, the historic bayfront towns lining Route 6A, and the beaches fringing both sides of the Cape offer quick escapes from the hustle and bustle of this most heavily touristed area of New England.

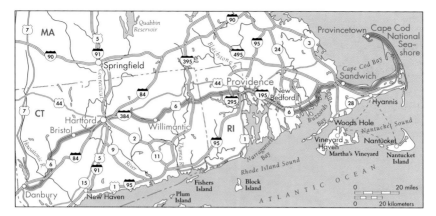

In contrast, the western section of US-6 travels through some of the most economically depressed cities in southeastern Massachusetts, places where the coastal lowlands have been paved over in the name of progress. Such picturesquely pleasing scenes as the ivy-covered brick of Harvard Yard or the weathered tobacco barns of the Pioneer Valley are far away, and even those sites further east in Massachusetts on US-6 might as well belong to another state. Or at least that's how it seems, as this route rolls by the harbors of retired naval vessels, acres of outlet malls, and hillsides of tight houses built for workers drawn to the great textile mills during the Industrial Revolution. While there are comely seaside towns just to the south (along what the tourist brochures call the Heritage Farm Coast), the 30 miles of US-6 between Cape Cod and the Connecticut border can only be appreciated by those with a romantic eye for commercial tackiness or by anthropologists studying urban decay. Although US-6 is worth picking up again through New Bedford, postcard-worthy views are few and far between.

Massachusetts is one of two states that grants private-property ownership as far as the low-tide line. For this reason, you should respect the No Trespassing signs you may encounter on some beaches. Fortunately, plenty of these signs are amended with Walkers Welcome.

When you reach Rhode Island, US-6 becomes a bit more enjoyable. Running along the foot of the low hills that fill the state's northern corners, US-6 takes you across Rhode Island in a half-hour. You drive through a quiet, mostly rural region until you reach the I-95 corridor at lively Providence.

US-6 then passes through some very pleasant rural landscape in Connecticut, a state that, especially if only seen from the freeways, can seem to contain nothing more than suburbs and office parks. From US-6 you can catch glimpses of expansive colonial farms and elegant frame houses as you skirt their typically well-patrolled boundaries. Additionally, numerous detours along lovely Route 169, the so-called Revolutionary Road, offer more satisfying tastes of this ultra-wealthy but frequently delightful state.

You'll miss everything that's nice about the Cape if you stay on US-6 or Route 28. Take a spin whenever possible along slow-but-scenic Route 6A or any of the hundreds of other country roads.

PROVINCETOWN

If not for its lack of freshwater, Provincetown, not Plymouth, would be the place we immediately equate with the Pilgrims. Way back in 1620, the band of religious travelers and fortune-seeking shipmates aboard the *Mayflower* landed here, expecting warm weather (in November, of all times) and good water. Neither was to be found and the Pilgrims sailed on, disembarking across the bay at Plymouth Rock. Thus, P-town (as natives and in-the-know locals call Provincetown) lost its chance to be enshrined as the cornerstone of Anglo-American civilization and has had to butter its bread with something other than the national creation story.

So P-town took to the water. For much of its history, the sea sustained the town, which became a trading spot, whaling village, and fishing port. As those industries tapered off, new ones arose to take their place. Art and tourism now keep P-town busy.

In 1901 Charles Hawthorne opened an art school here, bohemians followed, and the town earned art colony status that persists to this day. Among the artists and writers were John Reed, Eugene O'Neill, Susan Glaspell, and George Cram Cook, whose Provincetown Players made theater history. And on the heels of Greenwich Village's fashionable flock came the car-borne tourists, who have proven themselves as faithful as Capistrano swallows, returning year after year to this tip of the Cape. Provincetown is a particularly strong magnet for the East Coast's gays and lesbians, so don't be surprised to see as many rainbow flags as Stars and Stripes waving in the breezes.

whale-watching off Provincetown

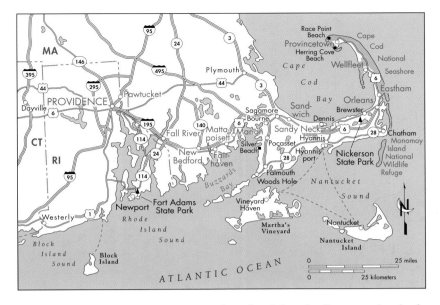

The summer trade prompts P-town to do its beach-boardwalk strut, as boatloads of day-trippers from Boston mob aptly named Commercial Street each afternoon, tanned couples mingle among the restaurants and outdoor cafes each evening, and fun-seekers fill up the bars and clubs each night. During any other season, however, the beach shuttle becomes a school bus, the wait for a table is negligible, and there's actually a chance that you'll find a place to park. Meanwhile, the off-season sunsets are still worth a visit to Race Point or Herring Cove Beach, even if they come at an earlier hour and require extra layers of clothing.

The most popular sunset-watching spots are also the prime suntanning beaches, which stretch around the entire tip of the Cape. Inland, 44,000 acres of sand dunes, forests of windbent oaks and stunted pines, cranberry bogs, and peaceful ponds are protected within the Cape Cod National Seashore, which boasts two long, clean beaches at **Herring Cove** (where's there food available in summer) and **Race Point,** where there's also a visitor center and a neat old Life Saving Station, moved here from Chatham in the 1970s. These two are the most popular stretches of beach because access and parking is easiest, but the entire beaches actually continue for miles all the way along the Cape. Another accessible beach is called the **Head of the Meadow,** located north of US-6 near North Truro, about five miles from P-Town proper. As at all Cape Cod beaches, there is a daily parking fee; annual Golden Eagle passes are accepted.

PROVINCETOWN PRACTICALITIES

After a day spent cycling amid dunes speckled with wild roses and beach grasses or admiring the handiwork of windowbox gardeners in P-town's cottage-lined lanes, you'll probably get hungry. Snackers may want to try the sugar-coated *trutas* (sweet potato fritters) from the **Portuguese Bakery** at 299 Commercial Street. However, if

The 252-foot Italianate tower over the town is the **Pilgrim Monument and Museum** (9 AM–5 PM, last admission at 4:15 PM, mid-March to Nov.; $5), with the best panorama on the Cape: in clear weather you can see the entire peninsula, as well as the mainland Massachusetts coast at Plymouth.

you have a bigger appetite and want a harborside table, consider the moderately priced **Lobster Pot** at 321 Commercial just east of MacMillan Wharf (enter through the kitchen; 508/487-0842) for heaping portions of time-tested local favorites such as cioppino or *sopa do mar,* veggie pastas, and of course, lobster every which way you want it. It's open year-round, too—an exception in these parts.

For livelier, less expensive dining, check out the multicultural menu—one of the few to please vegetarians—at **Napi's,** tucked away on Freeman Street at Standish (dinner only; 508/487-1145). South-of-the-border spices heat up the top-notch New American menu at **Lorraine's,** in the East End at 463 Commercial Street (dinner only; 508/487-6074), where you'll find some of P-town's best meals for the money. **Spiritus Café & Pizzeria,** at 190 Commercial Street (508/ 487-2808), is another good, low-cost savior, dishing up pizza, foccacia sandwiches, ice cream, and lattes to a steady clientele of tattooed young smokers and slackers until 2 AM on summer weekends.

If you're more in the mood for a linen and crystal celebration, look no further than the **Martin House,** 157 Commercial Street (508/487-1327). Fine fireside dining in cozy 18th-century parlors won't come cheap, but if you have reason to splurge, this is the place to do it.

Planning to spend the night? If it's a summer weekend, make reservations or you may spend your time searching for a bed rather than basking on the beach. Friendly and efficient, the staff at **Provincetown Reservations System** (800/648-0364) can help you for free to find accommodations to match your budget and taste. They can also help with travel arrangements and generally take the hassle out of a visit. Or you can make the calls yourself with the aid of the chamber of commerce directory, available from its **information booth** (508/487-3424) at Lopes Square on MacMillan Wharf. The comprehensive list of apartments, cottages, guest houses, inns, motels, and B&B rooms is extensive enough to make you wonder whether there is any house anywhere in town where visitors wouldn't be made welcome.

If you don't mind the occasional bout of late-night laughter from Commercial Street carousers, the **Somerset House,** 378 Commercial Street (508/ 487-0383), has comfortable rooms and a very central location in a old Cape Cod manse. Rounding out the lodging options are two Best Westerns and a Holiday Inn; two private campgrounds (**Coastal Acres Camping Court,** 508/487-1700; **Dunes**

Somerset House

Edge Camp Ground, 508/487-9815); and the bargain-priced shared little cottages of the **Outermost Hostel** (May–Oct.; $14; 508/487-4378) on Winslow Street past the Pilgrim Monument parking lot.

WELLFLEET

The town of Wellfleet (pop. 2,493) is one of the Cape's most picturesque communities, favored for some reason by writers, psychiatrists, and oysters. Although home to a cluster of fine art galleries, crafts and clothing shops, and pricey restaurants, the place succeeds handsomely in finding a niche between self-conscious quaintness and residential seclusion. It's also blessed by two additional rarities: **Mayo Beach** just west of the town pier, a public beach with year-round free parking; and **Painter's**, on Main Street beside the Duck Creeke Inn, a New American fusion-cuisine restaurant worth every dollar (dinner and Sunday brunch only; reservations 508/349-3003).

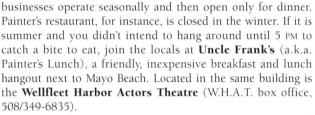

Alas, there are drawbacks. Most of the town's beaches are strictly for residents or local guests between late June and early September. Those that aren't off-limits charge $10. Other businesses operate seasonally and then open only for dinner. Painter's restaurant, for instance, is closed in the winter. If it is summer and you didn't intend to hang around until 5 PM to catch a bite to eat, join the locals at **Uncle Frank's** (a.k.a. Painter's Lunch), a friendly, inexpensive breakfast and lunch hangout next to Mayo Beach. Located in the same building is the **Wellfleet Harbor Actors Theatre** (W.H.A.T. box office, 508/349-6835).

While the Outer Cape has but one chain motel outside of Provincetown (a Sheraton on US-6 in Eastham), you'll still find plenty of characterful, locally owned accommodations, from little classic prewar dune shacks sitting cheek-to-cheek along the beach, to B&Bs nestled among the pines. Some of the more affordable rooms are available at the historic **Holden Inn,** 140 Commercial Street ($50–90; 508/349-3450), where you share bathrooms, the front porch, and the bay views.

The **Wellfleet Chamber of Commerce** (508/349-2510) has an exceptionally comprehensive directory of lodgings, available by mail or from its information booth on US-6.

CAPE COD NATIONAL SEASHORE

The outermost two dozen miles of Cape Cod, from Provincetown to Orleans, are protected from development as the Cape

In the 16th century, the Cape was covered with beech, white oak, juniper, and holly. Later, English colonists harvested the mature forests to satisfy their appetite for construction, firewood, turpentine, potash, and grazing land. In the early 1700s, tree and topsoil loss on the Outer Cape was so severe that homes had to be built on stilts to avoid being buried by blowing sand. Today's beech forests around Provincetown are the result of a major campaign begun in 1893 to save the town from a sandy grave.

If you want to save money, stay at the **HI Truro Hostel,** beautifully situated between cranberry bogs and ocean beach in a former Coast Guard station on N. Pamet Road in nearby Truro (late June to early Sept. only; $15, members $12; 508/349-3889). Reservations are advised. The 1930s beachfront cabins at **Days Cottages** ($75-120; 508/487-1062), along Route 6A in North Truro are another unusual option.

One of the finest biking or scenic driving routes on the Cape is the stretch of Old County Road that winds between Wellfleet and Truro, on the bay side of US-6. Here you can get a full sense of what the Cape is like, beyond beaches and bijou restaurants.

If you've never watched a movie in the comfort of your own car, it's time you caught up with lost pleasures at the **Wellfleet Drive-In** on US-6 five miles north of Eastham (508/349-7176), a genuine throwback to the era of roller-skating carhops and Mustang convertibles.

To at least vaguely disguise your off-Cape origins, you should know that Chatham is pronounced "CHAT-em," but Eastham is simply "EAST-ham."

Cod National Seashore, a 40-mile-long National Park Service property encompassing the whole of the coast. Pick up information detailing the various nature trails and interpretive programs at the **Salt Pond Visitor Center** (daily 9 AM–4:30 PM, weekends only Jan.–Feb.; 508/255-3421). You can also follow the prominent signs beside US-6 in Eastham, or the Province Lands Visitor Center on Race Point Road in Provincetown.

The park's highlights include miles of gorgeous beaches, harbor seals, and some of the Cape's best waves, which occur here because the south-facing beaches are blocked by the islands of Nantucket and Martha's Vineyard and the bayside is sheltered by the Cape itself. Another worthwhile scene is **Sunset Hill** in Wellfleet on Chequesset Neck Road heading toward Duck Harbor Beach. The late-afternoon views over Cape Cod Bay will reward the sedentary, while walkers will find a fine scenic escape along the Great Island Trail that begins from the hill's parking lot. Mind the tide tables if you do take a hike out to Jeremy Point, or you'll be wading on your return.

The classic Cape Cod dwelling—a porchless, rectangular, peak-roofed shed not unlike an oversized shingle or clapboard Monopoly piece—is a familiar feature of the Outer Cape landscape.

EASTHAM AND ORLEANS

Depending upon your direction of travel, Eastham marks either the beginning or the end of the Outer Cape. US-6, Route 6A, and Route 28 all coverge between here and neighboring Orleans, where the Cape narrows to its slender forearm. Here, too, the **Cape Cod Rail Trail** mingles with the road, which is why in summer the streets crawl with cyclists in search of refreshment. If that's your goal, too, look no further than **The Brown Bag Restaurant and Bakery** (daily until 3 PM), on the corner of West Road and Old Colony Way, for decent omelets, soups, sandwiches, and quiche. For something to fill the cup holder on your dash, stop in at the **Orleans Whole Food Store**, 46 Main Street (508/255-6540), a block south of the Rail Trail and Route 6A.

Campers will want to check out **Nickerson State Park** on Route 6A at the Brewster-Orleans line, one of the largest and most popular campgrounds in the state (year-round for RVs only, otherwise April 15 to Oct. 15; $6; reservations taken at 508/896-3491).

One of Cape Cod's many exquisite B&Bs is the **Whalewalk Inn**, 220 Bridge Road in Eastham ($120–195; 508/225-0617), where free bicycle rentals and delicious breakfasts make for an idyllic respite from the real world. Right next door on Goody Hallet Drive, budget travelers will be pleased to find the well-situated **HI Mid-Cape Hostel** (mid-May to mid-Sept.; $15, members $12; 508/255-2785).

ROUTE 28: SOUTHERN CAPE COD

For a taste of some of the best fried clams on the Cape, head to the **Kream 'n' Kone** (March–Nov.), opposite the A&P supermarket on Route 28 between Chatham and Harwich.

When people talk about Cape Cod—especially if they are complaining about terrible traffic, overdevelopment, and too many tourists—they're likely to be thinking about Southern Cape Cod, the densely developed corridor of resort areas along Route 28. The easternmost sections of Route 28, starting at Orleans and running south then west through delightful Chatham and a series of small picturesque ports, are pleasant enough. However, during the summer peaks, the far-western half can be pretty dire, with bumper-to-bumper traffic, overpriced hotels, and general desperation. Just about everything that can go wrong in a vacation destination seems to have gone wrong here, especially around Hyannis, the biggest city on Cape Cod. Which isn't to say stay away; just don't come expecting to relax and unwind.

Route 28's easternmost point is **Chatham,** probably the most popular and, to many, the prettiest of Cape Cod's many quaint communities. With the Cape Cod National Seashore stretching to the north, and isolated **Monomoy Island** drawing birds and bird-lovers to the south, it's easy to get away from all your fellow travelers. Midway along the southern Cape, thousands pass through Hyannis on their way to the upscale offshore islands of Nantucket and Martha's Vineyard. Thousands more come to Hyannis to pay homage to its most famous residents, the Kennedys, whose famous compound is southwest of Hyannis in the enclave of Hyannisport. You can't see it from land but you can catch a  glimpse of John F. Kennedy's Summer White House if you join one of the frequent boat tours that depart from Hyannis harbor. There's also a small **JFK Hyannis Museum** (daily 10 AM–4 PM; $3), mainly displaying photos of the Kennedy family vacations, on the ground floor of the old Hyannis Town Hall at 397 Main Street in the downtown business district.

Located at the bottom of Cape Cod, **Falmouth** was an early tourist destination and still attracts a slew of visitors, some bound for Martha's Vineyard, some to its dozen miles of beaches (such as **Old Silver Beach,** along Buzzards Bay in North Falmouth). Others come to enjoy the marine biology displays at the famous **Woods Hole Oceanographic Institution** (WHOI), in a clapboard building at 15 School Street (daily 10 AM–4:30 PM in summer, shorter hours off-season; $2; 508/289-2663). To find it, go four miles southwest from town to the busy port of Woods Hole. WHOI showcases marine flora and fauna and also has details on the discovery of the sunken *Titanic,* which was found in 1985 by Dr. Robert Ballard on a WHOI-run expedition using the deep-sea minisub *Alvin.*

SOUTHERN CAPE PRACTICALITIES

Route 28 is the fast-food of Cape Cod, and if it's a burger or a slice of pizza you're pining for, this is a good place to find satisfaction. In Falmouth, the nostalgia-fueled **Betsey's Diner,** 457 Main Street (508/540-0060) is handy, especially since real diner fans are still mourning the loss of Pocasset's wonderful **My Tin Man Diner** in a recent fire.

In Chatham, near the east end of Route 28, the ever-popular **Impudent Oyster** off Main Street (508/945-3545) has an unusual name but serves very traditional (and very good) seafood in a fairly serene, white-linen-tabled setting. Resist a restaurant dessert and make your way to South Chatham, where **Marion's Pie Shop** sells up truly wonderful lemon meringue, fruit, and pecan pies at 2022 S. Main Street (closed Mon; 508/432-9439). But be warned, when they sell out for the day, they close. The pies are take-away only but if you

Between Orleans and the Sagamore Bridge, the north shore of Cape Cod along Route 6A (Bayside) has more than a dozen beaches, most of which are found simply by turning north on whatever small residential or unimproved roads intersect the route. If you don't live here, expect to fork over a parking fee of at least $7 in season. Temporary residents and guests may obtain weekly or monthly permits; ask your hosts or the beach attendant to explain the procedure. One way to skirt the parking fees for beach use is to spend the night nearby and *walk* to the water.

don't mind the lack of cutlery, these treats can turn a beach picnic into an unforgettable experience.

For a taste of the real Cape between Falmouth and Hyannis, turn inland from Route 28 onto Route 130 to the historic, part–Native American town of Mashpee, where the very popular **Flume** (508/477-1456) serves great chowders and other seafood specialties from May to November.

Route 28 in general, and Hyannis in particular, has the most hotels and motel rooms of any place on the Cape, but few of them are places you'd want to spend much time in. They're mainly useful as staging posts for people traveling to and from the islands. Best Western, Comfort Inn, Days Inn, Super 8, and the other usual suspects have properties here, most of them charging a *lot* more than you might be used to; during the summer peak, the Super 8 gets $135 for a room that costs $35 in the off-season. There are also lots of mom-and-pop motels, including the irresistibly named **Americana Holiday Motel,** on Route 28 at 99 Main Street in West Yarmouth ($50–125; 508/775-5511 or 800/445-4497), which has hundreds of clean, quiet rooms set well back from the highway, plus three swimming pools. For an in-town place with more character, try the 150-year-old **Mostly Hall,** 27 Main Street ($65–125; 508/548-3786) in Falmouth.

For help and further information, contact the **chamber of commerce** in Falmouth (508/548-8500 or 800/526-8532) or Hyannis (508/362-5230 or 877/492-6647).

BAYSIDE ROUTE 6A

In total contrast to the high-speed US-6 freeway or the traffic-clogged, overdeveloped, and ugly Route 28, Route 6A shows off the Cape as it should be seen. Route 6A's winding back roads pass through small historic town after small historic town and are lined by seafood shacks, ice cream stands, high-style restaurants, colonial-era homes, village greens, stately churches—backed all the way by miles of bayfront beaches.

BREWSTER

Greetings from CAPE COD, MASS.

From Brewster in the east to Sandwich in the west, Route 6A offers a taste of what the Cape is all about. **Brewster** (pop. 8,440) has the 80-acre **Cape Cod Natural History Museum,** 869 Main Street (daily 9:30 AM–4:30 PM; $5) and the old-fashioned **Brewster Store,** 1935 Main Street, in business since the 1850s. **Dennis,** the terminus of the Cape Cod Rail Trail to Wellfleet, is also the setting for the nation's oldest professional summer-stock theater, the **Cape Playhouse** (box

A CAPE COD PRIMER

To avoid frustration and confusion when touring Cape Cod, it helps to understand its basic directions and seasons. The compass isn't your friend here, as you will discover when faced with highway signs stubbornly directing you *south* to Provincetown—when heading south would bring you sooner to Venezuela than to the Cape's northernmost town. Instead, the principal directions are up and down: up-Cape means generally westward, toward the mainland, while down-Cape means roughly east, toward the Outer Cape and Provincetown. Further confusion arises with the distinctions among the various coasts: *bayside* faces inward onto Cape Cod Bay, the *south shore* faces Nantucket Sound, while the *backside* braves the open Atlantic to the east.

If you're willing to pay a small price ($10–15) for the aid of a B&B reservation service, put yourself in the competent hands of **Bed and Breakfast Cape Cod** (508/255-3824 or 800/541-6226).

It's easier to keep track of Cape Cod's seasons. High season, when Cape-bound traffic can be bumper-to-bumper from before the bridge all the way to Hyannis, is basically from Memorial Day to Labor Day, with the summer vacation months of July and August seeing the highest hotel rates, the most crowded beaches, and abysmal traffic on Fridays especially, when most vacation rentals "turn over." That said, even at the worst of times you can still find peace and quiet if you're willing to walk, paddle, or bike a little way from your car.

office 508/385-3911), on Route 6A just east of the Mobil station. If you prefer film over stage, the **Cape Cinema,** on the grounds behind the Playhouse, specializes in movies you won't find at the mall. If you arrive late, stick around until the lights go up after the credits or you'll miss one of the Cape's best public artworks, the mural of Prometheus on the cinema's ceiling.

The next town to the west, **Barnstable,** is the second-oldest community on Cape Cod, founded in 1639, and it has managed to retain its historic core through the years. Continuing west on Route 6A from Barnstable, keep an eye out for Sandy Neck Road (next to the Sandy Neck Motel), the turnoff to **Sandy Neck** and its namesake barrier beach ($8 summer parking fee). Here, six miles of windswept dunes provide a picturesque backdrop for contemplating the changing light upon the relatively calm waters of Cape Cod Bay. Depending on season and time of day, you may catch sight of passing white-tailed deer or such endangered shorebirds as the least tern and piping plover.

BAYSIDE PRACTICALITIES

Restaurants and motels tend to gravitate toward Cape Cod's south shore along Route 28, and the few bayside establishments here along Route 6A seem determined to make up in total billings what is lacking in total volume. If, on the other hand,

Take in excellent Cape Cod views from atop **Scargo Tower** in Dennis, on Scargo Hill Road; turn toward South Dennis at the Mobil station, then follow signs.

you subscribe to the belief that a good meal is worth at least as much as a night's pampering at a little seaside inn, then treat yourself to sophisticated Italian cuisine at **Abbicci,** on Route 6A in Dennis (reservations advised, 508/362-3501). Don't be fooled by the down-home yellow-clapboard exterior; the interior is as contemporary and artfully designed as the food.

Instead of broiling yourself on the beach in a light marinade of SPF 45, enjoy one of the best Cape escapes on a bike. The **Cape Cod Rail Trail,** a 25-mile-long, fully paved pedestrian and bicycle path, runs between South Wellfleet and Dennis. If you're driving to the trail, you can usually find parking at either end, or in Nickerson State Park in Brewster, where the trail crosses under Route 6A. Bike rentals are available along the Rail Trail in Brewster at the **Rail Trail Bike Shop** (508/896-8200).

You can always balance your budget the next day with a visit to **Jack's Outback,** behind 161 Main Street (Route 6A) in Yarmouth Port (508/362-6690). The undisputed king of the Cape's white-bread cookery, Jack whips up basic breakfasts and lunches at rock-bottom prices—made possible in part by requiring that customers do everything but stand over the grill. Copious hand-lettered, phonetically spelled, construction-paper signs combine menu items, warnings about selling unattended children into slavery, and instructions for writing up your own ticket and busing your own dirty dishes. Follow these last to the letter or irascible ol' Jack will amuse his audience of regulars at your expense.

Between these two extremes is **Mattakeese Wharf** on Barnstable Harbor (turn at the traffic light east of Barnstable Village; open May–Oct. only; 508/362-4511), a casual, "You want fries with that?" kind of place elevated from the pack by its quality seafood and great location. Enjoying bouillabaisse on the deck while looking out over the marina in that golden light of a late summer evening is the sort of experience liable to have you planning ahead to your next Cape vacation.

One of many historic B&Bs along this stretch of the Cape is the **Isaiah Hall B&B Inn,** 152 Whig Street in Dennis ($75–95; 508/385-9928 or 800/736-0160), within walking distance of the beach and costing less than most meals at Abbicci.

For a full list of accommodation options, stop by a Cape Cod Chamber of Commerce **information booth** (508/362-3225), either at the Sagamore rotary just west of the canal or mid-Cape at the junction of Route 132 and US-6.

Not all of the Cape's glass furnaces have been extinguished: the glass blowers of the **Pairpoint Crystal Company,** on Route 6A in Sagamore (behind the Christmas Tree Shop), can be observed at work on weekdays.

Just south of US-6 from the Bourne Bridge, off Route 28 at the Otis rotary, the ultra-streamlined **My Tin Man Diner** was a delightful "diner with a heart," which, alas, burned down in November 2000.

SANDWICH

Although it rides the ridge of the Cape's terminal glacial moraine, the forest-clad US-6 (called Mid-Cape Highway in these parts) affords few good vistas. Traffic willing, you'll sail between the Sagamore Bridge and the Outer Cape in about 30 minutes, surrounded by more green than blue. One preferred route is parallel Route 6A. Never more than a mile or two away from US-6, this slower road is a good introduction to a part of the Cape that does its utmost to stay quaint without being too cute. Generally, it succeeds.

Take Sandwich, for example. When you reach the center of town, you'll come across a small, irregular green. Bordering it are a tall, white Christopher Wren–inspired church, a stately carriage-stop inn, and the Historical Society's **Sandwich Glass**

Museum (daily 9:30 AM–4:30 PM April–Oct., Wed.–Sun. only Nov.–March; $3.50). Although the town's various glassworks could and did produce consummate artistic pieces, they mostly created inexpensive, mass-market stuff—such as 10-cent oil-lamp chimneys—for household rather than decorative use. In other words, when you visit the museum, don't look for extravagant vases and other items. Rather, come prepare to view and appreciate such everyday works as lacy glass saucers, pressed plates, and molded jars. The vast majority of these are unmarked products of the Boston and Sandwich Glass Co., earliest and most famous of the region's 19th-century glass factories.

Dexter Grist Mill in Sandwich

Nearby on Pine and Grove Streets (follow signs from Route 130) is an even more diverse collection of Americana, the **Heritage Plantation of Sandwich** (daily 10 AM–5 PM mid-May to mid-Oct.; $9; 508/ 888-3300). Here nearly 80 landscaped acres surround collections of Currier & Ives prints, military miniatures, antique cars, cigar store figures, American primitive portraiture—more unflattering likenesses of children have never been conceived—and even a working 1912 carousel.

BUZZARDS BAY: MATTAPOISETT AND MARION

Skirting the major shipping port of Buzzards Bay, US-6 passes through residential Mattapoisett and Marion. These communities' modest appearances belie both property values and their residents' average incomes, just as the sandy soil and brittle-looking trees belie the original swampy conditions that made this coast so ecologically rich for its native inhabitants, the Wampanoag Indians. A half-dozen small rivers still drain these coastal lowlands, but despite the occasional stands of tall reeds, it goes almost without saying that here, as in far too many places along the Atlantic seaboard, wetlands have been drastically reduced. Modern developers aren't exclusively to blame, however; settlers have been accelerating nature's designs ever since 17th- and 18th-century colonists stripped the land of its rot-resistant Atlantic white cedars—old-growth giants found here near the northern extent of their range—and thus contributed to the silting-up of fertile fish-feeding marshes and ponds.

This stretch of US-6 is still fertile territory for the fruits of the sea, especially if it's fried, broiled, or served up in creamy chowder. Right on US-6 in Mattapoisett, the **Mattapoisett Chowder House,** 20 Country Road (508/758-2333), and **Oxford Creamery,** 98 Country Road (508/758-3847), are two particularly good examples, the best you'll find between here and the Outer Cape. The Creamery—which, as the name implies, also specializes in ice cream—is the more low-key of the two, downright fast-food-like; it also is only open in summer, daily until 10 PM.

If you're looking for a place to park the ol' RV for the night before or after hitting the Cape, you might choose **Scusset Beach State Reservation** (508/888-0859) in Sagamore, on Cape Cod Bay; $8 gets you a full hookup near the beach, across the canal from the power plant. More tent-friendly sites are found in **Shawme-Crowell State Forest** ($6; 508/888-0351) just over the bridge on Route 130 in Sandwich.

Although not as attractive to mansion-building plutocrats as nearby Newport, 19th-century Marion was still among New England's most prominent seaside resorts, attracting such visitors as President Grover Cleveland and novelist Henry James.

A clam-eater's key: Steamers are usually soft-shell (longneck) clams, preferably caught on a muddy rather than sandy bottom (unless you like grit in your teeth), steamed and served with their salty "liquor" and drawn butter for dipping. Fuller-flavored hard-shell quahogs ("KO-hogs" or "K'WOGS") are a chef's favorite chowder clam, although some folks will deep-fry or stuff and bake them, too. Cherrystones and littlenecks are small quahogs served raw on the half shell, or sometimes steamed. Bon appetit!

Mattapoisett means "place of rest" in Algonquian. The name originally applied to a small neck about 25 miles west on Mount Hope Bay, in what's now the town of Swansea.

To learn more than you ever thought possible about thermometers, pay a visit to **the world's largest thermometer collection** proudly on display in the basement of Dick "Thermometer Man" Porter's home in Onset; call 508/295-5504 for an invitation and directions.

The first Japanese resident of the United States, Manjiro Nakahama, lived in Fairhaven in the 1840s after returning with the whalers who rescued him from a shipwreck in the Pacific. Displays about "John" Manjiro and the town's sister city of Tosashimizu, Japan, are found in the Millicent Library.

FAIRHAVEN

There was a time when families could indicate that their lot was improving by moving away from New Bedford's hurly-burly mills and wharves and across the harbor to aptly named Fairhaven (stress the second syllable), which straddles US-6 within spyglass view of Johnny Cake Hill. Turn south on Main Street, at the intersection dominated by the palatial Italianate high school, and you'll discover a surprising amount of monumental Gothic-spired civic architecture. Most of it was generously donated in the early 20th century by Henry Huttleston Rogers, a native son and robber baron who made a mint as a director of John D. Rockefeller's Standard Oil Company. Stop by the marvelous Renaissance-style **Millicent Library** on Center Street —described as "a heaven of light and grace and harmonious color and sumptuous comfort" by Rogers's friend Mark Twain— for a **walking tour** brochure.

In addition to Portuguese and Cape Verdeans, Norwegians have been attracted to the local maritime trades. The Isaksen family is one example. Their waterfront restaurant down on Main Street, **Margaret's** (508/992-9942), is one of the hands-down best places for seafood in the area. If deep-sea scallops are on the menu—probably fresh off the family's own boats—don't pass them by; as anyone around here will tell you, the tiny bay scallops from Mexico and China served elsewhere can't compare to the more flavorful and meaty Atlantic variety.

NEW BEDFORD

Predominantly Portuguese New Bedford is remembered as a capital of the whaling industry back in the days when spermaceti candles and whale oil lamps were necessities, not antiques. The city's harbor at the mile-wide mouth of the Acushnet River was home port for the East Coast's largest commercial fishing fleet until nearly two decades of flagrant overfishing brought the industry to collapse in 1995. Now the community is trying to sail out of its troubled economic waters with the aid of tourism and the arts.

Studio artists are being invited to set up shop in vacant downtown buildings, an aquarium is planned for the waterfront, and the **New Bedford National Historical Park** showcases the immutable charm of downtown, its cobblestone streets and brick facades virtually unaltered since Herman Melville shipped out of here in 1847 aboard a whaler bound for the Pacific. For a good orientation, drop by the well-stocked **visitor center,** at the corner of William Street and North 2nd Street (508/996-4469), and join one of their free hour-long guided **walking tours.**

Before or after a stroll around town, head to the top of Johnny Cake Hill and visit the excellent **Whaling Museum** (daily 9 AM–5 PM; $4.50; 508/997-0046).

Perhaps H. H. Rogers's financial support for his hometown was compensation for the fact that his company's profits came at the expense of New Bedford's and Fairhaven's: the 1859 discovery of eastern Pennsylvania's oil fields dropped the bottom out of the market for whale oil and "coal oil" (coal-derived kerosene, a Fairhaven product).

Scrimshaw (carved whale ivory), tools of the whaling trade, historic photos, special maritime exhibits, and an 89-foot ship model are a few of the artifacts found in the not-to-be-missed museum collection maintained by the Old Dartmouth Historical Society. Across the street from the museum, the gorgeous little **Seamen's Bethel,** built in 1832 and featuring a pulpit shaped like a ship's bow, was featured in a chapter of Herman Melville's classic *Moby-Dick*.

NEW BEDFORD PRACTICALITIES

If the sounds of the seagulls' *scree*-ing around downtown whets your appetite for seafood, then drive down to **Davy's Locker,** 1480 E. Rodney French Street at Billy Woods Wharf (508/992-7359), where the ferry for Martha's Vineyard departs. There outside the rocky seawall you can watch the gulls soar over the harbor as you dig into some of the freshest seafood in town. Given that you're in a city that's 60 percent Portuguese, you might consider acquainting yourself with this local cuisine, although if you're a light eater, bring along a pair of friends to finish your meal. For maximum quality at a minimal (cash only) price, **Antonio's,** 267 Coggeshalle Street (508/990-3636) at N. Front Street, slightly northeast of the I-195/Route 18 interchange (exit 15), is a good choice, as is **Vasco da Gama,** 86 Dartmouth Street (508/993-4340) at Washington on the opposite end of town, a block south of Metro Pizza (look for the 7-UP sign over a plain brickfront, barlike place). Kale soup, rabbit or shellfish swimming in spicy tomato-based sauces, and of course *bacalhau* (salt cod) are typical menu items, in portions designed to thoroughly satisfy a boat crew's most mutinous rumblings.

New Bedford's Acushnet Avenue has a significant place in the world of late 19th-century American art: Albert Pinkham Ryder, visionary "painter of dreams," was born here, across from the childhood home of Albert Bierstadt, romantic painter of the American West.

Diner fans will appreciate New Bedford's offerings, too. The easiest diner to find is **Angelo's Orchid Diner,** 805 Rockdale Avenue (508/ 993-3172), a 1951 O'Mahony stainless-sided model; its menu is

solid short-order cookery enlivened by—you guessed it—a Portuguese influence. For a traditional Greek hand over the grill, check out the pristine **Shawmut Diner**, 943 Shawmut Avenue at Hathaway near Route 140 (daily 5 AM–7 PM; 508/993-3073), another 1950s O'Mahony; the neon Indian alone makes it worth a visit. The Shawmut also hosts dinerdom's popular radio program, **America, Good Morning,** a talk show that's broadcast all over the USA.

For a good example of the kind of down-home folk music performance found in church and grange halls throughout New England, check out New Bedford's **Tryworks Coffeehouse** (Saturday 8 PM, mid-Sept. to early May) in the First Unitarian Church on 8th and Union Streets.

Choices of accommodations are limited. The warmest welcome and greatest convenience to downtown attractions and restaurants is **Cynthia and Steven's B&B**, on 7th Street in the historic district (508/997-6433), where rooms with private baths go for $55–65. There's also a Days Inn on Hathaway Road by the airport, at I-195 exit 13B.

FALL RIVER

Cotton mills put Fall River on the map, and their demise nearly wiped it off again. One of the nation's leading industrial cities at the turn of the 20th century, Fall River (pop. 92,703) swiftly became one of the leading casualties of the Depression, propelled into a decade of bankruptcy by the triple whammy of mills' moves to cheaper Southern labor, a devastating downtown fire, and the Wall Street crash of 1929. Although receivership ended with World War II, the giant brick mills have only recently awakened from their decades of boarded-up slumber, reanimated by the factory stores that contribute to Fall River's new stature as southern New England's discount retailing center.

If 30 percent off assorted clothing and housewares doesn't lure you down the exit ramps, perhaps a fascination with warships will. A small armada awaits your exploration in **Battleship Cove** (daily 9 AM–sunset; $9; 800/533-3194), plainly visible from the Interstate bridge over the broad, brackish Taunton River: the

battleship *Massachusetts*, destroyer *Joseph P. Kennedy Jr.,* submarine *Lionfish,* and a pair of P.T. boats from World War II.

Along the waterfront, adjacent to the anchored ships, the galleries of **Fall River Heritage State Park** (daily 10 AM–6 PM in summer, till 4 PM otherwise; free) tell the city's story with excellent archival photos and period artifacts, one of nine such innovative parks dedicated to the state's industrial, labor, and immigration history.

While numerous eateries in this city subscribe to the four major food groups—salt, grease, sugar, and carbonation—decent dining does exist if you're willing to hunt around for it. Try the hearty, Eastern European, stick-to-your-ribs soups and meats

---

LIZZIE BORDEN

"Lizzie Borden took an ax/And gave her mother 40 whacks . . . ." If you've heard this couplet before, you're already acquainted with Fall River's most notorious citizen, a wealthy banker's daughter (and Sunday-school teacher) accused of the double murder of her father and stepmother on August 4, 1892. Lest children's rhymes prejudice your opinion of Ms. Borden, know that a jury of her peers returned a verdict of *not guilty*.

The **Fall River Historical Society** (Tues.–Fri. 9 AM–4:30 PM, weekends in summer only; $3.50) has a complete exhibit on the subject, including trial evidence and the alleged weapon, in its mansion headquarters at 451 Rock Street in the Highlands historic district. If you want more, you can tour the actual house where the murders occurred, or even stay the night at the **Borden Home Museum and B&B,** 92 Second Street (508/675-7333).

---

at the **Ukrainian Home,** 492 Globe Street off Route 138—just over a mile south of I-195, opposite Dunkin' Donuts (508/672-9677). The latest immigration trends are reflected in the tasty, inexpensive Southeast Asian cuisine found at the **New Phnom Penh Restaurant** in the Angor Plaza (closed Monday; 508/324-4909) on Quequechan Street, next to the huge Wampanoag Mill factory outlet mall.

This being Massachusetts, there's also a fine 1950s diner, **Al Mac's,** at the base of President Hill on US-6 at the junction with the Route 79/138 elevated highway. In great shape inside and out, this place not only serves coffee in pint-sized mugs, it stays open late: Sun.–Tues. 5:30 AM–midnight (until 10 PM in winter), Wed.–Thurs. till 3 AM, and Fri.–Sat. till 4 AM (508/679-5851).

If you don't fancy staying the night in Lizzie Borden's bed (if you do, see "Lizzie Borden" for more), a small rash of chain names among local accommodations include a Howard Johnson, a Hampton Inn, a Holiday Inn, an Econo Lodge, a Comfort Inn, and a Super 8.

Between Massachusetts and Connecticut, US-6 makes a quick run across Rhode Island, passing through or near Providence, Pawtucket, and Newport, all of which are covered in the US-1 chapter on pages 93–96.

ROUTE 169: WINDHAM COUNTY

Although the major Interstate I-395 cuts its way across eastern Connecticut from the coast, motorists rarely leave the fast lane long enough to take a peek behind the brow of the hills that border both the highway and the Quinebaug River, which are roughly parallel. If they did, they would find small valley towns raised around historic 19th-century milling operations

That tall ship sometimes anchored in summer near the mothball navy is the **HMS *Bounty*** (May–Oct.; $4; *508/673-3886*)—or, rather, the movie version, built from the original naval blueprint for MGM's 1962 production starring Marlon Brando and Trevor Howard. A fully functioning sailing vessel used for education and training, the replica makes frequent appearances at harbor and maritime festivals around New England and Canada, so call ahead for the port schedule if you don't want to miss her.

A quick trip south along Route 81 from Fall River to Adamsville, Rhode Island, will take you a bas-relief marker honoring the birthplace of the Rhode Island Red breed of chicken.

Across the river from Providence, overlooking Narragansett Bay, the mature greenscape of Crescent Park holds one of the finest old merry-go-rounds you'll ever see, an1895 **Looff Carousel,** still in operation most weekends for a fare of 50¢ a ride.

DINERS: FAST FOOD WORTH SLOWING DOWN FOR

Aaaah, the local diner! Throughout New England, these brightly lit establishments are magnets for folks weary of the dull predictability of the fast-food megachains. In contrast to the impersonality of those billions-serving burger factories, diners are low-key gathering spots where community gossip is shared and politics debated by a gang of regulars assembling around eight each morning. Where motherly waitresses (frequently named Mildred, Blanche, and Edna) wearing lace hankies pinned to their aprons are quick to offer refills on coffee. Where UPS drivers, Methodist clergy, morticians, and middle-school principals perched on adjacent stools know they can score decent hot roast-beef sandwiches or a great piece of fresh fruit pie. And where autumn leaf-peepers and other passers-through can inquire about local attractions or find out which nearby motels or B&Bs might still have empty rooms for that night.

The diner's lineage can ultimately be traced back to horse-drawn lunch carts selling sandwiches, pie, and hot coffee along the streets of such cities as Providence and Boston beginning in the 1870s. However, the prototypical New England diners are those built from the 1920s through the 1950s by the **Worcester Lunch Car Company:** barrel-roofed with colorful porcelain panels on the exterior, and plenty of varnished hardwood inside. Worcester made many of the places highlighted in this book, until it ceased operations in 1961. Other diners came from manufacturers headquartered in New York (**DeRaffele**) and especially New Jersey (**Mountain View, Fodero, Kullman, Paramount, Silk City, O'Mahony,** and many more). Each diner-maker trumpeted its own design innovations: streamlined metal exteriors, artful tilework, bits of elegant stained glass, distinctive built-in clocks, and more efficient floor plans. Some even included all necessary crockery, flatware, and cooking equipment, so that new owners could begin serving hungry locals on the very day set-up was complete.

Aficionados will be quick to inform you that real diners are roadside eateries whose component parts were fabricated in a factory, then shipped by road or rail for assembly onsite. Real diners, they'll insist, always have counters, with at least some cooking done within view of patrons. There'll almost certainly be booths, too, and a definite blue-collar, no-frills ambiance. Unlike their urban or roadside truck stop equivalents, few diners are open 24 hours; many in fact serve breakfast and lunch only, opening very early in the morning (around 6 AM) and closing around 2 or 3 PM. But not every place with the word "diner" in its name is the genuine article. Many places that call themselves a diner are as far removed from the classic prefab as IKEA furniture is from a handcrafted antique, and mavens regard diner-themed restaurants (like the current generation of Denny's) with considerable scorn. The smaller, the better, they say, with points deducted for any remodeling that disfigures the original design.

You needn't care about any of this lore, of course, to enjoy yourself. But after visiting your third or fourth diner, you may begin to notice similarities and differences among them. Curious about a particular establishment's history? Quiz the owner—more often than not, he or she will be happy to tell you all about the place, which may have started life with a different name in another town and been moved three or more times before it found its current home. Look for a "tag," the small metal plate (often affixed to the wall over the entry door) listing manufacturer, date, and serial number. And if you want to learn more, check these three outstanding resources for further diner information: an authoritative volume by Richard Gutman entitled *American Diner Then and Now* (published by Johns Hopkins University Press); the bimonthly magazine called (www.roadsidemagazine.com), and the long-awaited **American Diner Museum,** due to open in downtown Providence sometime soon (401/331-8575 or www.americandiner museum.org).

The best and most enjoyable way to learn about diners and diner culture is simply to spend time in them. New England has more good diners than anywhere else on the planet, and tiny Rhode Island is home to a surprisingly rich array of diner styles. Just north of Providence, there's the **Modern Diner** in Pawtucket, a maroon-and-cream 1941 single-ended Sterling Streamliner that was the first diner to be listed on the National Register of Historic Places; order the chowder. South of Providence, **Jigger's Diner** in East Greenwich is a 1950 Worcester that's justly celebrated for its cornmeal jonnycakes, a local specialty. Just outside upscale Newport, **Bishop's Fourth Street Diner** is a quintessential diner, an early 1950s O'Mahony that's perched outside the gates to the U.S. Navy base. In Providence itself, choose between the **Seaplane Diner,** another early 1950s O'Mahony, and the **Silver Top,** a 1939 Kullman. Located adjacent to Providence's city market, the Silver Top keeps odd hours: 11 PM to 6 AM only.

For more details on these or any of the dozens of other New England diners described in this book, look in the index under "Diner."

and railroad depots, and rural hill towns with farmland cultivated with corn since before the arrival of the *Mayflower.*

If you have the time and the inclination to explore, consider a detour through this historic landscape, either along Route 12, the mill town route, or Route 169, the old Norwich-Woodstock Turnpike, sometimes called the **Revolutionary Road.** One of the most scenic highways in the northeast, if not the nation, Route 169 intersects US-6 in **Brooklyn,** hometown to General Israel "Battle of Bunker Hill" Putnam, just five miles west of the I-395 freeway. A magnificent memorial to Putnam, who was second-in-command to George Washington, stands proudly at the center of Brooklyn, next to the town green along Route 169.

Brooklyn, an idyllic country hamlet that's about as opposite to its New York namesake as can be, also hosts the annual **Brooklyn Fair** the last weekend in August. Although there are rivals for the title, this town proclaims its fair America's oldest, and since its start in 1852, it has been held at the spacious fairgrounds south of town. Brooklyn also has a fine old-fashioned filling station, right on Route 169, and the Trinity Episcopal church has some Tiffany stained-glass windows.

North from Brooklyn, the Revolutionary Road heads off on a lovely, winding scenic cruise, passing well-manicured pastures and farms that seem more decorative than productive, the road bordered by dry stone walls. Two miles north of Brooklyn, stop at the **Lapsley Orchards** fruit stand for some exquisite peaches or other summer produce, or just follow along Route 169 as it winds through prestigious **Pomfret,** a historic getaway for Boston and New York elite, especially in the years after the railroad came through in the 1870s.

North and east of Pomfret, along US-44 just west of I-395, **Putnam** is a more typical Connecticut town, where former textile mills have found new life as antiques stores. Wander through the dozens of shops or along the nice path that follows the Quinebaug River.

At I-395 exit 93, one exit north along the freeway from where US-6 crosses the superslab, Dayville is home to **Zip's Diner** (860/774-6335), a 1949 O'Mahony that's one of the real gems among New England diners.

WINDHAM COUNTY PRACTICALITIES

A century ago, wealthy New Yorkers spent their summers in the northeast corner of Connecticut, particularly in and around tiny Pomfret; now they own second homes here and send their kids to one of the two prep schools in town. Besides contributing to the community's graceful architectural treasury, the schools help support the year-round existence of the fine **Vanilla Bean Cafe,** 450 Deerfield Road (860/928-1562) at the center of town; it's open till at least 8 PM most days, till 3 PM on Monday and Tuesday. If you aren't ashamed to park your beat-up Toyota next to new Jaguars and BMW convertibles owned by 17-year-olds, this casual counter-service eatery inside a restored old barn is worth a stop for excellent sandwiches, soups, and bakery goods, or for that eye-opening hit of espresso in the morning.

For a more down-to-earth meal, check out **Zip's Diner** off I-395 in Dayville (860/774-6335), or in between the antiques shops of Putnam, stop for a bite at **Nikki's Dog Place,** 35 Main Street (860/928-0252) next to the old train depot.

Predictably for such a lovely rural setting, there are plenty of

B&Bs tucked into the Windham hills, including the truly historic and very comfortable **Friendship Valley B&B** ($105–145; 860/779-9696), an antique-filled, 12-acre Quaker farm in Brooklyn, which once served as a main stop of the Underground Railroad. Some of the region's best camping is at the Wolf Den Campgrounds in **Mashamoquet Brook State Park** off Route 169/US-44 (open April–Oct. only; $12; 860/928-6121).

For a complete up-to-date list of restaurants, lodging, and attractions here in what the tourism authorities call the Quiet Corner, contact the **Northeast Connecticut Visitors District** (860/928-1228).

WILLIMANTIC

The 19th-century mill town of Willimantic (pop. 14,746) has been bypassed by the new four-lane freeway alignment of US-6. However, if you have an abiding interest in the lives and labors of the people who worked in early American industry, take a quick detour and stop by the small **Windham Textile and History Museum** (Thurs.–Sun. noon–5 PM; $3). It's located at 157 Union Street at the corner of Main Street, opposite the giant American Thread mill, which closed down in 1984 after doing business for 120 years.

> Besides a glimpse of Connecticut's rapidly vanishing working class culture, Willimantic also offers a thirst-quenching alternative to mass-market sodas: **Hosmer Mountain Beverages,** which produces more than 25 different types of refreshingly cold drinks, available at most area convenience stores.

Downtown Willimantic isn't in the doldrums by a long shot; the neoclassical former post office (with its 1930s WPA mural) has been reborn as a the **Willimantic Brewing Company,** 967 Main Street (860/423-6777), serving big plates of hearty food at low prices, plus an array of fresh microbrewed beers. Also worth visiting is the **Paradise Eatery,** serving healthy, vegetarian-friendly food at 713 Main Street (860/423-7682). For a taste of old-fashioned, all-American fun under the stars, head west of downtown, just north of US-6 along Route 32, to the **Mansfield Twin Drive-In** (860/423-4441), which shows alfresco movies every night in summer, weekends only in April, May, and September.

Between Willimantic and Hartford, old US-6 follows surface streets through a very nondescript urban landscape of 1940s housing and convenience stores from

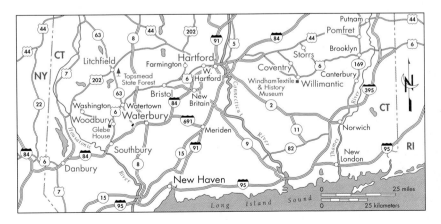

While it's not exactly open to the public, one of the old American Thread mill buildings is now used by T&M Distributors as a warehouse for a huge collection of old jukeboxes and pool tables. It's across from the Windham Textile and History Museum in Willimantic.

If you're not in any hurry to reach Hartford, you may want to follow Route 66 instead. No, it's not the one that winds from Chicago to Los Angeles, but it does offer a more scenic taste of central Connecticut, linking the two college town of Storrs and Middletown, home to the University of Connecticut and Wesleyan University, respectively.

the 1980s. If idling at red lights staring at cigarette and liquor billboards fits your vacation plans, go ahead and keep tracking US-6; otherwise, leave US-6 in Bolton and following I-384 and I-84 to the capital.

COVENTRY AND STORRS

A world away from the industrial history of Willimantic's mills, the rural town of Coventry (pop. 10,000) was the birthplace of colonial Connecticut's favorite son, Revolutionary War hero Nathan Hale (1755–76). A much-romanticized figure (best known for his last words, "I only regret that I have but one life to lose for my country," which he spoke on the gallows before being hanged by the British as a spy), Nathan Hale was born on the site of the grand **Nathan Hale Homestead**, 2299 South Street (daily in summer 1–5 PM; $5; 860/742-8996). Here you'll find displays of a variety of Hale family furniture and memorabilia in a house that was built a month after his death at the age of 21. Hale's early death is more tragic than heroic. He went behind British lines to gather information, posing as a schoolteacher (which he was), and carrying little more than his Yale diploma. He was relatively forgotten until the town of Coventry built a 45-foot-tall memorial to him, which stands near Lake Coventry.

Nathan Hale, Birth Place, South Coventry, Conn.

North and east of Coventry, the town of Storrs (pop. 12,200) is home to the basketball-mad University of Connecticut. Founded as an agricultural college, the university still feels like a farm, with cows wandering at the fringes and prominent signs pointing you toward the Dairy Products Store (which turns out to be a good, cheap, ice cream bar). However, the school has grown considerably in recent years, with a number of uninviting brick-and-glass hulks scattered along Route 195. There's very little college town ambiance and the campus seems to merge into the neighboring state prison and state police academy, but there is one unique draw: the **Museum of Puppetry,** off US-44 (Thurs.–Sun.; $2; 860/486-4605). If you've ever enjoyed TV's *Sesame Street,* a Balinese shadow puppet, or a Punch & Judy show, you'll appreciate the variety of puppets on display here, collected and made by students and faculty of the nation's only accredited degree program (B.A. through M.F.A.) in the puppet arts.

The Connecticut capital, Hartford, is covered in the US-5 chapter on pages 214–15.

BRISTOL

Heading west from Hartford toward the New York border, the upscale influence of the Litchfield Hills region may be seen in the comparative dearth of billboards, the subdued signage, and the fact that national chain stores don't blanket the highway like tickertape at a parade. But even Litchfield's refinement and taste can't totally restrain the welter of Petro Pantries and other caterers to the convenience of the populous Connecticut River valley. For the first 15 miles from the I-84 off-ramp in Farmington, this route becomes the playground of paving contractors and outdoor-lighting salespeople. Unless you're out shopping for mufflers, videos, hardware, sub sandwiches, or discount clothing, driving the route becomes an act of penance.

South of Bristol, off I-84 exit 31, **Lake Compounce** (860/583-3300) is the oldest amusement park in the United States, open since 1846. After surviving some financial difficulties in the 1990s, it has added a host of new rides to its historic charms.

Of course, behind the highway clutter are several attractions worthy of the name—two alone in the heart of Bristol, for example. Two blocks off US-6, the **American Clock and Watch Museum** at 100 Maple Street (daily 10 AM–5 PM March–Nov.; $4; 860/583-6070) has exactly what you'd expect—room after room of timepieces, more than 3,000 in all. Still, expectation can't begin to detract from the ingenuity and craftsmanship on display. And yes, most of the collection keeps the correct time, as you'll find out at the top of the hour; stand in the newer wing of the building to catch the best cacophony of striking, chiming, and ringing. Not very far away, **The New England Carousel Museum,** 95 Riverside Avenue (Route 72), will charm any kid alive, even if the kid in question is old enough to remember Joni Mitchell's refrain about painted ponies going up and down. The beautiful collection of colorful antique jumpers and prancers is augmented by artisans doing restoration work or carving new carousel animals at one end of the long gallery (Mon.–Sat. 10 AM–5 PM, Sun. noon–5 PM; $4; 860/585-5411).

Sports fans will know Bristol as the world headquarters of ESPN.

You'll find the nation's largest collection of locks, keys, and Victorian hardware behind the plain brick facade of the **Lock Museum of America** (Tues.–Sun. 1:30–4:30 PM, May–Oct.; $3; 860/589-6359) in Terryville, opposite the Congregational church at 230 Main Street (US-6).

TOPSMEAD

Just east of Litchfield off of Route 118 lies Topsmead, the former summer estate of Edith Morton Chase, daughter of a Waterbury brass magnate. Miss Chase bequeathed her hilltop Tudor mansion to the people of Connecticut after her death, along with more than 500 acres of wooded and landscaped grounds. Now **Topsmead State Forest** is one of the crown jewels of the state park system, ideal for rambles down to the bird blind in the woods, picnics upon the expansive lawns, or—if you packed your horse—afternoon canters along tree-lined farm lanes. Its status as a hidden treasure is due in no small part to the absence of good signage, but heading east on Route 118 from Litchfield, take a right on East Litchfield Road, another right at Buell Road, and you won't miss the stone-gate entrance. Topsmead is open year-round until sunset, with house tours

Topsmead doesn't permit camping, but two nearby state parks do: **Black Rock** on US-6 east of Watertown, and **Burr Pond** just off Route 8 north of Torrington. For current fees and site reservations, call the state parks division at 860/566-2304.

Litchfield must have something to recommend it: Eugene Fodor, well-traveled founder of the guidebook line that bears his name, calls it home.

For further information on activities and services, or for a brochure of local auto tours, contact the helpful folks at the Litchfield Hills Travel Council (P.O. Box 968, Litchfield, Connecticut 06759; 860/567-4506).

noon–5 PM on alternate weekends, June–Oct. (860/567-5694). By the way, that white house opposite the parking lot is private property unrelated to the state forest; please don't confuse its inhabitants with park rangers.

LITCHFIELD

This section of US-6 skirts the edge of Litchfield County, bucolic home to Manhattan-accented money, manners, and food (but mostly money), conspicuously framed by the white clapboard facades of some of New England's signature towns. Detour up Route 63, for example, and get an eyeful of the county seat of Litchfield, whose tidy green, stately old residences, and photogenic churches epitomize the area's attractions.

Some exceptional meals are to be had in this place, but don't expect any early-bird specials around here. Local restaurateurs can and do charge exactly what they think the meals are worth. And given that their regulars include a fair number of big names from major Manhattan publishers to major Hollywood movies, you can bet self-esteem is not in danger of any downswing in *these* kitchens.

West Street Grill, 43 West Street (860/567-3885) on the Litchfield Green, is widely considered one of the best restaurants in the state. If triple digits won't make you flinch at the end of your dinner, then lucky you won't have to worry whether to skip the appetizers or skimp on the wine simply to afford that fine crackly creme brulee or those tropical fruit sorbets for dessert. If you aren't so well heeled, drop by for lunch and sample haute bistro cuisine and service as impeccable as the town is pretty, and maybe, just maybe, walk out with change for that

Litchfield Law School 1784 (First in America)   Litchfield, Conn.

$20. If you still want to be able to afford one of those lobsters by the time you reach Cape Cod, West Street's owners have a more *rustique* wood-fired, brick-oven pizza place called **Grappa,** in the Litchfield Commons shops just west of the town center on Route 202 (860/567-1616); no one will question your expense report if you enjoy yourself here instead.

One place to rent a bike in the Litchfield Hills is the friendly and knowledgeable **Cycle Loft,** located among the shops of the Litchfield Commons on Route 202 in Litchfield (860/567-1713; $6 an hour or $20 a day).

WASHINGTON: THE INSTITUTE FOR AMERICAN INDIAN STUDIES

Long before the Bill of Rights was signed, the land around the Litchfield Hills was farmed and hunted by Algonquian tribes like the Pootatucks, who finally "sold" it to colonial settlers in 1659. The Institute for American Indian Studies (Mon.–Sat. 10 AM–5 PM. Sun. 1–5 PM; except Jan.–March, closed Mon.–Tues.; $4; 860/868-0518), has extensive exhibits on who these people were, what they did, and how anthropology and archaeology have brought some of this information to light. The IAIS also reminds visitors that not all Indians are casino owners and that traditional Native Americans continue to live and work here; crafts and technology demonstrations, performances, and workshops are offered. The museum is located 11 miles southwest of Litchfield via Route 202 and Route 47 in the hamlet of Washington. To get here from Woodbury take Route 47 to Route 199; the IAIS sign is about halfway between the Washington/Roxbury town line and the Route 47 junction.

WATERBURY: HOLY LAND USA

About 10 miles due east of Woodbury, or 10 miles south of Terryville via busy Route 8, the large old manufacturing city of Waterbury (pop. 109,000) is home to Holy Land USA, above I-84 on the hill—look for the giant illuminated cross. Plaster, carpet remnants, reflective mailbox-style adhesive lettering, plastic dolls, and biblical scripture are some of the basic ingredients in this folk art extravaganza built in the 1950s and '60s by a very, very dedicated Christian, Waterbury lawyer John Greco, who died in 1986 at age 91. The fact that an order of nuns runs the place has not kept vandals from having their way with it since Greco's demise,

but the general decay doesn't deter devout pilgrims and the utter ruin should certainly appeal to anyone with a dark, well-honed sense of irony and metaphor. Holy Land, which looms over the southeast edge of downtown, is easy to see from the freeway (impossible to miss if you're heading east on I-84), but getting there can be a little complicated. You have to follow a series of residential streets winding up the hill; the park itself is officially closed, but you can easily walk around the gates and explore. It's safe enough during the day but not at night (when you couldn't see anything, anyway).

WOODBURY

Woodbury's long Main Street (US-6) is loaded with so many antique and collectibles shops that the town has trademarked itself as the official Antiques Capitol (sic) of Connecticut. If you get hungry ogling at all of the old chairs and crockery, Woodbury also has a very nice grocery store in the middle of it all: **LaBonne's Epicure Market**, 690 S. Main Street (203/263-3632), ideal for picking up a deli sandwich or some picnic goodies.

Take some horse farms with lush green fields outlined by neat stone walls or zig-zagging knit-pole fences, mix in big old clapboard colonials with wide lawns and wood split-shingle roofs, add a couple of needle-spired churches and historic burial grounds beneath the tall maples and oaks, and you have all the trappings of a place that should live by the gentle stroke of a tall grandfather clock rather than the nervous second-splitting tick of a stopwatch. Alas, all of the Woodbury residents who keep time by the old Seth Thomas wind-ups must be at home taking naps, while all the sprinters caught up in lives like 100-meter dashes are out taking turns trying to get close enough to read the fine print on your rear license plate.

Since the rush of traffic on US-6 makes architectural appreciation impossible without suffering whiplash, stop by Woodbury's town office building on Main Street and pick up a free brochure detailing two local **walking tours** around the former sheep-raising capital of the American colonies, which is still liberally endowed with fine 18th- and 19th-century structures. One colonial home open to the public is the restored **Glebe House** (Wed.–Sun. 1–4 PM, April–Nov.; 203/263-2855), on Hollow Road (Route 317) in southern Woodbury. The first Episcopalian bishop was elected by a secret meeting of clergy at this minister's farm in 1783 and consecrated by Scottish Anglicans a year later. This was an extraordinarily radical act in that age, because it required accepting two unorthodoxies: religious freedom (the Anglicans, after all, were the official church of the defeated enemy), and the separation of church and state. These liberties weren't enshrined in the Constitution, by the way, until three years later.

To go with all the antiques and civil liberties, Woodbury has some nice places in which to eat and drink, like the friendly **Good News Cafe,** serving everything from meatloaf and onion rings to wok-fried shrimp on US-6 at 694 Main Street (203/266-4663).

Besides ecclesiastical history and colonial crafts, Woodbury's Glebe House also possesses the only remaining garden in the nation designed by Gertrude Jekyll, the horticulturist who perfected what's known as the English country garden.

South of Woodbury, US-6 joins up with the I-84 freeway at Southbury, where a huge IBM office complex and an equally huge shopping center have paved over the once-rural town's pastures and pumpkin fields. US-6 is pretty well submerged beneath I-84 between Southbury and the New York state line, and given the abutters vying for your business along every inch of the old road, you may actually find the Interstate more scenic. Amid all the convenience stores and corporate headquarters, US-6 skips off on its own for a few miles for a glimpse of upscale residential Newtown, only to merge again with the Interstate on the far side of the town's huge flagpole.

Midway between Southbury and the New York state line, Danbury marks the place where US-6 and I-84 cross US-7, a scenic route that winds north through the Berkshires to the Green Mountains of Vermont.

GREEN MOUNTAINS, BERKSHIRES, AND LITCHFIELD HILLS: US-7

GREEN MOUNTAINS, BERKSHIRES, AND LITCHFIELD HILLS: US-7

f you like the idea of cruising through miles of scenic countryside, with mountains rising to one side and lakes to the other,
you'll probably like US-7. Running between Canada and the
coast of Connecticut, US-7 manages to avoid the freeways, shopping malls, and other signs of the modern world, opting instead
for dairy and horse pastures and dozens of truly quaint small
towns, all framed by nearly nonstop natural splendor.

Starting in northwestern Vermont between the Green Mountains
and the shores of Lake Champlain, US-7 runs through the twin
towns of Winooski and Burlington, which share a scenic setting
as well as one of the New England's most enjoyable minor-league
baseball teams. Continuing along the lake, US-7 takes a look at the
wonderful folk art collected at the world-class Shelburne Museum,
before heading on to the college town of Middlebury and the
enticing mountain passes (known here as "gaps") that may tempt
you to detour to the east. Attractive as the mountains are, they
have to compete for your attention with the country towns of
the valley below, places like Arlington, longtime home of artist
Norman Rockwell; and Manchester, a plush resort that marks
the shift into the high-tone tourism of the Berkshires, south of the
Massachusetts border.

The Berkshires, as the entire far-western section of Massachusetts is often called, are roughly equidistant from New York City and Boston, and for more than a century have drawn flocks of migratory culture vultures from both places. Home to some of New England's most respected summer arts festivals, the Berkshires have long been a summer escape for urban elites, but they're not totally exclusive—just very popular, so make plans as soon as you can.

Like the neighboring Berkshires, Connecticut's Litchfield Hills are a traditional retreat for discerning city dwellers. The area is rich in forests, farms, and picturesque little towns laden with antique shops. Fast food and discount shopping are as alien to this landscape as affordability, so if your purse strings are tight you'll want to keep moving; otherwise, linger a while and enjoy some of the rural charm so prized by those people you see on the cover of *Business Week*.

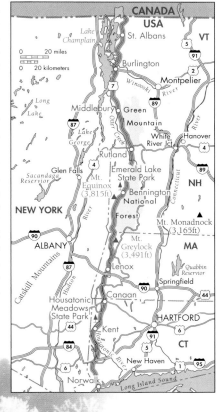

St. Albans was the site of the most northerly "battle" of the Civil War: in 1864 a band of Confederate soldiers came down from Canada, held up a bank, stole $200,000, and killed a man. Soon afterwards, 22 of the raiders were captured and tried in Canada and finally acquitted when their deeds were judged to be legitimate acts of war. St. Albans Raid is re-created every year during the town's Civil War Days, in late October.

ST. ALBANS AND FAIRFIELD

A busy railroad (and Underground Railroad) center back in Civil War times, St. Albans (pop. 7,300) is still more industrial than is most of Vermont, but its setting between the Green Mountains and Lake Champlain can make it seem quite idyllic. The well-traveled orator Henry Ward Beecher said that St. Albans sat "in the midst of a greater variety of scenic beauty" than anywhere else in the USA, and if you look across at Lake Champlain or up into the Green Mountains from Taylor Park, at the center of St. Albans' historic business district, you might see what he meant.

These days St. Albans has places to eat and sleep and is less expensive than many more-interesting towns. Despite the upscale name, rooms at the **Cadillac Motel** ($40–60; 802/524-2191) at 213 S. Main Street are plain but clean.

East of St. Albans via Route 36, the rural hamlet of Fairfield was the birthplace of Chester A. Arthur, who served as president from 1881 until 1885. Son of a Baptist minister, Arthur was born in 1829 in a parsonage that has been preserved as a museum (Wed.–Sun. 11 AM–5 PM; free; 802/828-3226). The adjacent church, where his father preached, has also been preserved in period condition and now holds a small display describing the variety of church and meetinghouse architecture in Vermont. Noted for his work in improving civil rights and reforming government bureaucracy, Arthur (who became president when James Garfield was assassinated) is something of a marginal figure among American presidents, but there are some interesting tales revolving around him. For instance, his own party didn't even offer to nominate him for a second term, and there are historians who believe he was born across the border in Canada, and as a Canadian citizen legally was not eligible to serve as commander-in-chief.

Midway between St. Albans and Burlington and a little east of US-7 and I-89, the town of Fairfax was home to the last U.S. factory making tiles for the popular word game Scrabble, but the factory closed down in 1998.

The engaging towns of Winooski, home to the Vermont Expos, and Burlington, home to University of Vermont, are covered in the US-2 chapter on pages 133–35.

SHELBURNE

One of the most popular and enjoyable stops in the state of Vermont sits just five miles south of downtown Burlington on the shores on Lake Champlain: the **Shelburne Museum** (daily 10 AM–5 PM, mid-May until mid-Oct. only; $17.50; 802/985-3346). The museum presents perhaps the best and certainly the most unusual agglomerations of fine art, folk art, and

general oddities you'll find anywhere. These toys, dolls, trade signs, and weathervanes (and much, much more) really do defy classification, but there's more here than a riot of garage-sale stuff. Assembled over a lifetime by heiress Electra Havemeyer Webb, whose parents introduced America to the art of the French Impressionists, the Shelburne collection includes paintings by European and American masters (Rembrandt, Monet, Manet, and Winslow Homer to drop a famous few names). However, it is most interesting for its unique Americana: old fire trucks, handmade quilts, and a world-class collection of cigarstore Indians (not to mention a model of a circus parade that's more than 500 feet long).

There are also some three dozen historic buildings brought here from all over New England: a covered bridge, a round barn, a lighthouse, a railroad depot, even a complete side-wheeled Lake Champlain steamboat, the *Ticonderoga*. The buildings, which all house different parts of the expansive collection, are spread over 40 acres of lawns and formal gardens, and there's so much to see you may want to save some for another visit, which you can do since tickets are good for two days.

Northwest of the Shelburne Museum, 1.5 miles from US-7 via Bay and Harbor Roads, **Shelburne Farms** is a 1,400-acre farm and nonprofit environmental center with eight miles of hiking trails on a promontory jutting out into Lake Champlain. The grounds were laid out by landscape architect Frederick Law

Olmsted to take full advantage of the natural topography (and to maximize views across the lake toward the Adirondack Mountains). In recent years, Shelburne Farms has become a

SHELBURNE FARMS

leading force in the movement toward sustainable agriculture, and you can taste the results in their fabulously flavorful cheddar cheeses, available nationwide. Free tastings are available here at the Farm Store, where you can also join a 90-minute guided tour ($10; 802/

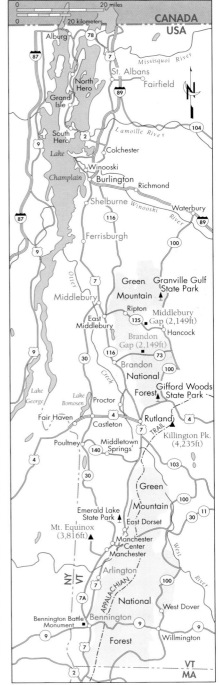

Charlotte is also the home of the **Vermont Wildflower Farm,** a carefully groomed six-acre garden (daily 10 AM–5 PM; $3; 802/425-3500) run by the producers of "America's Favorite Wildflower Seed."

In 1777, Vermont banned slavery in its original constitution, the first of the former British colonies to do so. Great Britain (and thus Canada) banned slavery in 1834, and the United States finally prohibited slavery with the 13th Amendment, which was ratified at the end of 1865.

The drive along US-7 between Burlington and Middlebury is pleasant enough, but numerous detours are at hand if you feel tempted to explore. Route 17 through Bristol, for example, will take you east to picturesque old redbrick towns and on into the Green Mountains. Route 17 heads northeast up and over scenic Appalachian Gap before dropping down into Mad River Glen toward Waitsfield, while a wilder road heads southeast over Lincoln Gap to Warren. To make a loop, follow Route 100 between Waitsfield and Warren.

The Morgan horse is the official state animal of Vermont, and you can see exemplars of this tough, strong breed three miles northwest of Middlebury at state-run **Morgan Horse Farm** (daily 9 AM–4 PM; $4; 802/388-2011). The historic farmstead where the horses were first bred is in Weybridge, well-signed along Route 125 and Route 23 from US-7 and the center of Middlebury.

985-8442) and explore the entire property. Included on the tours is a stop at the old mansion at the center of the estate, now the **Inn at Shelburne Farms** (May–Oct.; $90–175; 802/985-8498), where you can stay overnight or enjoy a wonderful meal (or three). There are also concerts, children's programs, and a variety of educational workshops held at Shelburne Farms throughout the summers.

South of Shelburne, just east of US-7, the historic crossroads hamlet of **Charlotte** used to be as big as Burlington, owing to its presence on the main stagecoach route to Troy, New York. Some of the Charlotte's historic buildings, including the main tavern, have been removed to the Shelburne Museum, while the Town Hall and others have been preserved *in situ* as minimuseums.

FERRISBURG: THE ROKEBY MUSEUM

Rokeby Museum, located right on US-7 in the town of Ferrisburg (pop. 2,300), preserves the home and farm of the Robinsons, a Quaker family who lived and raised sheep here for four generations, from the 1790s until the mid-1960s. Among many prominent Robinsons who lived and worked here were the staunch abolitionist Rowland T. Robinson, born here in 1797, and his son Rowland E. Robinson (1833–1900), a respected folklorist, natural historian, illustrator, and author. The museum (Thurs.–Sun. 11 AM–4 PM; $4; 802/877-3406) serves as a fine introduction to Vermont country life of a century or two ago, with its rooms full of furniture, tools, and domestic goods, not to mention the occasional living history events held on site. A visit here also provides an insight into one special aspect of the place: thanks to the efforts of Rowland T. Robinson, the house was a primary stop on the Underground Railroad, the network of abolitionists who helped slaves in the South escape to freedom. Escaped slaves were welcomed by the Robinsons, who paid them to work on the farm and helped them to establish independent lives. Many escaped slaves continued on to Canada, but many others remained here in Vermont, where abolitionist sentiments were strong.

MIDDLEBURY

The quintessential New England college town, Middlebury (pop 8,034), is set on rolling hills between the Green Mountains and the waters of Lake Champlain, making it a lovely place to explore. Home to its namesake liberal-arts college, where poet Robert Frost taught for many years, Middlebury is also a real town, with the remains of old marble quarries and mills lining the banks of Otter Creek, which tumbles in a broad waterfall at the heart of town.

Middlebury's many bike shops and bookshops owe their existence to the approximately 2,000 students lucky enough to attend **Middlebury College,** a spacious 500-acre campus spreading southwest of the town center along Route 30. Visitors are fortunate, too, as the rolling green open spaces are all generously provided with Adirondack-style wooden chairs, so you can take a break from your wandering and make yourself comfortable with a book or a beverage. Among the college's claims to fame is that it graduated the first African-American student in U.S. history. Middlebury College also stakes a claim to being the birthplace of the Frisbee and has a statue of a dog leaping to catch one of these flying discs on its main quadrangle, in front of Monroe Hall.

> If you want a cow-related souvenir of Vermont and have had enough Ben & Jerry's, stop into **Holy Cow,** 44 Main Street in Middlebury (802/388-6737), where artist Woody Jackson makes all manner of bovine-related mementos.

Back along US-7, the center of Middlebury is an odd-shaped green, dominated on one side by the landmark spire of the Congregational Church and on another by the historic **Middlebury Inn** ($80–160; 802/388-4961), which has been welcoming travelers since 1827. For budget travelers, a warm welcome awaits you at Middlebury's **HI Covered Bridge Hostel,** 62 Seymour Street ($20; 802/388-0401), a small, six-bed home-hostel named for and located near Vermont's oldest covered bridge, a mile or so northwest of town. Campers may want to head west from Middlebury to Lake Champlain, where the **DAR State Park** ($12; 802/759-2354) southwest of Addison, has camping, hot showers, and a lakefront swimming area.

Places to eat include the family-friendly **Fire and Ice,** north of the green at 26 Seymour Street (802/388-7166), and a well-preserved **A&W Root Beer** burger stand, on US-7 two miles south of the green.

EAST MIDDLEBURY, RIPTON, AND MIDDLEBURY GAP

South of Middlebury and east of US-7, a pair of roads offers two very different looks at the Green Mountains. Running along the foot of the mountains, Route 116 is an idyllic rural cruise, passing the 400-acre old-growth forest of Battell Biological Preserve on the way to Bristol, at the western foot of an unpaved road over sublime Lincoln Gap. Route 125, in contrast, climbs up along the banks of the Middlebury River to Ripton, where poet Robert Frost spent his summers late in life. Across Route 125 from the **Robert Frost Wayside** parking lot, 2.1 miles east of Ripton or 3.8 miles west of Middlebury Gap, an easy, mile-long interpretive nature trail through dense forest and riparian marshland is highlighted by plaques quoting excerpts from his poems. The first quarter of the trail takes a boardwalk across a beaver pond, and the far end of the trail passes through an old field where wild blueberries and huckleberries grow ripe in late summer.

Continuing uphill to the east, the yellow clapboard cottages of a former resort have been converted into a campus by Middlebury College. In midsummer the campus is home to the respected Bread Loaf Writers Conference, which since its founding in 1920 has been drawing editors, agents, writers, and aspiring writers to this idyllic mountain setting.

Another dozen miles to the east, Route 125 passes through 2,149-foot Middlebury Gap and crosses the hikers' Long Trail, then drops down toward Route 100, another great scenic drive, covered on pages 183–84. Before reaching Route 100 at

Rated among the World's 100 Best for 2001 by the gourmet-minded magazine *Saveur*, the idyllic **Blueberry Hill Inn** ($195-250 for two; 802/247-6735 or 800/448-0707) is a trim clapboard B&B offering the ultimate in Vermont country getaways. Located deep in the tranquil Green Mountain National Forest, the inn serves famously great good, locally grown food (dinner and breakfast included in the rates), and is well placed for day's spent hiking, cycling or cross-country skiing.

If you ever saw Bob Newhart's second-best TV show, *Newhart,* the inn used for exterior shots was and is the **Waybury Inn** (802/388-4015), on Route 125 southeast of Middlebury.

Along US-7 between Middlebury and Brandon, the hamlet of Salisbury is worth a stop to snap a photo of a giant **King Kong holding up an old VW.** The big ape stands in front of Pioneer Auto Sales used car lot, five miles north of Brandon.

the crossroads town of Hancock, Route 125 runs past **Texas Falls Recreation Area,** where a series of cascades drops down over a stack of glaciated boulders and water-worn potholes. Officially it's closed to swimming, but you can definitely plunge your toes in and relax in the enveloping white noise.

ROUTE 30: MIDDLEBURY TO BENNINGTON

If you're doing a circle tour of the Green Mountains area, there's no reason to double back on yourself to get home; with so many delightful drives, there's always an alternative. Here in the open rolling plains of the Lake Champlain Valley on the west side of the mountains, a very fine alternative to the US-7/Route 7A corridor between Middlebury and Bennington is Route 30. Besides giving access to **Hubbardton Battlefield,** site of the July 1777 defeat of a rag-tag band of Americans by British and Hessian forces, Route 30 passes by the pretty resorts lining Lake Bomoseen (where Harpo Marx had a summer home) through Castleton and the junction with US-4. (US-4 is covered in full on pages 170–87.) The main public access to Lake Bomoseen is at Crystal Beach ($1.50 adults, 50¢ kids), midway along the lake's eastern shore, where there are picnic tables and a children's playground along a sandy beach.

South of Castleton, Route 30 runs through Poultney, where the Taconic Mountains begin to rise up over the New York border before ending up at the artsy community of **Dorset,** a dozen miles north of Manchester Center and the junction with US-7 and Route 7A. Dorset makes a nice quiet base for exploring the region, especially if you manage to stay at **Inn at West View Farm,** a half-mile south of the Dorset village green at 2938 Route 30 ($120–165; 802/867-5715), a converted farmhouse that's been welcoming guests since the turn of the 20th century.

BRANDON AND BRANDON GAP

The trim little colonial-era town of Brandon, on US-7 between Middlebury and Rutland, was the birthplace in 1813 of Stephen A. Douglas, the 5-foot 2-inches tall political adversary of towering Abraham Lincoln during the elections of 1858. Douglas's home is just north of town, along US-7 next to a Baptist church.

Climbing up into the Green Mountains east from Brandon, Route 73 slices through beautiful Brandon Gap, which crosses the mountains and ends up near Rochester on Route 100. At the crest of the road, Route 73 cross the famous **Long Trail,** and a trailhead gives access to one of the best views of the Greens, from atop Mount Horrid. It's a short (quarter-mile) but steep climb, following the Long Trail to a blue-blazed spur trail that leads to some excellent views; note that the cliffs here are sometimes closed to protect nesting peregrine falcons, who call this home.

The big (for Vermont) city of Rutland marks the junction of US-7 with east-west US-4, which is covered on pages 170–87.

ROUTE 7A: MANCHESTER CENTER AND MANCHESTER

South of Rutland, US-7 becomes a four-lane freeway, and although there are some pretty stretches (especially around Emerald Lake State Park), there's not a lot to stop for until you reach the outskirts of Manchester. Here, historic Route 7A cuts off to the east, following the older alignment of this busy highway. As soon as you turn off US-7, you are transported into the heart of horse country, with estate homes set on manicured ranches. If you're here in midsummer, don't be surprised to see people dressed up like English aristocrats in full riding regalia, taking part in show-jumping or faux fox hunts.

On US-7 nine miles south of Brandon, the **New England Maple Museum** (daily 10 AM–4 PM; $1.25) sells Vermont's trademark product, and displays inside the long blue shed show how it gets made.

Wallingford, 10 miles south of Rutland on US-7, is the place where the hardware brand True Temper got its start. It was also the birthplace of the Rotary International organization.

ORVIS
5% FOR CONSERVATION

An aberration along generally rural Route 7A, the former milltown of Manchester Center (pop. 3,622) is now marked by acres of minimalls and upscale factory outlets such as Ralph Lauren and Calvin Klein. It's a lot like Freeport, Maine; the only real difference is that in place of L. L. Bean, Manchester Center has Orvis. Orvis, which got its start here along the trout-rich Batten Kill River in the 1800s, operates the **American Museum of Fly-Fishing,** where you can admire the rods, reels and fly-tying skills of the rich and famous, including Bing Crosby and Ernest Hemingway. The museum, which houses the world's largest collection of fishing gear, is on Route 7A next to the landmark Equinox Hotel (daily 10 AM–4 PM; 802/362-3300).

A total contrast to Manchester Center but just another half-mile south along Route 7A, the town of Manchester is the blue-blood social center of southwestern Vermont. With a genteel feeling more akin to a Berkshire resort with many grand summer homes, Manchester is something of an anomaly in Vermont, but if you can afford to spend some time here, there are lots of enjoyable ways to get rid of your spare cash. One pricey but down-home place to eat is **Quality Restaurant** on Main Street (802/362-9839), with cozy wooden booths that Norman Rockwell loved to sit in when he lived at nearby Arlington. The traditional cafe menu has seen the addition of such foodie faves as scallops over pesto fettuccine, but Quality is still a great place for breakfast. It's even better for pie: since 1920, it's been baking great, flaky, gooey treats, including fantastic apple pie (served with that only-in-Vermont slice of cheddar cheese).

Midway between Wallingford and Poultney, Middletown Springs is a one-time resort that has faded back to rural peace, set in the midst of rolling countryside. If you like the look of it, kick your shoes off and stay a while at the friendly **Middletown Springs Inn,** 4 Park Avenue (802/235-2531). Middletown Springs hosts the summertime **Vermont SolarFest,** a solar-powered festival of music, art, and crafts.

An overnight stay in town will set you back a ton of money, especially at one of Vermont's plushest old hotels, the white-columned **Equinox** ($200–350; 802/362-4700 or 800/362-4747), which has stood here since 1769. Your only hope for affordable lodgings are at family-owned **Aspen Motel** ($60–100; 802/362-2450) or the cozy **Wedgewood Motel** ($50–80; 802/362-2145), both of which are set back from Route 7A.

Just south of Manchester along Route 7A, the Georgian Revival mansion known as **Hildene,** built by Abraham Lincoln's son Robert Todd Lincoln, features some original furniture and family mementos.
Fisher-Scott Memorial Pines, west of Route 7A two miles north of Arlington, are 13 acres of the largest white pines in Vermont, with some measuring up to 120 feet tall.

Arlington's connection to the arts go back way beyond Rockwell—the landscape depicted on the Vermont state seal is based upon an engraving of the view west from what is now the town's train station.

In Arlington, on old Route 7A, stop by the 1962 **Snow's Arlington Dairy Bar** (802/375-2546) for a chili dog or an excellent milk shake, best enjoyed at one of the picnic tables next to dense woodlands.

The peak looming to the west of Manchester is **Mount Equinox;** the 3,816-foot summit is reached by a steep, five-mile toll road ($6) that starts midway between Manchester and Arlington. The drive to the top gives some nice views but the summit itself is disappointing—especially since the communications towers and inn (closed at time of writing) block the full panorama.

ROUTE 7A: ARLINGTON

One of the prettiest drives in southwest Vermont follows Route 7A, the old alignment of US-7 between Manchester and Bennington. The drive itself won't take much longer than the modern freeway version of US-7 but if you have time to stop and enjoy the scene, this 20-mile cruise could easily fill a leisurely afternoon. Midway between Manchester and Bennington, the main stop along historic Route 7A is the tidy village of Arlington (pop. 2,299). At the heart of Arlington, a converted church holds the **Norman Rockwell Gallery** (daily 9 AM–5 PM; $2; 802/375-6423), a small but sincere tribute to the artist and illustrator who lived and worked in Arlington during the peak of his creativity, from 1939 until 1952. Some of the rather elderly but still enthusiastic guides served as models for Rockwell's artworks, and they will no doubt share stories of him, making for a much more sincere and appropriately homespun tribute to the man who did so much to give Americans an image of ourselves and our country.

Another classic slice of Americana, a covered bridge over the Batten Kill River, can be enjoyed if you travel west from Arlington along Route 313 for about five miles, where the photogenic bridge is joined by a small green and a white-spired church. Also here: the **Inn on Covered Bridge Green** ($80–150; 802/375-9489), which offers four B&B rooms in a 1792 home set on five acres of apple orchards.

BENNINGTON

By far the largest Vermont town south of Burlington, Bennington (pop. 16,451) is a bustling little manufacturing and commercial center. It was named for a significant victory against the British-paid Hessians in 1777 during the American Revolution, a sweet morale-booster that contributed to the defeat of General "Gentleman Johnny" Burgoyne's army of Redcoats at Saratoga. In the subsequent centuries, Bennington's name became synonymous with art: the decorative arts of the antebellum United States Pottery Company; the liberal arts of Bennington College, one of the nation's most expensive and exclusive private colleges; and the folk art of Mary Robertson "Grandma" Moses.

The largest public collection of Grandma Moses's beguiling work is on display in the **Bennington Museum** (daily 9 AM–5 PM; $6), whose white-columned, ivy-covered edifice is found up the hill on West Main Street (Route 9) in the graceful old part of town. Along with 30 Grandma Moses paintings and the rural schoolhouse she attended two centuries ago, the museum also has a wide variety of historical artifacts, examples of early Bennington pottery, and the sole survivor of the fabulous motor cars once made here in Bennington by the Martin Company: a 1925 Wasp.

From the Bennington Museum, walk north toward the 306-foot obelisk that towers over the town: the **Bennington Battle Monument,** erected in 1891 to commemorate the Revolutionary War victory, which actually occurred west of town over the New York border. (For $2, from mid-April to Nov. 1, an elevator will take you to an observation room near the top of the tower for a great view up and down the valley.)

If anyone starts erecting monuments to good dining instead of old wars, this town would have another tower of stone beside the **Blue Benn Diner** (802/442-5140), on US-7 north of downtown. The fact that it's a vintage 1940s Silk City certainly gives this cozy nonsmoking joint character. But what earns the seven-days-a-week (from 6 AM!) loyalty of its patrons is the top-notch short-order cooking: from baked meat loaf and roast pork to broccoli stir-fry and multi-grain pancakes, the food's good, cheap, and served up so fast you'll barely have time to choose between Sinatra or Soundgarden on the wall-box juke at your table.

A 20-foot-tall chair built in the 1940s to show off civic pride in local manufacturing, still stands outside the Haynes & Kane Furniture Store on Route 7A in Bennington.

Between North Bennington and Manchester, **Vermont Valley Flyer** offers scenic railroad trips on restored 1930s trains ($14; 802/463-3069 or 800/707/3530).

Bennington is the final resting place of poet **Robert Frost,** whose tombstone in the burial ground alongside the Old First Church, at Church and Monument Streets, says: "I had a lover's quarrel with the world."

Whether or not you need gas, those interested in old cars and automobilia will want to stop by the full-service, re-created Sunoco filling station and antique car collection (7 AM–10 PM every day) at **Hemmings Motor News,** 215 Main Street in Bennington (800/227-4373). This re-created gas station also sells a full range of car-collecting books and memorabilia, including Hemmings' wonderful antique car calendars and their photography collection *Abandoned Autos: An America-Wide Appreciation of Aesthetically Abandoned Ancient Automobiles, Artfully Assembled (and Alliteratively Annotated) for the Astute Automotive Aficionado* ($19. 95), one of my all-time favorite car culture books.

By the early 19th century, farmland and pasture had replaced 75 percent of Berkshire County's forests. Now forests have reclaimed that 75 percent and more, but innumerable dry stone walls sticking up in thick groves of trees serve as reminders of the once-vast cultivated fields pioneer farmers cleared here—and all over New England.

Most of Bennington's **accommodations** are strung along Route 7A to the north and US-7 to the south of downtown, all local names but for the Ramada and Best Western inns found on 7A. If you are in the market for a distinctive B&B, push on the dozen miles to Williamstown, Massachusetts.

BERKSHIRE COUNTY

Hemmed in by the daunting topography of its many mountains, western Massachusetts is a world apart from the rest of the state. It's blessed with an easygoing small-town character so dissimilar from that of the metropolitan seacoast that locals compare it to southern Vermont or upstate New York, or anything, in fact, but Massachusetts. Given Boston's perennial neglect of the region, constituents often seem to wish that it *were* another state. Berkshire County might find the political clout it has so long sought if representation were based on culture and the social register rather than population. The region has been a magnet for performing arts and artists for over 150 years, and a playground for the rich and famous for over a century. To better sample this heritage and the associated culinary attractions, our route busies itself with the more populous valley floor. But remember, it never takes more than a few strategic turns to find splendidly rural back roads through woods as deep and undisturbed as those enjoyed by hikers along the Appalachian Trail, which parallels US-7 most of the way.

WILLIAMSTOWN

To the visitor it appears as if stately Williamstown (pop. 8,220) is simply a nickname for the immaculate and graceful campus of Williams College—even the main commercial block is basically the corridor between dorms and gym. From their common 18th-century benefactor, Ephraim Williams (who insisted the town's name be changed from its original West Hoosuck), to the large number of alumni who return in their retirement, "Billsville" and its college are nearly inseparable. The town-gown symbiosis has spawned an enviable array of visual, performing, and edible arts, yet fresh contingents of ingenuous youth keep all the wealth and refinement from becoming too cloying.

Two of the town's crown jewels are the **Clark Art Institute** on South Street (Tues.–Sun. 10 AM–5 PM; $5; 413/458-9545) and the **Williams College Museum of Art** (Tues.–Sat. 10 AM–5 PM, Sunday 1–5 PM; free; 413/597-2429) on Main Street opposite Memorial Chapel (a Westminster Abbey knock-off). They make an outstanding pair: the Clark with its extraordinary collection of Impressionist paintings, including more than 30 Renoirs; and the WCMA with its emphasis on changing exhibits of contemporary and non-Western art, set within gallery spaces that are themselves artfully conceived.

Winslow Homer's "Saco Bay" is part of the collection at the Clark Art Institute.

Another singular collection is stashed away on the second floor of Stetson Hall, the ivy-covered redbrick building furthest behind Memorial Chapel's gothic bulk. If you can find it, the **Chapin Library of Rare Books** (Mon.–Fri. 10 AM–noon, 1–5 PM; free; 413/597-2462) will reward you with a display of all of our nation's important birth certificates: the Declaration of Independence, the Articles of Confederation, an annotated draft of the Constitution, George Washington's copy of the Federalist Papers, and two early versions of the Bill of Rights (one with 17 and the other with 12 amendments).

Williamstown can claim another gem, this time in the natural art of relaxation. Luxurious Cuinard Lines used to serve its ocean-going passengers water exclusively from Williamstown, whose Sand Springs thermal mineral waters are as pure as any known on the planet. The 74° spring waters, still used by some hospitals and distributed by a small commercial bottler, have been enjoyed by bathers since at least 1762. The current bathhouse on the site is the **Sand Springs Spa,** 158 Sand Springs Road (Memorial Day to Labor Day; $7.50 single-day swim pass; 413/458-2833) on the north side of town; its genial owners Fred and Helen George bought the place during their honeymoon visit back in 1950.

WILLIAMSTOWN PRACTICALITIES

For breakfast, head to US-7 on the north side of town, where the popular **Chef's Hat,** 905 Simonds Road (413/458-5120), preserves a 100-year-old counter and other parts of its original diner incarnation. Also good, the **Clarksburg Bread Company,** at 37 Spring

Street (closed Sun. and Mon.; 413/458-2251) serves up soups, sandwiches, and a wealth of delicious baked goods until 4 PM. The hands-down best takeout pizza joint is **Hot Tomatoes**, 100 Water Street (413/458-2722), and in mild weather the nearby streamside park is well suited to lolling picnickers if you don't mind perfuming your car with pesto or spicy sausage on the way.

Tony continental dining suitable for starched alumni banquets abounds in Williamstown, but if you're looking for truly fresh, interesting food, skip the inns and go to the **Wild Amber Grill**, 101 North Street (413/458-4000). **Wild Oats**, the natural food store in the Colonial Shopping Center east of town on Route 2 at 248 Main Street (daily till 6 PM, Thursday till 8 PM), has a big selection of bulk items that will appeal to campers and hikers.

HANCOCK SHAKER VILLAGE

Just five miles west of Pittsfield on old US-20, Hancock Shaker Village is one of the best-preserved remnants of the religious sect known popularly as Shakers but formally as the United Society of Believers in Christ's Second Appearing, whose utopian communities flourished in the years before the Civil War. Shakers, as outsiders called them because of their occasional convulsions during worship, were dedicated to a communal life conspicuous in its equality between men and women, a natural corollary to their belief in parity between a male God and a female Holy Mother Wisdom.

The English-born leader of the group, Ann Lee, was in fact regarded by Shakers as the female, and second, incarnation of Christ. Although Puritan theocracy was ending, preaching this gospel did not endear her to many New Englanders in the decade following her arrival just prior to the American Revolution. During that war, Lee and her "children" sought their "Heaven on Earth," as seen in her visions. Mother Ann died near Albany, New York, in 1784, before any communities based on her precepts could be founded.

Hancock Shaker Village, third among the 24 settlements built in the nation by Lee's followers, was founded in 1790 and survived 170 years, outlasting all but two other Shaker communities. It's now preserved as a living museum (daily 9:30 AM–5:30 PM April–Oct.; $13.50; 413/443-0188 or 800/817-1137), with exhibits, tours, and working artisans interpreting the rural lifestyle and famous design skills of the Shakers. Appreciation of the efficiency, simplicity, and perfect workmanship consecrated within the "City of Peace" can quickly fill a couple of days if you let it. For a special treat, secure a place at the candlelight Shaker dinners held on Saturday evenings; you can also sample Shaker cuisine in the Village Cafe.

The center of Shaker activities was just west of Hancock, across the New York border at New Lebanon, where a few buildings still stand today. Other large Shaker communities in New England included Sabbathday Lake in Maine (see page 120), one at Enfield, New Hampshire (see page 177), and another at Canterbury, New Hampshire (see page 153).

HANCOCK SHAKER VILLAGE

A drive along Main Street (Route 2) will give you a view of most of Williamstown's accommodations, from the on-campus **Williams Inn**, 1090 Main Street ($150–195; 413/458-9371) to the small motels out on the eastern edge of town. North of downtown, the **River Bend Farm**, 643 Simonds Road ($60–125; 413/458-5504) offers reasonably priced B&B rooms in a historic farmhouse, but for a real treat consider **Field Farm** ($115–175; 413/458-3135) at 554 Sloan Road in South Williamstown, five miles south along either US-7 or scenic Water Street (Route 43). Occupying the 254-acre former estate of Pacific Northwest lumber tycoon Lawrence Bloedel, the main house, designed in 1948, is a striking example of American modern architecture. If you have any love of Frank Lloyd Wright or Charles and Ray Eames, you'll be delighted by this live-in museum of contemporary design, with its huge picture windows, proto-Scandinavian furniture, and Lucite fixtures, its walls adorned with selections from Bloedel's extensive 20th-century art collection. There are also tennis courts, a swimming pool, nature trails, and breathtaking views of Mount Greylock across the valley.

Singer Sewing Machine heir Robert Sterling Clark's huge art collection ended up in Williamstown in part because of the Cold War. In the late 1940s and early 1950s, the threat of a Russian nuclear attack seemed real enough that being as distant as possible from likely bomb targets was a critical factor in choosing a permanent repository.

One of the few bicycle shops offering rentals in this part of Massachusetts is **Spoke Bicycle & Repair**, at 618 Main Street in Williamstown (413/458-3456), which also carries copies of the handy *Bike Rides in the Berkshire Hills* by Lewis Cuyler.

Additional information is available from the **Chamber of Commerce Information Booth** (413/458-9077) at the center of town, or by picking up the latest copy of the free *Guide to Williamstown* from racks in local shop and restaurant vestibules.

East from Williamstown, Route 2 follows the route of the historic Mohawk Trail over the mountains from North Adams to the Pioneer Valley. The western half of this route is covered in the Appalachian Trail chapter on page 303; the eastern half is described in the US-5 chapter, on page 207.

PITTSFIELD

Once-thriving Pittsfield (pop. 48,622) is a classic example of a single-industry city on the skids. Having first lost its commercial center to a giant mall in a neighboring town, Pittsfield then watched its major employer, General Electric, proceed to consolidate, cut back, downsize, and otherwise all but lock up and turn out the lights. Compared to the carefully preserved Norman Rockwell simplicity of many of the surrounding small towns, Pittsfield's aging industrial cityscape has made it the place most Berkshire weekenders strenuously try to avoid, despite the fact that its size and the valley's topography make this nearly impossible unless you have a resident's familiarity with the backroads. That said, however, there are actually some good reasons to pay the place a visit.

If you can't make it to a Pittsfield Astros game in person, tune in to **WBRK 101.7FM** for the play-by-play.

Baseball, for example. Catching a home game with the professional (Short Season Class A) minor league **Pittsfield Astros** in Wahconah Park is widely regarded as an exemplar of the American pastime as it used to be: gregarious fans, decent players, and cheap admission ($3–7; 413/499-6387). Wahconah Park, built in 1919 off North Street, has a charm of its own, with plastic owls hanging from the rafters for pigeon scarecrows; a mascot that looks like Mr. Potato-Head with baseball stitching; cheesy sing-alongs; and the famous Sun Delay, when play is suspended until the setting sun stops shining in the batter's, catcher's, and umpire's eyes.

"Play ball" isn't the only phrase you'll likely to use to describe Pittsfield. A line from *The Graduate* may also come to mind: "One word: plastics." This piece of advice offered to Dustin Hoffman in that film will likely make sense to you while taking a tour of General Electric's **Living Environments concept house,** located on New York Avenue across from parent GE Plastics. Primarily a laboratory for testing high-tech materials and technologies for home construction and consumer products, the "Plastics House" has attracted so much attention from folks wanting to window-shop the future that weekly reserved tours are offered to benefit the local chapter of the United Way (Thurs. afternoons and some Sat. mornings; $6; 413/442-6948 or 800/696-6948 for reservations).

If associating plastics with Pittsfield seems novel, what about whales? Head out to Holmes Road, at the city's rural southern edge, and maybe you too will see the resemblance between the leviathan and the imposing outline of Mount Greylock, particularly if you view it from the study window of Herman Melville's **Arrowhead** (daily 10 AM–5 PM Memorial Day to Labor Day,

Arrowhead

Fri.–Mon. remainder of the year; $5). That salty masterpiece of digression and most unloved of high school reading assignments, *Moby-Dick*, was indeed written in this landlocked locale. While foremost a literary shrine, the spacious farm is also home to the Berkshire County Historical Society, whose well-curated exhibits are always interesting.

PITTSFIELD PRACTICALITIES

As with its other attractions, when it comes to food Pittsfield has some real out-of-the-way gems. In the acute angle between East and Elm Streets, for example, is the semicircular facade of the **Pittsfield Rye Bakery,** a 1950s flying saucer of glass and blue tile with big bright cases of fresh muffins, bagels, and breads beckoning within. Farther along East Street, past the mammoth GE Plastics plant, you'll find a pair of Italian places around the corner from one another; both serve good food, sometimes great food, at unusually low prices. The one you won't want to miss is **Elizabeth's,** 1264 East Street (413/448-8244), where all the pasta dishes are accompanied by fistfuls of crusty bread and wonderful salads, leaving little room for fine appetizers such as the *bagna caoda*, a must for anchovy lovers. For excellent pasta, pizza, and pub grub at a great small-town price, step around the corner to the **East Side Café,** 378 Newell Street (413/447-9405), a neighborhood bar whose comfort food and convivial atmosphere attract a family clientele.

Places to stay include a large **Holiday Inn Crowne Plaza** ($119–249; 413/499-2000) and other chains, plus the pleasant

Many an American industrialist's fortune came to rest among the Berkshire Hills, but the county's connection to the nation's wealth goes to the very fiber of the dollar. Crane & Co. of Dalton, just east of Pittsfield, has produced the paper for all U.S. currency since 1879. See the Appalachian Trail chapter for more.

Serious pilgrims on the path of Ishmael and the great white whale will want to visit the **Melville Memorial Room** on the upper level of the Berkshire Athenaeum, Pittsfield's public library.

Berkshire Inn, 150 W. Housatonic Street ($75–125; 413/443-3000), on US-20 a half-mile west of US-7.

LENOX

During the Gilded Age, the Berkshires were known as the "inland Newport" because of the opulent "cottages" that dotted the South County landscape, principally around Lenox (pop. 5,100). Some 75 of these giant mansions still stand, built for an era in which "society" was a respectable, full-time occupation for

The Mount, novelist Edith Wharton's home

folks with names like Carnegie and Westinghouse. Many of the houses have been converted to palatial inns, spas, or private schools; others are home to organizations whose presence makes Lenox a seasonal epicenter for professional performing arts. Besides **Tanglewood,** the local culture roster includes the **National Music Center** (800/872-6874), the **Berkshire Opera Company** (413/243-1343), and **Shakespeare & Company,** theatrical summer residents of novelist Edith Wharton's estate, The Mount.

The Lenox area also hosts **Jacob's Pillow** dance festival in Becket (413/243-0745) and the **Berkshire Theatre Festival** in Stockbridge (413/298-5576), so you can understand why such a small town is such a big magnet for East Coast culture vultures.

Wharton, the first woman to win a Pulitzer Prize for her 1920 novel *The Age of Innocence,* drew upon local people and incidents in many of her works, including two of her most famous: *House of Mirth* and *Ethan Frome.* The house she designed and built for herself in 1902, called **The Mount** (Tues.–Sun. 10 AM–2 PM in summer only; $6; 413/637-1899), is just south of central Lenox, well signed off Plunkett Street.

Tanglewood occupies the former Tappan Estate, a Berkshire cottage whose grounds included the Red House, in which Nathaniel Hawthorne wrote *House of the Seven Gables* during his brief Berkshire residency.

The annual influx of cosmopolitan concert-goers affects everything in southwestern Massachusetts, most obviously the local restaurants, half of which cater to seasonal immigrants from Boston and New York. If you aren't counting nickels, try the eclectic American menu at the **Church Street Cafe,** 65 Church Street (413/637-2745), where the tastes from the kitchen and accents from the diners are unmistakably reminiscent of some big-city bistro. Other major contenders for the town's gourmet dining crowd lie within the same two-block area. At the other end of the price spectrum is the mostly takeout **Salerno's Gourmet Pizza,** tucked away at 18 Franklin Street (413/637-8940), whose plain fast-food–style decor masks a practitioner of the delicious *abbondanza* school of pizza.

Lenox brims with more than 20 handsome B&B inns attractively situated amid wide lawns and gardens. Try the **Birchwood Inn,** 7 Hubbard Street ($80–180; 800/524-1646), opposite the Church on the Hill; or the **Brook Farm Inn** on Hawthorne Street (413/637-3013), which offers more than 700 volumes of poetry in the library, poetry on audiotape, poetry readings on Saturday, and poems *du jour* for perusal before breakfast. Another popular option, right at the center of Lenox, is the **Village Inn,** 16 Church Street (413/637-0020), built in 1771 and featuring clean, comfortable rooms and a very good restaurant at moderate prices—from $55 a night when Tanglewood is *not* in season.

Of course, if you prefer the anonymity of your favorite chain motels you'll find Susse Chalet, Quality Inn, Best Western, and Super 8 scattered along US-20 between the Pittsfield/Lenox line and the I-90 interchange in neighboring Lee. For a complete list of these local accommodations, or for help with last-minute lodging referrals, call the **Lenox Chamber of Commerce** (800/255-3669) or visit their office in the Lenox Academy Building on Main Street across from the Post Office plaza.

STOCKBRIDGE

If the main street of Stockbridge looks vaguely familiar, perhaps it's because the town made its way onto Norman Rockwell canvases during the final decades of his career, when he lived and worked here. You may dismiss his illustrations as the

TANGLEWOOD

To cognoscenti, Tanglewood is the name of an expansive hilltop estate with concert halls and sloping lawns that are home to the Boston Symphony Orchestra and a plethora of visiting artists for 10 weeks each summer. To everyone else it's the one-word explanation for the long restaurant lines, flash floods of weekend South County traffic, and un-  ceasing No Vacancy signs. From the end of June through to the beginning of September, anyone looking for a room will be guaranteed maximum frustration. If you want to be sure of a weekend room in and around Lenox during summer, reserve it in early spring, after which any places with the least bit of charm and comfort will have their weekends booked solid. The end of summer also is rather predictable, so there's no excuse for delaying your fall-foliage reservations.

While indoor tickets to Tanglewood performances are available in advance by fax, by mail, or through Ticketmaster (surcharge added), tickets for the lawns surrounding the Music Shed and Concert Hall are only available in person. For $13–20 you can buy an orchestral serenade beneath the stars—an exceptional value if the clouds don't burst (no rain checks are given), especially when accompanied by gourmet victuals from a local deli or restaurant. This is why you'll see most Tanglewood patrons sensibly outfitted with lawn chairs, blankets, and baskets instead of top hats and tails.

For complete program and ticket info, call **Symphony Charge** (888/266-1200), or write the Boston Symphony Orchestra, Symphony Hall, Boston, Massachusetts 02115. From early June through Labor Day, you may also call the Tanglewood **box office** (413/637-5165). Once the season begins, weekly program updates are available (413/637-1666).

epitome of contrived sentimentality, but the only people who don't find themselves grinning after a stroll through the unparalleled collection of **The Norman Rockwell Museum,** (daily 10 AM–5 PM May–Oct. and weekends year-round, otherwise 11 AM–4 PM; $9; 413/298-4100), on Route 183 two miles west of town, have hearts of solid flint. The town itself is worth a stroll, too, particularly past the grand houses along Main Street deliberately frozen in an idyllic past.

While most of the large estate homes are not open to the public, one of the county's more extravagant "cottages" is **Naumkeag** (daily 10 AM–4:15 PM late May to Labor Day, weekends only through Columbus Day; $7, or $5 garden only), an 1885 mansion on Prospect Hill Road less than a mile north of downtown Stockbridge. The mansion, designed by Stanford White for Joseph Choate, a lawyer who later served as U.S. ambassador to Britain, amply illustrates why this region was regarded the state's Gold Coast a century ago. The impressively landscaped grounds are an attraction in their own right.

Sculpture is the highlight of **Chesterwood** (daily 10 AM–5 PM May–Oct.; $7.50), off Route 183 just south of the Rockwell Museum. The residence was the summer home of **Daniel Chester French,** one of the most popular contributors to the fin de siècle American renaissance. French arrived on the art scene with a bang, sculpting Concord's *Minute Man* statue at age 25, but he is best remembered for his statue of the seated president in Lincoln Memorial in Washington, D.C. A tour of French's studio and house (now a property of the National Trust) or a walk around the 122 wooded acres graced with works of contemporary sculptors, quickly confirms why the sculptor once called his seasonal visits, "six months… in heaven."

HOUSATONIC

The few miles of Route 183 between the museums in Stockbridge and the town line are a prime example of the Berkshires' back-road charms. Wrapping around an old mill dam on the Housatonic River, the road tags along beside the water as the rounded bulk of Monument Mountain rises to the east, followed quickly by the dark brick hulks of the old Monument Mills. Entering Great Barrington, reads the sign, although the first glance suggests otherwise: if this place ever saw greatness, it was back in the era of steam locomotives. But looks deceive. Properly known as Housatonic, this village is becoming the funky country cousin of Manhattan's gentrified TriBeCa, with a cluster of working artists' studios among those old cotton mills along the river and storefront galleries in the old commercial block beside the railroad trestle.

Park by the schoolyard or the lumber mill and stroll around. The **Front Street Gallery** and **Le Petit Musée** are typically open weekends (noon–5 PM), but serendipity is the operative concept in this town, so take a look anyway if you visit

Know that Rockwell painting of the runaway kid with the policeman? The lunch-counter setting was inspired by **Joe's Diner,** 85 Center Street (413/243-9756) in nearby Lee, a Berkshire institution favored by everybody from local factory workers to New York celebrities.

The Stockbridge Indians, a band of Mahicans who some of the town's earliest settlers tried to convert to Christianity, were forced from this region in the 18th century. Their descendants now reside in central Wisconsin.

Stockbridge's Main Street hasn't always been the exclusive province of boutiques for coffee, curtains, and AARP members. Once upon a time it was also home to the eatery immortalized as the place where "you can get anything you want" by Arlo Guthrie in his 1967 antiwar folk song, "Alice's Restaurant Massacree."

on a weekday in case somebody happens to be around. **Spazi Contemporary Art and RiCA,** on the east side of the river above the lumberyard and in the old trolley barn down the road, respectively, keep somewhat longer hours (Spazi: Thurs.–Sun. noon–5 PM; RiCA: Wed.–Sun. noon–5 PM). Staff at these galleries can inform you of the open studio schedule for artists who work nearby.

When hunger pangs begin to diminish your art appreciation, step over to **Christina's Just Desserts,** 218 Pleasant Street (daily 10 AM–6 PM; 413/274-6521), across from the schoolyard, for tasty lunch fare and pastries. Or start a picnic basket with delicious, fresh, crusty sourdough from the **Berkshire Mountain Bakery,** 367 Park Street (Sun.–Thurs. 10 AM–10 PM; 413/274-3412), less than a mile south of the village on Route 183. To complete the basket, follow the highway another mile south to the **Taft Farms** roadside market at 119 Park Square, near Great Barrington. During apple-picking season Taft's wooden crates full of orchard-fresh fruit aren't to be missed.

Jutting up sharply north of the market parking lot, **Devil's Pulpit** on Monument Mountain is a good spot to enjoy your repast, which will be well earned by the half-hour climb to the rocky ledge with its unspoiled westward views (the eastern vista is scarred by gravel pits). Trailhead parking and picnic tables appear rather abruptly on the downhill side of US-7 north of the Route 183 junction; look for the Monument Mountain Reservation signs (donations appreciated).

GREAT BARRINGTON

While most South County towns have been spruced up like precious antiques, Great Barrington, with as many hardware stores as chic boutiques, is like grandma's comfortable old sofa, still too much in daily use to keep under velvet wraps. The town doesn't deplore the few tacky commercial lots around its fringes, perhaps because they can't detract from the handsome buildings at its core. Prime among these buildings are the 1905 **Mahaiwe Theater,** now a triplex (schedules 413/528-8885), all marble and gilt trim behind its marquee; the stone churches on wide Main Street; and imposing Searles Castle, a former Berkshire cottage turned private academy, which is generally closed but sometimes open for preconcert touring as part of the summertime **Stockbridge Chamber Music Festival** (413/528-8227).

The center of Great Barrington has a lot to offer hungry travelers. Fussy early-risers seeking their cappuccino and muffins, or picnickers needing the makings of a great spread will want to check out **The Berkshire Coffee Roasting Company,** at 286 Main Street, which serves up espresso drinks, teas, and bakery items, with the added benefit of the South County's best let's-hang-out atmosphere. **Bev's Homemade Ice Cream,** around the corner at 5 Railroad Street, is another source of caffeine, light lunch fare, and sugar, too, by the rich and creamy coneful.

Monument Mountain was where Herman Melville and Nathaniel Hawthorne first met on an outing arranged by a New York publisher in 1850, the year the two writers took up residence in the area. Melville, who dedicated *Moby-Dick* to his friend, was disconsolate when Hawthorne later moved away without notice.

Looking for a distinctive, out-of-the-way B&B? Consider using a booking service such as **Berkshire Bed and Breakfast Agency.** Owner Eleanor Hebert represents unadvertised and reasonably priced properties all along our route through the Berkshires. Call 413/268-7244 (Mon.–Fri. 9 AM–5:30 PM) or write P.O. Box 211, Williamsburg, Massachusetts 01096. Rates at represented properties run $60–300 a night for two people.

If you're looking for a last-minute room, save yourself a walk through the Yellow Pages with a single call to the **Lodging Availability Hotline** of the Southern Berkshire Chamber of Commerce (413/528-4006).

The first black man ever to earn a Ph.D. from Harvard, writer W. E. B. DuBois was born in Great Barrington in 1868.

Across from Bev's is **20 Railroad Street,** *the* place for burgers, sandwiches, and soups; its lively bar is the closest native example of a honky-tonk.

SHEFFIELD

Between Great Barrington and the Connecticut state line, US-7 winds through Sheffield and is lined by dozens of antique stores, earning this stretch the nickname Antique Alley. Sheffield also has a faded gray covered bridge, just 100 yards east of US-7 on the north side of town. At the south edge of Sheffield, just west of Ashley Falls village, **Bartholomew's Cobble** ($3) is a designated National Natural Landmark where geology and weather have conspired to produce an outstanding diversity of flora—more than 700 species—within a relatively small pocket of fern-covered boulder outcrops and broad meadows.

When people think of electricity they think of Thomas Edison and light bulbs, but the roots of your local utility lie here in the nation's first commercial electrical system, created by transformer inventor William Stanley for Great Barrington's downtown in 1886.

If you want to see for yourself how well suited the Housatonic River is for recreational canoeing, set up a rental with **Gaffer's Outdoors** on US-7 in Sheffield (413/229-0063). Rentals go for around $25/weekdays, $35/weekends, or $35 for van shuttle and six hours of paddling time.

The last battle of Shay's Rebellion, an uprising of farmers demanding reforms to prevent foreclosures after the American Revolution dried up English credit, was fought in a field south of the village on Sheffield Road. A small stone obelisk marks the spot, coincidentally adjacent to the Appalachian Trail.

NORTH CANAAN

Crossing into Connecticut from the north on US-7, the first thing that will catch your eye is the stainless-steel siding of **Collin's Diner,** in the heart of North Canaan (860/824-7040). A classic 1940s prefab diner, Collin's has all the usual diner standards, and its big parking lot (shared with the neighboring historic railroad depot) is frequently full of equally classic cars, whose owners congregate here on summer afternoons. The rest of North Canaan—a couple of clothing stores and an old movie theater—is anything but prissy, a refreshing change of pace from the overly tidy tourist towns that dominate the surrounding region.

Salisbury's Lakeville Furnace was the armory of the American Revolution, supplying George Washington's troops with almost all of their arsenal of artillery and ammunition for the duration of the war.

US-44 DETOUR: SALISBURY

After extensive touring around New England, you risk taking white columns, wide porches, picket fences, and the obligatory Congregational steeple for granted. Even then, prim little Salisbury, a half-dozen miles west of US-7 at the junction of Route 41 and US-44, still may elicit reveries about what small-town America would look like if strip malls ceased to exist.

Spend an afternoon sipping cardamom-scented tea in tiny **Chaiwalla,** at the head of Main Street (US-44), or step over to Academy Street to nosh on a stylish lunch at the **Harvest Bakery** while regulars banter with the owner as they stock up on the delicious breads and desserts, and see if you don't conclude that franchising of fast food should be declared a misdemeanor.

LIME ROCK PARK

On Route 112 a couple of miles west of US-7 you'll find **Lime Rock Park** (860/435-0896 or 800/722-3577), an automobile racetrack made famous in part by classic car rallies, a mid-May Grand Prix, the Skip Barber Racing School (800/221-1131), and the occasional appearance of celebrity drivers like Paul Newman and Tom Cruise. The sharp, twisting descent from nearby Lakeville to the raceway is one of the prettiest back-road drives in the area.

Interestingly, Salisbury was once a heavily industrialized center of 18th-century iron mining and manufacture, with ore pits, forges, and blast furnaces nestled amid hills whose forests were chewed down to the rocky soil by the incessant appetite of the wood-burning smelters. That this Pittsburgh of the American colonies has become tidy and quaint 200 years later could suggest a moral about resilience and resurrection, but perhaps more germane is that Salisbury looks the way it does now because residents were willing to question whether land development is an inalienable right.

US-44 DETOUR: NORFOLK AND WINSTED

From North Canaan, about 15 miles east of US-7, US-44 visits another pearl even more manicured than Salisbury—Norfolk. But unlike Salisbury, at least Norfolk has an auto-body shop and lopsided old American sedans amid the imports on the roads. If any town has capitalized on being far removed from trading floors and board meetings, it's this one. With three public parks and the largest private forest in the state, Norfolk has considered its sheer scenic beauty a stock in trade for nearly a century. Between late June and early August, residents and their guests enjoy the Yale School of Music's **Norfolk Chamber Music Festival** on the Ellen Battell Stoeckel Estate opposite the village green; phone for schedule and ticket information (860/542-5537 during the festival season, or 203/432-1966 Sept.–May). Even when there's no music, the green is worth a quick stop, so you can see the folksy road sign that points the way with pictures of rabbits and other cute creatures.

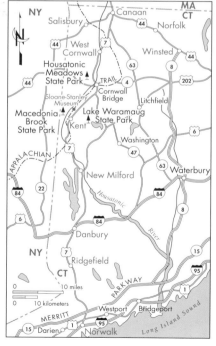

If good beer is a stronger incentive than sonatas or waterfalls are, you'll want to make a beeline for **The Pub,** in the handsome commercial brownstone at the center of town. With more than 150 excellent brews from around the world, it almost wouldn't matter whether the grub's any good but fortunately it is. The Cajun specials (Wed. and Thurs.) are a particularly good value. As befits such an oasis as Norfolk, there's a handful of B&Bs in town costing $120 a night or more, mostly catering to couples in search of the consummate we-deserve-it getaway. Bask in the rich Tudor woodwork and Tiffany windows of the **Manor House** (860/542-5690) while sipping tea by the fireplace—or between naps in your Jacuzzi, if your credit can stand it.

Continuing east from Norfolk, US-44 remains a very scenic route as far as Winsted, where Hartford-bound backroads aficionados should detour north onto Route 20 for a winding ride across the top of Connecticut. Winsted itself is the birthplace of

consumer advocate and Green Party presidential candidate Ralph "Unsafe at Any Speed" Nader, who has been working to establish a museum that would trace the history of product liability and other lawyerly themes. At the heart of Winsted, you can enjoy the all-American **Winsted Diner,** "Home of the Ra-Doc-a-Doodle Sandwich," on US-44 at 496 Main Street (860/379-4429).

WEST CORNWALL

Rivers are consistently some of the most attractive driving companions you could ask for, a fact proven once again as US-7 rejoins the Housatonic south of Lime Rock. The highway's scenic miles are further enhanced by the sudden appearance of a barn-red covered bridge, which since 1837 has served as the one-lane gateway to idyllic West Cornwall. This is the kind of place that would tar and feather the first vinyl-siding salesperson to walk into town, lest harm befall its antiquarian bookshop or other clapboard buildings bearing signs from previous commercial lives (although the old meat market is now a video store).

South of town, **Housatonic Meadows State Park** offers riverside camping (mid-April to mid-Sept.; $10), perfectly situated for anyone considering a canoe or kayak rental from adjacent **Clarke Outdoors** (860/672-6365). Bring mosquito repellent if you're planning to spend time near the water.

The park includes a short, three-mile round-trip trail up 1,160-foot Pine Knob, which offers fine views from its summit. Just south of the Housatonic Meadows park boundary, the Appalachian Trail crosses US-7 and the Housatonic River at the hamlet of Cornwall Bridge, then runs alongside the river for some eight miles, the longest riverside cruise in the trail's entire 2,100 miles.

SLOANE-STANLEY MUSEUM

If you like your history presented with a dash of artistic eccentricity, you'll probably enjoy the unusual display curated in this interesting little museum (Wed.–Sun.

10 AM–4 PM; $3; 860/927-3849). The museum is located along US-7 just north of Kent village, near the ruins of an early American iron foundry. The collection consists mainly of old tools—planes of all shapes and sizes, plus handsaws, augurs, clamps, and other woodworking devices—all arranged by local artist and author Eric Sloane (1905–85), whose books and prints are available in the gift shop. The "Stanley" in the museum's name comes (surprise, surprise) from the famous Stanley tool company, based in nearby New Britain, who donated the land and the museum building. Stanley tools make up a significant portion of the collection, but many others are handmade tools, some of which date back to days when colonial-era craftsmen forged their own tools to suit their specific needs.

Besides the tool collection, the museum also protects the remains of the 19th-century Kent Iron Furnace, now overgrown but slated for restoration.

Kent Falls State Park, along US-7 about five miles north of Kent, is a nice place to take a break from behind the wheel. Along with the namesake cascade, the park includes a short path through dense woods.

Running south of Kent, parallel to US-7 for about six miles along the west bank of the Housatonic River, Schagticoke Road is a slower, much more scenic route that gives a up-close look at the rugged geology beneath the trees. The route crosses the Schagticoke Indian Reservation and passes an old Indian cemetery before rejoining US-7 via a covered bridge on Bull's Bridge Road, three miles north of Gaylordsville.

KENT

Like many of its Litchfield-area neighbors, Kent (pop. 2,918) had a thriving iron industry until competition from larger Pennsylvania mines—with better access to post–Civil War markets—forced the local furnace to close. Now it's a bustling, upscale market town, its main street (US-7) lined with antique shops, galleries, and boutiques that have replaced blacksmith shops and wheelwrights. Examples of these new, higher-priced establishments include the New York–Paris-Kent art gallery in the old Pullman car behind the ice cream shop—née-depot; the gallery of African and Asian artifacts upstairs from the Foreign Cargo store; and the estate jewelry at Pauline's Place on the north side of town.

But not every price tag around here ends in triple zeros. For proof, step into **The Villager,** on North Main Street (860/927-3945) smack in the heart of town, where your scrambled eggs and burgers come as plain as you'd like or gussied up with andouille sausage or avocado and salsa. "Reliable" is the word that comes to mind for an oasis like this: open daily, with prices that are rarely seen these days outside of the Midwest.

Camping is available all summer in state parks alongside Route 341 on either side of Kent: to the west in **Macedonia Brook State Park** (860/927-3238); and to the east in **Lake Waramaug State Park** (860/868-2592), whose campsites share the water's edge with a handful of posh inns and exclusive homes. For indoor lodging, a nice option is the **Fife 'N' Drum** along US-7 at 53 N. Main Street ($75–95; 860/927-3509), which has motel-type rooms and a friendly restaurant and tavern.

NEW MILFORD

The Appalachian Trail crosses the New York state line near Bull's Bridge south of Kent, and so should you—on Route 55 or Route 37—if you want to enjoy a landscape that offers more fields and trees than guardrails and parking lots. Technically speaking, there's still a large swath of New England between New York and New Milford, but most of this has more in common with the Indianapolis beltway than with the Vermont countryside.

The infidels of prefab modular construction may be pounding at the gates, but aptly named Milford Green is still framed by a well-preserved backdrop of classic 19th-century architecture, from the church to the hardware store. New Milford also is a good place to grab a bite of Eastern European, Greek, or Tex-Mex food on block-long Bank Street or around the corner on Railroad Street. Mellow **Bank Street Coffee House,** 56 Bank Street tucked below street level (860/350-8920), can satisfy cravings for steaming latte or icy granitas. If you crave a memorable meal, check out **The Bistro Cafe,** 31 Bank Street, across from the black-glass, white-tile art deco cinema (860/355-3266), serving nori-wrapped tuna and oven-roasted duckling among the $15-and-up entrees of New American food. If you seek a feast for the senses, it doesn't get much better than this.

For accommodations, try the **Homestead Inn,** 5 Elm Street at the north end of the green ($85–115; 860/354-4080), within walking distance of dinner or a movie.

Wander amid the century-old ghosts of the region's iron industry at **Mine Hill Preserve,** the state's largest set of ore pits and furnace ruins, just off Route 67 between New Milford and Route 199. To get there, turn north on Mine Hill Road immediately west of the Shepaug River bridge.

DANBURY AND RIDGEFIELD

Approaching I-84 and for most of the way south to the coast, US-7 runs through what has become one vast and very wealthy suburb of New York City, and there's very little there to tempt you off the blacktop. Danbury (65,500) is now indistinct from any other suburb around the country, but it used to have a unique distinction of being the hat-making capital of the world. Exhibits tracing this and other aspect of Danbury's past can be seen at the **Danbury Museum,** downtown at 43 Main Street (Wed.–Sun. 2–5 PM; donations; 203/743-5200).

Continuing south toward the coast and I-95, US-7 manages to stay a two-lane most of the way, despite obvious pressure to become yet another turnpike. There's not much en route, but if you veer to the west along Route 35 to the town of Ridgefield (pop. 20,900), you can have a look at the colonial-era **Keeler Tavern,** 132 Main Street, which has a Revolutionary War cannonball lodged in its walls. Then walk a block to the **Aldrich Museum,** 258 Main Street (Tues.–Sun. 1–5 PM; $3; 203/438-4519), which displays contemporary art in a colonial-era house and high-quality sculpture in a two-acre garden behind.

After its long scenic run south from Canada, US-7 finally hits the end of the line at Norwalk, turning into a freeway near its junction with the historic Merritt Parkway and continuing toward Long Island Sound and the junction with US-1. Norwalk and the rest of this stretch of coastal Connecticut is covered on pages 106–07.

APPALACHIAN
TRAIL

APPALACHIAN TRAIL

The longest and best-known hiking trail in the country, the Appalachian Trail winds from the north woods of Maine all the way south to Georgia. Dozens of guidebooks cover the hiking trail but provide no description of how to follow the route in a car. The following scenic roads come fairly close to paralleling the pedestrian route, taking in a number of fascinating

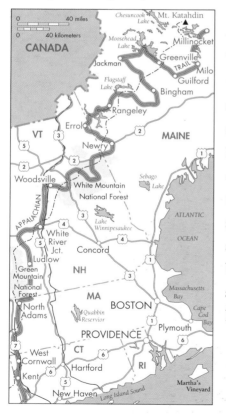

cities, towns, and historic sites along with the almost-continuous natural beauty. Where these roads cross the trail, I've detailed the best day hikes, so you can hike off into the woods and enjoy a taste of Mother Nature's bounty within a short walk from the car. Best of all, with very few exceptions, the route follows magnificently scenic two-lane roads all the way across New England, offering the best fall color imaginable, plus a look at parts of the region only locals usually get to see.

Although the Appalachian Trail runs within day-hiking distance of more than 25 million city dwellers, most of the route is intensely solitary and driving these roads will make you feel as though you've got the country all to yourself (though you may have to share the road with an occasional moose). Starting near Mount Katahdin, deep in the Maine Woods that even such a nature lover as Henry David Thoreau found dauntingly wild and remote, the route winds through rugged forests with signs of civilization—a backwoods mill town or a hunting and fishing resort area—spaced every few dozen miles. Some of the most beautiful places sit along the shores of inland Maine's major lakes, like Greenville on Moosehead Lake, or the vacation resorts ranged around Rangeley Lake. The wilds of Appalachian Maine also offer some of the best skiing in the nation, at Sugarloaf/USA, Sunday River, and other resorts. In the summertime you can take your pick of mountain biking, canoeing, river rafting, and of course hiking along the hundreds of miles of trails.

Whether you're a casual day-hiker or a seasoned backpacker, **Exploring the Appalachian Trail** by David Emblidge, et al. (Stackpole Books, 1999) is the best available guidebook to this legendary trail. Two titles in a series of five books cover New England; all of the guides have clear maps, charts showing elevation gain and loss, lots of good advice, and enough description and information to entice you safely and comfortably off the road.

Driving north to south, you could follow the fall color in leisurely moves south; heading south to north, you'd be assured of catching the peak season at least somewhere.

In New Hampshire, the Appalachian Trail reaches a peak right from the start: atop rugged Mount Washington. The mountain is in the heart of the Presidential Range, the tallest mountains in New England (at 6,000 feet) and has some of the hardest and most durable rocks on Earth; it's also known for having the worst weather on Earth. But the weather doesn't deter tourists from visiting. In fact, Mount Washington is one of New England's longest-standing attractions, and is accessible via a historic carriage and motor car route to the summit that is joined by a coal-fired, steam-powered railway, which climbs up an intensely steep incline—a Victorian engineering feat. The Presidentials and the surrounding White Mountains are also among the most popular vacation destinations in New England, but if you can avoid the peak times and busiest places, you can find hundreds of less-traveled roads and trails.

Some of the nation's wealthiest enclaves are found in the northern Appalachian region, but these rural idylls often brush up against some of the most economically depressed towns. It's common to encounter an exclusive resort and retirement community just a few miles away from a tumbledown old mill town, which is now as financially dependent upon three-season tourism as it once was upon the land and its resources.

Southwest of the White Mountains, the Appalachian Trail route takes a breather, winding through the idyllic charms of the rural Connecticut River Valley and its summer homes and liberal arts–college communities. Crossing into Vermont, the route parallels the busier US-4 highway through Woodstock but follows several country roads, maintaining the rural feel. Climbing up into the Green Mountains, the Appalachian Trail passes through one of the prettiest and most historic places in New England, the dairy-farming homestead of former President Calvin Coolidge, whose family still makes cheese and other Vermont country staples the old-fashioned way. Beyond the Coolidge farm at Plymouth, the Appalachian Trail follows scenic Route 100 along the spine of the mountains, passing by ski resort after ski resort that pack the slopes above still-quaint country hamlets.

Crossing into Massachusetts, the Appalachian Trail runs high above the high-toned resorts of the Berkshires, the summer destination of the Boston and New York upper crust for almost two centuries. Our driving tour does its best to avoid the increasingly suburban, densely developed corridor of vacation resorts here, but the closer we come to being within weekend escape distance of New York City, the more the towns become prissy and pretty as evidenced by the Litchfield Hills

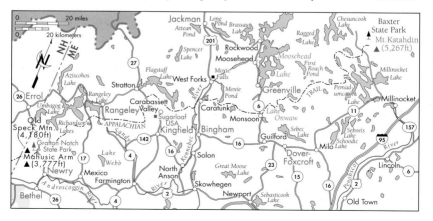

antique shops just across the Connecticut border. After a last run along the lovely Housatonic River, the Appalachian Trail disappears across the New York border, hidden away among the deluxe estates of Dutchess County.

Whether or not you come for fall color, the Appalachian Trail is an amazing drive. At any time of year, even a short drive here will be an enduring highlight of a New England tour.

MOUNT KATAHDIN

Mount Katahdin (pronounced "ka-TAW-din") is a real wilderness, with no paved roads but 175 miles of hiking trails (and LOTS of bugs). It is about 20 miles northwest of the nearest town, Millinocket (which is described in the US-2 chapter), but don't expect to drive to the summit. Only hikers—and few and brave they are—may climb to the top of Katahdin, Maine's highest peak and the northernmost trailhead of the backpackers' holy grail, the Appalachian Trail.

Mount Katahdin and its environs have managed to retain its natural vitality thanks to the foresight of former Maine Governor P. P. Baxter, who bought the land himself and donated it to the state after failing to convince legislators to ante up the cash. As a condition of the bequest, Baxter insisted that the land around Mount Katahdin (now called Baxter State Park) remain wild, so most trappings of the modern world, including radios, cell phones, even seeing-eye dogs, are prohibited. There's just one rough road around the park's perimeter plus a few cabins, so to see Baxter properly you'll have to hike and camp. Day-use fees are $8 per vehicle, free for Maine residents. Bring food, water purifiers, and plenty of insect repellent, and be prepared for any and all weather conditions. Abundant wildlife, amazing wildflowers, powerful waterfalls, and breathtaking views will reward your efforts.

For details, or to make camping reservations (June–Oct. only—no refunds!), write or visit the **Baxter State Park Authority,** 64 Balsam Drive, Millinocket, Maine 04462 (207/723-5140).

From Katahdin and Baxter State Park, the hiking trail winds south and west along the shores of a series of lakes, a difficult and isolated trip (dubbed the "100 Mile Wilderness") that can take a week or more before the next real sign of civilization. If you prefer to drive but aren't brave enough to embark upon some very remote logging roads, take Route 11 on a loop from Millinocket south to Milo, where it joins Route 6 toward the resort towns of Greenville and Bingham, both of which are within easy striking distance of the backwoods hiking trail.

DOVER-FOXCROFT: ENCHANTED FOREST

In the furniture mill town of Dover-Foxcroft, along Route 16 between Milo and Bingham, the Maine Woods hold a delightful little place that locals have dubbed the **Enchanted Forest.** Set back in a pine grove, this magical garden (officially

Just under five miles west of Dover-Foxcroft, toward Guildford on Route 16, is historic **Low's Bridge,** a registered national landmark. The original bridge was built in 1830 but destroyed by a flood in 1987. The 130-foot-long replica standing today was made in 1990. The road here runs alongside the Piscataquis (pronounced "pis-CAT-uh-quis") River, and thick stands of trees line the road as its curves up, down, and around the many hills.

called the Forest of Dreams and Meadow of Enchantment, according to the sign at the entrance) contains numerous small (3- to 4-foot-tall) brightly painted statues standing among the trees. The figures are actually tree stumps, carved to resemble Charlie Brown and Snoopy, the Statue of Liberty, Santa Claus, and other recognizable characters. The figure of Paul Bunyan even has a removable ax (don't worry, the blade isn't sharp).

The Enchanted Forest is more than a little out of the way but it's a popular destination, especially for local families. To get there from Route 16 in Dover-Foxcroft, follow US-7 south, turning right onto Pine Street (just before the Robinson Oil Company). From here, go 3.4 miles; the Enchanted Forest is on the right side at the bottom of a hill, just before the road crosses a bridge over the stream that runs through the property (free).

Back in Dover-Foxcroft, **Pat's Dairyland** at 55 South Street (207/564-2520) serves scallop and lobster rolls, and great shakes (available in regular, thick, extra-thick, and extra-extra-thick blends!). On a hat rack in the corner, the slogan says: Young at Heart. Slightly Older in Other Places. For a place to stay, try **The Foxcroft,** 25 W. Main Street ($50–60; 207/564-7720), a nice B&B located right in downtown Dover-Foxcroft, in an 1840s home.

GREENVILLE: MOOSEHEAD LAKE

Located along Routes 6/15 at the southern tip of massive Moosehead Lake, Greenville (pop. 1,600) is the center for backwoods recreation in this wild and wooly part of Maine. As you might guess from the name, the lake and surrounding lands are prime habitat for moose, which can be seen along the shores and rivers. In May and June, the region comes down with a contagious case of **MooseMainea,** a festival celebrated with moose safaris, moose parades, and other moose-themed activities (call 207/695-2702 for details). Moose or no moose, one of the best reasons to make the trek to Greenville is the chance to ride on the historic lake steamer *Katahdin,* which takes visitors on sightseeing tours (daily at 12:30 PM; $16; 207/695-2716) around the lake. Alas, the boat is now diesel powered but the

the steamboat Katahdin *on Moosehead Lake*

roughly three-hour cruise is still a real treat, especially during the fall foliage season in September.

Greenvile has more hotel and motel beds than residents, so finding a base here shouldn't be too hard. For a true taste of Maine, it's hard to beat **The Birches** ($40–180; 207/534-7305 or 800/825-9453), which has a lakeview restaurant (complete with massive moose head and fireplace) plus every conceivable type of accommodation, from tents to log cabins to a few rooms in the main lodge. The Birches is located in Rockwood, about 20 miles north of Greenville. Also in Rockwood are a few cabin courts, such as the quaint **Rockwood Cottages** ($65; 207/534-7725), which has a waterfront sauna; it also rents canoes. In Greenville proper there are a number of modern motels and some family-friendly, no-frills restaurants like **Auntie M's**, on Main Street (daily 5 AM–7 PM, till 9 PM in summer; 207/695-2238) across from the *Katahdin* dock.

The Appalachian Trail crosses Routes 6/15 a dozen miles south of Greenville at **Monson** (pop. 725), a historic little place famous for its slate quarries, which since the 1830s have provided the stone for the nation's sinks, roofs, blackboards, as well as the grave markers of JFK and Jackie O. These days, Monson is a legendary resting place for thru-hikers on the Appalachian Trail, most of whom plan on a layover at **Shaw's Boarding Home**, just west of the highway ($15–25; 207/997-3597). The friendly owners serve breakfast and dinner, and have a variety of beds and bunks (and hot showers!) available. Another food stop in Monson is the **Appalachian Station**, right on the main highway.

Moosehead Lake is the largest in Maine, with more than 400 miles of shoreline. The main landmark is a 750-foot chunk of volcanic rhyolite known as **Mount Kineo**, which stands on the midpoint of the eastern shore, across the water from the resorts and motel cottages at Rockwood, 20 miles north of Greenville on Routes 6/15.

BINGHAM

Deep in the heart of Maine, alongside US-201 on the banks of the Kennebec River, Bingham (pop. 1,200) is a pretty little town. In recent years, it has become a very popular destination for city dwellers wanting to ride the whitewater rapids of the mighty river that runs through it. For food, join the locals at **Thompson's**, on upper Main Street. Bingham also has one very nice B&B: **Mrs. G's**, on Meadow Street (207/672-4034), just east of Main Street. Rocking chairs on the front porch and boundless hospitality make for a true welcome. The reasonable prices don't hurt, either: $25 for a single bed, and children are charged by their age—$8 for an 8-year-old.

Bingham is located right on the 45th Parallel, midway between the Equator and the North Pole, as the Welcome to Bingham sign proudly proclaims. It's roughly 3,000 miles to either, but if you're here any time but the hottest day of the year, you'll probably think the North Pole is much closer than the Equator is.

North of Bingham, the hiker's Appalachian Trail crosses US-201 near Pleasant Pond and Caratunk, where a handful of old houses and an 1881 post office line the "old road" loop just east of US-201. Stop at the **Caratunk General Store** for a taste of local life. From Caratunk, US-201 stays alongside the Kennebec through the straggling community known as The Forks, which is little more than a few lodges and campgrounds catering to the many rafters who come to ride the river. One of the largest rafting companies is **Northern Outdoors** (207/663-4466 or 800/765-7238), now in their 25th year of running trips here.

Further north, near the Canadian border, scenic US-201 earns its nickname "Moose Alley" on the trip to and through the town of **Jackman,** one of the most remote places in this already remote region.

roadside art along US-201

To get across the broad Kennebec River at Caratunk, hikers avail themselves of a free canoe-ferry that is operated most summer and fall mornings by a local gentleman named Steve Longley (207/663-4441).

One of the highest waterfalls in Maine, **Moxie Falls** tumbles 100 feet down Moxie Stream. The falls are fairly easy to reach. From US-201 at The Forks, turn east onto Lake Moxie Road and follow that to a signposted trailhead; from there the waterfall is less than a mile ahead.

The stone-pile islands you often see in the middle of Maine rivers are the remains of the boom piers logging companies formerly used to separate various company's timbers that floated downstream during log drives.

KINGFIELD: STANLEY STEAMERS

From Bingham, Route 16 runs along the west side of the Kennebec while busier US-201 winds along its east side downstream toward Skowhegan and US-2 (see page 116 for more). The two roads finally go their separate ways at **Solon,** site of a lumber mill that specializes in engineered wood products, such as tongue depressors and popsicle sticks, according to the fellow who filled my gas tank and scraped the squashed bugs from my windshield. Continuing west, Route 16 winds past a "monster truck" speedway, some abandoned school buses, and thick fields of wildflowers all along the very pretty Sandy Stream toward Kingfield.

Kingfield (pop. 1,100) is in many ways the epitome of back-country Maine. It doesn't look like much—barely two blocks long, with a church, a general store, and two old-fashioned inns lining the main road—but the closer you look, the better it gets. Classic car fans may be surprised to learn that two of the more creative minds of the early automotive age, twin brothers Francis E. and Freelan O. Stanley, were born and raised in this middle-of-nowhere locale. The small but engaging **Stanley Museum** (Tues.–Sun. 1–4 PM; $2; 207/265-2729) has some displays on their exploits, and shows off three of their steam-powered cars (one of which the brothers navigated up Mount Washington, becoming the first of many to drive to the top of New England's highest peak). There are also some fascinating old photographs; before they started work on their motor cars, the brothers invented a form of dry-plate photography they later sold to George Eastman, of Kodak fame.

It's not a museum, but it could be: the funky **Herbert** on Main Street ($55–125; 207/265-2000) is a well-restored older hotel that greets guests with not one but two giant moose heads in its lobby (plus real live dogs splayed out in front of the desk). You can relax in the lobby or on one of the comfy chairs set out on the open-air veranda upstairs. The inn also has a very good restaurant, and rates include a continental breakfast. Rates are considerably higher in the winter than they are in summer, thanks to the Herbert's location within striking distance of the slopes of Sugarloaf/USA, the massive ski area just north of town via Routes 16/27. The inn serves a big dinner (for around $25), or you can eat calzones at **Anni's Market** across the street.

SUGARLOAF/USA

Sugarloaf/USA (207/237-2000 or 800/843-5623) is one of the largest and most popular ski areas in New England, on a par with Killington in quality if not size. It draws skiers back time after time, thanks to its welcoming feel—and its 2,820-foot vertical drop and 45 miles of trails. Sugarloaf doesn't close up shop entirely for the summer months but it might as well. Winter is its season.

The drive past Sugarloaf along Route 16 is pretty. An added bonus is a herd of moose, which are often sighted around the bogs at the foot of the mountain. From Stratton, where Route 16 diverges from Route 27 and heads southwest to Rangeley, however, the drive becomes less interesting, with clear-cut forests barely disguised by a thin curtain of roadside trees.

RANGELEY

Rangeley (pop. 1,090) is a down-to-earth sportsman's town that boasts a swell backyard: brawny Rangeley Lake, peeking from behind the stores on Main Street. The town has a few tourist shops selling the usual array of scented candles and moose paraphernalia, but it's mostly a practical, no-nonsense base camp for the outdoorsy type: fly fishermen who come for brook trout and salmon stocked in the region's many lakes; canoeists bound for those same lakes; mountain bikers, who cruise the logging roads and downhill runs at nearby Saddleback and Sugarloaf ski resorts; plus a fair number of AT hikers in desperate need of a shower.

The no-frills but fun city park, just off Main Street, is a good place to start your Rangeley experience. Not only is it near the town's main **information center** (207/864-5364), but it features a "swimming pool in the lake"—a roped-off, lifeguard-supervised

The hiker's Appalachian Trail cuts across the road to Farmington, Route 4, a few miles south of Rangeley, and across the road to Rumford, Route 17, a dozen miles southwest of Rangeley.

South of Rangeley, the townships are named by letter —Township C, Township D, etc,—which helps to explain the sign you'll see along Route 4, marking the otherwise invisible City Limits of the letter E.

Caution

X-ing

WILHELM REICH

No one seems to know exactly how or why he ended up here in the distant reaches of rural Maine, but the controversial psychotherapist Wilhem Reich (1897–1957) spent much of his later life in Rangeley. Depending on who you ask, Wilhelm Reich was an inspired visionary, a sex-obsessed quack, or a little of both. Reich, who studied for a time with Sigmund Freud, believed there is a universally present, primordial cosmic energy irrevocably linked with all matter; more contentiously, Reich believed that this energy, which he dubbed "orgone," was regulated for good health through the experience of sexual orgasm, the lack of which was the root cause of all psychological neuroses.

Reich fled Austria just before World War II and eventually set up his **Orgone Energy Observatory** (207/864-3443) for the study of Orgonomy on the property of his ranch, Orgonon, three miles west of Rangeley off Route 4. Reich had elaborate plans for Orgonon, including a hospital and training facilities for doctors. Back in Austria, he had argued in support of free, accessible birth control and abortion rights as early as the 1920s, and later studied cancer (which he believed were a result of disruptions in the release of orgone energy). In Maine, he took up cloud-busting, and attempted to use orgone energy to force rain to fall in drought-stricken areas. (His cloud-busting machines, one of which sits by his tomb overlooking the Rangeley Lakes region, were widely credited with ending a serious drought in the area back in the early 1950s.)

In the late 1940s the Food and Drug Administration began investigating Reich's activities, and in 1954 FDA scientists came to the conclusion that orgone energy didn't exist and that Reich was a quack. The FDA then issued a cease-and-desist order against Reich, focusing on his now-infamous Orgone Accumulator, a box that people sat in that "charged" them with orgone energy like that which might be released during orgasm. (The machine inspired Woody Allen's "orgasmatron" in his movie *Sleeper*.) Many of Reich's Orgone Accumulators and some six tons of his books and pamphlets were destroyed as part of the settlement agreement, and Reich moved to the Southwest to continue his work. But when a student back at Orgonon moved an Orgone Accumulator across state lines into safekeeping somewhere in New York City in 1957, Reich was arrested and thrown into jail for violating the FDA's order. He died in a federal prison eight months later.

Guests at the Wilhelm Reich Museum are treated to a very serious and sincere slide show tracing Reich's life, followed by a partly guided tour to the lab and upstairs offices in the Orgone Energy Observatory. Reich's primitive, colorful paintings line the walls, and the roof observatory offers lovely views of Dodge Pond and the entire Rangeley Lakes region. And yes, there's an Orgone Accumulator on display.

area with a pier, diving boards, a tiny beach, and beachhouse. For a bit more adventure, you can rent boats, kayaks, and mountain bikes from the crew at **Rangeley Mountain Bike,** 53 Main Street (207/864-5799).

Wilhelm Reich Museum

And, for a truly unique experience, head to the north shore of Rangeley Lake, about four miles west from town along Route 4, and follow signs to the **Wilhelm Reich Museum** (Wed.–Sun. 1–5 PM in summer only; $4; 207/864-3443). It was here the Austrian psychologist spent most of the last years of his life, refining his theories of sexuality and neurosis on a verdant 175-acre lakeview estate.

Because the Rangeley area attracts so many visitors, it has a wide range of services, with many nice motels and older lodges like the **Rangeley Inn,** 51 Main Street ($40–75; 207/864-3341 or 800/666-3687), in business since 1907 with a newer motel adjoining the original hotel. For food, head to **Sarge's Sports Pub and Grub** or the **Pine Tree Frosty,** on Main Street. The lobster rolls, onion rings, Gifford's Ice Cream, and other Maine staples somehow taste better if you eat them while sitting at picnic tables out back overlooking placid Haley Pond. After dark, the **People's Choice Restaurant and Lounge** at the western end of Main Street (207/864-5220) has full dinners (the prime rib is particularly popular with snowmobilers), plus live bands and dancing every Friday and Saturday night.

GRAFTON NOTCH STATE PARK

From Rangeley Lake, there are two alternatives if you want to follow the Appalachian Trail route. You can head south to Rumford along scenic Route 17 and the Swift River, then take US-2 west into New Hampshire's White Mountains; or you can follow the wilder drive along Route 16, which becomes Route 26 across the New Hampshire border. Both roads take about the same time and distance to reach Grafton Notch State Park, the northernmost of the many rugged gorges or notches carved into the mountains by glaciers and eons of erosion. The hikers' Appalachian Trail intersects Route 26 at the center of the park, and some of the prettiest parts of Grafton Notch line the road south and east of where

Along with usual tourist clutter, downtown Rangeley also has some nifty shopping. Log benches and other rustic objects are on sale at the **Moose America** store, 73 Main Street; wild chainsaw carvings are made on-the-spot by **Rodney Richard, the Mad Whittler** just down the street at 123 Main Street.

About 12 miles southwest of Rangeley, Route 4 crosses the hikers' Appalachian Trail, just south of which you can enjoy a quick dip in the cool waters of **Small's Falls,** a funky roadside pull-off where slick, slanted rocks conveniently double as short waterslides. Climb up along the slightly scary rocks at the fence line to the waterfall's top and you can see the stream tumble over the edge. Or follow the short trail into the woods to reach a more secluded stream that has a lot of places in which to wade around and splash about.

According to the Wilhelm Reich Museum, Reich's run-ins with the government resulted from bad dating experiences: "Human malevolence, which results from genital frustration, is so widespread in social relationships and institutions that Reich likened it to a plague—an emotional plague. The actions taken against Reich by the Federal Food and Drug Administration show many of the basic characteristics of this disease."

South and west of Grafton Notch State Park, the Appalachian Trail runs through one of its toughest sections through Mahoosuc Notch into New Hampshire. There's no road anywhere near here, so drivers wanting a quick taste of this impenetrable country will have to wind along the Bear River on scenic Route 26, then join US-2 for the drive through Bethel and Gorham, where the routes cross again.

the trail crosses. Along the road, a trio of waterfalls—Mother Walker, Screw Auger, and Step Falls—drop seemingly within reach of the roadway, and short, well-maintained paths lead to them from well-signed parking areas.

Along the northeast side of the White Mountains, between Grafton Notch and Mount Washington, the Appalachian Trail parallels the route of US-2, which is covered on pages 110–30. For lodging and dining suggestions in this region, check out the historic Maine resort town of Bethel and the New Hampshire logging towns of Gorham and Lancaster.

MOUNT WASHINGTON

The star attraction of the White Mountains' Presidential Range, 6,288-foot Mount Washington stands head and shoulders above every other peak in New England. East of the Mississippi, only Mount Mitchell in North Carolina's

Blue Ridge and Clingman's Dome in Tennessee's Great Smokies are taller. Despite its natural defenses—such as notoriously fierce storms that arise without warning—Mount Washington is accessible to an almost unfortunate degree. The **Mount Washington Auto Road** (weather permitting, mid-May to mid-Oct; $15 car and driver, $6 each additional adult; 603/466-3988) was first opened for carriages in 1861 and still switchbacks up the eastern side, climbing some 4,700 feet in barely eight miles. A marvel of engineering, construction, and maintenance, the Mount Washington Auto Road offers a great variety of impressions of the mountain, and wonderful views from almost every turn.

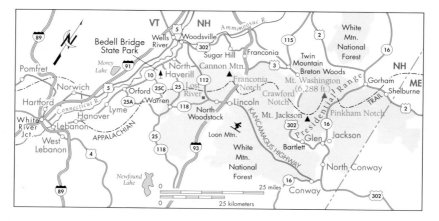

TIP TOP HOUSE, SUMMIT OF MT. WASHINGTON, WHITE MTS., N. H.

Route 17, running along the Swift River south from Rangeley toward the paper mill town of Rumford, is a wonderfully wild and scenic drive. Route 17 crosses the Appalchian Trail at what's known as the Height of Land. Besides being the highest section of highway in Maine, this stretch of road was named by *Reader's Digest* as one of the best places in New England to "leaf-peep" during the late September fall foliage season. The views from here are striking, with miles of verdant mountains, lakes and ponds shimmering in the sun, and the White Mountains not too far off in the distance. Further south along Route 17, midway to Rumford in the heart of a former gold-mining district, the **Coos Canyon Cabins** in Byron ($70; 203/364-7446) offer accommodations year-round.

If the weather's clear, you can see the Atlantic Ocean from the top of the mountain; in summer, mornings tend to be clearer, and sunny afternoons turn cloudy and stormy on the summit, complete with lightning and thunder. At the top, be prepared for winter weather any time of year (it can and does snow here every month of the year), and be sure to have a look inside the Summit House, which has displays on the historic hotels and taverns that have graced the top over the years. Visited by hundreds of people every day throughout the summer, since the 1850s the summit of Mount Washington has sprouted a series of restaurants and hotels—even a daily newspaper. The most evocative remnant of these is the recently restored **Tip Top House**, "the oldest mountaintop hostelry in the world," still open for tours if not food and drink (which is available, dully and expensively, in the Summit House cafeteria).

Cyclists and runners regularly race each other up the road to the summit, but there is another "easy" ride to the top: the **Mount Washington Cog Railway** ($39; 603/846-5404), which climbs slowly but surely on its steam-powered, coal-fired way, straight up and down the mountain's western slope from Bretton Woods.

HIKING MOUNT WASHINGTON

The best way to appreciate the granite cliffs, steep ravines, tumbling cataracts, and fragrant pines of Mount Washington is on foot. Besides the **Appalachian Trail**, which takes a 10-mile horseshoe-shaped route up from the AMC's Pinkham Notch hostel, hikers will find a smorgasbord of routes to the summit, including the country's oldest continuously maintained hiking trail, the **Crawford Path**, in use for over 175 years (for more, see "Crawford Notch," page 291). One-day ascents of Mount Washington are possible, most popularly by the **Tuckerman Ravine Trail** from the east. But don't be

If you're driving an RV with a wheelbase over 155 inches, are pulling any kind of trailer, or for any other reason don't feel like driving up and down Mount Washington, you can park at the bottom of the road and take a guided van tour (daily 8 AM–5 PM; $20; 603/466-3988). In winter, these tours will take you above tree line and give you the option of skiing or snowshoeing back down.

MOUNT WASHINGTON WEATHER

A mountain barely over 6,000 feet hardly deserves the same respect as the 20,000-footers in the Patagonian Andes, yet people die from exposure on the slopes of Mount Washington every year. Easy access invites complacency and a tendency to ignore trailside warnings advising retreat if you're unprepared for bad weather. But do respect the facts of nature: simply put, the Presidential Range of the White Mountains experiences some of the worst weather in the world, rivaling both Antarctica and the Alaska-Yukon ranges for consistently raw and bone-numbing combinations of gale-force winds, freezing temperatures, and precipitation. Lashings by 100-mph winds occur year-round on Mount Washington, whose summit holds the title for highest sustained wind speed on the face of the planet (231 mph in April 1934). Cloudy days outnumber clear ones on the peak, where snowstorms can strike any month of the year, and even in the balmiest summer months the average high temperature at the summit hovers around 50° F. Compounding the weather's potential severity is its total unpredictability: a day hike begun with sunblock and short sleeves can end up in driving rain and temperatures just 10° above freezing, or worse, in a total whiteout above tree line, even as a group of hikers a couple miles away on a neighboring peak enjoys lunch under blue skies and warm breezes.

The bottom line is, listen to what your mother always told you: be careful, and don't take chances. Learn to recognize and prevent hypothermia. Figure out how to read your trail maps and compass *before* you get caught in pelting sleet above tree line. Better to feel foolish packing potentially unnecessary wool sweaters and rain gear for a hike in July than to have your name added to the body count.

deceived by short trail lengths, as the elevation gain and frequent rough terrain can be quite taxing. The Tuckerman route mustn't be confused with the roughly parallel Huntington Ravine Trail, whose exposed ledges and steep pitches are strictly for vertigo-resistant hikers skilled at free climbing.

Beset by tundra conditions more typical of terrain a thousand miles to the north, the Presidentials are noted for their alpine gardens and *krummholz*, wind-stunted trees that try to eke out a living among the boulders and ice-shattered rock above timberline. Hikers seeking these sorts of wilderness should consider ascending a neighboring peak rather than Washington's fully developed summit. Some of the alpine areas on Mount Washington are off-limits to visitors, due to their fragility beneath too many hiking boots. As a general rule in any wilderness area, be mindful of the stress plants constantly face from the weather, and try not to tread on the vegetation above treeline.

PINKHAM NOTCH

South from the turnoff for the Mount Washington Auto Road, Route 16 passes through Pinkham Notch, a mostly undeveloped stretch of the White Mountains lined by forests and a few ski areas. First of these is **Great Glen** (603/466-2333), a cross-country ski area and summertime mountain bike center, which also serves as a convenient base for hiking around Mount Washington.

Continuing down Route 16, about four miles south of the Auto Road is the Wildcat Mountain ski area, across from which is Grand Central Station for Pinkham Notch, the **Pinkham Notch Camp.** Operated by the venerable Appalachian Mountain Club (AMC), the year-round trailhead facility offers topographical maps, guidebooks, weather updates, and precautionary advice, as well as limited gear. The camp also offers snacks, a cafeteria, a 24-hour hikers' pack room with bathrooms and showers, scheduled shuttle van service, and the **Joe Dodge Lodge** ($65 bed and board; 603/466-2727), a modern hostel with shared bunk rooms, a few private doubles, and great views from the library. For extended stays be sure to inquire about the significantly discounted package rates, or consider AMC membership ($40 yearly), which yields up to an additional $7 discount on all overnight stays—including package prices—at any AMC property.

MOUNT WASHINGTON VALLEY: JACKSON

Dropping sharply away to the south of 2,032-foot Pinkham Notch is the Ellis River, along whose banks sits the northern gateway to the Mount Washington Valley, resort-dominated Jackson (pop. 678). Given the number of lodgings among the attractive century-old clapboard homes, it seems the principal village occupation is innkeeper. The quantity of porches, gables, and chimneys hint at standard country B&B charms: lazy breakfasts in summer, nooks and crannies brimming with

The first automobile ascent of Mount Washington was made in 1899 by none other than F. O. Stanley, piloting one of his namesake Stanley Steamers.

To park a car at any trailhead in the White Mountains National Forest, you'll need to buy a **pass** from one of the information centers; these passes cost about $5, and are good for seven days.

Although clear-day views from the summit of Mount Washington are amazing, 9 days out of 10 the summit is socked in and cold, and snow can fall any month of the year.

If you're serious about hiking in the region, you won't want to be without the *AMC White Mountains Guide,* the most trusted source of trail and campsite descriptions and site-specific hiking advice since 1907. It's available at the Pinkham Notch Camp, or you can order it in advance by phone (603/466-2727) or by writing to AMC Books, P.O. Box 298, Dept. BC, Gorham, New Hampshire 03581-0298.

Just south of the AMC lodge in Pinkham Notch, Route 16 runs past the parking area for the short walk under Route 16 and downhill to **Glen Ellis Falls,** which tumble 70 feet down the southern slopes of Wildcat Mountain to a dark green pool. Beyond the falls, a much steeper climb follows the Appalachian Trail back up the eastern side of the notch, following Wildcat Ridge toward remote Carter Notch, with fine views of the Presidential peaks. If you want to cheat, you can ride the Wildcat Mountain gondola ($10) to the 4,397-foot summit and walk back down from there; if you want to linger in this comparatively little-visited corner of the White Mountains, stay a night or two at the very rustic, AMC-operated **Carter Notch Hut** (603/466-2727), which has a bunkhouse and a self-serve kitchen (bring your own food!).

cabbage roses, and crackling fires in your room at night. A covered bridge beside Route 16, taverns filled with antiques, and **winter sleigh rides** ($15; 603/383-0845) complete the postcard image of Merry Olde New England.

The Jackson area is not only pretty but also has a couple of northern New Hampshire's best places to eat, drink, and sleep. Just outside the southern edge of Pinkham Notch, at the junction of Route 16 and Route 16B, the **Shannon Door Pub** (603/383-4211) is usually just the right side of crowded—full of skiers, hikers, and other hungry folks enjoying hearty food, good beers, and frequent live folksy-bluesy music in a jovial setting. The grand hotel is Jackson is the stately **Wentworth** ($80–150; 603/383-9700), at the heart of the village, welcoming travelers since it was established back in 1880.

GLEN

South of Jackson along Route 16 or Route 16A, after a half-mile you pass the picturesque Jackson Covered Bridge, where the two alternates rejoin at the north edge of tiny Glen, which in the short stretch between the bridge and the junction with US-302 has one of the more concentrated barrages of roadside clutter in the White Mountains. Glen is best known not for hiking or sightseeing but as home to the children's theme park **Story Land** (daily 9 AM–6 pm in summer only; $18, under 4 free; 603/383-4293), where among its many playfully designed and carefully coifed acres, the highlights include a boat ride, a raft ride, and a fake fiberglass cow that gives fake milk when you squeeze its fake udders. Next to Story Land, and operated by the same people, the simulated realities of

Heritage—New Hampshire (daily 9 AM–5 PM; $10; 603/383-9776) feature slightly animated mannequins that act out episodes from New Hampshire's past—from initial immigration to the New World, through the Revolutionary War, to a steam train ride through Victorian-era White Mountains. If you like Disneyland attractions (especially "Great Moments with Mr. Lincoln"!) you may well love it; if not . . . well, the White Mountains are right outside the gates.

A half-mile south of these twin attractions, Route 16 links up with US-302 at a cluster of shops, a grocery store, and a bank ATM. This jumble is also home to the **Red Parka Pub** (603/383-4344), a jolly, moderate-to-inexpensive place to eat and drink, with live music most weekend nights.

NORTH CONWAY

If you're overdue for a little retail therapy you might consider continuing south on Route 16 from the US-302 junction toward North Conway (pop. 2,200), one of the cornerstones of New England's factory-outlet circuit. City dwellers be warned: horrible flashbacks to your homeward commute may result if you venture into the shopping mall zone, where half-hour (or longer) crawls along a five-mile stretch of highway are not unheard of on holidays, weekends, afternoons, summers, springs, or autumns.

Besides factory-outlet stores, North Conway is also home to New Hampshire's most popular scenic railroad, running steam engines throughout summer and during the fall color season. Based out of Conway's downtown depot, the **Conway Scenic Railroad** ($8–40 depending on trip; 603/356-5251 or 800/232-5251 for schedules and fares) runs historic trains south to Conway, through Bartlett, and all the way to Crawford Notch via the historic Frankenstein Trestle, with special excursions available in addition to these frequent trips.

Finally, there's a small but enjoyable ski area, **Cranmore** (603/356-5543 or 800/543-9206), a family-oriented resort with mostly intermediate-level trails, a tubing park, and summer mountain biking, all just east of town.

Although all the tourists may well drive you away from North Conway, the town does have some good places to eat and drink, like **Horsefeather's**, a lively bar with a good restaurant on Main Street right across from the depot. If this is a bit rowdy (as it can be during Red Sox–Yankees games), head up the street to **Elvio's Pizza**, where you can get slices or full pies, submarine sandwiches, and big salads, plus wine and beer.

There are lots of accommodations on and off Route 16, from old cabin courts to anodyne motels, but the most interesting place has to be the Civil War–era **Cranmore Inn**, a quick walk east of Route 16 at 24 Kearsarge Street ($50–95; 603/356-5502). Although brochures on North Conway and the White Mountains fill motel lobbies from Boston north, if you need more information contact the usually helpful **Mount Washington Information Booth** (603/356-3171) on Route 16.

CONWAY

Conway, five miles further down Route 16 at the south end of the scenic railroad line, is a nicer, littler town, with a couple of restaurants, a post office, and the very clean and very friendly **HI White Mountains Hostel**, in the heart of town at 36 Washington Street ($18 a night; 603/447-1001). If you have your doubts about hostelling, this place is sure to dispel them; run as a sustainable living center, it's as clean as it is serene, and besides saving money staying here, you're apt to meet like-minded fellow travelers over breakfast or relaxing in the game room.

Up Washington Street from the hostel (head north from Conway's only stoplight), you can visit a pair of scenic covered bridges, a large one spanning the Saco River toward Route 16 and the outlet hell of North Conway, and an older bridge spanning the Swift River, just upstream from its confluence with the

If you can turn a blind eye to all the retail frenzy, North Conway's central park offers one of the best views of Mount Washington, and the baseball diamond here hosts some pretty intense games.

The back road between Glen and North Conway, Route 16A is a much more pleasant drive, winding past a series of older resorts along the pastoral **Intervale Loop**. Another quiet alternative route to hyper-developed Route 16 is the **West Side Highway,** which runs south from near the Attitash Bear Peak ski area on US-302 all the way down the valley to Washington Street in Conway. Passing Diana's Baths, the climber's mecca, Cathedral Ledge, and lovely little Echo Lake State Park, the road runs along the west bank of the Saco River the whole way.

Just over the Maine border, about 10 miles east of North Conway via US-302, the town of **Fryeburg** hosts a weeklong agricultural fair during the first week in October that's one of the most popular in New England—packed with tractor pulls, horse racing, lots of music, even a pig scramble (a contest, not an egg dish).

Up in the hills above Conway, off Route 16 one mile south of the Kancamagus Highway at the edge of the White Mountains National Forest, the **Darby Field Inn** ($100–150; 603/447-2181) is a B&B open year-round for skiing, hiking, and great après-outdoors meals.

Fall foliage is at its best when warm clear days are followed by cold nights that stop the essential pigment-producing sugars from circulating out of the leaves. Sugar production is low on cloudy days, while warm nights allow the sugars to disperse before the brightest colors are produced. For **New Hampshire Fall Foliage Reports** (Sept. and Oct. only), call 800/258-3608.

The name Kancamagus honors the local Indian chief who controlled the area when the first European settlers began arriving at the White Mountains in the 1680s. The roadway was not paved until 1964, and was declared a National Scenic Byway in 1989.

Parking along New Hampshire highways is illegal, so don't be tempted to leave your car beside the road while you take a hike up that nearby hill—you may return to find it's been towed to some town 20 miles away.

Saco. Continuing north, the road becomes the West Side Highway, running along the Saco River all the way north to US-302.

DETOUR: THE KANCAMAGUS HIGHWAY

Running east-to-west from Conway over the mountains to Lincoln, the 34-mile **Kancamagus Highway** (Route 112) is one of the most incredible drives in the White Mountains. Much shorter and a lot less traveled than the prime tourist route along US-302 and US-3 through Crawford and Franconia Notches, the Kanc, as it's often called, takes you up and over the crest of the peaks, giving grand vistas over an almost completely undeveloped landscape—great for fall color leaf-peeping. Fall is definitely prime time for the drive, but any time of year (except maybe winter, when it can be a bit hairy) it's a lovely trip, lined by lupines in early summer and raging waterfalls in the spring.

Since it's part of the White Mountains National Forest, there's no gas, food, or lodging along the way, but if you bring your own food and water (or other beverage of your choice) there are many great stops. Climbing slowly up from Conway along the banks of the Swift River, Route 112 passes the USFS-run Covered Bridge Campground, which offers some 50 sites and access to the scenic **Albany Covered Bridge** over the Swift River. If you want some time off the pavement, the old Dugway Road winds from here back down to Conway along the north bank of the river.

Back on the Kanc, about three miles west of the covered bridge the road passes through the Rocky Gorge. From a well-signed parking area, the fairly easy **Champney Falls Trail** heads southeast toward Mount Chocorua, reaching the namesake cascade after just under a mile.

Near the midpoint of the Kanc, the **Russell Colbath Historic House** dates from the early 1800s and now houses a small museum (daily 9 AM–4 PM; free) with exhibits describing the lives of the White Mountains' early settlers. From the house, a short loop trail explores the effects loggers had on this region in the 1890s, when everything you see along the Kanc (and most everywhere else) was devastated by clear-cuts.

Three miles further west, just east of the crest and an easy half-mile walk from the well-signed parking area, **Sabbaday Falls** is a lovely little waterfall roaring through a narrow gorge. In a series of noisy, splashing cascades, the river drops down through a polished pink granite gorge, barely 10 feet wide but surrounded by dense forest. It's an ideal picnic spot and only 10–15 minutes from the road.

Ten miles east from Lincoln, about 25 miles west from Conway, the 2,855-foot crest of Kancamagus Pass marks the divide between the Saco River and Pemigawasset River watersheds. West of here, the Kanc drops steeply down past **Greeley Ponds,** where a two-mile trail leads south to a series of swimming holes in a cleft between Mount Kancamagus and Mount Osceola, before heading on past Loon Mountain into Lincoln.

CRAWFORD NOTCH

US-302 between Glen and Twin Mountain winds west around the southern flank of the Presidential Range, then heads north through Crawford Notch, another of the White Mountains' high passes and centerpiece of the Crawford Notch State Park. The road closely follows the Saco River through new-growth forest; the oaks and white pine of the lower valley give way to more birch and spruce as you gain elevation. Come autumn, the entire forest is a riot of color: the northern oaks' dark reds, the birches' and aspens' golden yellows, purples from the white ashes and sumacs, and most brilliant of all, the blaze of orange from countless sugar maples, which set New England's fall foliage apart from the crowd. From mid-September through Columbus Day weekend, be prepared to slow down and take it easy on the roads as the so-called leaf-peepers drive like grandmothers. If you don't want to face a lot of No Vacancy signs, book your fall weekend accommodations as far in advance as possible, since throughout New England autumn ranks as the year's busiest season for motels and inns.

South of Crawford Notch, five miles west of Glen on US-302 near Bartlett, **Attitash Bear Peak** (603/374-2368 or 888/554-1900) is a popular ski area with an unusual summer attraction: a nearly mile-long "alpine slide" ($9 per ride, or $21 all day) dropping down the mountainside—at speeds of up to 40 mph (unless you hit the brakes on the sled!). There's also a water park, mountain bike rentals, a climbing wall, and a trampoline—fun for the whole family.

Crawford Notch offers good day hikes to various waterfalls and vantage points such as **Frankenstein Cliff,** named for an artist whose work helped popularize the White Mountains, and 200-foot **Arethusa Falls,** the state's highest waterfall. Both trails pass near the historic **Frankenstein Trestle,** an impressive wood-and-steel engineering work still in use by the Conway Scenic Railroad; and during high spring runoff or after storms, Arethusa and nearby Ripley Falls on Avalanche Brook are among New Hampshire's most dramatic sights.

Camping is available at the state-run **Dry River Campground** (mid-May to mid-Oct; $12; 603/271-3628), a primitive tent-only facility opposite the trailheads to both Frankenstein Cliff and Arethusa Falls. A modest step up from tents is the $18-per-night **AMC Crawford Hostel** (603/466-2727); its large, spartan (but heated) bunk rooms, $1 showers, and self-service kitchen are open year-round beside US-302. Information about trails in the area may be found at the hostel, along with some minor supplies, although **Pinkham Notch Hostel** (on the other side of Mount Washington) is still the overall best resource for hikers in the White Mountains region.

North of Crawford Notch the highway joins the Ammonoosuc River headwaters as they flow toward the Connecticut River, passing Bretton Woods and the access road for the Mount Washington Cog Railway. The giant **Mount Washington Hotel** (800/258-0330) dominates the surrounding plain, its Victorian luxury no longer standing in such grand isolation below the peaks of the Presidentials now that a ski resort sits across the highway, and motels and condos squat around its skirts. Built at the turn of the 20th century by Pennsylvania Railroad tycoon Joseph Stickney, the Mount Washington Hotel received its most lasting recognition as host of the 1944 United Nations International Monetary Conference, the historic meeting of financiers from 44 nations that established the World Bank and pegged the price of

The first known ascent of Mount Washington was made in 1642 by Darby Field of Durham, who historians believe followed a route near that of today's Crawford Path.

Built in 1869, the **Mount Washington Cog Railway** has a maximum grade of 37.5 percent, surpassed by only one other nonfunicular railway in the world, high up in the Swiss Alps. Burning a ton of coal with each trip, the cinder-spewing engines of this historic Railway to the Moon take over an hour to ratchet up the three-mile track. Trips run from mid-May to mid-Oct. and cost $44; phone 603/846-5404 or 800/922-8825 for further information.

Among the peaks of the southern Presidential Range overlooking Crawford Notch is Mount Jackson, named for neither the seventh U.S. president, Andrew, nor for the Confederate general, Thomas "Stonewall," but for a former state geologist, Charles.

gold to the U.S. dollar. Since it recognized the United States as the strongest postwar economy and chose the dollar as the global standard for trade, the conference was perhaps even more influential than military victory in guaranteeing the longevity of U.S. dominion over the postwar world. Wander around the hotel's public areas and enjoy the grandeur (or a meal or a drink), but room rates are definitely in the "if you have to ask, you can't afford it" category.

CRAWFORD PATH: LAKE OF THE CLOUDS

For ambitious and well-prepared hikers, the north end of Crawford Notch is the start of the oldest and perhaps grandest walking trail in the country, the Crawford Path up towering Mount Washington. A strenuous, demanding, and potentially dangerous route, the Crawford Path is also breathtakingly beautiful, and a walk along it gives an almost complete picture of the White Mountains —sparkling brooks, fields of wildflowers, and glorious mountaintop panoramas. The hike is about eight miles each way, and it would take a very full day to do the round-trip climb of the 6,288-foot summit, which is nearly a vertical mile (well, 3,400 feet) above the trailhead. Once you've packed up all your essential supplies (winter clothing, waterproof everything, first-aid kit, water, food, map, and compass), head across US-302 from the AMC's **Crawford Notch Hostel,** which is a good place to spend the night before or after this hike. From the hostel, a set of wooden steps marks the start of a steady three-mile climb up Crawford Path toward the 4,310-foot summit of Mount Pierce, which was originally called Mount Clinton (in honor of the New York Governor DeWitt Clinton, not our ex-president, Bill). This is where the Crawford Path joins up with the main Appalachian Trail, and the two routes run together for the next five miles, passing over three more Presidential peaks (Mounts Eisenhower, Franklin, and Monroe), before dropping down to the enormously popular, AMC-run **Lake of the Clouds,** where you can make reservations for meals and a bed if you want to have a more leisurely trek. From the Lake of the Clouds hut, the summit of Mount Washington is under a mile (and more than 1,200 vertical feet) away, but many hikers prefer the comparative calm of Mount Monroe—ideal for appreciating the sunset without the crowds and cars that can diminish the pleasures of Mount Washington's top-of-the-world view.

The very beautiful (and very popular) section of the drive through Franconia Notch, between Crawford Notch and the towns of Lincoln and North Woodstock, is covered in the US-3 chapter on pages 143–48.

HIGH MOUNTAIN HUTS AND LODGES

The **Appalachian Mountain Club** (AMC) has made itself synonymous with backcountry recreation in New England for well over a century. The group maintains trails; operates a network of accommodations; sponsors educational programs; publishes maps and guides for hikers, canoeists, and kayakers; and performs other services for a region spanning from Mount Greylock, Massachusetts' highest peak, to Maine's Acadia National Park.

Many of AMC's overnight properties are lean-to's and tent platforms, but some, like the High Mountain Huts, are complete mountain-top hostels. Eight staffed alpine cabins are strung out roughly a day's hike apart along the Appalachian Trail between Carter Notch, east of Route 16, and Lonesome Lake, just west of US-3 in Franconia Notch. Several are easily accessible, but others are strenuous hikes from the nearest trailhead; some are below tree line, while others lie well up in the clouds. All offer bunk rooms, cold-water bathrooms, and two hot meals a day during their full-service periods. None has heat or showers. Most are open only during the summer months, but two are open on a self-service basis year-round. Adult rates run from $18 (winter, self-serve) to $64 per person (peak times, including breakfast and dinner), although extended stays and member discounts are available. All huts generally require reservations months in advance (603/466-2727), but it never hurts to ask if there are spaces available. If you're flexible about dates and locations and can visit midweek, you can usually find a bunk somewhere even with no advance planning.

For detailed descriptions of the huts and their access routes, talk to AMC staffers at the Pinkham Notch **visitor center** (603/466-2727), or consult either the *AMC White Mountain Guide* or *High Huts of the White Mountains*, available from AMC Books.

LOST RIVER GORGE

With five main roads and countless minor ones connecting the Franconia Notch area with the Connecticut River, there are nearly endless ways to get between these two places while staying more or less on the path of the hikers' Appalachian Trail, which disappears into the woods for most of the way. All of the roads are partly pretty and partly yucky  in about equal degrees, but one of the easiest to follow is Route 112, which runs west from North Woodstock along the Lost River, hopping over the crest and dropping down along the Wild Ammonoosuc River. (This is not related to the larger Ammonoosuc River in northern Maine.) The main stop along this route is the privately owned gorge known as the **Lost River** (daily 9 AM–6 PM; $8; 603/745-8031), where you can explore the jumble of glaciated granite boulders that seem to swallow up the river, giving it its name. Many of the big, moss-covered boulders have been given names (Guillotine Rock and Lemon Squeezer, to name two), and you can see these (and smell the fragrant pine trees) from the comfort of a wooden boardwalk or go wild and explore some of the many caves formed by the huge piles of rocks.

When the weather's fine, one of the most popular day hikes along this part of the Appalachian Trail is the climb up 4,802-foot **Mount Moosilauke** (alternately pronounced "moo-sa-LOCK" and "moo-sa-LOCK-key"), a fairly strenuous six-mile climb that ends with one of the great panoramas in New England. The hike, which starts from a parking area along Route 25 a half-mile northwest of Glencliff, climbs 3,500 vertical feet, is well signed and well traveled all the way. (Dartmouth College students treat the mountain as a second home.) You can also reach the summit by climbing four miles up from the Beaver Brook trailhead on Route 112 west of Kinsman Notch, but this is a much steeper slog and can be scarily slippery on the downhill.

Continuing west from Lost River Gorge, which sits at the top of Route 112's spectacular run through wild Kinsman Notch, the highway drops down into the Connecticut River watershed toward the Vermont town of Wells River, which happens to be home to the best truck stop in all New England, the **P&H Truck Stop Cafe** (802/429-2141) at I-91 exit 17, where you can enjoy fine chowder, charbroiled cheeseburgers, and great pies (and walls covered with images of Peterbilts and Mack trucks)—24 hours a day. After eating here, backtrack four miles to the river and follow scenic Route 10 along its east bank, winding south toward Hanover. The route along the Vermont side of the river, through the town of Fairlee (which has a nice diner and a unique drive-in movie theater/motel) is described in the US-5 chapter.

If you feel like following another route between Franconia Notch and the Connecticut River, it's fair so say that any way you go—on Routes 112, 166, 118, 25, 25A, or 25C, or any combination of these—you're likely to pass through some very characteristic (if not exactly idealized) New Hampshire scenes. Instead of shoppes and pubs, you'll pass snowmobile dealers and mobile homes, old pickup trucks, and shingles slung below mailboxes advertising homemade maple products, roofing contractors, small engine repair, and computer support. Houses nestled among the hardwoods spend nearly half the year wearing their insulation on the outside, the brunt of winter kept at bay by Tyvek swaddling and huge piles of split cordwood ready to stoke the stoves. Leaving the steep slopes of the western White Mountains, all of these routes start to level off as they descend into the Connecticut River Valley, passing small Christmas tree farms and hamlets composed of little more than a church, some houses, and a place to drop off the mail.

Between Wells River and White River Junction, US-5 runs parallel to this AT route, along the west bank of the Connecticut River. The Vermont side of the river is covered in the US-5 chapter, on pages 196–200.

ROUTE 10: NORTH HAVERILL AND LYME

In case you're worried, Lyme, New Hampshire, is not the place the tick-borne disease was named for; that Lyme is in Connecticut. That said, you still need to be on the lookout for these devilish little creatures.

While hikers along the Appalachian Trail have to struggle up and over several mountaintops, we drivers get to amble along a few miles to the west, following scenic Route 10 along the east banks of the lazy Connecticut River. Winding past pastures and cornfields, Route 10 is a nonstop pleasure to drive (or cycle); uneventful perhaps, but giving seemingly endless pastoral views framed by white rail fences, occasional farmhouses, and the voluptuous peaks that rise to the east and west. The first hamlet you reach along this part of Route 10, North Haverill, is a real museum piece, with a necklace of distinctive colonial-era homes flanking a oval town green and one of New Hampshire's oldest cemeteries close by. Continuing south, Route 10 runs past Haverill (there's also a Center Haverill and an East Haverill), where a well-signed turnoff west from Route 10 leads to what *used* to be the **Bedell Bridge**. The bridge washed away in 1979, but the pilings have been preserved as an unusual state park, with a riverside picnic table where you can enjoy the rippling waters.

A much more placid sort of water can be enjoyed at nearby Loch Lyme, where the rustic lodge and cabins of **Loch Lyme Lodge** ($100–150; 603/795-2141 or 800/423-2141) have been welcoming generations of New Englanders since 1946. Swim, sail, or float out on the small lake, which has an idyllic location between the mountains and the river.

A mile south of Loch Lyme, eight miles north of Hanover, the tidy town of Lyme presents yet another Kodak-worthy scene, with a Soldiers and Sailors Monument standing at the center of a slender green, a large church at one end and equally large stables at the other. According to a plaque, the stables were built in 1810 to shelter the horses of people attending the church, where Sunday sermons could easily last for five hours or more.

Lyme, which feels more like a part of the Virginia hunt country than New England, also has a fully stocked general store and a pair of nice places to stop for a night or three. The 1809 **Alden Country Inn** ($125; 603/795-4712), with period-decorated rooms, a very fine restaurant, and a cozy pub with a heartwarming fireplace, is not cheap but it is definitely special. If you want to build up an appetite before dinner, the innkeepers will rent you a bike and point you toward some of the area's best routes. The same owners also run the equally pleasant white clapboard **Dowd's Country Inn** (603/795-4712) across the green.

HANOVER: DARTMOUTH COLLEGE

Dartmouth College is the principal resident of attractive little Hanover (pop. 9,212) and it shows. Even people who attended schools cloned from office parks recognize Baker Library's tall clock tower and Georgian brick symmetry as the visual expression of everything collegiate. When school is in session, the cafes hum with undergraduate discourse, the downtown teems with students, and a varsity air envelops the historic campus and its sturdy neighbors. Between terms, however, the town's metabolism drops toward hibernation levels, which means there's no line for espresso.

That there *is* espresso at all is attributable to the Ivy League influence, just like the local architecture, dress, and cultural diversions. Concerning the last, Dartmouth's **Hood Museum of Art** (Tues.–Sun. 10 AM–5 PM; free; 603/646-2808), on the southeast side of the green and housed in a modern gallery designed in part by Charles Moore, shows a changing selection from its permanent collection but mainly hosts visiting exhibitions. Connected to the Hood, the **Hopkins Center** (603/646-2422 for schedule and tickets), is the uncontested local hotspot for performing arts and film; it also has a cafe.

That **Titan rocket** in the middle of wide-spot-in-the-road Warren, on Routes 118/25/25C, is a keepsake from a local gent's career in the Army's Missile Command down in Redstone, Alabama. Another unusual place to see in this part of New Hampshire is in the town of Glencliff, where the AT crosses Route 25: the small **Museum of American Weather** (July and Aug. only; 603/989-3167) in the home of hiker and historian Roger Bricker, who sometimes invites AT thru-hikers to shower and sleep in his ad hoc hostel.

A few miles west of the clearly signposted Appalachian Trail crossing, east from the Route 10 town of Orford, Route 25A passes the **Sugar House** at Mount Cube Farm. When the maple sap begins to run in early spring, this rudimentary wooden shed is transformed by the heady aroma of boiling syrup—a bright event in what is otherwise known as mud season. This rite of spring depends entirely upon the weather: warm days and cold nights keep the sap flowing, while too much cold or warmth shuts it off. Generally the sugar season lasts from mid-March through April. If you spot the steam from the evaporator, stop by for a sample or, come summer, enjoy a full breakfast of fresh pancakes swimming in that New England elixir (Thurs.–Sat., 4th of July weekend to Columbus Day weekend; 603/353-4709).

Although Ivy League Dartmouth has a $2 billion endowment and a conservative reputation, it has also had some interesting students, including children's stars Dr. Seuss, Captain Kangaroo, and Mr. Rogers, the latter two both dropouts. The poet Robert Frost was another famous nongraduate.

More contentious art can be experienced at the very center of Dartmouth where, in the lower level reading room of Baker Library, the walls are covered with a set of frescoes by **José Clemente Orozco**: "An Epic of American Civilization." Painted during the depths of the Great Depression from 1932 until 1934, when Orozco was a visiting art teacher here, these dramatic, brightly colored murals are the Mexican artist's only commissioned work in the United States. Like the work of his more celebrated colleague Diego Rivera, Orozco's mural is blatantly political, seeming to question the very foundations of an elite, private institution like Dartmouth. One panel goes so far as to show a cadre of skull-faced college professors resplendent in rich gowns and trampling on a bed of dusty, unopened books.

If it's too nice a day to stay indoors and contemplate society's ills, rent a bike and ride north to Lyme and back, or borrow a canoe or kayak from Dartmouth's **Ledyard Canoe Club** ($5/hour; 603/643-6709), located on the river just north of the Route 10A bridge, and play Huck Finn for an afternoon. Or you can take a hike.

With the **Dartmouth Outing Club** responsible for maintaining hundreds of miles of trails, including more than 75 miles of the Appalachian Trail, a part of which runs right through town, it's no surprise that Hanover is something of a hiking center. There's an AT marker embedded in the sidewalk in front of the Hanover Inn, from where the hiking trail runs west across the bridge to Vermont, and east down Main and Lebanon streets to the town of Etna, before climbing the 2,280-foot peak of Moose Mountain. Various hiking maps and guides are available from the Outing Club's office in Robinson Hall (603/646-2428) facing the green, and from the Dartmouth Bookstore on S. Main Street. Ambitious day-hikers should head east toward the Dartmouth Skiway (yes, the college has its own ski area), which serves as summertime trailhead for the short (1.4-mile) but steep hike up to **Holts Ledge**, an Appalachian Trail summit that gives a splendid panorama.

HANOVER PRACTICALITIES

A predominantly undergraduate student body means that double cappuccinos and lattes are the tipple of choice for the majority of Hanover's scholars. This is why the **Dirt Cowboy Cafe** at the head of S. Main Street is usually a live wire until their 2 AM closing, tendrils of cigarette smoke and conversation weaving amid the earnest note-takers and book-readers. If you prefer French press over Krups drip, **Rosey's Cafe** is the coffeehouse for you, at the corner of Lebanon and S. College Streets at the downstairs rear of the Rosey 'n' Jeke's clothing store. Rosey's mocha in particular is more European (bitter chocolate, not semisweet) than those offered by cafes bowing to the American sweet tooth.

Espresso, yes, and sandwiches, too: on S. Main across from the Ledyard Bank, **Patrick Henry's** offers decent soup-salad-sandwich fare in a mellow, fraternity-free setting. If you prefer thick-crust pizzas and calzones garnished with everything from kielbasa and sauerkraut to pesto chicken, try **Foodee's** at 45 Lyme Road, a New Hampshire–based chain with a local outlet just north of town on Route 10 in a modern building next to the Exxon station. When it comes to Italian, though, the last best word on the subject is the menu at **Café Buon Gustaio**, 72 S. Main Street

The Hanover Inn

A few years after New Hampshire and the other 12 American colonies began their revolt against mother England, Hanover and a handful of neighboring towns divorced themselves from New Hampshire to join Vermont. That short-lived association fell apart in 1782, leaving the towns independent for four years before they reunited with New Hampshire.

(Tues.–Sun. dinner only; 603/643-5711); its cuisine earns top honors and commands top dollar for both preparation and presentation.

Generations of Dartmouth students have survived their college years thanks in part to the generous portions served up at **Lou's**, 30 S. Main Street (603/643-3321). Hardly changed since it opened in 1947 and famed for their magical strawberry rhubarb and other fresh-baked pies, Lou's does great big breakfasts, lunch-time soups and burgers, and early dinners (they close at 5 PM, 3 PM on Sundays). Best of all, there's not a fluorescent light to be seen.

For accommodations around Hanover, there's the stately, Dartmouth-run **Hanover Inn** facing onto the Green ($250–350; 603/643-4300); for affordable rooms, however, look in nearby West Lebanon or across the river in White River Junction, Vermont.

Around Hanover, this Appalachian Trail route crosses paths with our road trips along US-4 and US-5. The towns of Lebanon, New Hampshire, and Woodstock, Vermont, and the ski resort of Killington, are covered in the US-4 chapter on pages 178–83. The Connecticut River towns of Fairlee and White River Junction are covered in US-5 on pages 197–200.

INTO THE MOUNTAINS: NORWICH, HARTFORD, AND POMFRET

From the Hanover area, into Norwich, Vermont, the most direct driving tour approximation of the hikers route is to follow US-4 west through Woodstock toward Killington, a route described

Before Vermont joined the union in 1791 as the 14th state, it spent 14 years as the independent Republic of New Connecticut. Its name comes from the French *verd mont*, meaning "green mountain," and appeared on maps as early as 1780.

In his book *Great American Motorcycle Tours* (John Muir Publications/Avalon Travel Publishing, 2000), author Gary McKechnie says this about the section of Route 100 around Plymouth and Killington: "Never before in the history of motorcycling has one road done so much for so many."

Vermont has a statewide system of color-coded roadside commercial signage that makes it easy to find B&Bs and other services off the main roads, although the sign space is paid for and therefore shouldn't be mistaken for a comprehensive guide to what's out there. For a good guide to the state's many fine restaurants, contact the **Vermont Fresh Network** (800/658-8787), which publishes a free booklet listing restaurants that use only the freshest local produce.

in the US-4 chapter. The hiking trail, however, runs further north, and passes through a series of pretty foothill villages that are well worth searching out on your way to the heart of the Green Mountains.

At Norwich, just uphill from where the Appalachian Trail crosses the Connecticut River along Route 10A on a broad low bridge from Hanover, you might want to while away a rainy afternoon at the interesting **Montshire Museum of Science** (daily 10 AM–5 PM; $6; 802/649-2200), which has more than 100 educational exhibits focusing on natural history, as well as aquariums showcasing fresh- and saltwater creatures. The next town the AT passes through is West Hartford, on the banks of the White River upstream from I-91 along Route 14.

From West Hartford, you can circle around (on unnumbered and rather rough-surfaced country roads) through North Pomfret, Pomfret, and South Pomfret, passing dairy farms, quaint barns, and one post office per town, coming in through the backdoor to upscale Woodstock, where this AT route links up with US-4 (see page 179 for more). From South Pomfret, a quaint little hamlet that's also home to the Suicide Six ski area, the hiker's Appalachian Trail heads up into the mountains through a long, roadless stretch before crossing Route 100 at Sherburne Pass. The only real driving route follows Route 12 south into Woodstock, which is covered in the US-4 chapter.

PLYMOUTH AND PLYMOUTH NOTCH: CALVIN COOLIDGE COUNTRY

COLONEL JOHN COOLIDGE, FATHER OF PRESIDENT CALVIN COOLIDGE AND CALVIN JR.
PLYMOUTH, VERMONT

Running a twisty seven miles south from US-4 and Bridgewater, Route 100A passes through beautiful scenery and Plymouth Notch, birthplace of Calvin Coolidge, the only U.S. president born on the 4th of July. The small hilltop clutch of buildings is so little changed by the 20th century, it's a wonder there aren't horses with carriages parked behind the visitor center instead of Subarus. One of the most evocative and simply beautiful historic sites in New England, the Coolidge Homestead has been restored to its 1923 appearance when Colonel John Coolidge administered the oath of office to his vacationing son, the vice president, after President Harding died unexpectedly in San Francisco. The homestead, his father's general store (named for a later owner, Florence Cilley), and the cheese factory (run by Calvin Coolidge's old son John, over 90 years old, who hand-makes some of Vermont's most delicious cheddars) are three of the 10 buildings open to the public (daily 9:30 AM–5 PM, Memorial Day to mid-Oct. $5; cheese factory open year-round, free). There's also a mile-long nature trail offering fine views of the Notch and its surroundings.

If you're looking for accommodations out where there are more stars than streetlights, try the **Salt Ash Inn** (doubles $85–165; 800/258-7258), an 1830s stagecoach stop at the junction of Routes 100A and 100 in Plymouth Union. Although Woodstock, Killington, and Ludlow are all within scenic 10- to 15-mile drives, surrounding mountains keep the 21st century a world away. Alternatively, for a true night under the Milky Way, pitch your tent in **Coolidge State Park** (late May to early Oct.; $11) off Route 100A in Plymouth.

ROUTE 100

Known as the Skiers' Highway, serpentine Route 100 manages to pass the base of nearly every major ski resort in Vermont. Joining it midway through the state, this Appalachian Trail driving route follows a favorite stretch for cyclists, a mostly level dozen miles through the small farms (some of which sell maple syrup in spring) and posh-looking lakeside resorts of the Black River valley. Route 100 ends up in **Ludlow**, at the foot of Okemo (oh-KEY-mo) Mountain. Any doubts that skiing is the cash cow of the state's most lucrative industry—tourism—are quickly dispelled by just one look at the wall-to-wall inns, sportswear shops, vacation real estate offices, and restaurants along Ludlow's main drag. The town's star attraction is that 3,300-foot peak with its hundreds of acres of ski trails serviced by state-of-the-art *everything*, although seven other ski areas cluster like the Pleiades within a 25-mile radius.

Between the end of ski season and the beginning of fall foliage, Ludlow's pulse nearly flatlines. Flocks of elderly, low-tipping Floridians migrate to the vast strings of condos around Okemo, actually adding to the summer slowdown. In recent years mountain bikers and inn-to-inn cyclists have become a source of some life, but overall, Ludlow, like many other Vermont ski towns, spends the warm months convalescing.

Fortunately yuppie recreation requires yuppie food, so when it comes time to do your pre-ride carbo-loading or aprés-ski whistle-wetting, you won't have to resort to a hamburger that's identical (or worse!) to those other billions and billions served. **Nikki's**, 44 Pond Street in the shopping plaza next to Okemo's access road (802/228-7797), is your best bet for creative continental cuisine—from the pizza del mar appetizer to the no-holds-barred white chocolate mousse. Good wine list, too. If Momma Valente's homemade lasagna or eggplant parmigiana is more your speed, continue south to the traffic light downtown and let her son welcome you into **Valente's** (802/228-2671), next to the park on the corner. Or if you're looking

"Silent Cal" Coolidge was famous—perhaps unjustly—for being a man of few words. A White House dinner guest is said to have bet that she could make the president address her with at least three words; when confronted with this challenge, Coolidge replied, "You lose."

President Coolidge recollected in his autobiography: "No doubt there have been kings who have participated in the induction of their sons into their office, but in republics where the succession comes by election I do not know of any other case in history where a father has administered to his son the qualifying oath of office. . . . It seemed a simple and natural thing to do at the time." His father, when later asked how he knew he could administer the oath, replied, "I didn't know I couldn't."

When garnished with Vermont-made Ben & Jerry's ice cream, apple pie à la mode is certainly nothing to sneer at, but if you really want to try apple pie the Vermont way, ask for a slab of sharp cheddar on the side instead of ice cream.

Okemo and its central Vermont sisters are best for intermediate skiers, although each has a few black diamond trails for experts, and Killington has more than just a few, if you don't mind sharing them with half the state of New Jersey on weekends. Skiers looking for more than a couple of hours of challenging downhill terrain will get more for the price of their lift ticket among the half-dozen ski areas around Stowe and Waterbury, a couple of hours farther north, where Route 100 crosses US-2 and I-89. See page 130 for more.

For a long-distance leaf-peepers update on the progress of Vermont foliage, call the state's **fall foliage hotline** (24-hour recording, Sept. and Oct. only): 802/828-3239.

Buffalo Brook, which drains into Lake Echo north of Ludlow, was for almost 30 years the site of a gold-mining operation in the mid-19th century.

If your supply of driving music is getting stale, visit the gift shop at the **Weston Priory,** three miles north of town, and pick up a tape of something truly inspirational. To hear the resident Benedictine monks live, consult the bulletin board by the parking lot for a schedule of their public devotional services. From the Route 100/155 junction, take Route 155 north; the priory's driveway is the first left.

for a decent inexpensive breakfast, try **The Hatchery** across the street, 164 Main Street (802/228-2311).

Accommodations run mostly on the flashy side with either antique-filled Victorian inns or "modern rustic" motels and chalets, but there's also the very reasonable **HI Trojan Horse Lodge** (802/228-5244; $15–20 per person; closed April), with its shared or private rooms in a converted barn beside Route 100 less than a half-mile south of the main street. (They offer canoe rentals in season, too.) Otherwise, for a place to stay expect to shell out anywhere from a summertime low of around $50 to a fall and winter weekend high of over $200.

A little way east of Ludlow, follow the Black River along Route 103 to Proctorsville, where the **Golden Stage Inn,** 399 Depot Street ($90–120; 802/226-7744) offers cozy rooms in a colonial-era coaching inn, now set in four acres of lush gardens.

Turning south out of Ludlow opposite the Black River Brewing Company, Route 100 wanders along the eastern edge of the Green Mountains' high spine through one town after another. With the exception of well-to-do **Weston,** a small place that makes a big business out of its candy-filled Vermont Country Store, skiing is clearly the name of the game for most of them: **Londonderry,** below Big Bromley; **Jamaica,** near Stratton Mountain; and **West Dover,** sandwiched between the impressive Mount Snow/Haystack complex. All the ski areas, of course, bubble with the usual superlatives about snowmaking, grooming, and fast chair lifts, while the towns boast colonial frame houses, snowboard shops, cafes, and country inns with discreet hand-carved wooden signs out front. Notice the details of this Vermont landscape: Saabs or pickups in the driveways, cupolas and weathervanes on the barn roofs, and fashionable Kubota tractors for mowing the fields that, no longer belonging to working farms, are groomed to postcard perfection.

If you don't mind the slightly synthetic airs of the area, one very nice place to stay a while is along Route 100 in the heart of Jamaica: the **Three Mountain Inn** (802/874-4140), a 200-year-old inn with a small restaurant serving food so good it's been raved about in *Gourmet Magazine*.

ROUTE 30: NEWFANE

The quickest way between I-91 and the Route 100 ski areas is scenic Route 30, which winds along the banks of the West River between Brattleboro and Jamaica. Just east of Route 100, near the big dam that blocks the river at West Townshend, the **Townshend Dam Diner** (802/874-4107) is an unpretentious place to check in with the mostly local crowd, who come here for Dam Big Burgers and other tongue-in-cheekily named culinary creations. Route 30, which runs diagonally across southcentral Vermont, ending up near Lake Champlain at the college town of Middlebury, holds one more unusual spot: the one-time home of writer Rudyard Kipling. Kipling settled in West Dummerston, above Brattleboro, after marrying a local woman. While living here in Vermont, at a house he dubbed **Naulakha,** he wrote some of his best-known works, including *Captains Courageous* and parts of the *Jungle Book.* The house is not generally open to the public but is preserved by the British nonprofit organization, **Landmark Trust,** through which you can rent the entire property (for $750–1200/week; from the United States dial 011-44-1628-825-925).

The main attraction along Route 30, however, is the town of Newfane, roughly midway between Route 100 and I-91. With a white church and cupola-bearing county courthouse surrounding a pristine village green, Newfane is one of those Vermont places that make visitors stop and think about how they can manage to stay just a little longer. One great reason to linger here is the Greek Revival–style **Four Columns Inn** ($110–195; 802/365-7713 or 800/787-6633), facing the green from behind the courthouse. The 10-room inn has a great restaurant (one of the best in the state), and the grounds cover 150 acres with trout streams and country gardens.

A nice drive north from Newfane along Route 35 brings you to Grafton, another picture-perfect Vermont village, covered in the US-5 chapter.

ROUTE 11: THE IDEAL TOUR

During the early years of motor touring, when cars and road trips first came into vogue, the scenic drive over the Green Mountains along Route 11 was one of the most popular routes in New England. Today, this route across the southern Green Mountains still offers incomparable views and access to some of the state's premier resorts and vacation destinations. Starting in the west at upscale Manchester Center, and winding into the Connecticut Valley via bellowing Bellows Falls, Route 11 crosses Route 100 at Londonderry, five miles south of Weston.

East from Londonderry, Route 11 runs through the heart of scenic Chester then edges northeast, dropping down into the Connecticut River valley along the Black River, near Springfield off I-91 exit 7. If you're fond of sharp cheddar, consider taking a particularly scenic south from Chester to historic Grafton. For more on Chester and Grafton, two of the prettiest villages in Vermont, see the US-5 chapter.

WILMINGTON AND ROUTE 9

Route 100 leaves its panoramic view of Mount Snow as it descends into Wilmington (pop. 1,968), another picturesque village of 18th- and 19th-century shops and houses built along the Deerfield River. For delicious pancakes served with a half-dozen toppings, stop at earthy **Sonny's Cup 'n' Saucer,** 159 N. Route 100 (802/464-5813). The chamber of commerce is named after the local ski resort rather than the town, so you know who pays the bills around here. Nevertheless, the warmer months see a fair bit of activity in the galleries and antique shops, and for classical music lovers, the **Marlboro Music Festival** marks summer's zenith at

Vermont has been synonymous with skiing since the beginning of the sport, with credit for both the first ski tow and first chair lift in the United States.

The ski town of West Dover is home to an unusual sight: the **World's Largest Bee,** made as an eye-catching marker for a failed honey museum. The bee now stands in the back yard of local resident Jerry Costello, who runs the **Deacon's Den Tavern** on Route 100 (802/464-9361), one of the region's livelier nightspots. Recent reports (courtesy of the ever-fascinating folks at roadsideamerica.com) say the bee has broken its front legs and is lying face down in the mud—a free gift is hereby offered to anyone who provides me with a reproducible photo of this semiforsaken creature.

Marlboro College, a dozen miles east toward Brattleboro on Route 9. Between mid-July and mid-August several score of the world's finest classical musicians perform here in one of the nation's most distinguished annual chamber music series (for schedule and ticket info, call 802/254-2394).

Heading westward toward Bennington, Route 9 crosses the diffuse southern edge of the Green Mountains. Unlike the well-defined ridges in the northern part of the range, the southern Greens spread out over a fairly wide area, and roadless tracts between the Big Bromley ski area and the Massachusetts state line are quite visible as large blank spots on the map. **Woodford State Park** on Route 9 is a good base for hikes into these areas, either along the AT or tributary trails; besides camping at the park (late May until early Oct.; $13–17), there's a seasonal HI hostel at Prospect Ski Mountain's **Greenwood Lodge** (late May until late Oct.; 802/442-2547; $14–17 per person), about three miles farther west on Route 9.

If you want to follow the hikers' Appalachian Trail south into Massachusetts, you have two parallel choices. You can continue west on Route 9 to Bennington, and follow US-7 south through Williamstown, bending back to rejoin the AT east of that well-groomed college town. (The US-7 route is described in the previous chapter.) Or, you can make your south through the much-less developed areas along Route 8 and Route 100, which take you through rural Heartwellville and Stamford before hitting the heavy-duty mill town of North Adams, across the Massachusetts border.

It ain't Texas or even Cincinnati, but chili fans who find themselves near Mount Snow on the second Saturday of each August should be sure to drop in on the annual **Vermont State Chili Cookoff** (802/464-3333 for details).

Brigham Young, the man who led the Mormon exodus to Utah, was born in Whitingham, fewer than 10 miles south of Wilmington on Route 100, at the south end of the Harriman Reservoir. There's a small commemorative monument and picnic area on the Town Hall Common.

Next-door neighbors could hardly be more dissimilar than Williamstown and North Adams, the working-class, former company town of North Adams faltering just a few miles upstream of all that collegiate gentility.

NORTH ADAMS

After a long, mostly rural cruise across Vermont, maybe joining the occasional bus tour for a visit to the North River Winery down in **Jacksonville,** your arrival in Massachusetts at industrial North Adams may be something of a shock. Nearly from its inception North Adams tied its fortunes to major manufacturing plants, churning out printed cotton until textiles went south, then rolling out capacitors for everything from the first atomic bomb to the television sets of the 1950s and 1960s. When electronics went solid-state and overseas, North Adams nearly died clinging to the belief that some new assembly line would come fill its sprawling 28-building, 19th-century mill complex on the Hoosic River next to downtown. The long-awaited reprieve from welfare and unemployment finally seems to be taking shape, but folks who remember days of industrial wages on a union scale have a hard time envisioning their city being salvaged by . . . *art*. Conceived over a decade ago and then nearly aborted by the recession of the early 1990s, the first 200,000 square feet of the Massachusetts Museum of Contemporary Art—**Mass MoCA**—have finally started to fill parts of the old Sprague Mill, on Marshall Street just north of Route 2 (Tues. –Sun 10 AM–5 PM; $8; 413/664-4481). If the master plan is ever fully implemented, the 13-acre "multidisciplinary cultural center" will become one of the world's largest art museums.

In the meantime, the region's historic gravy train is faithfully recollected in the galleries of the **Western Gateway Heritage State Park** (daily 10 AM–5 PM late May to early Nov., closed Tues.–Wed. rest of the year; donations; 413/663-

8059) on Route 8 just south of the Route 2 overpass. Occupying the renovated freight-yard buildings of the Boston and Maine Railroad, the park's visitor center highlights the landmark construction of the five-mile-long Hoosac Tunnel and North Adams's front-row seat on the Boston-to-Great Lakes rail connection it made possible.

ROUTE 2 DETOUR: MOHAWK TRAIL

Running east of North Adams toward Greenfield and I-91, and taking its name from the warpath used for raids against Algonquian settlements along the upper Connecticut River Valley, the Mohawk Trail (Route 2) was one of the nation's first scenic highways, improved and paved as early as 1914 as part of a massive state effort to lure tourists into this cash-deprived farm belt of New England. If you're driving an overloaded or underpowered vehicle, you'll appreciate the thrill and radiator-popping risks that once attended the slow switchback grind up around the attention-getting Hairpin Turn at the edge of the Western Summit. The turn is so tight that signs insist on a 15-mph speed limit, and people who don't abide by the rules are likely to find themselves screeching around past the sightseers at the **Golden Eagle Restaurant.** Further up, at the top of the hill, the tidy **Wigwam Summit Motel** ($50–60; 413/663-3205), one of many photogenic old motor courts along the route, have been taking in guests since the road was built. Don't be fooled by the short stretch of gentle ups and downs east of the summit over the glacier-flattened mountain peaks of the Hoosac peneplain: the route east along the tortuous Cold River ravine quickens the pulse even in these days of power steering and anti-lock brakes, especially if you get sandwiched between a pair of 18-wheelers, whose burning brakepads sometimes scent the air all the way down the valley.

It was during the blasting of the Hoosac Tunnel that nitroglycerin was first used as a construction explosive. And just so you know, the river is the Hoosic, the mountain range is the Hoosac.

Adams profited mightily from the protectionist trade policies of **President William McKinley,** which is why his statue—by Augustus Lukeman, who also carved Atlanta's *Stone Mountain*—stands at the north end of Park Street. The work was commissioned by a local mill-owning friend after McKinley's 1901 assassination.

East of the summit, dropping down into the valley of the Deerfield River, you pass groups of kayakers and some roadside stands offering rentals of inner tubes-the whitewater equivalent of a La-Z-Boy, and the preferred mode of transport for those interested in relaxing and enjoying the ride. More serious river runners may want to sign up for one of the trips offered by **Zoar Outdoors** (413/339-4010). There are also some enticingly kitschy old Indian Trading Posts, packed full of postcards, plastic tomahawks, and moccasins; my personal favorite is the Big Indian, fronted by a historically inaccurate, politically incorrect, and photogenically irresistible 35-foot-tall statue of a Plains Indian. Another giant Indian statue, a half-ton bronze entitled *Hail to the Sunrise*, stands along Route 2 just west of the town of Charlemont.

You'll find excellent wooded streamside campsites in **Mohawk Trail State Forest** ($12; 413/339-5504) just above where the Cold River empties into the Deerfield. There are five year-round rustic log cabins, too, but make reservations well in advance ($30; 413/339-5504) if you have your heart set on staying in one.

The stretch of the Mohawk Trail dropping down to the Pioneer Valley east of Charlemont, around the picturesque towns of Shelburne Falls and Colrain, is covered in the US-5 chapter, on pages 208–09.

ADAMS: THE MISS ADAMS DINER

Back along the Appalachian Trail, to carbo-load before hiking Mount Greylock, or for an indelible sample of New England local color, head down Route 8 about five miles from burly North Adams to the spiffy little town of **Adams,** birthplace to suffragette Susan B. Anthony and present home to the incomparable **Miss Adams Diner** (413/743-5300). Sitting opposite the Congregational church on downtown Park Street, this handsome Worcester lunch car was beloved for its steak and eggs, Blue Plate Specials, and tapioca pudding you'd expect from a place with a 1949 pedigree. Whether or not the Miss Adams is open (and at time of writing, it had recently reopened after closing down in 1999), Adams is a nifty little town, so feed the meter with your extra pennies—yes, 12 minutes' parking costs but one cent—and stroll around the restored commercial district, guided around by one of the free **walking-tour** brochures put out by the local Historical Commission. The town hall just a couple doors down from the Miss Adams has a ready supply, accompanied by friendly suggestions.

NO SASSING YOUR WAITRESS

an admonition from the menu at Miss Adams Diner

MOUNT GREYLOCK

Massachusetts' tallest peak is the centerpiece of 12,500-acre **Mount Greylock State Reservation,** one of the state's largest and most popular possessions. More than 50 miles of trails, including some thigh-burning mountain-bike routes, wander along the reforested slopes, most of which were heavily logged for fuel and

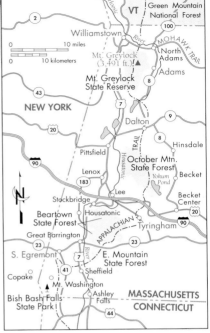

pulp back in the 19th century. Rock ledges provide great views of the Hoosic River valley to the east and the Housatonic valley to the south, when the namesake mists aren't keeping the 3,491-foot summit wadded up in a damp ball of dingy cotton. During warm months access is a cinch: century-old Notch Road snakes its way steeply up through the birch and spruce from Route 2 on the north side, while Rockwell Road ascends more gently from US-7 along the flanks of Greylock's southern neighbors. Combine these roads' 17 miles and you'll enjoy the most scenic driveable mountain ascent in New England, although keep in mind that both roads are narrow, rumble-stripped with frost-heaves, enlivened by occasional hairpin turns, and-especially at dusk-prone to wandering wildlife. If you want to see over the forest, climb the 105-foot **War Memorial Tower** on the summit. If the weather is good, you'll have a panoramic view from New Hampshire to Connecticut.

A stone's throw from the granite tower is the AMC's **Bascom Lodge** (mid-May to late Oct. only; 413/ 443-0011), a beautiful old stone and timber structure with private rooms, shared bunk rooms and cold-water baths, overpriced at $30–65 but for the location, which is sublime despite the nearby TV relay mast antenna.

ROUTE 8 TO DALTON: CRANE & CO. PAPER

A less traveled but not that much less scenic alternative to the busy US-7 corridor is to follow Route 8 south from North Adams through Adams, along the banks of the Hoosic River. With good views of Mount Greylock tempered by semisuburban sprawl of storage centers and used car lots, the route gives a good sense of what the other, less well-heeled half of the Berkshires looks like. The old railroad tracks, which run between Adams and Pittsfield, are in the process of being cleared and converted into a hiking and cycling Rails-to-Trails route, but for now Route 8 is best used as a shortcut. Coming down from Greylock, the hikers' Appalachian Trail crosses Route 8 in **Cheshire,** north of where **Whitney's Farm Stand** sells sandwiches and fresh-picked blueberries in summer. Pick up a bite and have a quick picnic along the shores of the Cheshire Reservoir.

You may not know that all of the paper used in all of the money printed in the USA comes from a mill here in the backwoods of Massachusetts, but if you spend any time here in Dalton (pop. 7,200), you'll learn. In fact, Crane & Co., which makes the 100 percent cotton paper used in U.S. currency, also makes some of the world's finest stationery, at a series of historic mills in this small Berkshire town, along Route 8 just east of Pittsfield's ever-increasing sprawl. The company's **museum** (Mon.–Fri. 2–5 PM in summer only; free; 413/684-2600), housed in the Old Stone Mill at the center of town, traces the history of the Crane Company in particular, and of American paper-making in general.

South of Dalton, Route 8 continues to parallel the Appalachian Trail, with some brief stretches of rural beauty around the hamlet of Hinsdale. After passing by a number of children's summer camps, it finally links up with US-20 near Chester.

Possibly the most detailed and well-written guide to exploration of the Berkshires on foot is Lauren Stevens's *Hikes & Walks in the Berkshire Hills,* usually available in local bookstores and gift shops, or directly from Berkshire House Publishers, Box 915, Great Barrington, Massachusetts 01230.

For an up-to-the-day report on the spread of autumn color through the Berkshires during September and October, call for the local **foliage report:** 800/343-9072 from out of state, or 800/632-8038 within Massachusetts.

Near where Route 8 and US-20 intersect, just east of the I-90 Massachusetts Turnpike, the outskirts of Becket are home to the **Jacob's Pillow Dance Festival** (413/243-0745), a 12-week celebration that since its beginnings in the 1930s has evolved into the nation's premier dance festival.

TYRINGHAM

Route 8, US-20, and the Mass Turnpike all cross the Appalachian Trail at Greenwater Pond east of Lee, but a much more

scenic stretch of the trail can be accessed south of here in the village of Tyringham (pop. 370). Site of a Shaker community in the 1800s and later a popular artists colony, this small hamlet is situated in a delightfully rural landscape of small farms and rolling pastures. The main sight here is an odd one: **Santarella** (daily 10 AM–5 PM; $4), the hand-hewn home and studio of British sculptor Sir Henry Kitson, whose many works include the Pilgrim monument at

SANTARELLA
Museum & Gardens

Plymouth and the *Minute Man* at Lexington Green. His house is a place where the *Hobbit's* Bilbo Baggins would feel at home, with its sculpted rocks, twisting beams, and organic-looking pseudothatched roof.

South of Santarella, beyond the ever-quaint center of Tyringham, a signed parking area marks the crossing of the Appalachian Trail, which you can follow on a short (three-mile round-trip) hike through fields of wildflowers up through Tyringham Cobble to a ridge giving a good view over this pastoral valley, which feels far more remote than it really is.

West of Tyringham, the Appalachian Trail crosses Route 23 just east of Great Barrington and the Butternut Basin ski area, then crosses US-7 and the Housatonic River via Kellogg Road in Sheffield. For more on Great Barrington and Sheffield, see the US-7 chapter on pages 266–67.

SOUTH EGREMONT TO THE STATE LINE

While US-7 gets the most tourist traffic, the more pastoral of the two roads into Connecticut follows Routes 23/41 from South Egremont, another of those well-preserved villages entirely ensconced in the National Register of Historic Places, which is hardly a rare honor in Massachusetts. While the custom of baptizing property with cute monikers has seized altogether too many New Englanders, this is one place that genuinely deserves appellations such as Huckleberry Hollow, the Birches, and Wheelbarrow Hill Farm.

South Egremont is the northern gateway to the state's remotest corner, the township of **Mount Washington** (pop. 120). Within its wooded boundaries, Bash Bish Falls State Park, Mount Washington State Forest, and Mount Everett State Reservation all provide fine hikes on and off the Appalachian Trail. You can pick up a free trail map covering all three properties at State Forest Headquarters (413/528-0330). Take the signposted turn

The mountainous section of US-20, north of the Mass Turnpike between Huntington and Lee, is one of the oldest auto roads in New England, originally called **Jacob's Ladder.** Older and in some ways prettier than the busier and much more famous Mohawk Trail across the state's northwestern tier, Jacob's Ladder is centered on the quaint town of Chester.

from Route 41 west of South Egremont Village, and follow the road past signs for Bash Bish Falls and Copake, New York, until you reach the end of the paving nine miles later. The Bash Bish waterfall is no Niagara, but it's a nice place to while away a hot summer's afternoon.

Back in South Egremont, **Mom's Country Café** (413/528-2414) at the center of town is a friendly choice for a bite before or after a hike; you'll find country breakfasts, burgers, pasta, and soups. Inexpensive, too. **The Gaslight** (413/528-0870), a few hundred yards farther east, is worth a stop for its pies alone, but you won't be disappointed with by omelets, sandwiches, and salads.

In a class by itself is **John Andrew's,** serving dinner and Sunday brunch at the corner of Route 23 and Blunt Road, almost at the New York state line. The small, seasonally adjusted menu may be laced with the familiar—wild mushrooms, baby greens, balsamic this, wild thyme that—but the sum of the parts is without peer. For such an experience, even $30 a head will seem an absolute bargain; reservations are advised (413/528-3469; closed Wed. off-season).

Besides South Egremont's two 200-year-old inns—**The Weathervane** ($115–140; 413/528-9580) and the **Egremont** (413/528-2111)—accommodations in the vicinity include several B&Bs, three of which lie along Route 41 in adjacent Sheffield, en route to Connecticut. If you want to linger over the excellent hiking without resorting to a tent, consider the **Race Brook Lodge** on Route 41, roughly six miles south of Route 23 ($80–155; 413/229-2916). With a connecting path up to Mount Race right outside the front door, this cheerfully rustic, chintz-free zone makes a perfect base for loop hikes along the AT.

From South Egremont, the Appalachian Trail follows Route 41 south to Salisbury, Connecticut, where it rejoins our US-7 route. The southernmost sections of the AT, running alongside the Housatonic River and US-7, are covered in the US-7 chapter.

ROAD TRIP
RESOURCES

RECOMMENDED READING

NEW ENGLAND CLASSICS

Cider House Rules, by John Irving. By the writer who brought us *The World According to Garp, A Prayer for Owen Meany,* and other tales, this complex Dickensian novel is set in an orphanage and revolves around an unusual theme—abortions in 1940s New England. Another great New England read by this prolific author is the *Hotel New Hampshire.*

Complete Poems, by Emily Dickinson. Dickinson spent almost her entire life in the same house in the same small New England town—Amherst, Massachusetts. Almost none of her poems was published until 70 years after her death, yet Emily Dickinson (1830–86) is frequently hailed as one of the most significant and innovative American poets. This book has facsimiles of her diary pages, dozens of her letters, and 450 of her now-familiar little ditties, including this one:

Much madness is divinest sense
To a discerning eye;
Much sense the starkest madness.
Tis the majority
In this, as all, prevails.
Assent, and you are sane;
Demur, you're straightaway dangerous,
And handled with a chain.

Literary critics with a sense of humor have said that the best way to get to sense of the rhythm of Emily Dickinson's poems is to read them to the tune of the folk song "Yellow Rose of Texas."

Ethan Frome, by Edith Wharton. Born in 1862 and reared in a upper-class family in Gilded Age New York City, Edith Wharton (1862–1937) lived for years on an estate in the Massachusetts Berkshires before finally settling in France, where she wrote her most successful books. The first woman to win the Pulitzer Prize for Fiction for her 1920 novel *The Age of Innocence,* in 1911 Wharton wrote this uncharacteristically bleak novella, which was recently made into an engrossing film. Set on an impoverished Massachusetts farm in the bleak gray of midwinter, this poignant story traces the loves, and lack of love, of the title character.

Little Women, by Louisa May Alcott. Part of the fertile literary and cultural scene that was centered on mid-1800s Concord, Massachusetts, Alcott based this tale of female adolescence in part on her own life, growing up as one of four sisters.

Moby-Dick, by Herman Melville. OK, so most of it takes place at sea, far away from New England, but this great whale of a book was written in western Massachusetts, starts in New Bedford, and stands as one of the great literary monuments of a region that takes writing very seriously. A similar New England classic—written partly in Vermont, of all unlikely places—is Rudyard Kipling's classic tale, *Captains Courageous,* which described the adventures of a spoiled rich boy rescued by a Gloucester fishing boat after falling from a luxury cruise ship.

North of Boston, by Robert Frost. Available for $1 at bookstores and most of the Robert Frost (1874–1963) sights in

New Hampshire and Vermont, this slim volume contains the poet's first and in many ways most remarkable works. His *Collected Poems* includes later poems like the famous "Road Less Traveled" (reprinted on page 157), but these early ones are also fine.

The Wood-Pile

"The Wood-Pile," (1913) my favorite Frost poem from *North of Boston*, nicely encapsulates the persistence of things past all over New England:

Out walking in the frozen swamp one grey day
I paused and said, "I will turn back from here.
No, I will go on farther—and we shall see."
The hard snow held me, save where now and then
One foot went down. The view was all in lines
Straight up and down of tall slim trees
Too much alike to mark or name a place by
So as to say for certain I was here
Or somewhere else: I was just far from home.
A small bird flew before me. He was careful
To put a tree between us when he lighted,
And say no word to tell me who he was
Who was so foolish as to think what he thought.
He thought that I was after him for a feather—
The white one in his tail; like one who takes
Everything said as personal to himself.

One flight out sideways would have undeceived him. And then there was a pile of wood for which
I forgot him and let his little fear
Carry him off the way I might have gone,
Without so much as wishing him goodnight.
He went behind it to make his last stand.

It was a cord of maple, cut and split
And piled—and measured, four by four by eight.
And not another like it could I see.
No runner tracks in this year's snow looped near it.
And it was older sure than this year's cutting,
Or even last year's or the year's before.
The wood was grey and the bark warping off it
And the pile somewhat sunken. Clematis
Had wound strings round and round it like a bundle.
What held it though on one side was a tree
Still growing, and on one a stake and prop,
These latter about to fall. I thought that only
Someone who lived in turning to fresh tasks
Could so forget his handiwork on which
He spent himself, the labour of his axe,
And leave it there far from a useful fireplace
To warm the frozen swamp as best it could
With the slow smokeless burning of decay.

On the Road, by Jack Kerouac. What the Beatles were to music, the beats were to literature, and this wild ramble of a road story was Lowell, Massachusetts native Kerouac's first Number One hit, inspiring a generation or two to hightail it along America's highways in the tracks of Sal Paradise and Dean Moriarty. Before and after *On the Road,* Kerouac wrote a set of semi-autobiographical stories recounting his growing up in Lowell, including *The Town and the City, Doctor Sax,* and *Vision of Gerard.*

BACKGROUND

American Diner: Then and Now, by Richard J. S. Gutman (Johns Hopkins, 2000). A lushly illustrated, encyclopedic history of that great American roadside institution, from its humble beginnings in the lunch wagons of the late 1880s to the streamlined stainless-steel models so beloved of art directors and style gurus. The bible of diner lovers everywhere, this recently revised edition contains a state-by-state listing of all the diners still in business.

Common Landscape of America, 1580 to 1845, by John R. Stilgoe (Yale University Press, 1982). Tracing the evolution of the American landscape, this eye-opening and engagingly rich book explores the varied forms and meanings of wilderness, roads, towns, and everything else we so often take for granted. The early chapters on New England are especially captivating, exploring the interplay of man and nature, on the ground and in the nascent national imagination.

Open Road: A Celebration of the American Highway, by Phil Patton (Simon and Schuster, 1986). An energetic account of how the American roadside landscape, especially in the Northeast, came to look the way it does today. Masterfully blending a discussion of the economic and political forces behind the nation's highway network, the book expresses a contagious enthusiasm for the inherent democracy the automobile embodies.

The Perfect Storm, by Sebastian Junger (W. W. Norton, 1997). Before it was turned into a major motion picture, this book spent over a year at the top of the best-seller lists for its painfully vivid descriptions of fishermen and sailors lost in the torrential storm that hit northern New England around Halloween in 1991.

TRAVELOGUES AND TRAVEL GUIDES

The American Guides. Often called the WPA Guides, these state-by-state guidebooks were written in the mid-1930s by workers of the New Deal–era Works Progress Administration, and paint a detailed picture of New England (and the whole country) in the years between the world wars. The history and culture sections are revealing, but the best things about these books are the detailed touring itineraries, which criss-cross the states following the old main roads. Most are of out of print, but copies are generally available at libraries.

Blue Highways: A Journey into America, by William Least Heat Moon (Little, Brown and Company, 1982). One of the best-selling travel books ever written, this intensely personal yet openhearted tale traces the path of a part-Indian, part-time English teacher who travels the back roads "in search of places where change did not mean ruin and where time and men and deeds connected." His travels across New England take in a tour of Woodstock, Vermont, maple sugaring in New Hampshire, and fishing for flounder off Kennebunkport, Maine.

Exploring the Appalachian Trail, David Emblidge et al. (Stackpole Books, 1999). Whether you're a casual day hiker or a seasoned backpacker, this is the best available guidebook to the most famous trail in the country. Two titles in a series of five books cover New England; all have clear maps, charts showing elevation gain and loss, lots of good advice, and enough description and information to entice you safely and comfortably off the road.

The Maine Woods, by Henry David Thoreau (Penguin Books, 1988). If you ever catch yourself thinking that Maine's Mount Katahdin is a long way from civilization, read this account of a series of trips the renowned nature writer took there in the 1850s. Thoreau's philosophies are better absorbed by reading *Walden,* which describes his two years living in a simple cabin outside Concord, Massachusetts.

The Plant Explorer's Guide to New England, by Raymond Wiggers (Mountain Press, 1994). This is a unique guide covering the many different plants and trees of New England through a series of different "road trips" around the region. Along with the geological and botanical expertise, it has many good maps and enough illustrations that you'll soon be able to tell red oaks from black locusts and Saint-John's-wort from Queen Anne's lace.

Roadside Geology of Vermont and New Hampshire, by Bradford Van Diver (Mountain Press, 1987). One of a series of illustrated guidebooks detailing the geology of the ancient mountains at the heart of New England, this book will tell you everything you ever wanted to know—and much more—about the impressive geology of the White and Green Mountains. Other guides in the series do the same for rest of New England.

Travels with Charley: In Search of America, by John Steinbeck (Viking, 1962). Rambling around "this monster of a land" in his camper Rocinante, accompanied only by his eponymous French poodle, Steinbeck returns to California after self-imposed exile in New York to find that, even if you can't go home again, there are many intriguing things to see and to think about along the way. His grand circle routes starts off on the ferry from Long Island to Connecticut, winding up through Maine where he watches the last of the log drives, then takes him to Sunday service at a country church in Vermont.

PERIODICALS

Roadside Magazine. For the past 10 years, *Roadside* has covered the back roads and small-town Main Streets, with a particular focus on diners, those uniquely American institutions that are a traveler's best friend. Along with articles aimed at "getting America out of the franchises, the malls, the Interstates," and back into the real things that foster community and make this country interesting, each issue includes a Diner Finder, which lists, locates, and describes the make and models of all the surviving diners in a certain area. For more information, contact: Coffee Cup Productions, P.O. Box 20652, Worcester, MA 01602, 508/791-1838 www.road sidemagazine.com.

Yankee Magazine. Since the late 1940s *Yankee Magazine* has been a veritable *Reader's Digest* of everything to do with New England. More than 600,000 copies of this homespun journal circulate every week, reminding locals and telling outsiders what's so great about this most historic and characterful corner of the country. For more information, contact: P.O. Box 520, Dublin, NH 03444, 603/563-8111.

"What's a Yankee?: To a European or Asian, a Yankee is an American; to a southern American, a Yankee is a Northerner; to a Northerner, a Yankee is a New Englander; to a New Englander, a Yankee is a Vermonter; to a Vermonter, a Yankee is a person who eats apple pie for breakfast; to a Vermonter who eats apple pie for breakfast, a Yankee is someone who eats it with a knife."
—*Yankee Magazine*

TRAVEL INFORMATION

Maine
Maine Publicity Bureau (207/623-0363 or 800/533-9595)
www.visitmaine.com
Road Conditions (207/287-3427)
Bureau of Parks and Lands (207/287-3821)

New Hampshire
Office of Tourism (603/271-2666 or 603/271-2343 or 800/386-4664)
www.visitnh.gov
Road Conditions (603/271-6900)
State Parks (603/271-3556)

Vermont
Office of Tourism (802/828-3237 or 802/828-3236 or 800/837-6668)
www.travel-vermont.com
Road Conditions (802/828-2468)
State Parks (802/241-3655)

Massachusetts
Office of Tourism (617/727-3201 or 800/447-6277)
www.mass-vacation.com
Road Conditions (617/374-1234)
State Parks (617/973-8700)

Rhode Island
Office of Tourism (401/222-2601 or 800/556-2484)
www.visitrhodeisland.com
Road Conditions (401/222-2545)
State Parks (401/222-2632)

Connecticut
Office of Tourism (860/270-8080 or 800/282-6863)
www.tourism.state.ct.us
Road Conditions (860/594-2650)
State Parks (860/424-3200)

ORGANIZATIONS

Automobile Club of America (AAA)
There are two excellent reasons to become a member of this national automobile club. One is the peace of mind you get knowing that if something goes wrong with your car, AAA folks come out and help you 24 hours a day, 365 days a year. Even better, for information hogs like myself, is the wealth of maps and guidebooks they publish, all of which are free to members. Join your local club (look under "AAA" in the white pages), and once you're on the road in New England you can avail yourself of the 70-odd local offices in almost every town, or the main one in Boston, 125 High Street (617/443-9300).

Appalachian Mountain Club (AMC)
5 Joy Street
Boston, MA 02108
www.outdoors.org
617/523-0636
Founded way back in 1876, the Appalachian Mountain Club is the driving force behind the protection and public enjoyment of New England's wilderness and outdoor areas. Their most prominent service is the provision of rustic accommodation in the White Mountains area of New Hampshire, where they operate a number of cabins and huts for hikers and other outdoor-minded visitors. The club also organizes trips, fixes trails, and publishes hiking guidebooks.

Green Mountain Club
4711 Route 100
Waterbury Center, VT 05677
www.greenmountainclub.org
802/244-7037
Since its creation in 1910, the Green Mountain Club was worked to plan, build, maintain and protect the Long Trail, which runs along the spine of the state from Canada to Massachusetts.

Hostelling International/American Youth Hostels (HI/AYH)
733 15th Street NW
Suite 840
Washington, D.C. 20005
www.hiayh.org
202/783-6161
Dedicated to the proposition that travel helps people gain a richer understanding of the world, Hostelling International helps people travel by providing inexpensive

and welcoming places to stay. Originally intended for young people, hostels have broadened their mission to include everyone—in fact, a large proportion of hostel guests are closer to 70 than to 17—and they make great places to meet fellow travelers and maybe make new friends.

Society for Commercial Archeology (SCA)
c/o Dept. of Popular Culture
Bowling Green State University
Bowling Green, OH 43403
www.sca-roadside.org
Do you like diners? Drive-ins? Neon signs? Roadside attractions? Relax—you're not alone. The Society for Commercial Archeology, made up of hundreds of like-minded enthusiasts, is organized under the auspices of the Smithsonian's Museum of American History and works to preserve, interpret, and promote enjoyment of this sort of roadside Americana.

INDEX

COVERED BRIDGES

MUSEUM HIGHLIGHTS

RAILROAD HISTORY

SKI AREAS

WATERFALLS

MAP INDEX

SPECIAL TOPICS INDEX

Jamie Jensen has been immersed in road trip culture from an early age, thanks to a childhood spent drinking drive-in milk shakes and riding roller coasters in Los Angeles—before they tore everything down—and family road trips up and down the California coast, to the Sierra Nevada national parks, and all over the Southwest. After a three-year stint bumming around the country, making hay in Kansas, sailing boats on the Chesapeake Bay, painting houses in Boston, and living in the storeroom of a Manhattan music studio, he returned to California and earned a degree in Architecture from U.C. Berkeley. Rather than get a real job, he then moved to England, where he began writing about America. He now lives in Northern California, at the west end of US-50.

PHOTO AND ILLUSTRATION CREDITS

Denise J. R. Bass 27, 34 (all), 62, 95, 234 (top); **Arthur Boufford/NHOTTD** 207; **David Brownwell/NHOTTD** 286; **Priscilla Carton/Clark's Trading Post** 146; **Clark Art Institute** 259; **Kindra Clineff/Massachusetts Tourism** 23, 28, 30, 91, 158, 159, 163, 165 (bottom), 166 (top), 167, 209 (all), 222, 231, 233 (top), 234 (bottom), 306, 308; **Buz Cochrane** 119; **Diane Cook & Len Jenshel** 15, 108, 136, 168, 188, 246, 272; **Larry Cultrera** 162; **Fairbanks Museum** 123; **Bob Grant/NHOTTD** 122; **Jeff Greenberg/Maine Tourism** 278; **Bill Griffith/King Features Syndicate** 217; **Jamie Jensen** 18, 19, 21, 32, 35, 36, 37, 38 (all), 48, 56 (all), 63, 67 (all), 70, 71, 75, 76, 80, 86, 88, 89, 91, 94, 96, 97, 101, 104, 107, 112, 120, 127, 129, 131, 134, 140, 142, 144, 147, 150, 151, 152, 154 (all), 156, 161, 165 (top), 166 (bottom), 171, 172, 173, 175, 177, 180, 183, 184 (top), 185, 186, 191, 192, 193, 194, 195, 196, 197, 201, 203, 204 (all), 205 (all), 206, 207, 212, 214, 224, 228, 236, 238, 242 (bottom), 243, 248, 250, 254, 256, 257 (all), 269, 275, 277, 285, 298, 303, 304, 305; **Len Jenshel** 2, 44, 218; **JFK Hyannis Museum** 227; **Library of Congress** 17, 23; **Litchfield Hills Travel Council** 24, 239, 242 (top), 244, 245, 268, 271; **Lost River** 293; **Maine Office of Tourism** 26, 33, 49, 52, 61, 72, 115, 117, 279, 280, 281 (all), 283 (bottom two); **Massachusetts Historical Society** 17; **Massachusetts Tourism** 23; **Jim McElholm** 12, 27 (bottom), 81, 83, 85, 86; **Ralph Morang/NHOTTD** 153; **New Bedford Whaling Museum** 233 (bottom two); **Norman Rockwell Museum** 184 (bottom); **Rhode Island Tourism** 39, 96, 99; **Rock of Ages** 128; **Ronald Saari** 87, 93, 179, 217, 237; **Wilhelm Reich Museum** 283; **Steven Ziglar** 263

The images that serve as chapter front pieces throughout this book were all made by New York City–based photographer Len Jenshel, whose pictures are well worth the proverbial 1,000 words. Original prints may be available through the Yancey Richardson Gallery (212/343-1255).

NOTES

NOTES

AVALON
TRAVEL
p u b l i s h i n g

How far will our travel guides take you? As far as you want.

Discover a rhumba-fueled nightspot in Old Havana, explore prehistoric tombs in Ireland, hike beneath California's centuries-old redwoods, or embark on a classic road trip along Route 66. Our guidebooks deliver solidly researched, trip-tested information—minus any generic froth—to help globetrotters or weekend warriors create an adventure uniquely their own.

And we're not just about the printed page. Public television viewers are tuning in to Rick Steves' new travel series, Rick Steves' Europe. On the Web, readers can cruise the virtual black top with Road Trip USA author Jamie Jensen and learn travel industry secrets from Edward Hasbrouck of The Practical Nomad. With Foghorn AnyWare eBooks, users of handheld devices can place themselves "inside" the content of the guidebooks.

In print. On TV. On the Internet. In the palm of your hand.
We supply the information. The rest is up to you.

Avalon Travel Publishing
Something for everyone

www.travelmatters.com

Avalon Travel Publishing guides are available at your favorite book or travel store.

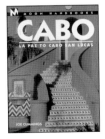

MOON HANDBOOKS

provide comprehensive coverage of a region's arts, history, land, people, and social issues in addition to detailed practical listings for accommodations, food, outdoor recreation, and entertainment. Moon Handbooks allow complete immersion in a region's culture—ideal for travelers who want to combine sightseeing with insight for an extraordinary travel experience in destinations throughout North America, Hawaii, Latin America, the Caribbean, Asia, and the Pacific.

WWW.MOON.COM

Rick Steves shows you where to travel and how to travel—all while getting the most value for your dollar. His Back Door travel philosophy is about making friends, having fun, and avoiding tourist rip-offs.

Rick's been traveling to Europe for more than 25 years and is the author of 22 guidebooks, which have sold more than a million copies. He also hosts the award-winning public television series *Rick Steves' Europe.*

WWW.RICKSTEVES.COM

ROAD TRIP USA

Getting there is half the fun, and Road Trip USA guides are your ticket to driving adventure. Taking you off the interstates and onto less-traveled, two-lane highways, each guide is filled with fascinating trivia, historical information, photographs, facts about regional writers, and details on where to sleep and eat—all contributing to your exploration of the American road.

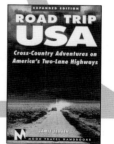

"[Books] so full of the pleasures of the American road, you can smell the upholstery."
~BBC radio

WWW.ROADTRIPUSA.COM

FOGHORN OUTDOORS guides are for campers, hikers, boaters, anglers, bikers, and golfers of all levels of daring and skill. Each guide focuses on a specific U.S. region and contains site descriptions and ratings, driving directions, facilities and fees information, and easy-to-read maps that leave only the task of deciding where to go.

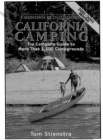

"Foghorn Outdoors has established an ecological conservation standard unmatched by any other publisher."
~Sierra Club

WWW.FOGHORN.COM

TRAVEL SMART guidebooks are accessible, route-based driving guides focusing on regions throughout the United States and Canada. Special interest tours provide the most practical routes for family fun, outdoor activities, or regional history for a trip of anywhere from two to 22 days. Travel Smarts take the guesswork out of planning a trip by recommending only the most interesting places to eat, stay, and visit.

"One of the few travel series that rates sightseeing attractions. That's a handy feature. It helps to have some guidance so that every minute counts."
~San Diego Union-Tribune

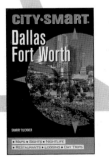

CiTY·SMaRT™ guides are written by local authors with hometown perspectives who have personally selected the best places to eat, shop, sightsee, and simply hang out. The honest, lively, and opinionated advice is perfect for business travelers looking to relax with the locals or for longtime residents looking for something new to do Saturday night.

U.S.~METRIC CONVERSION

1 inch = 2.54 centimeters (cm)
1 foot = .3048 meters (m)
1 yard = 0.914 meters
1 mile = 1.6093 kilometers (km)
1 km = .6214 miles
1 fathom = 1.8288 m
1 chain = 20.1168 m
1 furlong = 201.168 m
1 acre = .4047 hectares
1 sq km = 100 hectares
1 sq mile = 2.59 square km
1 ounce = 28.35 grams
1 pound = .4536 kilograms
1 short ton = .90718 metric ton
1 short ton = 2000 pounds
1 long ton = 1.016 metric tons
1 long ton = 2240 pounds
1 metric ton = 1000 kilograms
1 quart = .94635 liters
1 US gallon = 3.7854 liters
1 Imperial gallon = 4.5459 liters
1 nautical mile = 1.852 km

To compute celsius temperatures, subtract 32 from Fahrenheit and divide by 1.8. To go the other way, multiply celsius by 1.8 and add 32.

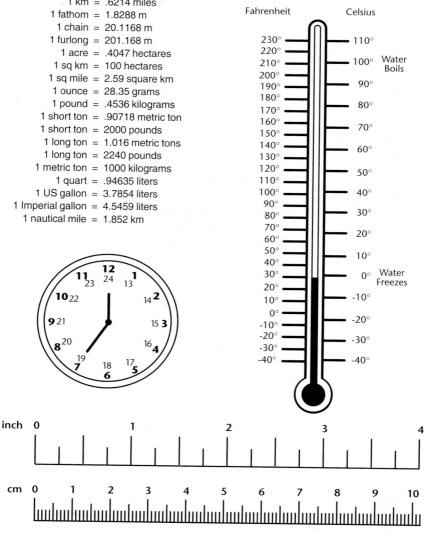

HOSTELLING INTERNATIONAL
choose BOSTON

HI-BOSTON

The best hostels in the best places!

Hostelling International–Boston is centrally located downtown in the Fenway and is within walking distance to museums and nightspots. Walk along the Freedom Trail, stroll around the Boston Common, or take in a Boston Pops concert. Go back in time and experience 17th-century colonial America. Join in on one of our many events and guided tours.

Open 24 hours.
12 Hemenway Street,
Boston, Massachusetts 02115.
For toll-free reservations within the U.S.
call 800-909-4776. code 07
Telephone: 617-536-9455.
bostonhostel@bostonhostel.org
www.bostonhostel.org

Just $24-26 a night!

www.hiayh.org

HOSTELLING INTERNATIONAL®

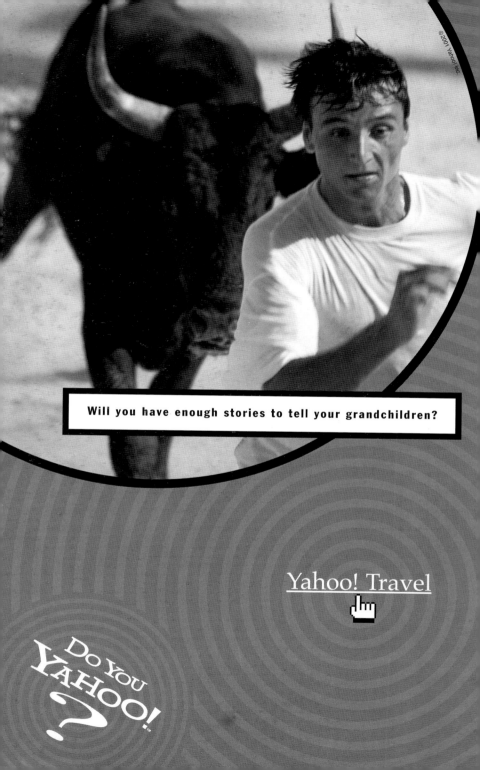